# Reason &
# Reenchantment

David Griffin

November 2013

# Reason & Reenchantment

## The Philosophical, Religious, and Political Thought of

# David Ray Griffin

John B. Cobb, Jr.
Richard Falk
Catherine Keller
Editors

Process Century Press
Claremont, CA

REASON & REENCHANTMENT
The Philosophical, Religious, and Political Thought of
David Ray Griffin

Process Century Press
An Imprint of the Center for Process Studies
A Program of Claremont Lincoln University &
Claremont School of Theology
1325 N. College Avenue
Claremont, CA 91711

Cover photo:
*Northern Lights* (Lofoten Islands, Northern Norway)
Bjørn Jørgensen/www.arcticphoto.no
Used with permission.

ISBN 978-1-940447-00-1

Printed in the United States of America

# CONTENTS

## PART THREE: RESPONSES AND REFLECTIONS

## APPENDIX

NOTES

BIBLIOGRAPHY OF DAVID RAY GRIFFIN

CONTRIBUTORS

# Preface

## John B.Cobb, Jr.

There are many introductions to Griffin's thought in this volume. Gary Dorrien's is the most comprehensive, but since one can approach Griffin from many angles, others will prove more accessible for some readers. There is no need for another introduction. So what is left for a preface? Perhaps some comments by one who has worked closely with Griffin in a diversity of roles over many years will be in order.

I knew him first as my student. Like many graduate students, he was already in that capacity my teacher. He was also unusually helpful to me in my writing and in project-inPrefacePrefaceg a future for process thought. Accordingly, when the opportunity arose to have a Center for Process Studies that would include a colleague for me who would also administer the Center, I turned immediately to Griffin, and he happily accepted. Since then we have been colleagues and co-workers in an institution that is dear to us both. We have continued to contribute to each other's thinking, but I suspect that he has been my teacher more often than I, his.

I have tended to divide my academic colleagues, the really good ones, into two groups: the intellectuals (or critical thinkers) and the scholars. Intellectuals meditate on large topics and seek to understand the reasons for diverse answers. This means that much of their work is the critique of assumptions and the clarification of their own. Usually they deal with questions that the current situation in the world or in their own lives makes important. Scholars focus on particular problems that present themselves as important in the current discussions in their fields or disciplines. They seek to advance their fields by critically evaluating the work of others in the field and building upon it. Their discussions of specific problems are typically exhaustive and rigorous.

Of course, most intellectuals do some scholarly work, and most scholars are influenced by the discussions of intellectuals. Like other such typologies, this one has quite limited usefulness. But it helps me to understand myself and my view of research universities today. I am troubled that the disciplinary organization that pervades these universities encourages superb scholarship, but discourages real intellectual life. To illustrate what seems to me a broad change since my own time in graduate school, I will speak of professors in departments of philosophy. At the University of Chicago, when I was a student in the years right after World War II, this department was staffed by philosophers. Philosophers as such are intellectuals. Rudolf Carnap, Richard McKeon, Charles Hartshorne, and Charles Morris were all philosophers. Of course, they were well-versed in the history of philosophy, but what we learned from them was primarily what they thought and why. It is my impression that that kind of a department is rare today. People are employed to teach about particular types or periods of philosophy. The primary task of professors is not "to profess" but to explain well what others thought.

All of this is to raise a question about Griffin. Is he an intellectual or a scholar? To an extent that is rare in the Anglo-Saxon world, he is fully both. As an intellectual, his choice of topics is based on the importance of the issues for himself and for the world. He seeks what he can affirm as the truth. Imagination, insight, and speculation play their roles. He is a true intellectual. However, he engages in the pursuit of answers through a thorough and remarkably rigorous and exhaustive study, both objective and critical, of what others have said. He excels in scholarship. But the scholarship is not in the service of an academic discipline. It serves to advance his intellectual enterprise.

Both his intellectual enthusiasm and his scholarly rigor were applied in the planning of Center for Process Studies conferences. We would identify a topic that we considered important. David would then engage in extensive study of the literature related to that topic in order to decide whom we should invite. Of course, we usually knew a few people in our own process family who we wanted to involve. But we wanted others who were doing creative work on the topic that had some congeniality with process thought and who would at least be willing to discuss our proposals as we discussed theirs.

Griffin's scholarly thoroughness played two roles in preparing for these conferences. First, he studied the writers who had dealt with the topic to identify the appropriate invitees. Second, he often wrote a paper to help those invitees to understand the process perspective on the topic.

Usually this process worked well. On one occasion, however, it backfired. The topic of the conference was the body/mind relation. This problematic emerges in diverse academic disciplines, and Griffin found interesting writers in several fields. He set out to write a paper to explain the process view to those who accepted his invitation. Of course, this involved describing the way the problem was formulated in various disciplines as well as the process response. It was an enormous topic. Griffin approached it as usual with scholarly thoroughness and wrote a manuscript of some five hundred pages that he sent to those who had agreed to come. This did not make for a good conference, since no one read it in advance. However, the quality of this paper, written for the participants in this conference, was such that it was published by the University of California Press under the title *Unsnarling the World-Knot: Consciousness, Freedom, and the Mind-Body Problem.* The book is a masterpiece in both its intellectual and its scholarly dimensions.

The present book as a whole consists of responses to Griffin's writing. I am noting that hardly less important to the scholarly world, and certainly to the process community, were the many conferences he organized. Those he organized for the Center for Process Studies advanced process thought over a wide range and established connections with many who would otherwise have given it little attention. Sometimes, as in the instance just noted, Griffin was able to connect his authorship of books with his organization of conferences. In other cases, he edited collections of papers that grew out of conferences. But for the most part the history of his writing and of the conferences he put on for the Center for Process Studies are distinct.

Teaching, writing books, administering the Center, and organizing conferences for the Center still did not exhaust the creative energies of this remarkable man. He married a woman who lived in Santa Barbara, and he began to commute to his work in Claremont. Rather than take advantage of this arrangement to have more time to do his own writing, in 1983 he created another institution in Santa Barbara, The Center for a Postmodern World. This Center sponsored numerous distinguished speakers and two large conferences. Its audience was the thoughtful public rather than academia, and its name points to its focus on the changes needed in public thought, institutions, and policies.

The choice of "postmodern" in the name of his organization could suggest that he wanted to be identified with a growing global movement centering in France. Derrida, Foucault, and Deleuze were among those who had popularized this term, and many North American scholars were beginning to use it. But Griffin's case was different. Along with Whiteheadians in general, he was sharply critical of the Cartesian thought that still, and perhaps increasingly, shaped the American university. He noted that a few Whiteheadians had for decades described their position as "postmodern." He recognized that there were commonalities in the critique of modern thought by Whiteheadians and the French postmodernists. But he also saw a very fundamental difference. The French celebrated "deconstruction." This left us with only "local knowledge." It abandoned and often rejected efforts to gain an overview of what is happening or a coherent picture of the natural world. In these respects it continued and carried to its logical limits tendencies that Griffin identified with modernity. He sometimes called deconstructive postmodernism "most-modern" thought. For Whiteheadians, the critique of modernity was for the sake of constructing a better conceptuality and overarching vision. To distinguish Whiteheadian postmodernism from the French form, he introduced the term "constructive postmodernism."

He arranged with SUNY Press to edit a whole series: SUNY Series in Constructive Postmodern Thought. This grew directly out of his work in Santa Barbara, especially the two conferences. The first of these conferences, "Toward a Postmodern World," provided materials for the first two books in the series: *The Reenchantment of Science* and *Spirituality and Society.* The second conference, "Toward a Postmodern Presidency," gave birth to *Postmodern Politics for a Planet in Crisis.* Still another book in the series, *Primordial Truth and Postmodern Thought,* grew out of a visit, as lecturer, by Huston Smith.

Identifying a sharp disjunction between deconstructive and constructive postmodernism expresses an important characteristic of Griffin. I can make it clear by speaking first of a common characteristic among Whiteheadians. We know that our position is in tension with the prevalent ideas in almost all departments of American universities. We hope for more acceptance. This leads us to build bridges toward the mainstream discussion wherever that seems promising. For example, in the early years of my career, we found we could agree with much that was being done by existentialists. We worked hard to bring our Whiteheadian ideas into a form that existentialists could appreciate.

In recent decades, the overlap of interests and concerns with the dominant school of postmodernism has seemed highly promising. Some Whiteheadians have adapted their formulations to express congeniality so as to participate in the postmodern conversations. But Griffin sees that such adaptation can work against making the full contribution of which Whitehead is capable. In any case, politics, including academic politics, is for him fully subordinate to questions of truth. Whiteheadians know that all thought is perspectival, but Whitehead, nevertheless, taught us that the realization of this relativity can lead us to a self-criticism that opens us to being enriched by what others offer. It is a step toward a wider, more inclusive, and better vision. It should not be used to weaken our claims to the truth of what we offer, or to turn our proposals for change of public policy into highly tentative suggestions. Griffin's firm affirmation of the whole Whiteheadian vision is sometimes a source of embarrassment to other Whiteheadians.

An example is in the field of parapsychology. In contrast with Bergson and James, this was not one of Whitehead's major interests. Also, it is a generally unacceptable topic in the university. So Whiteheadians who wish to reduce the offense of Whitehead in the university usually ignore it. But in fact

Whitehead's ontology allows for a certain type of action at a distance, and Whitehead believed that this occurs. What in fact happens and what does not are empirical questions for Whitehead, not to be decided by a metaphysics that rules out the possibility of action at a distance or of mental acts playing a role in the physical world.

The increasing exclusion of the study of parapsychology from American universities was for Griffin a reason to study the evidence for and against it. He did so and found the evidence for some parapsychological phenomena fully convincing. He wrote an important book on this topic. Obviously, this did not improve his standing among academic colleagues, but it evoked an appreciation and respect among those engaged in the field to which chapters in this book give evidence.

An outsider might suppose the topic of parapsychology and the related topic of what happens to people after death would be of interest in the theological community. However, this has not been the case. Theologians, for the most part, share the dominant culture of the university, and in any case are eager to be accepted there. Accordingly, they downplay aspects of Christian belief that are not acceptable in academic circles. Griffin himself began his research with considerable skepticism about life after death, but he was led by the evidence to positive convictions. He presented his conclusions on this subject in the same way as on others—clearly, unambiguously, and firmly. His strong affirmation of evidence for life after death has been received by theologians more as an embarrassment than as a gift. Griffin, however, refuses to be embarrassed about stating what he finds the evidence to support. The truth of a statement is more important to him than its acceptability in one community or another.

The term "constructive postmodernism" has had some resonance in the United States. Some persons with strong ecological concerns are glad to work with Whiteheadians under that banner. The same is true of some feminists. Even though Griffin did not invent the term for the purpose of building connections, he has been happy to find allies in this way. But overall his work on this topic has, as of yet, had minor impact here.

On this point, China provides a marked, and quite wonderful, contrast. Many Chinese intellectuals were troubled that China was so wholly dedicated to modernization—capitalist or Marxist—when many Western intellectuals were devoting their careers to critiquing modernity. Accordingly, some of them sought new directions in the postmodern literature. However, the deconstructive focus did not help them much. The most glaring problem with Chinese modernization was ecological, and the French postmodernists did not give them much guidance on this point.

This need and frustration opened Chinese thinkers to the idea of "constructive postmodernism." The first book in the SUNY series *(The Reenchantment of Science)* had trivial effects in the United States, but in China it evoked national conferences. One of the leading Chinese postmodernists, a member of the Academy of Social Sciences, was Zhihe Wang, who has contributed to this book. He came to Claremont to study with Griffin. His wife, Meijun Fan, professor of Chinese aesthetics in Beijing, later joined him. Together they have established constructive postmodernism, or process thought, as a major cultural and intellectual movement in China. In all probability, if future historians assess the career of David Griffin, his influence in China will be of the highest importance. It is continuing and growing.

Most people, if they saw that at last there was a large community of great global importance that appreciated their work and was open to their guidance, would drop everything else to take advantage of the situation. But that is not Griffin's style. He saw that others could carry on in China what he had begun, and I had the great good fortune to be included among these others.

Meanwhile, he had come across a topic in which deception was being perpetrated on the American people and indeed on the whole world. Since the topic was being carefully avoided by the academic community, his study and writing were needed if truth was not to be totally silenced. I refer, of course, to the official story of the events that took place on September 11, 2001.

My mention of the conferences he organized in Santa Barbara and the books that followed in the SUNY Series indicated a growing interest in world order. Griffin was convinced that a world in whose history war is a fundamental determinant cannot survive. We must envision a world order in which decisions are made in other ways. He began to write about global democracy. In the process, his usual thoroughness led him to study a great deal of history, including the history of the way the United States dominated Latin America. I believe this removed any illusions he may once have had about the moral virtue of United States foreign policy.

In this stage of his thinking, along with many of us, Griffin immediately interpreted the destruction of the World Trade towers as "blowback," that is, as revenge for American actions in other parts of the world. But unlike most of us, he felt the need to study the event more carefully. He came across material that showed inconsistencies in the dominant account. These piqued his interest further. Additional study, rather than supporting the "blowback" explanation, pointed to the involvement of elements of the United States government. This intensified his commitment to get to the bottom of things, in so far as that was possible.

There was nothing surprising to those of us who knew him that Griffin would tackle a taboo topic, fully recognizing that he would be tagged as a "conspiracy nut." That was in character. But some of us were concerned that in this case it was not only status in the academic community that was at stake but also, perhaps, his life. We were vaguely aware that accidents all too often befall those who dig into topics the interpretation of which the elite want to control. Griffin was not unaware of danger, but he judged that that the government's policy was to have as little public attention directed to these issues as possible, with the great majority of people led to believe that any suggestion of government involvement was ridiculous. The accidental death of a major writer in the field would increase suspicion that the government had something to hide. I believe his judgment was accurate. Ironically, the modesty of his public achievements and the success of government censorship and control of public opinion kept him safe.

Griffin thought that he was more likely to be the victim of a true "nut" who was angered by his charges against the government. For a while he avoided television, thinking that as long as he was not physically recognizable by most people, there was not much danger. But before long he threw caution to the winds.

I said above that in terms of world history his most important legacy will be in China. There is, however, the possibility that another legacy will exceed even that. I will offer a fantasy of how that could happen. I choose "fantasy" so that no reader will suppose I predict anything of this sort. My respect for the power of our elite to control events precludes any such expectation.

Fast forward to 2021. Imagine that the work of Architects and Engineers for 9/11 Truth has grown to such a point that the discussion of who was really responsible for the destruction of the World Trade Towers has become politically inescapable. Imagine that some of the media, which has long worked with the government to censor news in this area, has decided that, in order to maintain any credibility with the public, it must begin to participate in serious research and reporting about what happened. Imagine that the official story crumbles and finally the government establishes a blue-ribbon committee and provides it with the resources to undertake a serious investigation.

Now imagine that the American people are awakened to the way they have been duped by the power elite. They come to see how their acceptance of the lies that have been fed them by their government and the media has supported American imperialism abroad and the loss of freedom at home, while impoverishing the majority of the people and concentrating wealth in the hands of one percent of one percent. Imagine that this new awareness generates a new political movement that sweeps away the established power structure of Democrats and Republicans alike.

If all this should happen, and historians should seek to understand how it happened, they would likely give primary and direct credit to Architects and Engineers for 9/11 Truth. That would be entirely appropriate. But they would probably also judge that this organization would not have succeeded, perhaps would not even have come into existence, if it had not been for the work of David Griffin. It was he who for a decade was the most persistent and reliable writer in this field.

I have called this a fantasy. Twenty years ago I would have called any notion that Griffin would play an important role in China a fantasy. Some fantasies are actualized in the course of history. I will not give up hope for this one. The sustainability of the planet requires some such drastic change in the course of U.S. history. Even if the chances of its occurrence are very slight, Griffin's willingness to devote so much effort to discovering the truth about 9/11 and making it public was a gamble worth taking. I deeply appreciate his judgment and his courage.

There is another possible future whose realization would owe much to Griffin. I will not call this a "fantasy," since I think in some measure, perhaps small, it will be realized. Griffin himself raised our sights to this future in 1998, at the Third International Whitehead Conference, of which he was the major organizer. He told us that the twenty-first century would be the Whiteheadian one. I am sure he expected laughter from the people in the audience, all of whom felt that their Whiteheadian interests caused them to be marginalized. He got the laughter, but he also stimulated serious thought about what was happening and what would happen.

A Whiteheadian century would be above all a transformation of the modern ones (dualistic and materialistic), whose thought forms have been largely Cartesian. Future historians may judge that the influence of Cartesian thought forms reached its apex in the twentieth century. For example, the organization of the university and the methods employed by the academic disciplines that make it up became Cartesian to the core. At the same time, historians may recognize that the limitations of Cartesian thought became highly visible, and that creative intellectual life broke out of bondage to it. In the sciences, Cartesian habits dominated, but the evidence and new developments did not fit. The dualism of nature and spirit that organizes the universities crumbled. Postmodernism arose and captured the imagination of many.

If we ask what is succeeding modernism, the answer may be further fragmentation and trivialization of knowledge and the abandonment of any quest for wisdom. But insofar as we look to positive new directions, Whiteheadians see some commonality with their vision in much that is happening in the sciences. Whitehead's emphasis on organisms and relations fits better with emerging insights than do the material objects of the modern world. The primacy of events over things is gaining in plausibility. The boundaries between mind and matter are eroding. Even panexperientialism does not seem as unthinkable as was once the case.

Psychology and sociology fit better into a Whiteheadian context than a Cartesian one. Interest in process thought is emerging in circles of political theory and international relations. Mainstream economics, which is the triumph of Cartesianism in the social sciences, is losing its credibility as its theories guide the world into financial and ecological disaster. Ecological economics, already connected to Whitehead's thought, may become increasingly influential.

Something similar can be said in relation to the professions. Whitehead's vision of education may catch on. Whitehead's thought is allied with those agriculturalists who seek ecological farming instead of industrialized forms. Although process theology is still rejected by most theologians, its competitors seem to lack a convincing alternative. In the fields of administration and management, process thought has already made great headway. Insofar as there develops a concern for a coherent unification of these developments in an emerging worldview, Whitehead has few competitors.

To claim some sort of victory for Whitehead over Descartes would be extremely premature. It may never happen. But to see promise for the movement of thought in that direction is not simply fantasy. It is not impossible that within a generation, few advocates of Cartesian thought will admit to that preference. Whitehead's name may be treated with respect. And even if it is not, Whiteheadians may be able to identify with the cutting edge of thought in many university departments.

To whatever extent a scenario unfolds in this direction, and we ask how this came about, the name of Griffin will figure prominently. He was the key figure in the organization and operation of what was once properly called "The Center for Process Studies." This center helped to preserve the visibility of process thinking when it faded at its former center at the University of Chicago. Much of what has happened in other countries, including the forming of the International Process Network, has been facilitated or supported from this center.

David's work in the establishment, development, and dissemination of process thought has not been a lonely task. It has been more the work of a team player. But if the potential of Whitehead's philosophy to change the climate of scholarship and of intellectual life is realized, there will be no one to whom more credit will be due than David Griffin.

# PART ONE

# Philosophical and Religious Perspectives

# 1. God, Power and Evil: David Griffin Revisited

## Catherine Keller

I gladly accepted the assignment of reconsidering Griffin's game-changing thought on the problem posed by the God/power/evil complex. Theodicy is of course only a part of the awe-inspiring and ongoing contribution to theological doctrine and transdisciplinary investigation that this symposium honors. Griffin's process theodicy is arguably the linchpin—what keeps the wheel from spinning off—of his entire constructive postmodern theology. Indeed, it does not only found his own project but may be said to offer a logic that keeps the wheel of theism itself from falling off—off the cart of intellectual credibility. But since we really do come to praise Griffin, not to bury him, we know he will see right through the ceremonies of our adulation to the structures—and flaws—of our argument.

So it seems only fair to begin with a syllogism:

A   The problem of evil is susceptible of rational solution.
B   Griffin has provided a rational solution.
C   Therefore there is no problem of evil.

Oops. There still seems to be a problem: Evil did not disappear like Rumpelstiltskin on being properly named. And of all people Griffin has not ceased to expose and combat the most insidious forms of evil, because they are far from being solved in reality or in practice. But we are speaking of a *rational* solution to the problem—the familiar theo-logical one nicely popularized in the 1950s in Archibald MacLeish's play *JB,* where the character of that nickname for Job is tormented by the ditty:

> If God is God God is not good.
> If God is good God is not God.[1]

In other words, godness is not goodness but power.

In *God, Power, and Evil* (1976),[2] Griffin worked out his famous 8-point elaboration of the problem of evil, which had traditionally been captured in the simpler syllogism: God is good, God is omnipotent, evil exists, therefore no God. With that syllogism, theodicy comes asymptotically close to theocide!

Griffin did not offer his 8-point solution in the form of an alternative syllogism,[3] although his logic remains formidable throughout the process theodicy he does offer.

He later refined his theodicy in *Evil Revisited* (1991),[4] answering criticisms that honored the importance of his contribution with the seriousness of their own arguments. With characteristically swashbuckling lucidity, he answers them all. And do not forget the inexpensive little Process &Faith booklet,[5] which I confess to having assigned recently to seminarians, knowing no more economic way to break open the problem of evil for them—to expose the logic of theodicy *as* a problem liable to intellectual solution. And break it open one must, if one teaches folk who presume some version of traditional Jewish, Christian or indeed Muslim theism. For the unsolved problem of evil routinely causes the more thoughtful members of this population—precisely the ones capable of turning their tradition toward a more con-vivial messianicity—demoralization and pacification.

My silly syllogism suggests, however, a familiar misunderstanding of the whole project of a theodicy: that it rationalizes or makes light of suffering, that it does not recognize the mystery of evil, that it undermines hope, et cetera—a poignant history of misunderstandings. One can only respect the passions, griefs, advocacies and yearnings that produce impatience regarding any abstract approach to suffering; and theologies driven by that impatience were gripping my generation during the couple decades in which Griffin's theodicy was being received, sometimes more indirectly than explicitly, along with process theology as a whole. In other words, the overlapping movements of postholocaust, feminist, and liberation thought, however marginal in power, nonetheless dominated progressive theological discourse. And they had little tolerance for any syllogisms, for any appeal to rationality, for any claim like Griffin's, that "[i]t is precisely in regard to issues . . . with which we are most passionately engaged . . . that we must try the hardest to achieve a properly philosophic state of mind."[6] He is there defending his argument in advance from those (he names existentialists) who find its insistence on philosophical consistency deadening of passionate concern. And beyond existentialism, and a certain neo-orthodox fideism, the social movements were just coming into theological strength. They brought their own suspicion of rationality, "our passion for justice" (Carter Heyward); and over a decade they would be spiked with deconstruction.

Methodologically speaking, in other words, the project was destined to a certain incompatibility with precisely those theologies that most needed it. To suggest as much is a version of my larger claim as to the linchpin of theology itself. I am in a good position to address that need, as my own voice came into its own, if it did, as a member of that impassioned emancipatory collectivity and an adherent to its experiments at the poetic edge of rationality. The actual theo-logical content, however, that underpinned the shifting image of God and the branching

politics was for me, and for many of us, that of process theology
(in my Claremont experience such content was delivered
with remarkable male encouragement of feminist qualms
and queries, and no one more concretely than Griffin, despite
or because of this difference of style and method, supported
my own development—this is too much autobiography.) And
process theology already turned on its defiance of the classical
omnipotence that deifies power. The emancipatory theologies
more broadly were nothing if not critiques of power.

The feminist implications of process theology had in fact
already been compactly explicated in the Cobb-Griffin *Process Theology* (also 1976!).[7] If, because of its undisguised rationalism, *God, Power, and Evil* did not get the recognition it
deserved in its own period, it nonetheless exercised tremendous indirect influence—not just spooky action at a distance,
but lodging in the minds of a branching multitude of feminist
thinkers, directly and indirectly involved in process thought,
a counter-logic, a systematic alternative, to the numbingly
standard assumption that God = Power.

These issues may seem rather distant now. But it is my
hunch that the progressive cogitations will perform their
agitations more effectively in this millennium insofar as we
come to terms with the role of rationality in our own theo-logies, and thus, pivotally, in our theodicies—even if some of us
some of the time supplement theology with theopoetics.

This is not to say that we should go back and replay the other
kinds of reception that *God, Power, and Evil* did get, especially
the tremendous caliber of critical engagement and debate
from (white male) non-process thinkers. This stimulated the
writing of *Evil Revisited.* In such dialogical dialectics, Griffin
exemplifies a kind of argumentative exposition that once
comprised the genius of Christianity, not just scholastic but
speculative, which Protestantism partly undermined and the

social movements further disdained—but without which I suspect no thinking Christian will want to remain a Christian—whether or not we would or could quite emulate the style.

Coming to terms with reason will not undo the political and the poststructuralist deconstructions of the power drives of western Reason itself—in the image of a supreme Indifference—or the diversity of styles they made possible for theology and even philosophy. It is the reasoned content delivered through Griffin's theodicy that I am suggesting we always needed—and that will continue to provide a crucial argument, indeed a crux (or cross), of theological thinking. Whether theological thinking itself is needed on other fronts—ecologically, sexually, economically, politically, aesthetically, even spiritually—is another argument, which I may manage to avoid here. But insofar as we are engaged in *theistic* discourses, whether out of sincere belief, strategic rhetoric, or experimental polydoxy, I do not see any way around Griffin's theodicy. Let me designate two axes of it that no sane theology can do without.

According to the first axis, one does not need to speak of a God beyond the classically omnipotent One as powerless—as the powerless power (Moltmann) or the "Weakness of God" (Caputo). It is not that Griffin's God just has *less* of the sort of power we attribute to divinity. It is a *different sort* of power, the power of persuasion rather than coercion. But why isn't God *more* persuasive, then, when it comes to genocides, et cetera? The answer is indelible: because "the greatest conceivable power a being can have cannot be equated with all the power."[8] With Hartshorne, Griffin argues that a "perfect agent" cannot "unilaterally bring about that which it is impossible for one being unilaterally to effect."[9] No, that is not a circular argument. It entails that no being can "guarantee that the other beings will avoid all genuine evil. The possibility of genuine evil is necessary."[10] This does not mean that *actual* evil is necessary, which would make God, after all, culpable. Something more subtle is in play. God is responsible but not indictable for evil—but not because the evil is ultimately unreal. It is real: the universe would be better without it. So he suggests "C omnipotence" (coherent omnipotence).[11]

?

I find such language strategically helpful with adherents of the Abrahamisms (as opposed to just cancelling the omnipotence premises). I also suggest a different translation of *omnipotens*—as 'omnipotentiality.' As sheer potentiality, it is what I have elsewhere identified as the *tehom* or deep of a *creatio ex profundis,* a hermeneutical (or -nautical) theopoetic variation on the theme of Griffin's creation from chaos. He demonstrates in his process theodicy that the *creatio ex nihilo* implies classical omnipotence, as C-omnipotence is implied by the biblical creation from chaos. The potential for evil lies within its urging. But whether the potential is realized in good or evil ways depends upon the joint actualizations of creatures. Creatures are responsible agents.

And here is where Griffin's brilliant "metaphysical correlations of value and power" come into play.[12] In a nutshell: free agents have the capacity to actualize evil or else they are not free. One then asks why would God bring forth free creatures at all; why not just bring forth good ones who may think they are free but are only free to do the good? His answer is "that God could not create such beings."[13] Not because of a deficiency of divine capacity, but because such beings are a contradiction in terms. They cannot exist. To exist as a creature at all in this metaphysics is to be partially *causa sui,* participant in the infinite creativity, of which what we call God is the everlasting embodiment. So God is not unilaterally *making* but *calling forth* creatures from the deep, from which God comes forth simultaneously. (Both creating and creatable, and neither, said Nicolas Cusa in 1453.) Creatures come forth in the irreducible spontaneity marked at the elemental level as quantum indeterminacy. Why couldn't we all be kept at the harmless lower levels of agency, of capacity for evil, then? Wouldn't it be worth it, to prevent the horrors and the holocausts of history? But this also will not work—by definition. For evil is understood not only as destructive discord; but as triviality, the inhibition of complexity and so of The intensity of experience.[14]

So to say "God cannot produce a world without evil" is not to impugn the power or goodness of the creator. Freedom is dangerous. Creation is a high-risk endeavor. This is not an unbiblical thought, after all: The creation from chaos suggests neither divine mistakes nor divine innocence, but co-creative adventures that mount in complexity to the "very good" of all the critters together. And the sin and problems that follow reinforce the aura of risk. Nor is it an unpreachable thought, should this be a concern: "Grace is dangerous," pointed out William Sloane Coffin. It can get you crucified. Not because "God the Father" wills "his Only Begotten" to be tortured to death for the good of us sinners. But because making transformations in our creaturely arrangements, especial when they are human and larded with imperial habits, is felt as dangerous to the human powers and thus is highly risky for the agents of change. As Griffin well knows.

Divine power, in other words, must be read as radically relational: It empowers, and thus does not contradict the divine attribute about which the bible gets definitive: love. (As Anna Mercedes names her new theology *Power For*, not power over.[15]) But Griffin would hasten to insist that although this persuasive power may indeed be more akin to what we mean by good, his argument is metaphysical, not merely moral. I buy this too. I cannot be convinced by a moralist argument (God is good therefore God must use good, noncoercive power). No, coercive power has operated with tremendous selective advantages among prehuman creatures, suggesting no primly just Creator. And it is the resort to (truly) circular moralisms that inhibits the efficacy of the progressive theologies: God must be just, on the side of the oppressed, profeminist, black, et cetera, else we cannot worship him/her/it. That may be true, but it is not persuasive. And it is in this millennium no longer very interesting.

For this reason, I find more persuasive what Griffin calls the metaphysical argument. To paraphrase it: the texture of the universe is inherently relational. For this, there is immense *physical* testimony—indeed it lies at the base of Griffin's later work of reenchantment. And Karen Barad therefore finds as a physicist a responsiveness running through everything, down to the quanta in their indeterminacy of interconnection. Because of that relationality there is—Henry Stapp does this too[16]—a responsiveness in everything to everything else. A germ of responsibility. The existence of what we call God cannot be derived from anything about the universe; but if we find the God-metaphor still sometimes resonant, it will be all the more so when inferred from the universal process of relations. If divinity is entangled in this creation, then God is an empty trope when abstracted from the indeterminate interrelations that comprise everything. Therefore the *matter* of divinity, the body that we can figure as the body of God, depends upon those relations for its own experience. But *as* bodies we each can use a coercive power that is not part of the divine repertory; for the body of God would be the whole universe, with nothing outside to use itself *against*. This is all Griffinesque thinking, in slightly altered and *ipso facto* fuzzier language.[17]

In other words and in a certain way, the premises of my silly syllogism are, after all, true. Griffin did provide a "solution." For of course Griffin's theo-logic entails that there can be no solution—if that would mean the elimination of evil from the world. (The "final solution.")

But as it turned out in GPE's opening 4-point syllogism, a few more premises make their appearance. In this case:

A2. Rational solution cannot be complete—if it s rational.

B2. Griffin's rational solution illumines irreducibly extra-rational realities.

B3. Those realities include emotion, interest, concern, feeling, intuition, uncertainty.

B4. Rationality does not eliminate mystery, it eliminates contradiction (which is often masked as mystery).

B5. Mystery encompasses the indeterminacies of the world, the unknowns of divinity, and the enigma of their nonseparability.

As, however, Griffin is no friend of "mystery," which he does not distinguish from the mystification that acquiesces in contradiction, that last pair of premises may seem alien to his project. But as they are crucial to me and to many, I hope they appear as a friendly supplement.

Indeterminacy signifies uncertainties that, unlike a formulaic murder mystery, may or may not be solvable after the fact; "God" signifies mystery that escapes contradiction only insofar as it eludes but does not violate rationality. But of course it violates any rationality that denies mystery—that, in other words, posits complete rational solution rather than self-critical and open rational process. God does not escape thereby into nonentity but into metaphor, inasmuch as a figure or trope may hold within itself a margin of unknowability. Of course, process theologians on the whole and Griffin in particular are impatient with any such swerve to metaphor as well as mystery—they smell an excuse for lazy thinking, vague mysticism, undisciplined passions, and the failure to confront contradictions (such as God's godness and God's goodness). The history of the suppression of hard questions—political or theological—through "endless appeals to 'mystery' or 'paradox,'"[18] is one long justification of that impatience. Mystery then simply subserves the "inscrutable majesty" of coercive power.

Nonetheless, coercive power was usually exercised against and not by mystics. I am at any rate not able to "believe" in any version of a God I am supposed to believe in—that is, to take anything said about God as literally, definitively or prosaically true. No matter how "compelling" the argument. And fortunately we know that the whole schematism of process language relies on, in Whitehead's words, "metaphors mutely appealing for an intuitive leap."[19] For that reason, I have remained a follower of process theology, of its god and of the work and theodicy of Griffin. It is not founded on an appeal to belief, to propositions rational or dogmatic that one is to *believe.* The leap is invited by the muteness, a silence, an unspeakability that precedes speech and receives it back at moment's end. The apophasis [not-saying] of an ancient mysticism of negative theology here folds in and out of an affirmative cosmology. In that loop, which I call "apophatic entanglement," our nonseparability and our nonknowing meet. (I realize that my tangling metaphors cannot give joy to the author of *Unsnarling the World Knot.)* They meet at what complexity theory calls "the edge of chaos," and so actualize in thought the potentiality of the chaos of creation itself.

New knowledge takes place only in that meeting. Rationality if it is rational is nothing but attention to the specific relations of the already to the not yet knowable. And it knows that it does not know where the boundary lies between the not yet knowable and the unknowable. To repeat: that unknowing does not justify the repression or suppression of contradictions in any domain of discourse.

I consider Griffin's theodicy an important swathe of new knowledge. I do not consider it or any theology to be definitive knowledge about God, as though mirroring God in language. I know of no God—entity, being or object—that could be mirrored. It is knowing in the sense of Cusa's "conjecture," or Whitehead's "proposition"—more important that it is interesting "than that it be true.[20] But not thereby untrue. It is perhaps all the more true, the more it keeps faith with the margin of its unknowing amidst the density of its relations. And it is all the more interesting, the more it keeps mystery in play (which is perhaps why Griffin has been so gracious to the likes of me—never accusable of "dispassion": at least the theopoetics attracts some folk to process thought).

If Griffin has provided a rational solution to the problem of evil, it is so reasonable because it takes reason as far as it can go—and therefore releases a powerful intuition. For intuition remains uncritical opinion tinged with feeling if it has not exhausted its rational recourse. And it becomes mystification if it does not continue to test and apply, flying the little "aeroplane" on multiple quests.[21] So I hope it is evident that if the propeller does not fall off the plane when it is flying theological missions, it is because of the theodicy that Griffin has rendered so brilliantly persuasive. The unknowing with which I have smudged its contour is in service to its rationality; and especially to its persuasive power among an audience of thinkers involved in some sort of progressive religious praxis, but ever more in doubt about "God." I find that if they recognize the radicality of the apophatic underground of theism, they are granted the benefit of their doubt. And the benefit of the doubt is that it keeps rationality and uncertainty mutually attuned. This attunement may be all that permits the "tremendous psychic discipline" Griffin calls for at the end of *Evil Revisited,* teaching a noncoercive image of God that one might not yet feel in any way but intellectually to be true.[22] I find that the intellectual faith is everywhere drying out when left to itself; and that the mystical excess, the elusive "more," as seepage of the tehomic depth, may keep it moist and alive.

Griffin long ago moved on to other questions and domains of questions, in which theory has not just inspired practice but morphed into it. In a sense, his theology often has not-spoken itself (with little aura of mysticism, if a certain paranormal entanglement) not by losing faith but by thinking it all the way through. Every symbolic locus of theology depends upon this rethinking of power: creation, christology, eschatology, salvation. Whether or not we always call it C-omnipotence, it is with cogency, coherence, and creative force that Griffin has rolled through an immense Constructive manifold of themes that push beyond theology proper: especially in natural science, religious pluralism, and postmodern politics. In each case, however, the operation of his theologoumenon of persuasive power exposes the false flags and junk mysteries of the powers that be. And they *be* in the West above all in ontotheological and habitual *imitatio* of the great idol of omnipotence: "of God as the one whose 'mighty hand' controls all earthly forces, including the coercive power of an imperialistic state."[23] So the "problem of evil" that Griffin solves is the fabrication of the theologians who sanctify that coercion, and of the wishful-thinking of its victims. As long as godness means power in the civilizational imagination, sustained explicitly by theists and unconsciously secularized by the rest, it will undermine robust alternatives.

No one on the Earth has to my knowledge done more to actualize the postmodern potential, indeed the omnipotentiality, of the constructive alternative, than has Griffin. The linchpin holds. The wheel turns. Griffin has more missions to fly.

# 2. Rationalistic Panexperiential Panentheism:

## David Griffin's Whiteheadian Religious Philosophy

### Gary Dorrien

It is a privilege and delight for me to contribute to this celebration of David Griffin's work. My assignment is a bit puzzling, as I received three different requests. One asked me to speak about David's contribution to process theology, another asked me to discuss his rendering of the differences between Alfred North Whitehead and Charles Hartshorne, and the third vaguely asked me to discuss David's contribution to process thought. I might have taken this situation as license to do whatever I want, but instead, I have decided to take a shot at all three assignments. I am going to emphasize David's panexperientialism, rationalism, and panentheism, and I am going to begin by saying a word about Whiteheadian process theology in general before getting to David in particular.

There are many things that I admire about Whiteheadian thought. It has a genius philosophical founder in Alfred

North Whitehead. It offers a picture of a divinely influenced universe oriented toward beauty and the intensification of experience. It is consistent with the modern understanding of evolution as a long, slow, gradual process of layered stages in which complex forms of life build upon simple ones. It is consistent, for the most part, with relativity theory, in which the universe is dynamic and interconnected, space and time are inseparable, and gravity and acceleration are indistinguishable. It conceives events as the fundamental things themselves, the immanent movement of creativity itself, not as occurrences that happen to things or that enduring things experience.

All of this makes the Whiteheadian system the greatest metaphysical worldview of the past century, ready made for a theology in which God constantly absorbs the passing world and retains its variety in the immediacy and final unity of God's everlasting present. God is always in process with creation as the lure for feeling and creative transformation, the eternal urge of desire that lures us to make creative, life-enhancing choices.

But John Cobb, David Griffin and other process theologians did not rest with this pretty picture, so that many of us cut our teeth theologically on the early engagements of process theology with environmentalism, feminism, and liberation theology. From these beginnings in the 1970s, the process school has originated or produced a plethora of feminist and womanist theologies, new forms of environmental theology, Christian-Buddhist dialogue, various engagements with postmodern and poststructuralist criticism, an academic industry known as the religion-science dialogue, and significant inroads into China and South Korea. This school of theology, despite its abortive beginning, its notoriously unintelligible jargon, and its rather belated rebirth in the

1940s, has become the one indispensable school of thought for progressive theology as a whole.

Some Whiteheadians worry a great deal about the scientific standing of process thought and the referentiality of its claims, and some urge that Whitehead's concepts only matter if they work as generative and illuminating metaphors. But in both cases the Whiteheadian language of flux, order, and process is suited for interdisciplinary dialogue. Today at progressive U.S. American seminaries and divinity schools we say that we need to uphold the best of our traditions of social Christianity, ecumenism, feminism, and the many kinds of liberation theology, and we need to do it in a way that is global, connected to world cultures and societies, committed to the liberating perspectives of LGBTQ theory and criticism, and engaged in interreligious dialogue and theologies of world religions. Describing this ideal is not so difficult. Working out a viable model for it is very difficult. The best one that we have is the Whiteheadian model.

The process school has distinguished itself by taking the risks that go with holding large intellectual ambitions, grappling creatively with the hardest intellectual problems, thinking on a global and cosmic scale, and showing concern for the common good and the natural world. No one better represents the intellectual ambition of process theology than David Griffin. He has surpassed everyone in challenging the materialistic, atheistic modernism of the academy, and his work is prolific and wide-ranging to the point of being impossible to summarize.

As Catherine Keller's contribution shows, the major work of Griffin's early career was his important book on theodicy, *God, Power, and Evil*. It is strange that no process thinker of the prior generation had systematically taken up this subject— not Hartshorne, Bernie Loomer, Bernard Meland, Daniel Day

Williams, Norman Pittenger, or anyone else of that generation. It is strange because process theology offers a distinct
answer to the theodicy issue, and there is no issue that has
drawn more people to the process perspective than this one.
Yet there was no process theodicy until 1976.

Most of the time, authors hate it when you tell them that
one of their early books was the most important or influential one that they wrote. When you are fresh out of graduate school, you only know this much, you try to get as much
mileage as you can out of what you know, and it is galling to
be told, years later, that you made your biggest splash when
you were a half-informed youth. So, I stress that *God, Power,
and Evil* is not the best book that Griffin ever wrote. But it is
the book that launched a whole genre of process theology. It
evoked strong responses for over a decade. It established the
keynotes of Griffin's process theology. And it set off so much
discussion that he had to write a sequel in 1991 after trying to
withdraw from the back-and-forth over his position.

Griffin argued that Whiteheadian theism solves the perennial problems of theodicy because it distinctively holds
together the reality of true creaturely freedom, God's moral
goodness, and genuine evil. God does not control creatures
because God *cannot* control creatures. Creativity is a universal feature of actuality and is inherent in it. To be creative is
to possess real powers of self-creation and other-creation.
Therefore it is metaphysically impossible for God to possess a
monopoly of power, for God needs an actual world, and all actualities contain powers of self-determination and other-di-
rected influence. Embracing Whitehead's Platonist idea that
God's agency is persuasive, not coercive, Griffin grounded his
rejection of divine omnipotence on the metaphysical principle that the entire realm of actuality contains inherent powers
of creativity.[1]

Then he took a Hartshornean step beyond Whitehead. Whitehead had suggested that the metaphysical principles of reality were determined by God's primordial decision. Following Hartshorne, Griffin argued that the metaphysical categories "are beyond all decision, even God's." Whiteheadian theism is most coherent as a theory about the way things are necessarily. It is about the necessary metaphysical basis of this world and all others, and it is true or false on the basis of its account of the metaphysical principles of reality.[2]

Griffin's theodicy is a theory of persuasive efficient causation about a God that has no independent body distinct from the world. God provides an initial aim for each actual occasion, and relative coercion occurs in efficient causation, but God cannot exert coercion in an absolute sense. Absolute coercion requires having a body distinct from the creature's bodies, but God has no "hands" with which to make things happen. God has a body only in the sense that the world is God's body; God is the "soul of the world" whose causal relations are always directly individual-to-individual.[3]

There are plenty of theologians who believe that panexperientialism is the weakest and most dispensable part of Whitehead's system, but I believe that Griffin's stout defense of panexperientialism is one of the great strengths of his work.

Dualists fail to explain how such radically different things as mind and matter can causally influence each other, they violate the principle of continuity, and they violate the principle of the conservation of energy—that the energy of the universe has remained constant since the big bang. Materialistic theories fail to account for the unity of experience, the unity of bodily behavior, and the reality of freedom. If there is no mind, how do we possess a unified conscious experience? How can I orchestrate different physical actions at the same time? How can a personal center of consciousness be a wholly material being?[4]

Griffin counters that minds are real but thoroughly natural. The unsolved dilemmas of the dualistic, dogmatic materialist, and emergent materialist theories indicate that something is wrong with the reigning assumptions in the field. In Griffin's rendering, the debate between dualists and materialists is a "family quarrel" between theorists who take for granted the early-Enlightenment view that the basic units of nature have no experiential features. The Whiteheadian alternative naturalizes a really existing mind. If experiences are actual things and all actualities have experience, the aspect of the world that we know most directly—our own conscious experience—is not a supernatural or an anomalous phenomenon. Mind and matter go all the way down. The regnant theories commit Whitehead's fallacy of misplaced concreteness, failing to recognize that their basic notions are abstractions.

Panexperientialism replaces the substantialist premises of dualism and materialism with Whiteheadian process, showing that experiences have spatial extension and that bodies endure through time. It avoids the dualistic problems of discontinuity and interaction between ontologically dissimilar entities. It affirms and accounts for the reality of experience, freedom, and the unity of experience and behavior. The Whiteheadian approach does not have to solve the impossible problem of drawing a line between experiencing and nonexperiencing individuals, and it does not have to explain how experience can be generated by nonexperiencing entities or processes. More broadly, it offers a naturalistic, qualitatively monist form of realism that takes consciousness seriously and that regards everything in the world as real in some way.

I do think that rhetorically, and in living out your intellectual lineage, nearly all of you Whiteheadians wrongly play down the idealistic element of your position. You are so determined to claim the mantle of realism and to cut loose from

Cartesian anxiety and Kantian subjectivity that you misrepresent your relationship to German idealism. Most of you, including Griffin, have the trademark idealistic fixation with the importance of consciousness and freedom. To say, as you do, that nature is like human subjects, or that to be a person is to experience and be experienced, is to line up with Schelling and Hegel in conceiving reality as nothing less than the self-thinking of Spirit. Spirit empties itself into the real world of sensuous particularity in its creation of the world as an experience of itself, as in Hegel, or as the lure for creative transformation, as in Whitehead. Anyone who knows post-Kantian idealism and is not a Whiteheadian can see and feel the German idealism in Whiteheadian thought.

But I digress. Griffin makes the strongest case that I know of for the view that it makes more sense to say that all actualities have experience than to claim that experiences are not actual things. In his rendering, panexperientialism is not a form of vitalism, as it does not claim that a new causal force emerged when life broke into mechanistic nature, and it is not as implausible as dualism or materialism. Griffin emphasizes that the panexperientialist hall of fame includes Leibniz, Spinoza, Fechner, Lotze, James, Bergson, Peirce, Whitehead, Hartshorne, F.C.S. Schiller, C.H. Waddington, and David Bohm.

Unfortunately, some of these intellectual heroes—notably Spinoza, Fechner, and Schiller—taught that *all things* have feelings. This idea that rocks and minerals have feelings is the bane of good panexperientialism. Griffin follows Leibniz, Whitehead and Hartshorne in distinguishing between individuals that respond to their environment and mere aggregational entities that do not bear psychic life. A rock cannot experience because it lacks the coordinating and unifying occasion that would enable it to respond to its environment as a unity with any degree of freedom.[5]

Griffin's chief work on this subject, *Unsnarling the World-Knot,* argued vigorously that only the panexperiential option integrates scientific knowledge with the core beliefs that are necessary to rational thought, because only panexperientialism reconciles the element of truth in dualist theory (that mind and brain are distinct and interact) with the element of truth in materialist theory (that all actual things are physical). Since the prevailing scientific picture of reality finds no place for consciousness or freedom, something has to be wrong with it. The key to making science more true and real is to make experience a fundamental category.

There is a connection between Griffin's emphasis on the unreality of materialism and the increasing emphasis in his later works on the existence of hard-core commonsense truths. His concept of what he calls "constructive postmodernism" has always included a belief in hard-core commonsense, but by the end of the 1990s it was the centerpiece of his argument.[6]

Philosophically this position is rooted in Scottish commonsense realism, and Griffin stresses that Whitehead, also, believed in universal truths of experience. In *Process and Reality*, Whitehead declared that all thinking must bow to the presuppositions that are necessary "for the regulation of our lives" and that all "such presumptions are imperative in experience."[7]

Like Thomas Reid and the Scottish moralists, Griffin contends that certain common presumptions are universally presupposed in practice even when they are denied in theory. Most commonsense ideas are culturally conditioned, but some are universal facts of experience. In Griffin's early version of this argument, he described causality, freedom, genuine evil, and the existence of an actual world as commonsense universals: All rational people practice the conviction that every event is influenced by other events. Our behavior is at least partly self-determining. Some things happen that should not have happened. And real things exist external to one's consciousness.

Griffin contends, very much like Reid, that these ideas are common to all human beings at the presuppositional level and are inevitably presupposed in practice. Moreover, they cannot be denied verbally without self-contradiction. One assumes causality in the act of causing one's self or others to doubt causality; one uses one's freedom in the act of renouncing the idea of freedom; even professed solipsists assume an actual world when they drive a car or question the existence of others. Expanding on this theme, Griffin added that time, axiological realism, the correspondence of interpretive ideas to the real world as the measure of truth, and the ultimate meaningfulness of life are also universal truths. Everyone distinguishes among the past, present, and future, and recognizes that some things are better than others. The ultimate test of any philosophical position is whether it does justice to the hard-core ideas that are inevitably presupposed in practice by all human beings.

That is a thoroughly rationalist claim—that thinking must attempt to integrate the universal facts of experience. By this definition, Whitehead and Hartshorne were unyielding rationalists, although both of them had room for Peirce's falliblist principle that all notions must be subject to doubt. To Griffin, this means that precise *formulations* of hard-core ideas are always fallible. Moreover, Peirce affirmed the existence of universal facts of experience; "commonsense" was one of his central doctrines.

Whitehead, by making the inevitable presuppositions of practice crucial to his system, adopted a defining feature of Peirce's and James' pragmatism. To Griffin, this combination of metaphysical and practical reason is what is needed to ward off the skepticism and nihilism of radical postmodern theory. Constructive postmodernism refuses the fashionable indulgence of doubting things that must be presupposed to be true in the very act of doubting. Theology cannot go down the road of radical postmodernism without playing into the hands of sophisticated fundamentalists and nihilistic relativists. If religion is not an important mode of knowledge, it deserves to be marginalized as it has been under modernity.[8]

Knowledge consists of beliefs that are well-founded and true—"justified true belief"—and religion cannot get along without justified beliefs. Griffin rejects the postmodern claim that all "facts" are theory-laden products of prior conceptual and cultural systems. If each worldview creates its own facts and we never experience any data directly, we have no reason to reject theologies assuming a geocentric universe or biblical inerrancy.[9]

To Griffin, the crucial theological task is to rehabilitate theism while adhering to the formal standards of modern philosophy and science. Process thought holds in view the same naturalistic world described by modern science and philosophy, but it teaches that human beings directly intuit divine reality at all times. God is the really existing soul of the world that acts throughout the entire evolutionary process and directly influences higher-level actualities. Put differently, God is the supreme Holy Reality that is directly and constantly prehended by human beings.[10]

That comes pretty close to what Alvin Plantinga calls a "properly basic" claim—that belief in God is properly held without appealing to inferential evidence. Plantinga says that believing in God is on the same level epistemologically as believing in the existence of other minds, the past, or an external word, and Griffin says that Plantinga goes overboard in two respects: (1) his God is too traditionally Christian to be properly basic, and (2) the existence of an external world is knowable through perception and is thus a fact of experience. But Griffin espouses an ostensibly generic version of Plantinga's argument that belief in God is constitutive in the foundations of knowledge. The sense of a Holy Reality *is* properly basic to human experience; thus, a generic form of the Holy Reality experienced by people from various traditions would be, and is, universal.[11]

Griffin's early version of this claim described God as the supreme, nonderivative, Holy Power that is alone worthy of worship and ultimate concern; the purposive creator of the world, perfectly good, and source of moral norms; and the ultimate guarantee of life's meaning and hope of ultimate victory of good over evil. That ruled out the idea of God as a cluster of ideals, the identification of God with anything imperfect, definitions devoid of aim such as "being itself," any identification of God with evil impulses, and all forms of "might makes right" theodicy. In his later versions, Griffin adds that God is a personal being; perfect in love, goodness, and beauty; supreme, "perhaps even perfect" in power; omnipresent; and necessarily and everlastingly existent.

I fail to see how this is not a quite specific God, even if one grants Griffin's claim that it is too generic to be a *doctrine* of God—a specific version of belief in a Holy Reality. I am going to circle back to this point in a moment, but I am overdue to complete my assignment about Whitehead vis-á-vis Hartshorne, on which Griffin usually sides with Hartshorne when there is a difference. No one has contributed more than Griffin to our understanding of the differences and similarities between Whitehead and Hartshorne. In Griffin's definitive account, Whitehead and Hartshorne held different views of divine dipolarity, eternal possibilities, secondary qualities, metaphysical principles, philosophic method, the perishing of actual occasions, and objective immortality. Most importantly, they differed about the nature of divine reality, though not in the way that process theologians favoring Hartshorne often say.[12]

Griffin shows that so-called "dipolar theism" is actually doubly dipolar, and Whitehead and Hartshorne both had versions of both kinds. Whitehead famously distinguished between God's primordial and consequent natures, conceiving God as influencing the world (primordial) and as being influenced by the world (consequent). Hartshorne distinguished between God's abstract essence and concrete states, conceiving God as unchanging (abstract essence) and as changing as part of the temporal process (concrete states). Against the tendency of many process thinkers, Griffin plays up the differences between these models, where there are two kinds of dipolarity at issue. One is about God influencing and being influenced, the other is about God changing and not changing. With differences in emphasis, Whitehead and Hartshorne both affirmed both kinds of dipolarity, but Whitehead's version was flawed because he tried to account for both dipolarities under the primordial/consequent distinction. Under the primordial category Whitehead described God as unchanging *and* as influencing the world; under the consequent category he described God as changing *and* as influenced by the world.[13]

To Griffin, that overtaxes the primordial/consequent distinction. According to Whitehead, the initial aims through which God influences the world come from God's primordial nature alone, but Whitehead also described God's primordial nature as an abstraction, "a mere factor in God, deficient in actuality." If the primordial nature is an abstraction, Griffin reasons, it cannot be the source of initial aims, for Whitehead taught (as a metaphysical principle) that only actualities can provide explanatory reasons. In this way, Whitehead's account of the primordial nature contradicted his maxim that God must not be treated as an exception to metaphysical principles. A.H.

Johnson pressed Whitehead on this point; Whitehead replied that it had been "a great carelessness" on his part to treat a mere abstraction in God as an actuality. Following Hartshorne and the early John Cobb, Griffin argues that if the initial aims come from God's *unchanging* primordial nature, they cannot be relevant to changing, specific situations in the world. Whitehead's account of the initial aims was contradictory; thus his concept of God had to be reconceptualized.[14]

Griffin embraces the Hartshornean view of God as an or-dered society of occasions of experience. If God is a society of events analogous to a human soul, the initial aims can be viewed as an act of God's entire being in the moment. In this view, God's consequent nature becomes simply the abstract principle that each new moment requires what Hartshorne called "a new Consequent State of deity." In each moment of the world process, God apprehends all the events that have just occurred, "then unifies all these prehensions into a divine satisfaction, which includes initial aims for the next moment of the universe." The idea of God's consequent nature is simply an abstraction from this process. God's initial aims combine God's primordial aims with the "sympathetic knowledge" that God gains from immediately past circumstances.[15]

Whitehead taught that the real enduring things in life are societies, and his ontology was based on the idea that enduring individuals are fundamentally relational, not single actual entities. Yet he described God as a single actual entity that is everlastingly growing together. Griffin counters that if God is everlastingly in concrescence, God must receive efficient causation and final causation simultaneously, unlike any (finite) actual occasion. Thus Whitehead made another metaphysical exception for God. Griffin accepts Hartshorne's proposal that God is a personal society of occasions of experience, a living person. But Hartshorne dropped most of Whitehead's doctrine of eternal objects, and he failed to develop a fully dipolar concept of God. Whitehead conceived the eternal objects objectively, as mathematical Platonic forms, and subjectively, as primordially envisaged means by which God lures the world to actualize values; Hartshorne accepted eternal objects only in the objective sense.[16]

Griffin compellingly combines both kinds of divine dipolarity: "We must think of God as both necessary and contingent, both absolute and relative, both unchanging and changing, both independent and dependent, both non-temporal and temporal." God's diverse aspects are God's abstract essence and concrete states. By the former, God is necessary and absolute; by the latter God is contingent and relative. God is unchanging with respect to character but changing in relation to the world process; God is a causal agent that infuses the world with ideals *and* a person who is affected by the world process.[17]

For Griffin, the reality of freedom, causality, the external world, the past, moral values, ultimate meaning, and the sense of Holy Reality are all certain, while his doctrines of God and immortality, being doctrines, are less certain. He claims "overwhelming probability" for naturalistic theism and "strong" probability for some form of continued consciousness beyond bodily death. For panexperientialism he claims the status of "best theory," though he notes that Hartshorne made a claim to certainty. Always, he argues, liberal theology should begin with the hard-core facts of human experience, then choose the best theories at hand, then refine and solidify probable convictions. The liberal principle of upholding the authority of reason and experience is indispensable. On the other hand, the liberal tradition wrongly capitulated to a sensationalist dogma limiting perception to physical sense and a mechanistic dogma rendering fundamental nature devoid of experience, spontaneity, self-determination, and final causation.[18]

Constructive postmodern liberal theology, in Griffin's telling, is a means of deliverance from that sorry and unreal world. It rests on the three p's of Whiteheadian theism: prehension (the idea of intuitive apprehension), panentheism (the idea that God and the world are internal to each other) and panexperientialism (the idea that all aggregate-transcending entities possess some measure of experience).

Griffin plays up Whitehead's rationalism about commonsense universals. The facts of experience, he says, provide a criterion for judging worldviews that is universal, not relativistic, and not culturally conditioned. Any philosophy that does not rest upon hard-core commonsense "cannot be a guide to practice." Certain truths of experience are transcultural and universal, standing in judgment over worldviews; any perspective that purports to say something worthwhile must assume and employ them.

I fail to see how that is not a type of foundationalism, even if it is not the type that builds a house on distinct first principles. Certainly, there is a meaningful difference between saying, as Thomas Reid did, that every house needs a foundation, and saying, as Griffin does, that thinking must begin wherever we happen to be. But to say that commonsense universalism is the only worthwhile way to do philosophy is to make an aggressively foundationalist claim. When he started on this path, Griffin made the criterion of self-contradiction central to its definition. Interpretation is variable and fallible, he allowed, but causality, freedom, an external world, and genuine evil are universal facts of experience that cannot be rejected verbally without contradiction. Later he added truth as correspondence to the actual world.

But universality is a powerful idea and Griffin's list kept getting longer; eventually it included the ultimate meaning of life and a sense of a supreme Holy Reality. With each addition his appeal to performative self-contradiction got weaker. Immanuel Kant was notoriously perplexed about causality, freedom, time, and radical evil, and the correspondence theory of truth is widely disputed. More importantly, many people hold with ample consistency that life has no ultimate meaning and there is no Holy Reality to experience. Whatever one makes of causality, freedom, time, and radical evil, Griffin's strongest argument for commonsense universals does not prove his ultimacy arguments. Ultimately, nothing may be important. All that Griffin can argue here is that his ultimacy arguments do not lack some power of necessity, for if nothing is ultimately important, life itself is ultimately meaningless.[19]

That is a Kantian argument. But Griffin avoids post-Kantian idealism like the plague, partly because Kant was notoriously critical of commonsense realism, never mind that what is ultimately at stake for Griffin and Whiteheadian theism is the same thing that German idealists fixated upon—the spiritual importance of freedom, feeling, consciousness, and moral value.

Kantian idealism was the wellspring of modern theology. The key to Kant's system, terrible ironies notwithstanding, was the emancipating and unifying reality of freedomeven as Kant admitted that he did not understand it. Kant's transcendental idealism laid the groundwork for all post-Kantian theologies by theorizing about the creative powers of mind and the categories of understanding as universal conditions of experience. That led to Schelling and Hegel privileging becoming over being, which yielded Hegel's concept of God as spiraling relationality embracing all otherness and difference. God's infinite subjectivity, in Hegel's idea, was an infinite inter-subjectivity of holding differences together in a play of creative relationships not dissolving into sameness.

German idealism put panentheism into play in modern theology by conceiving it as irreducibly dynamic and relational—the very things that supposedly distinguish the Whiteheadian school. God is the inter-subjective whole of wholes, not the Wholly Other. It was Hegel's fluid, spiraling, relational panentheism that changed the debate in theology about how God might relate to the world, offering an alternative to pantheism *and* the static being-God later rejected by Nietzsche, Heidegger, and Levinas.

There are Whiteheadians who draw upon the idealist wellsprings of liberal theology in their work, Philip Clayton most notably. But Griffin absorbed the aversion of his school to German idealism, even as he and his school refashioned its consuming preoccupations.

## THEOLOGY AND THE ACADEMIC STUDY OF RELIGION

One of the things I most appreciate about Griffin's work is his strong defense of theology as an academic field and his resistance to an exclusively religious-studies approach to religion. Religious thinkers should be able to discuss and defend religious ideas in the same way that philosophers and physicists pursue ideas in their fields. What would philosophy be if you couldn't make arguments about first-order truth claims? Physicists go on about electrons, quarks, black holes, and gravitons, and nobody tells them that they should stick to meta-descriptions.[20]

The study of religion cannot be a serious academic discipline if it is not permitted to pursue truth questions in the open, critical, position-taking manner of other disciplines. Moreover, theology cannot meaningfully address the modern crisis of belief if it shies away from making truth claims. Like Hartshorne, Cobb, and Bernard Meland, Griffin believes that naturalistic process theism is the answer to the crisis of belief.

Like Meland he looks for a way to warm the spiritual coldness of Chicago empiricism; unlike Meland he puts no stock in the resacralizing power of mythical symbolism. To Griffin, remythologization simply obscures the real problems of intelligibility and credible belief. If process thought is true, it is true fundamentally as a metaphysical description. Metaphysical principles trump any Meland-like claims that might be made about the evocative appeal of process metaphors.[21]

When I wrote about Griffin in volume three of my trilogy on liberal theology, I expected to press very hard on Griffin versus Meland and Marjorie Suchocki on this issue. But then I talked to him about it, and he said, you know, I have never said that there is anything wrong with appropriating Whitehead the way that Meland, Suchocki or Catherine Keller do. He reasoned that his rationalistic Whiteheadianism complemented the more aesthetic, pragmatic, and feminist forms of process theology: "The kinds of things I do seem to meet the needs of quite a number of people, and Catherine's and Marjorie's writings appeal to many people that mine don't. This is a Jamesian-Whiteheadian point, about different temperaments." Suchocki put it more sharply to me, describing Griffin as the "last important defender" of the rationalist approach to process theology: "The old preoccupation with finding the 'true' metaphysical system is fading away."[22]

So I went back to David; he was lecturing in Michigan at the time. What does it mean even to claim that you espouse the true metaphysical system? He waved it off. Griffin said, "When I get to heaven I don't expect to find that I had the true metaphysical system. But I do believe that Whitehead developed the best one, and I'm not going to sell it short."

Certainly no one could ever say, with any degree of justified true belief, that David Griffin sold short Whiteheadian theism or liberal theology.

# 3. Griffin's Panexperientialism as *Philosophia Perennis*

## Daniel A. Dombrowski

The title of David Ray Griffin's 1998 book, *Unsnarling the World Knot: Consciousness, Freedom, and the Mind-Body Problem,* alludes to a rope metaphor from Schopenhauer to the effect that the key philosophical problem since the seventeenth century—the mind-body problem—is, on prevailing assumptions, unsolvable.

### THE NEED FOR A RADICAL APPROACH

At the risk of mixing metaphors, one can highlight several different prominent contemporary philosophers of mind to illustrate why we have been tie≠d in a "world knot": William Seager claimed that we have no idea whatsoever how consciousness "emerges" from matter; Jaegwon Kim held that we have reached a "dead end" regarding the mind-body problem; Colin McGinn alleged that we will *never* be able to understand the emergence of consciousness from the brain; John Searle suggested that most of mainstream philosophy of mind is "obviously false"; and Galen Strawson maintained that only a "revolutionary" new way of thinking will enable us to respond adequately to the mind-body problem. Although Daniel Dennett has been a bit more optimistic regarding a solution to the mind-body problem on prevailing assumptions, even he portrayed consciousness as a "mystery."[1]

In full light of the enormity of the difficulty, Griffin hopes to "unsnarl" the world-knot. It might be assumed that this unsnarling is an instance of the new, *revolutionary* thinking called for by Strawson. But Thomas Nagel's phrasing of the same view may be more helpful when he says that *radical* speculation is needed in order to unsnarl the world knot (5). I am taking the etymology of the word "radical" seriously, in that it comes from the Latin *radix* for "root." That is, Griffin has offered an oxymoronic *radically new* approach to the mind-body problem, just as he is trying to revitalize an old solution to it. In the present chapter, I will be attempting to find for Griffin a place of honor within a perennial tradition that goes back to Plato. As Josiah Royce once suggested:

> Whenever I have most carefully revised my … standards, I am always able to see … that at best I have been finding out, in some new light, the true meaning that was latent in old traditions.… Revision does not mean mere destruction. … Let us bury the natural body of tradition. What we want is its glorified body and its immortal soul.[2]

Whitehead once made a similar point:

> Undoubtedly, philosophy is dominated by its past literature to a greater extent than any other science. And rightly so. But the claim that it has acquired a set of technical terms sufficient for its purposes, and exhaustive of its meanings, is entirely unfounded.[3]

But this gets us ahead of the story. Or better, it prematurely puts us behind it.

It will serve us well to get clear at the outset regarding what the problem is: How can experience arise out of, and act back upon, nonexperience? The two major contemporary responses to this question—dualism and materialism—engage in thinking that is both wishful *and fearful.* I see this addition ("and fearful") to be one of Griffin's most significant achievements, in that both of these responses are often driven by fears that are frequently not acknowledged. One does sometimes hear dualists express their fear that life would not be meaningful if human beings were put on a material par with clocks or computers, but it is also instructive to note that materialists are often fearful of a return to belief in supernaturalism and miracles if dualism is accepted. Hence dualism is to be avoided at all costs, according to fearful materialists like Dennett,[4] even if Dennett is apparently oblivious to the fact that there are defenders of theistic metaphysics like Griffin who are also opponents to supernaturalism and miracles, as the title of his 2001 book, *Reenchantment without Supernaturalism,* indicates.[5] By at least acknowledging the existence of wishful and fearful thinking in both forms, Griffin suggests, we might more easily work our way to a better solution to the problem.

## SOURCE OF THE PROBLEM

The root of the difficulty, if not of the solution, infamously goes back to Descartes and his enormous influence. Unlike most critics of Descartes, however, Griffin locates the problem not with Descartes' view of mind, but rather with his view of matter. This is another signal contribution from Griffin. Indeed, there are problems with Descartes' view of mind as constituted by a purely temporal inside with no spatiality, but even more problematic on Griffin's insightful reading are the issues concerning Descartes' view of matter as strictly outside, and hence devoid of internal relations, and purely spatial in the sense that it can be understood in an instant without temporal (and hence causal) relations (46-49).

The problems unique to dualism are well known. It cannot account well, or even plausibly, for interaction between mind and body; and it violates the understandable assumption that there is continuity in nature. Whitehead goes so far as to claim that the bifurcation of nature is vicious![6] And the problems unique to materialism are also well known, even if they are typically not proclaimed as loudly as those with dualism. Materialists have a devil of a time explaining the unity of experience if it is composed of billions of insentient neurons; it typically either leaves consciousness out of consideration or treats it as an (emergent or supervenient) afterthought; and it contradicts what Griffin calls certain hardcore commonsense notions like belief in human freedom (49-60). By the way, this is another one of Griffin's significant contributions: he distinguishes between certain "soft" commonsense notions, which apply only contingently in some circumstances but not others, and "hardcore" commonsense notions, whose denial is inevitably contradicted by our practice, such as belief in an external world, belief in human freedom (and hence responsibility), and belief in efficient causality from the past (15-21).

Contemporary philosophers of mind tend to emphasize either the problems unique to dualism or those unique to materialism. But from Griffin's radical panexperientialist standpoint, which lies outside the provenance of either dualism or materialism, it is clear that there are some problems that are common to *both* dualism and materialism. Among these are difficulties in determining where the line should be drawn between experiencing and non-experiencing beings (a difficulty that is avoided in panexperientialism, as we will see); in accounting for consciousness in some fashion other than as the Great Exception in nature; and in explaining how experience could emerge out of machine-like nonexperience (60-76).

All of these problems (those unique to dualism, those unique to materialism, and those shared by dualism and materialism) can be traced back to Descartes' views, especially to his view of machine-like matter. If mind is supposed to be pure temporality with no spatiality, and if matter is supposed to be pure spatiality with no internal duration and no experience of temporal passage, then the remarkable view of Whitehead embraced in a nuanced way by Griffin stands in stark opposition:

> The mutual structural relations between events are both spatial and temporal. If you think of them as merely spatial you are omitting the temporal element, and if you think of them as merely temporal you are omitting the spatial element. Thus when you think of space alone, or of time alone, you are dealing in abstractions, namely, you are leaving out an essential element in the life of nature as known to you in . . . experience.[7]

It should be emphasized that there is one sort of emergentism that is acceptable to Griffin: the emergence of complex experiences out of the simple experiences of actual occasions (or events, or microscopic organisms). What is unintelligible is the emergence of an experiential "inside" out of non-experiential bits of machinery governed strictly in terms of external relations. The latter sort of emergence would involve "sheer magic," as the panexperientialist geneticist Sewall Wright put it. Even the materialist J.J.C. Smart points out colloquially that no enzyme can catalyze the production of a spook (63, 71). That is, the conscious experience that arises out of the primitive, preconscious yet experiential organic reality of brain cells is, at least in principle, understandable. What is unintelligible is the idea that complex, conscious experiences arise out of completely insentient, non-experiential mechanical constituents.[8] Once again, the root of the difficulty is to be found in Descartes' view of matter as vacuous actuality devoid of temporality, experience, and internal relatedness to the past.

The debate between dualism and materialism is a family quarrel, on Griffin's view, in that the latter takes its meanings of both mind and matter from the former. Another way to put the point is to say that materialism just *is* dualism in disguise. Once the dualistic ghost in the machine is exorcized by the materialist, what is left is the same mechanized nature that characterized almost all of reality on the dualist's own terms, the exceptions being the relatively infrequent "ghosts" in a predominantly mechanical world (77-80).

We will see that Griffin's way out of these difficulties involves not only avoiding the view of matter as vacuous actuality (i.e., as devoid of any sort of internal becoming or experiential "mattering"), but also avoiding the view that insentient aggregates of sentient constituents (e.g., rocks, telephones) are the most concrete realities. This view is an instance of the fallacy of *misplaced* concreteness if the *res verae* are concrete occasions of momentary experience (117-24, 167). Another case of the fallacy of misplaced concreteness is found when high-level consciousness is seen as the primary, most "concrete" reality, when in point of fact such consciousness is rather rare and abstract in contrast to ubiquitous organic feeling of a more primitive sort. Both bottom-up (materialism) and top-bottom (dualism) approaches to the mind-body problem ultimately lead to insoluble problems regarding the initially excluded reality. Panexperientialism promises a higher degree of integration of our knowledge than its alternatives, but not at the expense of explanatory adequacy.

The Cartesian view of matter (as well as the reductionist's view of matter) as vacuous actuality is, it should be noted, never *experienced* by us. Belief in matter of this sort is the result of high-level abstraction involving *concepts* like extension and mass. It is precisely this "pulpy" character of vacuous actuality that makes the emergence of experience out of it difficult, if not impossible, to understand.

## BEING IS POWER

The thesis of my essay is that Griffin's unsnarling of the world-knot is a highly original (indeed courageous) presentation of a very old view that goes back to Plato. At one point in his book (230), Griffin acknowledges this in a reference to Plato (which unfortunately did not make it into the book's index). The passage in question is from the *Sophist* (247E), where the Eleatic Stranger (presumably Plato) offers the following definition of being:

> I suggest that anything has real being that is so constituted as to possess any sort of power either to affect anything else or (*eite*) to be affected, in however small a degree, by the most insignificant agent, though it be only once. I am proposing as a mark to distinguish real things that they are nothing but power *(dynamis)*.

Two terminological observations are needed. First, it is no accident that the Greek word for "power" *(dynamis)* is also the root of our word "dynamic," and it is precisely this identification of being with dynamic power that makes Plato's later metaphysics so appealing to process thinkers like Whitehead, Hartshorne, Griffin, and myself.[9] In these thinkers, dynamic power is the organic drive of the universe. Second, Plato's use of "or" *(eite)*, however, would have to be changed to "and" *(kai)* in order to be congruent with Griffin's view. This is because the mind-body problem cannot be solved as long as it is assumed that there are some beings that can act on others but nonetheless remain completely unmoved by others, on the one hand, while there are other beings (vacuous actualities) that can supinely be acted upon by others but that exert no agency, on the other. On Griffin's view, the primary beings are actual occasions that have *both* the dynamic power to receive influence from the past *and* the dynamic power to creatively render determinate in the present what were once future determinables.

Mainstream philosophers of mind need to be reminded that Griffin's view is not panconsciousness, but panexperientialism. Consciousness, when seen as a type of specialized experience that involves a contrast between affirmation and negation and that emerges only in those beings with central nervous systems, involves not only a high level of experience but also of spontaneity. Even though experience and spontaneity are distributed throughout nature, consciousness is not. This point is worth emphasizing because of the alleged implausibility of Griffin's panexperientialism, an implausibility that would be quite understandable if panexperientialism were to be equated with panconsciousness.

I suspect that panexperientialism would have fewer critics if they realized that it is a view that is part of the effort to thoroughly naturalize the mind, to rid it of both supernaturalism and its anomalous status when it is interpreted by the Siamese twins joined at the hip: dualism and materialism. That is, "naturalism" and "physicalism" are not synonyms for "materialism." Griffin's view is both naturalistic and physicalist. But it is not a type of "materialism," if this term refers to the Cartesian belief that matter consists in purely external relations with no internal relations or experience. That is, Griffin's view is not materialist, if "matter" refers to vacuous actuality.

Further, panexperientialism is not only a type of naturalism, it is a type of monism in that on its basis there is only one sort of actuality: actual occasions with a physical pole, which has the dynamic power to receive influence from the past, and a mental pole, which has the dynamic power to bring about at least a partially novel advance into the future. Because experience, which at its highest level gives rise to consciousness, is not the Great Exception to everything else that is going on in nature, panexperientialism provides hope that the mind-body problem can be solved (77-92).

Griffin starts from the realization that our experience is itself a part of nature. It is nature known from the inside (which does not commit Griffin to the dualistic implications often found in introspectionist psychology). Generalizing from this (experiential) nature that we know best, we can claim that experience is the very nature of nature. The feelings one has of what happened in one's past a second ago provide an analogy for what happens all the way down in nature. This view avoids the problems that are created in dualism and materialism when experience is, in effect, placed outside of nature. In a word, materialism is half-hearted. Or again, Griffin agrees with dualists and materialists that it is crucial that we observe nature, but he insightfully disagrees with them in claiming that the most direct way to observe nature is to observe it working in ourselves as experiencing beings (124-32).

The Platonic view that Griffin defends is metaphysical or transcendental in the sense that he is offering an account of the universal characteristics of *experiencing individuals* (which is something of a redundancy for panexperientialists). These characteristics would include *both* the dynamic power to feel causal influence from the past, to prehend the physical forces that impinge on an experiencing individual, *and* the dynamic power to add something new, in however slight a way. Griffin speaks of a perpetual oscillation in that there is a duality *within* each organic event wherein efficient causation from the past yields to a literal *de-cision,* a cutting off of some possibilities regarding the future, which then yields to efficient causation being exerted on future events, and so on *ad infinitum* (151-62).

Because *each* event is subject for itself and an object for others, no event is simply a subject or simply an object, contra dualism and materialism. Reality is characterized by the power in subjects-that-become-objects. This stance is compatible with the view that every event has a physical aspect of receiving efficient causality from the past, hence Griffin's position can be described as a type of "physicalism," even if it is not a type of "materialism" wherein there are vacuous actualities that are simply mechanical objects. Finally, this panexperientialist characterization of the real as constituted by dynamic centers of power applies to electrons, organelles, cells, simple animals, mammals, primates, and human beings, as the mental pole expands at each level, but never to the point where the physical pole vanishes (227-31).

The claim that being *is* power has clear theological implications. If there were an omnipotent being with *all* power, then such power would be exercised over absolutely nothing or over the absolutely powerless, neither of which makes any sense if any claim regarding what absolute nothingness *is* is itself contradictory and if being *is* power, respectively. Hartshorne puts the point in an insightful way:

> Whitehead does not "limit" the power of God as compared to some conceivably more powerful being; he merely points out that there is a social element in the very idea of power. . . . In Whitehead's terms every occasion is in some measure self-determining, and in some measure passive, receptive, toward the self-determinations of others. . . . Creativity is not a power, but just power.[10]

In a sense, to be is to create, and belief in a so-called "inorganic" nature is the result of the very slight degree of creative power found there.

## FROM PLATO TO DESCARTES AND FROM DESCARTES TO KANT

The question understandably arises: if Plato was close to a defensible position regarding the relationship between mind and body, what happened in the period between him and Descartes, and, by implication, between him and where we are today, with the mind-body dead end? A short answer to this question would point to Plato himself as the culprit. To be sure, there is much in Plato's dialogues that is congenial to Griffin's panexperientialism, in addition to the above definition of being as dynamic power in the *Sophist*. For example, there are passages in Plato's dialogues that hint at panexperientialism (*Phaedrus* 245E, *Laws* 896A, *Epinomis* 983D), in that psyche, defined in terms of self-motion, is required in order to understand the dynamism of the natural world. By contrast, there is also well-known evidence in Plato (and a great deal of it!) that supports the case for dualism. And it is this latter evidence that has been historically dominant, especially in terms of the efforts of St. Augustine and others to Christianize Plato or to Platonize Christianity. After all, the Cartesian dictum, often depicted as self-evident, that mind is inextended (in contrast to the more defensible view that experiences have *spatio*temporal relations) was Augustinian before it was Cartesian.[11] In this regard, Griffin is part of a tradition within process thought that has sought to uncover a lost process Platonism, a tradition that includes Whitehead, Hartshorne, Leonard Eslick, and others.[12]

To be precise, Griffin's panexperientialism is prefigured in ancient philosophy in terms of a conjunction of three different concepts. Granted, no single ancient author put these three points together, but when they are configured by a contemporary scholar one is able to see a strong resemblance to Griffin's panexperientialism: (1) Plato's discovery in the *Sophist* of the metaphysical concept that being *is* dynamic power; (2) his definition of psyche in the *Phaedrus* and *Laws* in terms of self-motion, a definition that is amplified, as we will see, by Aristotelian hylomorphism and *kinesis;* and (3) the Epicurean belief that ultimate reality is atomic in character. When these three concepts are put together, one derives a view wherein dynamic power and self-motion are seen to go "all the way down."

Because of Whitehead's frequent criticisms of the subject-predicate logic of Aristotle, based as it is on a metaphysics centered on the substance-accident distinction, some process thinkers have concluded that process metaphysics is completely removed from Aristotle and from those he influenced in medieval philosophy. But the situation here is just as complicated as it is regarding Plato.[13] For example, recently two very scholarly books have appeared, both written by Thomists heavily influenced not only by Aristotle but also by Whitehead.[14] And both are somewhat favorably disposed toward Griffin's view. These process-enriched Thomists try to rescue Aristotle and Thomas from the charge that there is insufficient dynamism in metaphysics, with Whitehead providing the inspiration for their efforts. In the Aristotelian-Thomistic tradition, on their interpretation, matter is not the vacuous actuality it is in Descartes in that it is always informed. Or again, the whole point to Aristotelian-Thomistic hylomorphism is to suggest that matter without form and form without matter are the results of abstraction in that concrete reality is populated by "formbodies" or "mindbodies" or "soulbodies," to coin terms that try to capture the non-dualistic character of hylomorphs. The Aristotelian idea that mind is, in a manner, all things is a protest against the view that mind is what is left over when one abstracts away from either behavior or matter; rather, matter in motion just *is* mind in some fashion.[15]

Griffin's view is also "medieval" in the sense that scholastic thinkers often distinguished (albeit inconsistently) between the *categories,* which were concepts that were applicable to all creatures but not to God, and the *transcendentals,* which were concepts that were applicable to all beings including God. It is often noticed that among the transcendentals were oneness, goodness, truth, and beauty. In addition, there was *power,* the ability to influence others, and, in the process thinking exemplified by Griffin, the ability to be influenced. That is, one way to interpret what Griffin is doing is to say that the dynamic power to receive influence from others, as well as the dynamic power to creatively advance beyond such influence—in that there are never sufficient causal conditions from the past to determine completely concrete actuality in the present, although there are necessary conditions of some sort—is a transcendental.[16]

As before, it is Descartes and his legacy regarding matter that is Griffin's adversary, not premodern philosophy, whether ancient or medieval. Whitehead, it will be remembered, thought of his philosophy as a recurrence to pre-Kantian modes of thought.[17] In this regard, it is instructive to remember that no less an authority than Ivor Leclerc thought of Whitehead as a dynamic hylomorphist.[18] My point here is to highlight the long tradition in philosophy that Griffin is not only revitalizing but advancing after a three-century slowdown, due to Descartes' influential view of matter as vacuous actuality. As Whitehead once said, and as I think Griffin should affirm, "nothing in thought is ever completely new."[19] Griffin is not being denigrated, nor is Whitehead, when they are seen as important footnotes to Plato.[20]

Although Griffin mentions only briefly the premodern roots of his panexperientialism,[21] he pays careful attention to certain developments in modern philosophy that indicate the pushback that has occurred (or that could occur) with respect to the Cartesian view of matter and its effect on dominant modern and contemporary views of mind. For obvious reasons, due to Leibniz's own panpsychism, especially in *Monadology,* Griffin notes the importance of this great thinker, but Leclerc also alerts us to Leibniz's similarity to Aristotle. Newton insisted that an active principle had to be operative *in* nature, and not *ex machina* as in Descartes. But Leibniz thought that Newton did, in fact, unwittingly fall victim to use of the *ex machina* device. Leibniz's defense of something fundamentally active in nature was seen by him as a return to the Greeks, specifically to Aristotle's idea that physical existents were characterized by *kinesis* and *dynamis*. On Leclerc's interpretation, which adds historical depth to Griffin's view, both Leibniz *and* Whitehead signal a revitalization of the Aristotelian doctrine of internal change and power in matter and a denigration of the Cartesian denial of internal change and power in matter, a denial, as Griffin notes, that has largely persisted to the present day.[22] As Hartshorne puts the point, "If upon the wreckage of Newtonian materialism a new world view is to arise, then Whitehead's system is the most important single indication of what that world view is to be."[23]

It is customary to emphasize the fact that Hume awoke Kant from his dogmatic rationalist slumbers that were induced by Leibniz, Wolff, and others. To view things exclusively in this way, however, is to fail to consider the possibility that the Leibnizian view may be more compatible with contemporary science than other modern views, including Kant's. Consider the idea that the usual classification of natural things as "inanimate" derives from a neglect of microscopic activity, as in the kinetic theory of heat or the view that even rocks are in motion in their microscopic parts.[24] That is, scholars tend not to accentuate the degree to which Leibniz's panpsychism had an influence on Kant. As a result, there is a perhaps understandable tendency to read Kant's phenomena-noumena distinction as being almost exclusively under the influence of Descartes.

It is one of Griffin's signal achievements that he makes a convincing case for the claim that Kant in his *Dreams of a Spirit-Seer* came closer to panexperientialism than most scholars realize, specifically in his discussion of what will later be called noumenal things-in-themselves in contrast to the phenomenal world as it appears to us. In this early work, Kant seems to think that *either* we should remain agnostic regarding things-in-themselves *or* we should agree with Leibniz that they are instances of psyche. As is well known, Kant eventually opted for the former alternative, but the prominent place given the latter alternative by Kant should not escape our notice, especially because it has not received the attention it deserves and hence may have unanticipated strengths. Kant appears to rebuke those who ridicule Leibniz's panpsychism because, *if* we had to state what physical reality is in itself, we would have to follow Leibniz.[25]

Consider the following: In *some* sense, we know ourselves from the inside and other beings from the outside. What are the latter like in themselves? Because we have *some* knowledge from the inside, in that we are intimately aware of our own experiences, one wonders if others have insides as well. We need not assume that our purely spatial and external awareness of these objects exhausts what they are in themselves. Indeed, it would seem extravagant to make such an assumption. What it would be like to have no inside at all, what it would be like to be a vacuous actuality, is beyond our ken, as Griffin holds and as Kant indirectly intimates (84, 98-103).[26] It is consistent with Griffin's view to emphasize that Kant refused to identify things-in-themselves with lifeless matter and left open the possibility that they were instances of experience.[27]

We should be clear that when we experience green in a grove of trees, our immediate sources for this experience are events that take place in living cells in our eyes and in the brain. Some quality is abstracted from these events and transformed into what we experience as greenness; Whitehead speaks of "transmutation."[28] This process of transforming many received data into one patch of experienced greenness is a mental operation that cannot be supposed to be enjoyed by cells in the optic nerve or in the brain in *exactly* the same way that it is found in human experience, but on the panexperientialist view there must be some quality *analogous* to greenness that the cells experience. Or again, if one has a toothache and if the transmission of the agitation from the cells in one's tooth to the brain is interrupted by an anaesthetic, the cells may continue to have the same feelings as before, even if they are not transmuted into human experience.[29]

Because a single, unitary experience of a human being is molded out of many stimuli (evidence from the five senses, thousands of influences from the past relayed via memory, billions of experiences exerting their influence via brain cells), mechanical or automatic predictability is not likely. That is, prediction is limited not merely by our ignorance, but is rather due to the creative synthesis that is experience itself. Those who come to appreciate Griffin's panexperientialism may very well be like the character in Moliere who did not realize that he had been speaking prose all his life.[30]

Of course there are many other insightful thinkers who have defended panexperientialism or positions that have a family resemblance to it. David Skrbina details many of these, who would include Peirce (perhaps) and several of the German romantics. Time does not permit me to treat all of them, an effort that would duplicate Skrbina's book.[31] Among those I will neglect are Wordsworth and the English romantic poets who, through Coleridge, borrowed freely from the German romantics. The central point here is to locate Griffin within an overall tradition that is quite old, a tradition that is continued in various ways in contemporary analytic philosophy through thinkers such as David Chalmers, Thomas Nagel, William Seager, and Galen Strawson.

## ANTICIPATING THE FUTURE

Because panexperientialism and positions that have a family resemblance to it have been around since the time of Plato, it is unlikely that they will go away soon. Indeed, in part because of Griffin, it is not hyperbolic to suggest that not only will they continue to hang around but likely will be taken more seriously in scholarly circles than they have been for quite some time. That is, having sketched the place of Griffin's panexperientialism in its historical setting, I would now like to very briefly mention two points regarding what its influence could be in the future.

First, from a phenomenological point of view, everyone can attest to the experience of *localized pleasure and pain,* which offers strong support for the idea that experience occurs at least as far "down" as cells. Although this phenomenological evidence does not exactly prove panexperientialism, it does ably counteract the still popular claim that panexperientialism is implausible. The hope is that even intuitions regarding implausibility will change over time, once the most egregious caricatures of panexperientialism are removed—for example, that telephones and rocks are believed by panexperientialists like Griffin to experience or even to be conscious. As Griffin argues, one pays a very stiff price for failing to distinguish adequately between mere aggregates and compound experiencing individuals.

This phenomenological evidence indicates, at the very least, that experiences of a subhuman kind (cells or smaller) are real. It is not only *we* who suffer, but also the microscopic living members of our bodies. "Our sensations are sympathetic participations in their feelings."[32] Griffin's case for panexperientialism is more likely to be persuasive when we focus on a mode of perception other than vision, which tends to play into the hands of modern dualists or materialists by giving us a static and apparently value-neutral concept of nature. By contrast, if we take as the quintessential example of direct perception a throb of localized pain or pleasure in an organism, we come to know that something is happening *in* the body that is not value-neutral. From this latter starting point, it is much easier to consider the merits of the claim that there is no inanimate matter, if this means inactive matter. A panexperientialist defends the stance that in a material being's microscopic parts there is self-motion in response to influence. Cells in particular resemble us in having feelings.[33]

It is true that we cannot quite discern the microindividual cells that constitute our bodies, but this should not conceal the fact that in vague outline we can demarcate localized feeling. In addition, it should not escape our notice that cells can in some vague way prehend us, in that psychosomatic illness would be practically inexplicable on any other basis.[34] The datum of pain experience is in the body, initially in cells and then in human experience or mind. "Hurt my cells and you hurt me."[35] A true solipsist would be someone who, if such were possible, never experienced localized pleasure or pain, in that localized pleasure and pain signal feeling *of* feeling of a microscopic sort.

Griffin's view is captured well in Hartshorne's claim that the prosaic or apathetic fallacy is just as misleading as the pathetic one. Granted, we should not attribute pathos to entities that cannot feel, such as aggregates and abstractions. But we should also avoid failure to appreciate microscopic sentiency when it is, in fact, present. Both primitive animism and seventeenth-century-inspired mechanism should be avoided in an accurate description of our own experiences and in our description of nature in general. And an accurate description of nature will involve not only theories in physics, but also those in biology and psychology. None of us simply decides what our cells will do. Rather, because they are not entirely mindless or insentient, they make their own decisions, in however slight a way. Not only are cells within a body alive, they are possessive of a rudimentary spontaneity.[36]

It will no doubt be objected that Griffin's theory might work as far "down" as cells, but that it does not work when trying to explain inorganic nature. However, if the bodily conditions of our feelings of "inorganic" nature are themselves feelings, then panexperientialism cannot be rejected as easily as these objectors suppose. If we learn about nature largely through sight, hearing, and touch receptors, and if these receptors genuinely relate us to things outside of the body, the relata cannot be entirely dissimilar. If sensation is human feeling of subhuman feeling, and if no feeling is solipsistic, then there is no radical difference in kind between cellular feeling and the self-movement in response to causal influence found in atoms. There is indeed "insentient matter," but this refers to a complex or aggregate whose constituents are primitive forms of sentience. As before, tables as unities are in fact insentient, but over a long stretch of time the changes that are constantly occurring *in* the table will clearly manifest themselves. For example, the wooden boat exhibited at the museum at Giza in Egypt, supposedly the oldest in the world, is now hardly recognizable as a boat.

To say in 17th-century fashion that matter is *absolutely* insentient is to proceed as if cell-theory and subatomic physics had not occurred. It is not hyperbolic to claim that we now know that nature is everywhere active. It is true that many materialists might try to conceptually sever the connection between activity and sentience by admitting that there is activity throughout nature, but insisting that there is zero sentience and zero novelty below a certain level. However, this distinction leaves the ubiquitous activity in nature unexplained. Panexperientialism provides such an explanation in terms of protean self-motion such that the slight level of novelty found in atoms should not be confused with the complete absence of such activity.[37]

As before, our physical feelings of our own past just a moment ago provide a powerful analogy for what happens all the way down in nature. What is *really* implausible is either placing experience outside of nature (as in dualism) or resting content with an explanatory scheme that leaves experience, especially conscious experience, unexplained (as in materialism). If even our bodily cells are prehenders with inner durations and experiences of qualia, and if all the information we have about nature is mediated through them, then understanding rests on our experiences *of* experiences at the microscopic level. To put the point in Platonic terms that Plato himself would never have used, human experience is re-collection of what is "collected" at the cellular level.

This takes us close to Griffin's panexperientialism. Once we are in the neighborhood of panexperientialism, there is no need to criticize physics as long as one realizes that it deals with abstractions and needs to be supplemented by an "inner physics" (as emphasized by Strawson) analogous to the "inner biology" with which we are all familiar via localized pleasure and pain. Granted, our localized pleasure and pain is still *somewhat* abstract, in that we cannot identify the specific microindividual cells that are harmed by intense heat, for example (see Plato's *Republic* 462c-d, regarding *neura* or "nerves"), but we do experience very small regions of cellular individuals and vicariously participate, via our central nervous systems, in their experiences.

In short, what we need is an enlarged conception of matter. Griffin will continue to help us figure out how to develop this concept. It should be emphasized, however, that on the basis of this enlarged concept of matter we can still say that the physical has priority over the mental, in the sense that even on a panexperientialist basis the mental pole in each actual occasion is derivative of the physical pole, but the physical pole involves powerful (Platonic) energy to be affected by others. To receive influence is oxymoronically a type of activity, as in working hard to hear the counterpoint in a difficult symphony or as in deliberately laboring to listen to what someone else is saying. *Purely* physical entities, on this view, are aggregates of active singulars. The robust character of the physical in panexperientialism, however, is expressed well by Whitehead when he says that "my theory . . . is ready to accept any outcome of physical research."[38]

Second, it is still unclear if the resurgence of panpsychism in philosophy of mind will lead to long-term productive conversation between process thinkers like Griffin and *mainstream analytic philosophers.* It is clear that the "explanatory gap" between first- and third-person accounts of consciousness derives from at least somewhat inaccessible experiential "properties" (with the scare quotes to be explained momentarily), which are at least somewhat analogous to the self-motions of Platonic souls. Panexperientialism is the view that these properties are everywhere. Because they are everywhere, panexperientialism is capable in ways that dualism and mechanistic materialism are not of understanding experience as an evolutionary process. That is, Griffin's view is well equipped to bridge the gap between functional or causal theories of mind, on the one hand, and subjective accounts of experience (including conscious experience), on the other, in a way that dovetails well with evolutionary theory.

Sequestering experience from the rest of nature prevents such a dovetailing, as Nathaniel Barrett notices in his insightful treatment of process panpsychism (or panexperientialism), which will inform much of what I have to say in the next several paragraphs.[39]

Unfortunately, the resurgence of panpsychism in analytic philosophy of mind usually rests on tacit substantialist metaphysical assumptions that are at odds with those explicitly operative in process philosophy (including process Platonism), as Barrett notices. In analytic versions of panpsychism, the mind-body problem is typically framed in terms of *properties.* These may be phenomenal, physical, or functional. Further, these properties are seen to have various kinds of relationship to each other: identity, emergence, supervenience, or reductionist. The explanatory gap mentioned above involves a seemingly irreconcilable difference between phenomenal properties and the rest. Griffin's view is that these phenomenal "properties" (variously described as "what it is like to be an X," or as qualia) are ubiquitous in nature, hence in one sense there is no gap to be bridged.

In Griffin's thought, however, feelings or experiences are not so much properties as they are the perspectives of momentary actual occasions. Feeling or experience is understood by Griffin within a framework that unfortunately tends to be ignored in analytic versions of panpsychism. Therefore, Barrett is astute to notice two different explanatory gaps: between process panexperientialism and analytic panpsychism and between first-person phenomenal and third-person accounts. Here we can see what could in the future be Griffin's major contribution to analytic panpsychism. When a "what it is like" feeling is *reified* into a special property, the particular perspective of an occasion of experience is in danger of being lost. Or again, if experience is viewed as a special property of the abstract entity "consciousness," what is lost is the distinctive dynamic perspective of a particular organic occasion. The danger is that differences in perspective and uniqueness of perspective would become reified under the special property of "experience" or "consciousness."

Experience is not so much a property that is added to physical processes (a view that Whitehead called the theory of psychic additions and that Hartshorne called the annex theory of value[40]), but is the very (Platonic) dynamic power of what exists both to assimilate its causal influences and to exert itself in response to them. Granted, it makes sense to distinguish between what it is like to be "in here" and what it is like to be "out there," as long as one realizes that these are selective abstractions from a single stream and as long as one does not assume that the latter is more real than the former, as Barrett emphasizes. By contrast, for example, Nagel seems to think that the shift from subjectivity to objectivity is a transition from one type of property to another, rather than the passage in a concrescing actual occasion from the clutch of vivid immediacy in the present to its superjective influence on later actual occasions.

There are untapped possibilities within Griffin's view for bridging phenomenal, functional, and even neurological descriptions. Because feelings always involve "something more," functional or reductionist descriptions all by themselves are especially incomplete. As Barrett emphasizes, in terms that seem to apply especially well in the case of Griffin's efforts to unsnarl the world-knot, "process panpsychism indicates a way forward by understanding the 'something more' of conscious feeling in terms of perspectivity rather than special properties."[41] Experience, including conscious experience, develops *over time* in ways that reified properties do not. The explanation of such experience will in the future require an up-to-date version of Plato's view of the one and the many, wherein a high degree of both integrity and diversity of participating neural populations are explicated, both philosophically and scientifically.

Barrett captures well both the spirit of Griffin's panexperientialism and the contribution it could make to the perennial project initiated by Plato to understand well the proper relationship between "the mental" and "the physical":

> Process panpsychism makes progress on the explanatory gap between functional and phenomenal accounts of consciousness because it registers not just the fact of qualitative experience per se, but the crucial additional fact that the qualitatively rich experience of consciousness is constantly changing. This dynamism arises from the particularity of conscious feeling, in both its clear and distinct aspects and its vast reserves of vagueness and triviality. In contrast, property panpsychism, like the analytic framework from which it is derived, deals only in static properties whose particularity is of no consequence.[42]

## HISTORICAL THINKING

Griffin's panexperientialism belies the famous (or infamous) quip allegedly made by Quine that there are two quite different reasons why people enter philosophy: to do philosophy or merely to do history of philosophy. It has been the purpose of the present essay to argue that, regarding Griffin's panexperientialism, these two are not mutually exclusive. That is, thinking about the mind-body problem *is* historical thinking via Plato and Descartes, whether philosophers of mind realize it or not. To admit this much, however, is not necessarily to commit to the intellectually conservative claim that we stand on the shoulders of giants (like Plato), in that it is equally true to say that we stand in their dark shadow. Once again, to be is to exhibit *both* the dynamic power to prehend causal influence from the past *and* the dynamic power to unsnarl knots.

What it means to be a process thinker in the wake of Griffin is to say not only that the reality of events is *successive*, but also *cumulative*. Through prehension of causal influence, the present, in a way, includes the past, hence we should be suspicious of thinkers who largely dispense with philosophers from previous centuries. Intellectual history is one of the principal sources for contemporary wisdom, including wisdom regarding what has come to be called "the mind-body problem." Or again, to be a process thinker in the wake of Griffin is to hold that becoming is both *cumulative* and *creative* in that the new at any moment is not already "in the cards" or entailed by previous events or conditions. Nevertheless, the cumulative character of process means that these conditions are in some sense contained in the new. In Hartshornean terms congenial to Griffin's project, each instance of becoming is a creative synthesis.

David Ray Griffin is to be thanked for alerting us to the fact that it is a new ballgame in philosophy of mind: panexperientialism is now a reputable player. Understanding this fact, however, is difficult without an awareness of earlier games and earlier players. It should be noted that process thinkers have defended this view throughout the 20th century. Griffin has shown that panexperientialism will not go away simply because it has been largely ignored for (a mere) three hundred years. To paraphrase Emerson: When the half-gods of dualism and materialism depart, the gods of panexperientialism can arrive.[43]

# 4. Griffin on Evolution

## John B. Cobb, Jr.

D avid Griffin's work on evolution is part and parcel of his work on science in general.[1] This has been motivated largely by his concerns as a Christian believer. However, his approach and proposals are deeply informed by his commitment to process thought. This has led to an approach that is rare and that has been pursued by Griffin with greater care and rigor than by anyone else. My approach is similar to his, but less rigorous, and it is indebted to him for central insights. We affirm the necessity of adapting Christian thinking to the data that science provides us. But we do not believe that all the theories that scientists have developed on the basis of reliable data are themselves reliable. The fact that there is a wide consensus among scientists on some of these theories does not convince us that we must adapt our theology to all of them. This is certainly the case with the neo-Darwinian theory of evolution. But before discussing that theory directly, I will consider some broader issues.

### THEOLOGY AND SCIENCE

There is no doubt that scientists have contributed enormously to our understanding of the world in which we live. There is also no doubt that the picture of the world that most of them adopt, at least when they are functioning as scientists, is markedly alien to the biblical one. Much of this difference simply reflects the ignorance of the biblical writers of what scientists have learned about the world. But this does not explain all the differences. The dominant worldview of modern science is not required as the only possible explanation of the facts science has discovered. This worldview was adopted partly because it fit well with the early stages of the development of modern science, but partly for other reasons. No one has contributed more than Griffin to sorting out these reasons and their influence in shaping what is often simply considered "the scientific worldview."

Of course, not all of Griffin's ideas are original with him. Historians studying the early development of modern science have provided him the basic information about the early history. Whitehead's *Science and the Modern World* encourages a critical stance toward the development of the dominant worldview. Nevertheless, I, as representative of a large number of modern people, long assumed that the worldview of modern science came into being largely because of its usefulness to scientists and the evidence that supported it.

Those Christians who have shared this assumption have struggled to relate their faith to a worldview that is inherently in marked tension with it. There have been three major ways of responding. Many have simply abandoned their faith, replacing it with ideas that arise from the modern scientific worldview. Among those who did not, some have argued that more of Christian belief can be made compatible to this worldview than is immediately apparent. They then shed those Christians beliefs that they find incompatible.

The third response has been to adopt some form of dualism. Descartes' dualism left to believers the realm of mind, while turning over to science the realm of matter. As this separation broke down, Immanuel Kant offered a different one in his *Critiques.* When we think as scientists, one world view is required. But when we think in terms of the practical issues of action in daily life, the questions that arise require that we think in a quite different way. As long as Christian thought recognizes that it deals only with the postulates of the practical reason, it can be free from the restrictions imposed by theoretical reason.

This distinction has provided a certain kind of peace. However, it tends to leave people with the sense that whereas science tells us the way things are, ethics and religion do not. They are allowed a certain importance, but not equality in the scheme of things. In later versions, science is accorded the world of facts, ethics and religion, the world of values. It is significant that modern research universities devote themselves to the facts and aim to be value-free. In excluding the realms allotted to ethics and religion, these universities do not understand themselves to be omitting anything important.

Some Christian thinkers seeking help in Kantian dualism found consolation in the linguistic turn. This did not give any support to the idea that religious thought dealt with reality, but it extended this abandonment of realism to all thought. According to this view, we must abandon the idea of there being a reality about which we are learning and with which we needed to come to terms. One could understand science as "a language game," one among others. The other language games could include ethics and Christian theology. If Christians join in the general abandonment of realism altogether, they can claim that their beliefs are on the same footing as any others, including scientific ones: Christian language can claim the same status as that of science.

For many Christians, however, this is not a possible solution. At a deep level, it is clear to many Christians that Christian faith inherently intends to speak of reality. To be told that it does not is disturbing, even when one is told that science does not either.

Conservative Christians have held to reality more firmly than liberals. Although liberals have generally held to the reality at least of human beings and human history, they have often been prepared to say that their further beliefs could be understood as a way that only *symbolizes* the ultimate mystery. Conservatives, on the other hand, were likely to claim that their language spoke quite directly of reality. Whereas liberals were strongly inclined to accept the authority of the scientific over a wide range of beliefs, conservatives would not agree to scientific affirmations that directly contradicted their convictions. This resistance to science came out clearly in the discussions of evolution.

Theologians influenced by Whitehead, most clearly and vigorously in the case of Griffin, rejected all these positions: We certainly recognize that reality is very mysterious, but we affirm that the mysterious world is very real and that the task of both scientists and theologians is to understand it as well as possible. We are convinced that science provides a great deal of information that responsible human beings, theologians especially, must accept and to which they must adjust Christian understanding of the world. For example, in relation to the debates about evolution, we are convinced that the descent of human beings from pre-human animals is a fact to be accepted and affirmed. But we do not believe that the only explanation of the facts is the one adopted by the great majority of scientists. Indeed, we do not think that scientific theory should be left to scientists. Historians, philosophers, and theologians should be involved.

In other words, we judge that theory always involves pre-judgments or assumptions, and that the fact that particular views are well-established in the various scientific disciplines does not mean that they are correct. We would have more confidence in the theories accepted in the scientific disciplines if there was more critical openness within them to alternative assumptions. But since many alternative possibilities are not considered within the scientific guilds, it is appropriate for historians, philosophers, and theologians to introduce them into the public discussion.

My own confidence in disagreeing with the consensus of scientists was greatly strengthened when I learned from Griffin that among the leading scientists in the early days of modern science there were those who retained an Aristotelian worldview and others who held to more organismic models as they studied alchemy. The victory of the clock model was gradual, and it did not imply that progress was lacking under the aegis of other models.[2] There is no question but that it provided a basis for fruitful research, but at least part of the reason for its growing dominance lay elsewhere.

Descartes play a large role in the victory of the mechanistic worldview. His preference for this view, at least in part, was that it offered more support than the other models to Catholic theology and the authority of the church. From Descartes' point of view, if nature is only matter in motion, it is utterly inconceivable that human experience and thought are part of nature. The human soul can and should be understood as completely free from the characteristics of nature. He followed Plato in declaring the soul immortal. The natural world, furthermore, is governed by laws that cannot be attributed to matter as such. It therefore requires an external creator.

Also, if nature is purely mechanical, it is not hard to show that there are events that are inexplicable naturally. The authority of the church rested extensively in the miracles worked by its saints. It was assumed that these miracles were acts of God. The assumption that some events are miraculous and that the miraculous requires God as a direct explanation is much better supported given this view of nature than if nature itself is accorded the remarkable powers that some scientists attributed to it.

Other early modern thinkers saw additional benefits in this view of nature. As long as the earth was understood as organic, it commanded a certain respect. Mining was felt to be a violation of the living earth. Human beings could feel freer to exploit the resources of the earth if they understood it to be simply matter in motion.

Still others saw another political advantage in this worldview: Employing an analogy to kingly establishment of law over subjects, this new view regarded God as the external authority who imposes laws upon nature. By contrast, if one viewed the "laws" of nature as regularities generated by the behavior of myriads of subjects, one might support more democratic views of the ideal society.

When I learned from Griffin something of this complex history of the rise of the modern scientific worldview, my hesitation to engage in the discussion of scientific theory fell away. Clearly the scientific worldview played a role in shaping scientific theory. If that worldview had achieved dominance simply because of its scientific superiority, then as an outsider it felt very presumptuous to criticize. But if theological and philosophical factors played a role in its adoption, then a theologian should be free to participate in the evaluation.

Of course, Descartes' mechanistic view of nature would not have won out had it not been brilliantly successful in interpreting the data and guiding new experiments. As more and more scientists adopted this worldview, obviously more and more of the findings of science were interpreted in this way. When the Royal Society in England committed itself to this kind of science, other approaches faded. In his early years, Newton engaged in alchemical experiments, but in the end he threw his prestige behind the Royal Society.

The brilliant successes of mechanistic science enabled it to ignore its obvious problems. Descartes left to his successors utterly puzzling ideas about the relation of the human mind (belonging to one order of reality) and the human body (belonging to another). Today the mechanists assure us that eventually we will be able to show that all causation is mechanistic, so our experience cannot be anything more than epiphenomenal. But their insistence that they themselves are machines speaking in ways that are determined by mechanical laws, rather than by thought, leaves one wondering why we should believe what they say to be true. The puzzle is hardly less today than when first posed by Descartes' metaphysics. It seems entirely reasonable to consider whether the data can be explained by other basic assumptions that do not call for endorsing such unbelievable notions. Obviously, the fact that Whitehead offers us a developed theory of a quite different type encourages us to engage in this approach to science.

Griffin has shown that it is possible today in the examination of scientific theories to distinguish between those that stay close to the scientific facts and those that are more influenced by the metaphysical view that has become dominant in the scientific world. One can then focus on the latter and propose alternatives that are no less adequate to the truly scientific theories than the ones around which scientists have formed their consensus.

It is important that we theologians do not press assumptions that fit poorly with truly scientific theories. But we process theologians believe that Whitehead's theories actually do more justice to what is truly scientific than the now dominant ones. We are also quite sure that they provide more scope for the confident articulation of basic Christian convictions.

There was only one topic on which Whitehead wrote at length in criticism of what was then a developing scientific consensus. He believed it important to develop a theory of general relativity that was free from what he saw as mistaken assumptions in Einstein's theory. Contemporary cosmology is based on Einstein's theory and, if Whitehead is correct philosophically, then it is faulty.

Two features of Einstein's theory especially bothered Whitehead. First, it illustrated for him the fallacy of misplaced concreteness. The notions of curvature and straightness apply to physical things, he said, but space is not—in the requisite sense—a physical thing. It does not make sense, therefore, to describe space as variably curved. As a mathematician, Whitehead asserted that any space that can be treated by Euclidean geometry can also be treated by elliptic and hyperbolic geometry. Indeed, the idea that something is curved presupposes a background of something that is not curved. The idea of the curvature of space does not make sense.

I am not aware of any critical response to Whitehead's point by Einsteinians, that is, by the overwhelmingly dominant community of physicists. For them, Einstein is to be followed because his theories have led to many proven predictions. The dominant view is that we must adjust our thinking to his formulae rather than adjust his formulae to beliefs established elsewhere.

Another feature of Einstein's thought that bothered Whitehead was that it does away with notions such as force and causality. These are ideas deeply rooted in experience, but excluded by Einstein's theory. Whitehead reintroduces them to replace the curvature of space in his explanation of gravity.

A different issue, but one that participates with Einsteinian relativity in the formation of the modern cosmological synthesis, is the interpretation of the red shift. This can be explained in various ways, but the explanation in terms of distance from the observer has been taken as the reliable basis for the development of cosmology. This leads to the conclusion that the universe is expanding and, when read backwards in time, to the Big Bang.

Many scientific theories encounter problems that require positing unproved or unknown entities or forces. This can lead to new testable theories, and the advance of science continues. The dominant cosmological model now works only by positing that most of the matter and energy in the universe is "dark." This dramatic addition to our cosmology has the disadvantage that reliable tests of the existence of this matter and energy are extremely difficult to envision. The rational move would be to consider that this fact renders the expansion model with its Big Bang quite uncertain. This should lead to considering other explanations of the red shift that do not require positing such dubious realities. But thus far the dominant community sticks with its biases and presents them to the public as scientifically established. The great body of discussion in the wider public continues as if the Big Bang were an established cosmological fact. This is psychologically and sociologically understandable, but these ideas actually remain interesting theories rather than established facts.

I mention this current issue only to illustrate the need to distinguish between evidence to which the philosopher and theologian should unquestionably adjust thinking and the established theories in the sciences that rest on thoroughly questionable beliefs. The consensus about these theories does not establish them as beyond questioning by outsiders. The scientific experts are not generally also philosophical experts. But many of their theories and beliefs are dependent on assumptions that students in other fields are better equipped to judge. This is all the more the case when scientists do not acknowledge their limitations. The disciplinary organization of knowledge obscures these relationships. The result is that whole fields of thought in the sciences develop over long periods of time on the basis of mistaken assumptions.

Change is likely to occur in the scientific guilds only when the gap between the theory and the evidence becomes very large. In my opinion, this is now occurring in cosmology in several ways. But the theologian who understands the way in which science works does not have to wait until the scientific consensus changes in order to disagree with leading scientists. To whatever extent what is offered us as science is in fact determined by doubtful assumptions, theology can be developed on the basis of more plausible ones. Of course, it is essential that these other assumptions be compatible with the scientific evidence.

## THEOLOGY AND EVOLUTION

*Scientific* cosmology has not been Griffin's special focus and is not the main topic of this paper. Whitehead noted that every cosmology suggests a religion; so we could spend time on how the Einsteinian cosmology has affected religious understanding and sensibility. But the connection between religious belief and evolutionary theory is more immediate and more glaring. It is this topic on which a deep rift arose in society, one that has not been healed. To this day we find a contemptuous hostility toward theology in research universities because of the conservative religious opposition to evolutionary theory, and we find large groups of people who reject the authority of science even in its proper sphere. Candidates for political office, even today, sometimes assure the voters that they do not "believe in" evolution.

I noted above that the liberal church, indeed, the dominant ecclesiastical establishment, hastens to reassure scientists that religious leaders give authority to scientists in their own fields. This means that they do not argue with the consensus reached among scientific experts. In evolutionary biology, this consensus is neo-Darwinism.

Griffin regards this liberal yielding of authority to scientific experts to be a mistake. In this respect, he sides with religious conservatives. But the conservative critique is often expressed either in the wholesale rejection of science or in the development of a pseudo-science out of traditional religious beliefs. Griffin, in contrast, engages in careful analysis of the distinction between the real needs of science and the evidence that must be affirmed, on the one side, and, on the other, the influence of problematic assumptions on the formation of theories, including those on which "expert" opinion among scientists has achieved consensus. I am one of those who believe that this is a very important task and essential in the long run for the health of Christian faith.

Recently, Griffin contributed two important chapters to a book I edited. The title is *Back to Darwin.* My intention in adopting that title was to make two things clear to any potential reader. The contributors all affirm the fact of evolution and that there is no debate about the importance in evolution of "natural selection." On the other hand, most of the contributors believe the consensus that emerged later among Darwinian evolutionists are seriously mistaken.

Of course, the title is not intended to imply that we ignored all developments since Darwin's time or that we agreed with everything he said. However, Griffin was bothered by the title. He, of all the contributors, had gone to the trouble of pointing out aspects of Darwin's beliefs and assumptions that the book as a whole rejected. The title ignored that careful work on his part. For this we owe him an apology.

In Chapter 17, Griffin identifies fifteen positions taken in the current consensus among evolutionary biologists that we label "neo-Darwinism." The first eight were shared by Darwin himself. Griffin begins with two "basic scientific doctrines," microevolution and macroevolution, that he agrees are well established. Darwinians have shown that species are not fixed and that they have descended from earlier ones over a long period of time.

Griffin then proceeds to identify five metaphysical doctrines shared by Darwin and neo-Darwinians. The first two he considers essential to science: naturalism, in the sense of exclusion of supernatural intervention, and ontological uniformitarianism. The latter doctrine is that nature has the same characteristics everywhere.

Griffin then identifies three additional metaphysical assumptions that biologists share with the wider community of science but that are not essential to science as such. The first two are the ideas built into the mechanistic model whose victory I discussed earlier. He calls them "positivism-materialism" and "predictive determinism." A great deal of the problem that Christians have with science arises from these, and of course Griffin is in the lead in showing how they influence scientific work and the conclusions that scientists draw from it.

The third metaphysical assumption that Griffin identifies is less often discussed by Christian critics. It is nominalism. This doctrine arose in the late Middle Ages and was called the "modern" way. Griffin identifies it as central to modern science and indeed to modernity generally. It had particular importance for Darwinians because they were overthrowing the idea that there are fixed species or types. The restoration of something close to a Platonic realism is a distinctive feature of Griffin's thought to which I will return.

Griffin calls the eighth point in his list, gradualism, a "derivative scientific doctrine." Both Darwin and the neo-Darwinists have affirmed that the emergence of new species occurs gradually through numerous small changes. Griffin regards this as a scientific theory that is not based on the evidence in any direct sense. Instead, it follows from a combination of the scientific point about the descent of contemporary species from earlier species, noted above, and the metaphysical beliefs he has identified.

This gradualism cannot claim to be derived directly from the empirical evidence, because even today the vast array of fossils that have been studied fall overwhelmingly into well-differentiated species. If the development of one species from another were gradual, one would expect to find transitional forms, but these are almost nonexistent. This is problematic, because abrupt jumps from one species to another do not fit the metaphysical assumptions of modern science fully shared by evolutionary biologists.

Griffin then turns to three specifically neo-Darwinian scientific doctrines. Darwin himself did not claim to know how the variations among which natural selection took place occurred. He was open to Lamarckian ideas without committing himself to them. Not claiming to know this, he also left open the possibility that the emergence of variations that led to the rise of a new species—that is, macroevolution—might be different from the variations known to occur within a species. The choice of *Back to Darwin* as a title was to reaffirm this openness to multiple theories as a place for a fresh beginning.

The neo-Darwinians closed the open doors left by Darwin. The first of three specifically neo-Darwinian scientific doctrines Griffin identifies is that macroevolution does not introduce any mechanisms of change different from those operative in microevolution. Note that calling a doctrine "scientific" does not mean that it is based on evidence, only that empirical evidence for and against it are, in principle, possible. In fact, although this particular doctrine is strongly held, there is little evidence supporting it.

The second of the doctrines in this list is the idea that the variations from which natural selection operates are all "random." The contrast here is partly with sexual selection, or Lamarckian views of the inheritance of characteristics acquired from the behavior of ancestors. Neo-Darwinists found in Mendelian genetics a basis for understanding that changes in genes led to diverse phenotypes and behavior, and these changes were random in a way in which animal behavior is not. This did not mean that at the physical level there were no causal explanations, only that their occurrence was random with respect to its biological outcome. Having found this as a way of explaining how evolution occurred, the dominant evolutionary community declared it the *only* way. The only justification I can see for this further statement is that it is the way that best fits with the assumed metaphysical principles.

Griffin's third uniquely neo-Darwinian scientific doctrine, which has a similar status, is that evolution is wholly undirected. Darwin himself was a deist who thought that the original creative act bestowed a certain tendency or direction to the created order. Whereas on the first two of these points the neo-Darwinists took positions that were far more restrictive than Darwin, they did not directly oppose him. On this point, they explicitly rejected his view.

David concludes this analysis with four items on religion and morality. Whereas the implications of the modern scientific worldview have always entailed the exclusion of God from the nature studied by science, there was a general openness to understanding God as Creator and Lawgiver and as directly involved with human beings in the field of morality. But neo-Darwinian evolution included human beings in nature and thus in principle excluded God from any relation to them as well. Darwin retained the notion of God's initial creative act, but neo-Darwinists rejected that as well. They declare themselves to be atheists and often imply that their science demonstrates that their atheism is correct.

Some atheists go to great lengths to show that this position does not undercut the meaningfulness of life and the importance of morality. They sometimes appeal to nature as in itself providing us with the meaning that we need. However, leading spokespersons for neo-Darwinism not only deny the existence of a deity but also reject the existence of meaning in nature. If we seek meaning, we must create our own. David lists the meaninglessness of the universe as his next point after atheism. Closely related to this is what he calls "amoralism": There are no moral norms.

Darwin saw an upward tendency in the course of evolution and attributed this to the way God created it. Neo-Darwinists deny any such trend. The very idea of progress is for them meaningless. The only evaluation of an organism they find useful is its adaptation to its environment. A very simple organism may be just as well adapted as a complex one. There is no basis for declaring the complex one "better."

Once the mechanistic view of nature is fully combined with the inclusion of human beings in nature, the religious and moral conclusions drawn by the neo-Darwinists are largely entailed. Does this mean that science as such implies the meaninglessness of life? Griffin's careful analysis shows clearly that it does not. What has become the scientific worldview is not based on scientific discoveries or empirical evidence. It is instead the dogmatic affirmation of a philosophical system whose connections with the evidence are highly problematic.

But this in no way implies we can dismiss science and go on our way. Scientists have learned much that is reliably accurate about the world in which we live and about its human inhabitants. David's extraordinary contribution is to guide us carefully and responsibly into sorting out what, on the one hand, responsible Christians and others should appropriate from the work of scientists and what, on the other hand, we can and should reject.

## PLATONIC REALISM

One of Griffin's great strengths is that he ignores questions of current acceptability of ideas. He seeks truth. He has given major attention to parapsychology when this topic has been almost taboo in scholarly and intellectual circles. He has given major attention to the question of what really happened on Sept. 11, 2001, when the government, the media, and the universities have joined forces to silence that question. He is my authority in both of these areas.

So when Griffin tackles the question of Platonic realism, I must pay attention. During my lifetime and long before, despite great respect for Plato, his realism with respect to ideas has been viewed as quaint rather than as something that can be taken straightforwardly. I have absorbed that bias and not seriously questioned it. I am even somewhat shocked by what Griffin writes on this topic.

There is no question but that eternal objects, collectively constituting the Primordial Nature of God, are an important part of Whitehead's philosophy. This places Whitehead broadly in the Platonic tradition and, more specifically, in the neo-Platonic one. I have often defended Whitehead's Platonism against those who wish to deny Platonic ideas any reality whatsoever. Nevertheless, Griffin's use of Whitehead at this point is surprising and somewhat disturbing to other Whiteheadians. My defense of Whitehead is in part the claim that his eternal objects are in fact very different from Plato's "ideas."

Plato took for granted that there are numerous species of things and that language identified these species. Although there are variations among members of a species, the characteristics common to all can be identified and better examples can be distinguished from inferior ones. Similarly, there are definite virtues, and we can discuss what constitutes them fully and perfectly. These ideal forms are much like mathematical objects. We can draw circles and can judge that some of our figures are better than others, even if no one is perfect. In mathematics, we can discuss the character of the circle as such.

It has been my understanding that modern logic has abandoned this pattern. In relation to the virtues, for example, there are as many eternal objects as there are ideas about virtue in human minds. The word "justice" does not refer uniquely to any one of these. It may have as many meanings as it has iterations, since absolute identity of meaning in changing contexts is rare. Of course, many of these meanings are very similar, so for practical purposes people often understand one another well enough. But there is no essence to which the word corresponds.

Similarly, in the world of manmade objects, there are no boundaries in the nature of things separating, for example, tables from desks. There are some objects that almost all speakers of the English language would agree are tables and others that almost all would agree are desks. But there are others on which there would be no such ready agreement. The disagreement is *not* about whether the object in question is *really* a table or a desk, because such a question has no answer. This is just a matter of the use of language. There are no essences corresponding to particular terms. In any case a single object may be classified as a member of more than one class of objects. A wooden table may be classified among wooden objects just as well as among tables. One cannot organize things uniquely in terms of species and genus with the understanding that this corresponds to an eternal and immutable order.

With living things, also, I have understood that whatever value the old system of ordering them in species and genera still has, it does not correspond to an eternal system of essences. I have supposed that there would always be the possibility, if not always the actuality, of organisms that were no longer clearly members of one recognizable species but not yet members of another. Drawing a line and saying that, at some moment the first human appeared, would be arbitrary rather than illuminating.

All of this is to say that I have thought that, while Whitehead's eternal objects are certainly in the Platonic tradition, they are radically democratic in the sense that they are not ordered in terms of better and worse. Every pure potential just *is* a pure potential. It is only with impure potentials, propositions, that potentiality takes on value.

Griffin has found statements in Whitehead that sound more Platonic than this. But more important, he sees the absence of transitional organisms in the fossil record as indicating a status for species that the dominant community of evolutionary theorists prefers to ignore. Once again, as often in the past, I see him forcing attention to matters that our dominant theories obscure. In this case, it is the explanation of the saltations, or jumps, that the fossil evidence suggests.

I remain hesitant to explain this absence of transitional types by any eternal ordering of the eternal objects. It seems to me that there are better approaches. For example, if a new species comes into being by symbiosis, as Lynn Margulis showed has happened, there might be a quite abrupt jump. And perhaps the disappearance of the food on which a species has depended in a particular locale might lead to the death of all except a few members that have a previously unused ability to procure a different kind of food. The necessity to live on this other food might produce quite rapid change, leading to the emergence of a different species with few transitional organisms.

But Griffin is well ahead of me in reflection on this problem. I follow Griffin in the judgment that neo-Darwinism is a massive failure. Griffin is correct that we cannot solve the problem by going "back to Darwin." The task of reconstructing evolutionary theory lies before us. I must pay more attention to the talk of "attractors." If that requires developing Whitehead's theory of eternal objects in a more Platonic direction, Griffin will again prove to have been our leader.

# 5. Scientific and Religious Naturalism

## Philip Clayton

I t is a joy to have this chance to respond to one of my favorite discussion partners. I dedicate this paper to those evenings in my first year as a CST professor when David and I used to share a glass of wine and conversations after the end of our Wednesday evening classes.

Each of the authors in this volume has been assigned a particular topic, and I ended up with the assignment of scientific naturalism—a welcome topic on which to engage David, actually. My premise will be that the specific features of a "naturalistic" methodology in contemporary physics, chemistry, and biology do not actually play a particularly strong role in David's thought. For this reason, I will instead concentrate on David's position on naturalism in general, which is not actually influenced to any significant extent by mainline scientific practices or by the self-interpretations of scientists. Once we have this position before us, I will move on to my own observations and evaluation.

### DAVID GRIFFIN'S NATURALISTIC PROCESS PHILOSOPHY OF RELIGION

Process philosophies have a longer history than is often acknowledged. One finds their origins in Heraclitus or Empedocles; one discovers parallels and antecedents in the emanation metaphysics of Plotinus and the Neoplatonic school;

and one can trace the increasing emphasis on temporality in Lessing, Schelling, Hegel, Schopenhauer, and their followers. As a school in contemporary philosophy of religion, however, process philosophy traces back to the work of Alfred North Whitehead, particularly his 1929 *Process and Reality*, and its influence. Whitehead and Russell's *Principia Mathematica* had a major influence in logic and the philosophy of mathematics, his work in the philosophy of education had major advocates,[1] and his philosophy of science continues to receive significant attention.[2]

But without question Whitehead's major influence has been within the philosophy of religion. By the late 1940s there was a strong Whitehead school at the University of Chicago Divinity School. During the 1950s and '60s, when Yale was widely heralded as the nation's leading philosophy department, several of the key figures were Whiteheadians, including Paul Weiss and William A. Christian. Since then, process philosophers have made significant contributions to a wide variety of debates within the philosophy of religion.[3] David Griffin's work stands as one of the most significant, if not the preeminent, contribution to this genre.

The starting point for this work is the metaphysical framework advanced in *Process and Reality*. According to this metaphysic, reality consists of moments of experience or "actual occasions." Actual occasions "prehend" the contents of previous occasions both physically and mentally. But each actual occasion, manifesting a process that Whitehead calls *concrescence*, also synthesizes its input into a unique perspective on the world. Thus each actual entity, as it concludes its process of becoming, bequeaths to the world a new synthetic perspective; as Whitehead famously put it, "The many become one and are increased by one" (*PR* 21).[4] The idealist tendency of this metaphysics is clear: reality is synthesized in the experience of each individual unit of reality; in some sense, reality *just is* the sum of these experiences.

This tendency may explain the attraction that this metaphysic has exercised on many philosophers of religion. God is an actual entity (or, for others, a series of actual occasions) and is describable using the same metaphysical principles exemplified by finite occasions. But Whitehead's God is also different in some noticeable respects. God's "primordial" nature includes the valuation of all possibilities and thus acts as a sort of axiological ground for all reality, that is, for all subsequent moments of experience. By contrast, God's "consequent nature" prehends, values, and retains the experience of all other occasions. God becomes the "fellow sufferer who understands." Whitehead realized that some sort of cosmic retention was crucial if a thoroughgoing process metaphysic was not going to devolve into nihilism. He wrote:

> The ultimate evil . . . lies in the fact that the past fades, that time is a "perpetual perishing." Objectification involves elimination. The present fact has not the past fact with it in any full immediacy. The process of time veils the past below distinctive feeling. There is a unison of becoming among things in the present. Why should there not be novelty without loss of this direct unison of immediacy among things? In the temporal world, it is the empirical fact that process entails loss: the past is present under an abstraction. But there is no reason, of any ultimate metaphysical generality, why this should be the whole story. (*PR* 340)

God preserves the results of all past experience, though not that experience in its subjective immediacy. No perspective is lost.

Charles Hartshorne tended to give this metaphysic a distinctively rationalist twist, whereas the thinkers of the

"Chicago School" read it in a more empiricist and naturalist fashion, even when they were doing theology. In works such as *A Christian Natural Theology*, John Cobb balanced the two strands, while also extending the results more deeply into Christian theology, interreligious dialogue, and the philosophy of science.[5] David Ray Griffin, Cobb's student, quickly became his most important partner in developing a coherent metaphysical account and extending it to a wide range of social, political, and cultural issues. Similar efforts were undertaken by process philosophers such as Lewis Ford, Robert Neville, Brian Henning, Daniel Dombrowski, Don Viney, and Jay McDaniel.[7]

## PROCESS PHILOSOPHY AND CHRISTIANITY

Clearly, Whitehead's theism diverges from classical theism. Hartshorne decided to call it "neoclassical" theism, and "process theism" eventually became the standard term. In order to understand and evaluate Griffin's naturalism, one must first determine to what extent process theism shares the supernaturalist assumptions of classical Christian theism and to what extent it breaks from those assumptions.

Some pretty clear evidence arises when one notes how many orthodox and evangelical philosophers of religion challenge process theism for being insufficiently supernaturalist—a requirement that they take to be central to orthodox theology and Christian practice. Process theology, they argue, is not (sufficiently) Trinitarian; a God who takes up all finite experience within God's self cannot be protected from the challenge of the problem of evil; Whitehead's "objective immortality" is not sufficient for the Christian hope, which presupposes subjective immortality; the uniqueness of Jesus Christ and his resurrection cannot be adequately conceived within the more naturalistic framework of process theology;

a God who persuades but does not coerce lacks sufficient (supernatural) power and cannot be counted on to "bring all things unto himself"; and prayer becomes impossible without a more robust understanding of miracles.

In a complex and sometimes technical philosophical dispute played out over some three decades, process theologians have responded to each of these charges. Many authors in the Bracken and Suchocki collection, for example, argued for one or another form of process trinitarianism.[8] Interestingly, while Cobb worked "to relativize the threeness of God," Griffin espoused a "naturalistic theism" as the basis for a "naturalistic Trinity," consisting of Divine Creativity, Creative Love, and Responsive Love.

It is false to say that the problem of evil is more pronounced in the Whiteheadian context. Instead, as Griffin shows, the rejection of supernatural omnipotence in process thought is probably the *only* way to avoid making God culpable for unnecessary suffering.[9] In *The End of Evil*, Marjorie Suchocki provided a sophisticated defense of the possibility of subjective immortality within a Whiteheadian framework[10]; a more recent anthology has offered defenses, elaborations, and criticisms of her attempt.[11] Numerous volumes have defended the compatibility of process theology with the biblical documents, with religious practices such as prayer, and with core motifs of Christian theology.[12]

The rich conceptual overlaps between process theology and "open theism" or "free will theism," starting in the 1990s, have spawned significant new work in philosophical theology.[13] Exchanges between Griffin and William Hasker, for example, open and close the Cobb and Pinnock volume on free will theism.[14] Further projects of this nature are today being coordinated by Thomas Jay Oord, whose work seeks to integrate process philosophy and orthodox Christian thought.

Oord's conferences, and his sessions on "Open and Relational Theology" at the American Academy of Religion attended by up to 500 people, have produced several new anthologies with important new work.[15]

The partnership between open theists and process thinkers reflects the (to my mind accurate) sense that there is significant common ground between the Whiteheadian view of God and the understanding of God in the biblical documents:

> [T]he love of God for the world . . . is the particular providence for particular occasions. . . . By reason of this reciprocal relation, the love in the world passes into the love in heaven, and floods back again into the world. In this sense, God is the great companion—the fellow-sufferer who understands. (*PR* 351)

Both open theists and process thinkers challenge the idea that God exercises unlimited power (though open theists insist that God could do so if God wished). Both affirm that it is difficult to defend a robust notion of human self-determination if God is held to pre-ordain all events and predestine the fate of all souls. On such a view, human existence appears more like a puppet show. Finally, both groups can appeal to common christological statements. As Hartshorne wrote, "To say that Jesus was God, then, ought to mean that God himself is one with us in our suffering, that divine love is not essentially benevolence—external well-wishing—but sympathy, taking into itself our every grief."[16]

The greatest tension between the two groups, I suggest, arises with the question whether an absence of supernatural miracles is an essential feature of the God-world relationship, or a voluntary self-limitation on the part of God. Open theists and many panentheists defend the claim that the creation of a natural order was a free decision by God, reflecting divine grace and providence, rather than a metaphysical necessity.

This is also one of the reasons that they affirm creation *ex nihilo*. On this view, God is essentially all-powerful, but God freely self-limits the divine power in order to allow for real agents to exist and to have a genuine role in co-determining their future. This view has come to be known as the "kenotic doctrine of creation," drawing from the notion of self-emptying (*ekenōsen*) in Phil. 2:5-8.

Griffin, like many process philosophers, replies that any such self-limitation would be a contingent and arbitrary move. If it results from a free divine decision, no adequate philosophical account can be constructed to account for it. Moreover, a God who arbitrarily limited God's power could also just as arbitrarily choose to exercise it again at some future point of time. Much more philosophically satisfying, Griffin argues, is a conception of God according to which it lies in God's essential nature to persuade rather than coerce. God is essentially, and hence eternally, limited by a world. For this reason, orthodox process thinkers share Whitehead's resistance to creation *ex nihilo*. God has always been accompanied by *some* world or universe, even though it may have been different worlds in different "cosmic epochs." This limitation on the divine power is an essential feature of God; like every other actual entity, God could not coerce even if God wished to. Put differently: because God as an existing entity is essentially similar to other entities, the limitation on divine power presupposed by genuine (bi-directional) interaction with others is a metaphysical given. This explains the famous six symmetries at the end of *Process and Reality:*

> It is as true to say that God is permanent and the World fluent, as that the World is permanent and God is fluent.

> It is as true to say that God is one and the World many, as that the World is one and God many.

It is as true to say that, in comparison with the World, God is actual eminently, as that, in comparison with God, the World is actual eminently.

It is as true to say that the World is immanent in God, as that God is immanent in the World.

It is as true to say that God transcends the World, as that the World transcends God.

It is as true to say that God creates the World, as that the World creates God. (*PR* 348)

This is one of the topics on which Griffin and I disagree. I will return to this topic below.

## ATHEISM AND NATURALISM IN PROCESS PHILOSOPHY OF RELIGION

Process naturalism represents a complex resource for philosophers of religion in part because it has been put to use not only by theists but also by agnostics and atheists, not only by classical theists and panentheists but also by humanists, not only by those affiliated with specific religious traditions but also by perennialists and philosophers with more purely metaphysical interests.

I earlier mentioned the bipolar theism that Whitehead advocated at the end of *Process and Reality* and that Charles Hartshorne and his followers elaborated in many later publications. But scholars have also noted that many features of Whitehead's theism were only introduced in the final stratum of the composition of *Process and Reality*.[17] His magnum opus was followed by two major works, *Modes of Thought* and *Adventures of Ideas*, in which theism plays little to no discernible role. Thus within a few decades one can find strong advocates of an atheist process metaphysics. I pause for a moment to consider this school because I believe that it sheds important light on Griffin's own naturalism.

Atheist process philosophers affirm a metaphysics of creativity as Whitehead's major contribution to philosophy, and then argue that Creativity has as much claim to ultimacy in Whitehead's writings as does the notion of God. Creativity *could be* an attribute of God, but it can also be taken as a basic metaphysical principle independent of God. (Consider the parallel: some Platonists locate the forms within the mind of God; others postulate that they exist in an independent realm, as in Roger Penrose's or Karl Popper's "third world.") If this argument is successful, the notion of God becomes optional for, if not actually counter-indicated by, Whitehead's notion of Creativity. Sherburne made this argument in 1967,[18] and one finds something like the same move in Gordon Kaufman's *In the Beginning—Creativity*, in which he makes Creativity his final theological resting place.[19]

As attention shifted from strict Chicago School process thought and Sherburne's more strongly atheist approach, the door was opened for defending process thought as a kinder, gentler form of naturalism. David Ray Griffin has led this charge (though certainly not without allies) in a number of publications, perhaps most brilliantly in his *Reenchantment without Supernaturalism*.[20] Griffin distinguishes the form of naturalism dominant in contemporary philosophy of science and, for example, the New Atheists—he calls it naturalism$_{sam}$—from the non-reductive naturalism to which process philosophy gives rise—naturalism$_{ppp}$. Naturalism$_{sam}$ is *sensationalist, atheist, and materialist*. That is, it accepts the representationalist and empiricist theory of knowledge that gradually emerged in British Empiricism from John Locke to David Hume and that unintentionally constructed an increasingly high barrier between the agent and the world she seeks to know.[21] Atheism is assumed in standard modern naturalism, but the God it rejects is a supernatural God who stands over against, and even tends to negate, the natural order. Finally, naturalism~sam~ accepts the Hobbesian assumption that all that exists is "matter in motion"; it thus perpetuates the materialist metaphysic that dominated much of modern European thought.

In contrast to naturalism~sam~, Griffin advances an alternative view, naturalism~ppp~, which is *prehensive, panentheistic, and panexperientialist.* Instead of the exclusively external relations presupposed in modern empiricism, Griffin affirms the Whiteheadian doctrine of "prehension," which presupposes internal relations between the knower and the things that she knows. Instead of atheism, he affirms panentheism: all is contained within the divine, although God is also conceptually distinct from the world. And instead of materialism, he affirms that all units of reality are themselves occasions, moments of experience.[22]

Some of Griffin's critics have responded that "theistic naturalism" is a contradiction in terms and that one cannot, Humpty-Dumpty-like, make a venerable philosophical term such as "naturalism" mean just anything. Still, the remarkable influence that Griffin's work has had turns in part on the sense that the modern battle between naturalism and supernaturalism—a distinction foreign to medieval philosophy!—is locked in a stalemate that neither side can break. Famously, Whitehead sought to conceive God not as "an exception to all metaphysical principles" but as "their chief exemplification." (*PR* 343). Of course, there is more than one way to break the stalemate. The "open panentheism" that I defend in *Adventures in the Spirit*, for example, is not identical to the orthodox Whiteheadian position that Griffin is proposing.[23] In arguing for the finite-infinite distinction in a (roughly) Hegelian fashion, I rely on essential distinctions between God and finite agents that Griffin does not endorse. Still, we remain allies within the broader movement in recent philosophy of religion that is seeking to undercut, and I think is succeeding at undercutting, the harsh natural-supernatural distinction that has tended to place religion at such odds with science.

Incidentally, the dualism of naturalism and supernaturalism is also left behind in recent work, led by Catherine Keller and Roland Faber, which seeks to synthesize process philosophy with contemporary French post-structuralist thought, especially Jacques Derrida and Gilles Deleuze.[24] This work challenges the very distinction between constructive and deconstructive philosophy (or theology). Wedding Whitehead, the systematic metaphysician, with Derrida, the deconstructer of systems, might at first seem like a surprising marriage—especially given that the best-known process thinkers of the previous generations were highly system-centric in their approaches (Hartshorne, early Cobb, Griffin, Ford). Yet Whitehead's late work in particular offers strong evidence that he placed process over systematicity; and the recent work by Keller and Faber may well represent the most philosophically sophisticated work in process studies published in recent years.

## REFLECTIONS AND CRITICISMS

Let me put my observations and concerns in the form of five questions:

(1) Does Griffin's use of "naturalism" really lower the walls of division between religion and science? I understand how the pragmatic empiricism of James and Dewey lessened the conflict by eschewing metaphysical claims. I understand how the socio-historical empiricism of the Chicago School lessened the conflict by historicizing, and thereby relativizing, the propositional claims of theologians. As William Dean writes in his classic text, American religious empiricism implies "that history constructs reality, that history is simply a

chain of interpretations, and that whatever might lie outside history lies outside religion, empirically considered."[35] But I don't believe Griffin would accept any of these three options as sufficient.

✓ I also understand how focusing on religion as a set of guiding value claims would reduce the conflict. This is the path of Henry Nelson Wieman's religious naturalism:

> It is impossible to gain knowledge of the total cosmos or to have any understanding of the infinity transcending the cosmos. Consequently, beliefs about these matters are illusions, cherished for their utility in producing desired states of mind. . . . Nothing can transform man unless it operates in human life. Therefore, in human life, in the actual processes of human existence, must be found the saving and transforming power which religious inquiry seeks and which faith must apprehend.[26]

A few decades later, another theologian at the Chicago School would likewise replace metaphysics with ethics; I am referring of course to Jean-Luc Marion in *God without Being*. But *this* is clearly not the path that David has followed!

Finally, I can understand how the turn to a purely aesthetic theology, or an apophatic theology, or particular forms of aesthetic theology (say, John Caputo) can tear down the dividing walls. But Griffin has embraced Hartshornean rationalism rather than one of these approaches. How does that move reduce the tensions with contemporary intellectual culture in ways that are analogous to what these thinkers and schools have done?

(2) One of the major growth areas in religion-science discussions today is the Cognitive Science of Religion (CSR). CSR asks about the functions of religious belief, drawing on recent work in the neurosciences, evolutionary theory, archeology, and the empirically oriented social sciences, such

as the biology of behavior.[27] One of the central questions is whether religious practices are adaptive, that is, whether they increase the odds that an individual or group will survive given the selection pressures placed upon them. Many scholars today would think of CSR as a paradigm example of the naturalistic study of religion. Yet Griffin's writings imply that he would be highly resistant to this naturalistic treatment of religious belief.

(3) The previous point surfaces one of the dangers in attempting to redefine previously existing terms, as Griffin has done with the term naturalism. It's just not true that most philosophers who use the term mean to include views that are "prehensive, panentheistic, and panexperientialist"—if anything, they mean to *exclude* such views! Does it help to promote clear philosophical discussion to take an existing technical term and employ it in a completely different sense? I remember when Nancey Murphy began using the term "postmodern" to refer to a set of assumptions that were diametrically opposed to the way that everyone else in the discussion was using the term.[28] It is just not clear that such an approach sheds more light than heat. Do we best challenge the assumptions of contemporary naturalism by taking an opposing position and branding it "naturalism"?

(4) Does David understand "naturalism" to mean the same thing as the many Chinese scholars and leaders who use the term? One could ask the same question about a related term, "constructive postmodernism" (建设性后现代主义). There is extensive, if anecdotal, evidence that a significant semantic gap opens up between David's panentheistic naturalism and its appropriation by (for example) Chinese scholars. Griffin's naturalism leaves a place for the pervasive influence of the Whiteheadian God, as it must; he is, after all, a Whiteheadian panentheist. By contrast, virtually none of the many Chinese

constructive postmodernists with whom we work is a panentheist in this sense.

(5) I've suggested that differences of meaning lurk just
beneath the surface in this murky topic of naturalism. We
all know that equivocation is the arch-enemy of analysis.
Semantic ambiguities have torpedoed many a careful argument. What should we do?

Well, if the term becomes the problem rather than the
solution, one can always let it go. What if we remove the term
"naturalism" altogether from David's analysis? If we do, what
remains is the contrast between David's two subscripts: *sam*
and *ppp*. Ah, interesting: we now have the battle between
sensationalist-atheist-materialism on the one side, and
prehensive-panentheistic-panexperientialism on the other.
And, ladies and gentlemen, here is a Battle of the Titans—
perhaps, quite literally, the battle of the century. This new
debate is no less a battle to the death than the battle between
naturalism and supernaturalism that preceded it, for *sam*
and *ppp* share virtually no common ground. Read Griffin
carefully: the two combatants are as diametrically opposed
as were their predecessors. Indeed, now there are not one
but three fundamental oppositions, for each of the three
letters abbreviates its own battle: *s* vs. *p, a* vs. *p, m* vs. *p*. To
paraphrase Tertullian, what has sensationalism to do with an
epistemology of prehension, atheism to do with panentheism,
or materialism to do with panexperientialism?

Griffin rightly recognized that the old battle of naturalism
vs. supernaturalism is outdated; it rests on that strange category of "theism" that philosophers in the late 17th century invented to save religion from the onslaught of Newton's mechanics
and Hobbes' "matter in motion." But who wanted that deistic
theism anyway, that disappointing *deus absconditus*, that ab-
sentee father/landlord? It's not a battle worth fighting—not

only because it is 350 years out of date, but also because that God has become much less credible in our day and age.

## Conclusion

As we reach the end of this essay, it is important to try to name the fundamental ambiguity that this chapter and its arguments have uncovered.

We have discovered that the contrasts between *sam* and *ppp* in David Griffin's work are no less stark than were the contrasts between naturalism and supernaturalism in the classical debate. Few SAMites convert to PPPites, and few PPPites are tugged at all by the arguments of the SAMites. Now many process readers will experience no conflict or disappointment when faced with this conclusion. After all, they may respond, is not it our goal to develop a radically different worldview, a "relational worldview for the common good"? Must not we challenge the dehumanizing reductionism that rules scientific circles? And is not David our Goliath in this battle? (Technically, of course, David should be their David, so we'll have to work a bit more on the metaphor.)

There will be other readers, however, who will feel some disappointment in this outcome. These readers—and I number myself among them—find it disturbing that the stance of process thinkers toward the mainline science of our day, and hence toward most contemporary scientists, is so consistently negative. Over the course of many years of conferences, the Center for Process Studies in Claremont has generally found some allies from within the sciences on each topic that has been studied. More typically, however, we have couched the proposals coming from the process philosophers and theologians as contrasts (and often as sharp contrasts) to the science endorsed by the vast majority of the scientists of our day.

In this paper I have sought to convey the reasons for my dis-ease with this approach, and with the new battle of the naturalisms that Griffin has launched: SAM vs. PPP. It's important, here at the end, to be explicit about why one might have these reservations. For many of us, the most relevant philosophical commitment is to the dialogical vision for philosophy most often associated with the work of Charles Sanders Peirce.[29] As is well known, Peirce linked success in science, success in philosophy, the core principles of rational discourse, and sometimes even truth, with consensus reached by "the relevant communities of inquiry" over the long term. When one loses contact with those who hold opposing positions, one also loses the ability to assess the strength of one's own arguments. To the Peircean, the resulting publications become tennis without a net.

In this respect, I am a Peircean before I am anything else in philosophy. Theologians have usually been committed to explicating the core beliefs of their own particular tradition. Philosophers, by contrast, generally claim to be motivated by the broader pursuit of truth, bringing to each new topic the best reasoning they can muster and an undying passion to know what is the case.

If you are a Peircean like me, you feel disappointment whenever you encounter fixed walls of opposition surrounding warring camps, with nothing but No-Man's-Land lying between them. You walk the desolate landscape, like Max von Sydow in Ingmar Bergman's *Seventh Seal*, looking for areas of inquiry that exist without fixed walls and dogmas, areas where discussion partners are working to establish genuine conceptual contact across differences.

Sometimes the results are incredibly encouraging. I think, for example, of the international discussions of science and religion in the 1990s, when scientists, philosophers, and religionists began to work out conceptual connections that had never been explored before. At other times the results are less encouraging. Numerous debates over the last few decades began in promising ways and then ended with a circling of the wagons. Among the examples are: Christian philosophy, first presented as an engagement of Christianity with contemporary culture, but then often devolving into a smug dismissal of alternatives, for example in the later work of Alvin Plantinga and many articles in *Faith and Philosophy*; the metaphysical debates of the American Catholic Philosophical Society, which often became exercises in orthodox Thomism for aging faculty at Catholic schools; the "Hegelian renaissance" in Germany in the 1980s and '90s, which devolved into Scholastic commentaries on philosophical minutiae; and, most unfortunately, the early science-and-religion debate, which moved from a period of genuine transformation on both sides to what is now a complete standoff between the New Atheists and the Intelligent Design theorists. (As a sign of the times, the Templeton Foundation now funds BIOLA, the Bible Institute of Los Angeles, at multi-million dollar levels but has no major new grants running at UCLA or UC San Diego.)

I close, then, with the hope of creating some level of sacred restlessness in my readers. Consider the Chicago School in the mid-20th century, where many variants of naturalized religion were developed that helped to change the face of liberal religion in the American public square. Consider the exciting philosophical renaissance that is occurring even now in China: Neo-Marxists developing Marxism for a postmodern context; science-religion discussions that draw deeply on Confucian, Taoist, and other distinctively Chinese wisdom traditions; and, perhaps most important, Chinese eco-philosophers who are integrating Whitehead with Chinese traditions to lay the foundations of an ecological civilization for a postmodern world. In each of these cases, old walls have come down and new alliances are being built.

Indeed, consider Griffin's own *God, Power, and Evil: A Process Theodicy*. That book had such a significant impact because it spoke to Christians and Jews whose assumptions had led them to an unanswerable problem of evil. Its more adequate model of God allowed them to solve inconsistencies in their own position while remaining Christian or Jewish in thought and practice. *The genius of the book is that it made contact.* SAM and PPP *seem* to make contact, because both are labeled "naturalism" and both reject the old supernaturalism. But, as we have seen, the labels actually name a fundamental difference; they do not help to build new bridges.

I close then with a call to retain (or regain) the prophetic spirit of the process tradition at its best. Prophets challenge norms and push back against the establishment. But they usually do this by making contact with that establishment and speaking to it in effective ways. Think of the metaphors of Jeremiah and Ezekiel. That is why their arguments hit home so effectively. Prophetic process thought has the potential to be transformative across a wide range of academic disciplines: philosophy, theology, ecology, economics, social theory, ethics, political theory . . . and, yes, the philosophy of science as well. This too should be a crucial part of David Griffin's legacy. It is our heritage as process thinkers—but only if we continue to practice the "skillful means" of making real contact across philosophical differences.

# 6. Non-Supernatural Naturalism and Deep Religious Pluralism

## Sandra B. Lubarsky

Whitehead once wrote, "It belongs to the self-respect of intellect to pursue every tangle of thought to its final unravelment."[1] I cannot think of a more concise description of how David Griffin has spent his considerable talents. He has pursued truth like a whistleblower calling all ill-conceived theological schemes to account. But like Whitehead, "unravelment" has been a method, not a goal. For Griffin, philosophical clarity is for the purpose of the wider goal of aligning human understanding with reality and with the moral and aesthetic dimensions of life. Religious pluralism is one strand in his lifework of shaping a constructive postmodern philosophy that offers "a vision of the harmony of truth"[2] (Whitehead's words) and a "vital spirituality"[3] (Griffin's words).

"To be loyal to God," Griffin declared at the conference in 2003 that led to the publication of his edited volume *Deep Religious Pluralism*, "is to be loyal to the world."[4] Knowing full well the power of false claims and the damage they have done when attached to religion (and politics), and mindful of the role religion might play—for good or for ill—in the coming era of environmental and social disruption, Griffin's attention to religious pluralism is an expression of his loyalty. It is a significant part of his contribution to a world desperately in need of durable sources of justice, love, and peace.

Griffin's two-pronged approach—a critical analysis of the arguments offered by leading theologians and a systematic construction of a process-based religious pluralism—sharpens a discourse that all too easily could settle into various versions of pluralism that appease the desire for tolerance but ultimately fail to produce the profound theological changes that it demands. Moreover, he has done much to raise the profile of the pivotal work of John Cobb, and, it is fair to say, to save genuine religious pluralism from a premature end.

Religious pluralism arose as a compelling response to the presence of diverse traditions and as an alternative to the deficiencies of exclusivism and inclusivism. In the 1980s, it received significant enthusiasm from both theologians and the public: John Cobb's *Beyond Dialogue* was published in 1982; Alan Race's *Christians and Religious Pluralism* came out in 1983; Paul Knitter's *No Other Name?* followed in 1985; and *The Myth of Christian Uniqueness*, co-edited by Knitter and John Hick, was published in 1987. These seminal works were accompanied by scores of institutional and grassroots efforts to engage in interreligious dialogue. Nonetheless, coming to terms theologically with both the sociological facts of religious pluralism and the theological demands that it imposes remains a challenge.

In religiously liberal circles—both Christian and Jewish—pluralism is now understood as consonant with what it means to be a right-minded member of the congregation. What that often means, however, is that, as Rabbi Susan Laemmle said, "all spiritual paths are finally leading to the same sacred ground."[5] This is a position that, despite being an advance over religious intolerance, has its deficiencies. Representing what Griffin calls "identist pluralism," it is subject to the charge of relativism. Amongst religious conservatives, the idea of religious pluralism remains a feckless compromise with modernity, undermining supernaturalism as well as leading to relativism. Griffin refuses either option. There is, he argues, a better option than the unstable seesawing between religious singularity (in its several varieties) and relativism. But it requires a rethinking of modernity's assumptions about naturalism, religion's assumptions about modernity, and theologians' assumptions about pluralism.

Just how important it is to deepen the discourse on religious pluralism is made clear in Robert Wuthnow's 2005 study of religious diversity in the United States. Most Americans, he found, "are, at one level, *tolerant* of people who may belong to religions quite different from their own, such as immigrants or people living in other countries who may be Muslims or Hindus or Buddhists," and 74% agreed with this statement: "All major religions, such as Christianity, Hinduism, Buddhism, and Islam, contain some truth about God."

But this affirmation is sown in thin soil. Wuthnow also found that between 50-60% of respondents favored government monitoring of Muslim and Buddhist groups; that 47% viewed Islam as fanatical; that 25% believed the same to be true about Hinduism and Buddhism; and that almost a quarter were in favor of making it illegal for Muslims, Hindus, and Buddhists to meet in groups in the U.S. Notably, animus toward Islam was not linked to 9/11 or a fear of terrorism but to a general belief that the United States is a Christian country. For that reason, a significant amount of ill will was extended to eastern traditions as well.

This antipathy was, moreover, reinforced by the fact that 60% of Americans can be described as either exclusivists or inclusivists (Wuthnow's estimate was 30% in each category), most of whom know next to nothing about other people's traditions. Not surprisingly, exclusivism correlates strongly with negative judgments about other traditions. It seems that Americans' tolerance for religious difference—even in the face of significant exposure to religious diversity in their daily interactions and even during a time of political and economic stability (2005)—is still rather marginal. There is little to sustain the good news that most Americans believe that there is some truth to other traditions when it is served up with a stew of other, less wholesome, ideas.

In one moving section, Wuthnow describes a Christian exclusivist who said that her best friend was a Jew. "She said her friend was a lovely woman, but then she broke into tears talking about how sad it was that her friend wasn't saved. The Bible says there's only one way: "It's written a million times—one way, one way, one way."[6] Of course, nothing like this is written "a million times" in the Bible, but that exaggeration captures her distress over a cherished friendship made vulnerable by the principles of a cherished faith.

Religious diversity calls for theological structures that can bear the weight of difference without demanding cognitive dissonance, emotional contraction, or religious infidelity.

Griffin takes on the project of religious pluralism for a number of reasons. It is, as he notes, "one of the central issues in contemporary religious thought," and he cites reasons it has become so: increased encounters with people from other traditions and awareness of the positive value they reap from their faiths; greater sensitivity to the harm caused by religious exclusivism; expanded recognition of the need for traditions to cooperate in the face of worldwide challenges; and the affirmation that divine love brooks no barriers. But Griffin's chief interest is in what he calls the "ontological reason," the reason that turns on truth-making and reality-formation and thus provides a philosophical ground for religious pluralism. The ontological reason involves the entwined relationship between science and religion in the modern era.

Griffin focuses on the ontological basis of religious pluralism not because he is indifferent to the other reasons for supporting the "pluralistic turn." In fact, many of the other areas of his work would lead him in the same direction. The power of love, for example, is absolutely central to Griffin's theodicy, for it is the way God acts in the world at every moment and in relation to every being. Moreover, his critique of American empire and nuclear armament, his concerns about ecological catastrophe, his profound belief that religion could be (although is not necessarily) an animating force for good: These are all points of contact with the conversation on religious pluralism.

But the ontological reason strikes at the heart of Griffin's larger project on constructive postmodernism. This project aims toward "a new unity of scientific, ethical, aesthetic, and religious intuitions,"[7] one that both celebrates modernist ways of thinking that have advanced human understanding and well-being and, at the same time, reconstructs those ways that have thwarted our ability to generate and sustain life.

Modernity has contended with religion for a host of reasons—including premodern assertions of religious absolutism—and it has triumphed. But this contest between modernity and religion is not the outcome of inexorable principles of logic. It is, rather, the consequence of a series of unnecessary assumptions that has led to a false opposition between religion and science. The "central question" of Griffin's 2000 book, *Religion and Scientific Naturalism: Overcoming the*

*Conflicts*, asks "whether there is anything essential to science that is in conflict with any beliefs essential to vital religion, especially theistic religion. My answer," he writes, "is no."[8]

This "no" is the wider context in which Griffin's work on religious pluralism must be understood. It constitutes the frame for his unique contribution to contemporary deliberations on religious pluralism. Simply put: religious pluralism hangs on a reconstruction of modern science as much as it does on a reconstruction of traditional theology; a vigorous form of religious pluralism cannot be achieved apart from this wider rethinking. Griffin's approach to religious pluralism exemplifies this rethinking, going beyond the shortcomings of modernity without forfeiting its successes. On the one hand, he argues against the tradition of absolutism; on the other hand, he argues against the moral relativism and atheism of modernity. Likewise, on the one hand, he advances a non-supernaturalist theology and, on the other hand, he takes seriously the existence of a divine reality and a value-saturated world. Griffin's argument belongs squarely to his efforts to, as Gary Dorrien has written, "rehabilitate theism while adhering to the formal standards of modern philosophy and science."[9] More accurately, it is a rehabilitation of *both* theology *and* science, undertaken to correct the overreach of modern science and "the timidity of [modern] religion" (Griffin's language).[10]

S. Mark Heim has accused religious pluralists of having failed to do what they set out to do: to honor real differences between religious traditions in terms of both their beliefs about ultimate reality and their efforts to achieve salvation. He argues that the focus on the commonalities between traditions has resulted in a homogenized version of a Western-style religion, that the diversity that pluralists had set out to affirm has been subverted by the assumption that all religions affirm the same ultimate reality and the same final goal.

His judgment is based primarily on the work of John Hick, whose version of pluralism Heim and many others deem to be the paradigmatic version of religious pluralism. Based on Hick's model, Heim concludes that this pluralism is so flawed as not really to be pluralistic at all.

Griffin shares Heim's critique of Hick's interpretation of religious pluralism—and then some. But he holds that Heim is mistaken on a much more fundamental point: Hick's "pluralistic hypothesis" should not be taken as the bench mark for religious pluralism. Not only is it flawed by the fact that, although Hick's theology is pluralistic (*contra* Heim), it is only shallowly so. But also, there is a far more robust form of religious pluralism: a model of *deep* religious pluralism, which is based on the philosophy of Alfred North Whitehead and draws on the further insights of John Cobb. This is a version of religious pluralism that is not susceptible to the charges raised by Heim (and others) against pluralism.

Moreover, this version provides a theology of religions that, by virtue of being part of a comprehensive philosophical system that affirms religious naturalism, is uniquely able to address some of the toughest challenges pluralism presents to religion. It is, as well, an approach to religious pluralism that is compatible with a variety of religious traditions, without claiming that they are identical down deep.[11]

Griffin's formulation of a postmodern constructive religious pluralism contains four elements: (1) an ontological and epistemological naturalism that rejects sensationism, atheism, and materialism; (2) the notion of divine power as persuasive power; (3) the affirmation of multiple ultimates; and (4) the affirmation of a pluralism of universalizable norms.

Griffin lifts up the encounter with modern science as the primary inducement for the contemporary development of theologies of religious pluralism. Most important in this regard is the rejection of religious supernaturalism. Scientific naturalism ruled out the possibility that a divine agent could disrupt the laws of nature through some form of supernatural revelation. Those religious traditions that sought to be compatible with modern science—which is to say, to be modern—had to relinquish supernaturalism.

Once supernatural intervention in nature and human history was abandoned, it was no longer reasonable to think that infallible and timeless truth could be unilaterally revealed at any single moment to any singular people or individual. The scientific worldview challenged revelatory truth based on divine activity of this sort and, in doing so, challenged all assertions of religious uniqueness and superiority established on this premise. Although the occurrence of revelation is not denied, *truth* is to be settled through experience and reason—both of which are historically conditioned and subject to error—and not by appeal to a perfect revelation. The affirmation of religious pluralism became a logical consequence of the rejection of supernaturalism in favor of a religious naturalism.

What Griffin calls "generic religious pluralism" is the affirmation that truth and salvific value are not limited to a single religious tradition. It is, instead, far more likely that there is truth and value in many traditions—certainly in traditions that have survived for long periods of time and offered guidance and consolation to generations of adherents.

Griffin makes it clear that the rejection of supernaturalism and the affirmation of naturalism are "crucial for explaining the rise of generic pluralism and for understanding its nature."[12] And, indeed, pluralistic theologians on the whole have embraced both the ontological and epistemic aspects of naturalism. (*Ontological* naturalism is the position that "there are *no* events devoid of natural, in the sense of finite, causes. ... [I]f there is divine causation in the world, it is integral to the world's normal causal processes, never an interruption of them." According to *epistemic* naturalism, "[a]ll claims to truth are to be judged in terms of experience and reason," so that any claims based on supernatural revelation are ruled out.[13]) By virtue of the acceptance of both ontological and epistemic naturalism, pluralistic theologians have aligned themselves with modernity. In so doing, however, a paradox has arisen: The very conditions of modernity that prompt religious pluralism seem to undermine the validity of religion. As Catholic theologian Paul Griffiths puts it: modernity is "voracious" and "omnivorous," with the result that its "surface tolerance of all religions is indistinguishable from a profound hostility to all."[14]

Griffin, however, disputes *this* conception of modernity, which he does by means of the unravelment of naturalism from the accumulated, but unwarranted, assumptions of sensationism, atheism, and materialism (which Griffin has abbreviated *naturalism$_{sam}$*). Naturalism of this kind does indeed invalidate the entire quest for religious pluralism, because it delegitimizes both religion and ethics. But *generic* naturalism, which entails only the rejection of supernaturalism, can be called "non-supernatural naturalism" (which Griffin abbreviates *naturalism$_{ns}$*). Naturalism in the generic sense, therefore, does not need to entail materialism. It need not abandon God and divine influence in the world. God, mind, freedom, and value can be understood as functioning in accord with natural causal processes.

Neither religious pluralism nor modernity requires the acceptance of atheism or materialism. But unless this clarification is made, so that non-supernatural naturalism is distinguished from the sensationist-atheistic-materialist version of naturalism, those who are drawn to religious pluralism because of the implications of modern science will find themselves endorsing a position that rules out religion as such. What Griffin does so well is to show how the various riddles of religious pluralism can only be solved by placing religious pluralism within a naturalistic framework that does not rule out God or God's agency in the world. This framework, he argues, is best described as a naturalism in which sensationism is replaced by a prehensive doctrine of perception (according to which sensory perception is derivative from a nonsensory type of perception), atheism is replaced by panentheism, and materialism is replaced by panexperientialism (which he abbreviates *naturalism$_{ppp}$*). This "3-P naturalism" explains how science and religion can be complementary approaches to reality, how religious truth can be pluralistic, how God can act in the world without violating the natural order, and how relativism can be avoided.

While the rejection of supernatural intervention leads to a rejection of revelation that is infallible and complete, it need not mean a rejection of divine agency. But because most theologians who have engaged with science have not differentiated *non-supernatural* naturalism from *atheistic* naturalism, it has been difficult for them to speak of God's activity in the world. One of the most important consequences of Griffin's distinction is that it makes it possible to talk about God's efficacious work in the world. Griffin argues that God *does* "intervene" in the world, but not in ways that violate natural causation. God's persuasive agency helps to explain the pluralism, mutability, and uniqueness of traditions. Giving up the doctrine of divine omnipotence helps to clarify the historical evolution of religions, while affirming divine persuasive influence in the world helps to clarify why the evolution of religions is not simply a matter of historical consequences.[15] God remains part of the ecology in which religions evolve.

It is also worth noting that Griffin's emphasis on God's persuasive power is important for not only explaining divine activity in a non-supernaturalist theology, but also for guiding human interaction. If God's way of acting in the world is as a persuasive power, those who seek to imitate God will endeavor, in all their relations—including interaction with people of different faiths—to act similarly.[16]

The most curious aspect of the discourse on pluralism is that, for so many thinkers, generic pluralism—the idea that there are multiple religions that possess truth and salvific value—morphs very quickly into identist pluralism—the idea that "all religions are oriented toward the same religious object . . . and promote essentially the same end."[17] It is this fact that makes the whole pluralist undertaking not only fail to be deeply pluralistic but, equally important, vulnerable to the charge, famously articulated by Alan Race, of "debilitating relativism." Indeed, any number of internet sites, dictionaries of religion, and encyclopedia essays move effortlessly from a preliminary explanation of religious diversity (the fact that many different traditions exist) to an affirmation of religious pluralism (the position that truth can be found residing in more than one tradition) to an unwitting slide into identist relativism (the idea that all religions are equally valid because they are essentially the same).

It is a misstep closely related to the popularity of the work of John Hick, who does exactly this in his writings. And it is a misstep seen also in the writings of those who advance the "perennial philosophy," such as Huston Smith. In both cases, one recognizes the differences between forms of religion that focus on a personal ultimate, perhaps called God, and forms that focus on an impersonal or formless ultimate, perhaps called Emptiness or Being Itself. But the urge to find common ground between them seems irrepressible. As Griffin points out, the tendency in the East has been to subordinate the personal God to impersonal ultimate reality; the tendency in the West has been the opposite. Hick's approach has collapsed the two forms of religious experience in another way: making both forms subservient to an ineffable "Real."[18] In all three cases—which are all forms of identist pluralism—difference is eclipsed by the desire to remake experience according to philosophical predilections.

In the face of the significant shortcomings of identist pluralism, Griffin demonstrates that a "different type of pluralism" is possible.[19] In line with the complementarity of science and religion and drawing on John Cobb's work, Griffin sets forth a way to understand competing religious truth claims as complementary. In this way, he is able to overcome the insidious assumption of identist pluralism, according to which diversity is not a fundamental feature of reality, and the long-standing habit of seeking religious uniformity.

Griffin's "different type of pluralism" does not attempt to controvert the experience of difference. It begins with the aim for adequacy to the facts of experience, taking seriously the reports of diverse apprehensions of reality and the possibility—even likelihood—that there is more than one ultimate. Drawing on his own fully developed critique of creation out of nothing, then on Whitehead's distinction between God and creativity, and then on Cobb's important insight that experiences of "in-formed reality" and "form-less reality" correspond to the distinction between God and creativity, respectively, Griffin shapes a religious pluralism that transcends the failings of both exclusivism (the failure to affirm pluralism) and relativism (the failure to maintain difference). He calls the resulting position "deep religious pluralism"—to distinguish it from Hick's real but shallow pluralism—maintaining that (1) different religions really are different; that (2) they may nonetheless reveal universally valid insights; that (3) these insights may be complementary rather than oppositional; and that (4) they, taken together, give us a richer understanding of reality than we might otherwise have.

Can deep religious pluralism also be deeply Christian, Jewish, Muslim, Buddhist, or Hindu? Can the affirmation of multiple ultimates and of multiple claims to truth be made alongside a vigorous commitment to one tradition? The affirmative answer to this question attests to the radical nature of a postmodern, constructive process pluralism. Griffin quotes Cobb: "[W]e do not need to relativize our beliefs." Rather, "[w]e can affirm our insights as universally valid! What we cannot do, without lapsing back into unjustified arrogance, is to deny that the insights of other traditions are also universally valid."[20] It is not necessary to give up claims to universally valid norms; it *is* necessary to give up the claim that what my tradition values is *the* universal value rather than *a* universal value. The shift from the definite article to the indefinite article is, as Griffin points out, a crucial modification.[21]

A relativizing of values arises only if, in the face of multiple truth claims, traditions decide to live side by side with each other, unaffected by a truth that is "out there," but not of consequence to one's own tradition. A value can, by contrast, be recognized as not only "good for them" but also "good for us" and thus be incorporated into a new theological landscape. In this embrace of values previously not recognized by a tradition, and in the subsequent angling toward an as-yet-undetermined shape, lies the radical sweep of religious pluralism. Having acknowledged that truth has not been revealed in any complete form or fully expressed by any particular human interpretation, those who remain committed to religious traditions must nurture an abiding loyalty to creative transformation. This is the process of deep religious pluralism.

Griffin lifts up Cobb's remarkable statement, highlighting (and celebrating) this point: "Pointing out that the task of transforming Christianity 'in relation to each of the great ways of humankind is a vast one,' Cobb says: 'We have barely begun to deal with the fundamental changes that must be effected within our Christian faith.'"[22] Of course, this vast task is in front of every tradition that recognizes the logic of deep religious pluralism. And yet, this "having barely begun" has advanced the conversation on religious pluralism significantly.

The genius of Griffin's philosophy of religion has been the cogent reworking of the relationship between modern science and religion. In distinguishing non-supernatural naturalism from sensationist, atheistic, and materialistic naturalism, Griffin makes it possible for theologians to develop spirited, compelling responses to the universal truths of modern science. Deep religious pluralism is one of these responses. It has generated multiple ways of ensuring that religious pluralism is truly pluralistic. Apart from the frame of non-supernatural naturalism, the idea that there are multiple ultimates would be so radical as to be either incomprehensible or in need of the authority of revelation. Within it, the idea of multiple complementary ultimates appears as a coherent consequence. The limitations of individual human psyches provide species-specific reasons. The place-based and historically conditioned nature of human cultures provides sociological reasons. God's ever-active, non-coercive influence in the world provides the theological reason. Non-supernatural naturalism provides the ontological reason.

Deep religious pluralism is, as Griffin has contended, a way of being loyal to both God and the world. Its yield exceeds religious tolerance. It is also an expression of the quest for truth, extending to the coordination of "the various deep truths to which the various religions of the world have called attention" and, beyond that, to an increase in "genuine knowledge."[23] The importance of cultivating it at this moment in human history cannot be overestimated.

# 7. The Vagaries of Religious Experience: David Griffin's Reenchantment in Light of Constructivism and Attribution Theory

## Nancy Frankenberry

David Griffin has tackled many of the most contested topics in the academic study of religion and explored with subtlety and nuance the most complex questions in the philosophy of religion. One of the many reasons for deeper interest in his philosophy of religion is appreciation of the alternative form of theism he defends. Before turning to my topic—religious experience—I want to remark on what I believe to be the single most important contribution Griffin has made to philosophical debates about religion. Vividly and persuasively, he has pleaded the case for process theism as a compelling third position beyond the usual suspects—*either* classical theism *or* atheism. Better than any other process thinker, with the possible exception of Charles Hartshorne, he has made the case that by excluding or marginalizing process theism, philosophers of religion have been guilty of perpetuating an unfair, incomplete, and false version of the intellectual options available in our time. With dogged devotion to what I am tempted to call the Law of the Occluded Muddle, he has been a brilliant critic of the Catch-22 in which opponents seek to pin process thinkers— as though anyone who writes about *real* theism must mean supernatural conceptions of deity, which are incoherent, and any coherent conception can be dismissed as not *real* theism.

Why should the default meaning of theism refer to the classical model of an omnipotent, omniscient, omnibenevolent personal Being outside of space and time, and yet mysteriously present to humans while exceeding human comprehension? Despite a long history of critique in the modern period, this presumption has curiously persisted, even as the default meaning adopted by New Atheists. Fortunately, against the ignorant and ahistorical assumptions found on both sides of the theism-atheism debates, David Griffin has continued to argue for the cogency of process theism as a third option, variously called "theistic naturalism" or "naturalistic theism," but in any case a revisionist theism that does not posit an omnipotent supernatural Being fully actualized and antecedent to the world. Against all who would reduce the intellectual options to only two, Griffin has issued a series of powerful arguments, most notably in *Religion and Scientific Naturalism* (2000) and *Reenchantment Without Supernaturalism* (2001), building on the work of Whitehead and Hartshorne.

Gary Dorrien depicts theological liberalism as a third way, rationally and experientially, between "authority-based orthodoxies," on the one hand, and "secular disbelief," on the other hand.[1] This does not quite fit Griffin's delineation of a third, overlooked theistic position, in my opinion. Although it should be generally classed with liberal theology, process theology is best described as a third option that lies *beyond* the sterile clash between orthodoxy and disbelief. It comes *after* them, to use the overworked preposition that appears in recent titles by Mark C. Taylor, John Caputo, and others. "Between" seems to conjure too much brokering, as though taking a little from authority-based orthodoxies, then allowing a little from secular disbelief, not quite siding with either. "*After* theism versus atheism" makes clear that process thought leaves both behind, attempting to find not a middle ground but a way to reframe the entire debate. No one has been more thorough or more convincing than Griffin in showing that any form of theism that upholds a single causal principle as the source, or sole creator, of the world is "shipwrecked upon the rock of the problem of evil," in the words of Alfred North Whitehead.[2] There is no middle ground to occupy here. Process theism takes the conversation *beyond* the choice between Vince Lombardi ("he's no good unless he's a winner") and Woody Allen ("it's not that God doesn't exist, it's just that he's an underachiever"). To suppose that the choice is between omnipotence versus impotence is to frame the debate still on the side of assumptions derived from the history of classical theism in the West. Griffin's achievement has been to show that a merely verbalizable, but not coherently conceivable, form of omnipotent power cannot be used as a standard by which to judge the God of a coherent conception either imperfect or impotent.

Indicative of the systematic character of his critique of standard philosophy of religion is a little-known review Griffin wrote in 1991 of Kai Nielsen's *God, Skepticism, and Modernity*.[3] First noting that Nielsen's critique of all forms of theism aimed to be exhaustive, Griffin then succinctly set forth the core of Nielsen's account in the form of seven propositions. He argued that Nielsen's case against theism, and his case in favor of atheism, were both incomplete.

According to Nielsen, nonanthropomorphic conceptions of God are incoherent; anthropomorphic conceptions of God may be coherent, but they are superstitious and involve false beliefs; and conceptions of God that are neither incoherent nor anthropomorphic are essentially atheistic, equating God simply with love or moral ideals. But this case against theism is not exhaustive, Griffin objected, because the conceptions of God referred to in Nielsen's theses are not exhaustive. The ideas of nontraditional theists, such as Whitehead, Hartshorne, Otto Pfleiderer, William James, and Frederick Tennant—who all agree that traditional theism is incoherent—are not encompassed. Did this critique register on Kai Nielsen? Interestingly, in a book published in 2001, Nielsen *agreed* that his case was not complete and that in order for it to be complete, he would need to consider the Whiteheadian-Hartshornean option of a God in process. Clearly nettled by Griffin's review, but not inclined to take up the exacting task of reading Whitehead, Nielsen devoted a total of seventy lines in one bulging footnote to refusing the task of investigating a naturalistic theistic option that purports to be logically coherent, congruent with scientific knowledge, and applicable to human experience. Why the refusal? Because we need to get rid of "metaphysical moonshine," he wrote.[4]

Moonshine or not, Nielsen's verdict that metaphysics is just what we need to get rid of is widely shared outside of the Whiteheadian world. Key elements of process theism clearly do rely on speculative philosophical claims that are controversial and that need to be independently evaluated. However, the fair appraisal of the philosophical adequacy of process theism has been arbitrarily impeded by the Catch-22 game. To the American pragmatist and historicist Jeffrey Stout, for example, it seems that revisionists like Griffin have to choose between *either* the distinctiveness *or* the conversability of their theological voice. To the extent to which the theological message carries relevance, Stout thinks, it is purchased at the price of redundancy, while its distinctiveness (from secular culture) can only be acquired with the risk of irrelevance.[5] To the religious naturalist Henry Samuel Levinson, Whiteheadian theism is a "halfway house" en route to its logical successor project, atheism.[6]

For the most part, it must be said, Griffin's work has been appropriated in theology and some areas of philosophy, but seems to have fallen on deaf ears in Anglo-American philosophy of religion and in the academic study of religion. These two areas currently share an overlapping reconsideration of the topic of religious experience, rife with a variety of methodological and theoretical avenues.

## RELIGIOUS EXPERIENCE

Turning now to the main concern of this paper, I will first encapsulate Griffin's development of a Whiteheadian account of religious experience, chiefly in *Reenchantment Without Supernaturalism* (2001), and then compare it with a very different methodology, cognitive theory of religion—particularly the constructivist approach associated with the work of Wayne Proudfoot and the attributional theory of religion best investigated in the recent work of Ann Taves. My aim is to show that Griffin's work can supplement and extend theirs, even as their methodological and theoretical proposals can give us the tools for specifying his process theology more precisely. Their two approaches thus map the distinction between doing theology and studying religion.

Religious experience, a concept that turns out to be of relatively recent origin, has presented several notorious problems to investigators. Two primary issues have emerged in Anglo-American philosophical circles over the last half-century, having to do, first, with the relation of concepts and experience, and second—derived from the first—with the nature of immediacy and inference. Debates over these two questions have gone through roughly three phases. First, in the 1960s and the '70s, the debate was focused chiefly on the cognitive versus the non-cognitive nature of religious experience and language. Meaningful propositions were said to be either analytic or capable of verification or falsification by experience. This sterile disjunction died out with the demise of positivism and the waning of the verificationist/falsificationist challenges, but not before raising in particularly sharp form doubts about the cognitive value of religious experience, the meaning of meaning, and the confirmability of "inferences to the best explanation" in the absence of sense-perception.

Second, in the 1980s and '90s, the main debate was framed between the constructivists and the perennialists, represented, respectively, by Wayne Proudfoot and William Barnard. In this stage, the constructivists, with their early version of attribution theory, won over most philosophers of religion with the argument that religious experiences are conditioned by the experiencer's cultural context and do not possess a perennial common core across traditions and times.

Finally, in the 21st century, cognitive studies of religion are now providing much of the theoretical leveraging for investigations of religious experience, drawing on experimental work in biology, psychology, and the new neurosciences. Although it is too soon to draw conclusions, one of the ambitions of the cognitive project is to find universal properties of human cognitive structures that shape, constrain, and generate religious systems.

To the first and second of these phases, Griffin has contributed valuable arguments, which I can only adumbrate here. To the third phase in which cognitive science is dominant, I believe that Griffin's approach can clarify an important area of uncertainty in attributional theory, an uncertainty that is also evident in the constructivist program.

Griffin's answer to the first phase can be found in his elaboration of Whitehead's nonsensationist doctrine of perception. In light of this analysis of perception, the chief problem with the verificationist/falsificationist phase of philosophy of religion was its exclusive concern with sensory perception, a secondary mode that is derivative from a more fundamental nonsensory "prehension" in the mode of causal efficacy. Griffin argued that the Whiteheadian alternative not only represents a more adequate epistemology, but also allows for a direct perception of a "Holy Reality."[7] In this vein, he demonstrated how perception in the mode of causal efficacy permits what he called "genuine religious experience" without violation of the 'good kind' of naturalism; and, in a discussion of the truths that Whitehead believed were derivable from religious experience—such as a sense of permanent rightness in the nature of things—Griffin defended the very thing that the verificationist disputes never considered, namely, the possibility that religious experience might have an objective ground in nature that transcends the subject's experience without, at the same time, being characterized as supernatural or non-empirical.

Griffin's answer to the debates between the constructivists and the perennialists in the second phase is more difficult to encapsulate but can best be seen in his treatment of Wayne Proudfoot's classic study, *Religious Experience* (1985). For Griffin, what constitutes an experience a "genuine religious experience" is that it is "understood as direct perception of a Holy Power."[8] For Proudfoot, according to Griffin, "What constitutes an experience as a *religious* experience . . . is not something inherent to the experience but the interpretive categories brought to it from the person's culture."[9] The chief source of Griffin's criticism of Proudfoot's project then appears in this complaint: "Rather than religion's being a product, at least partly, of religious experience, so-called religious *experience* is entirely a product of religious *beliefs*—which are themselves to be explained in nonreligious terms."[10]

This is a doubtful interpretation of Proudfoot's constructivism, but it does bring out the first hard question I have been leading up to: What is a proper understanding of the relation between concepts and experience? Do concepts, beliefs, and thoughts exhaust experience? Or does experience display at least some recalcitrance to some interpretations as well as some receptivity to others? Can we collapse "interpretation" completely into "experience"? Or, while recognizing an inexplicable matrix of interpretation-experience, should we resist any tendency to dissolve either category into the other? Can there be a non-conceptual element to experience? If so, is there perhaps a deeper, more fundamental aspect of religious experience, beneath the cultural variations involving Jesus, Krishna, or the Tao—something corresponding to what has been called the Sacred, the Numinous, the Holy?

The second, and related—if not identical—question can be put in terms of the nature of immediacy and the extent of inference. Is immediate knowledge ever had? Perhaps of our own mental states, in some privileged sense? Or is all knowledge inferential, so that even first-person knowledge is in principle the same as third-person knowledge? Applied to the epistemology of religious experience, this is the question whether the intentional object of religious experience is immediately "given," in some sense, or posited as the outcome of inferential movements around a web of concepts and beliefs. In relation to Griffin's philosophy of religion, it calls for a more explicit explication of two things: what he means by "givenness" when he writes that God is given to experience; and whether when he writes about "direct religious experience" he means "direct, but inferential" or "immediate, and non-inferential." *Reenchantment* made clear that Griffin affirms the view that our experience does contain data that are simply "given."[11]

For myself, I take it that no one has really worked out the *cognitive* dimension of anything called "direct experience" as a notion that transcends the futile dyad "either-immediate-or-inferred." The natural supposition that we might like to make, i.e., that neither *alone* is sufficient, still does not succeed as a proper formula for giving a convincing account of their status as together. William James's discussion of the *a priori* in the final chapter of his *Principles of Psychology* confronts this very difficulty—the problem of the concepts that begin with experience, but do not arise out of experience in the sense that we can find obvious originals for them in the stream of direct experience. Despite the richness of his radical empiricism with its connections and relations, James was misled in thinking he had to find counterparts in the stream of experience for every term. It led him only to a dead-end there, for the stream of experience does not contain all of the concepts and relations in terms of which it is to be understood and interpreted. Without concepts and logical operations involving abstract and generalizable terms, there could be no systematic interpretation or inferential judgments about experience. Experience is neither self-organizing nor self-interpreting. Not every concept employed in the description of the stream of experience or the chain of inferences about some aspect of it is related to the stream in precisely the same way. Some conceptual constructions are at the edge, and others are at more of a logical distance from the stream and we cannot find counterparts for them. The majority of the concepts required for doing theology are concepts that have empirical meaning and are thus not subject to treatment on the basis of logical considerations alone, and yet these concepts are not empirical in the sense that the stream of experience has them as "given," or just there to be read off.

Of course, these are longstanding and complex epistemological questions, that neither Griffin nor I are likely to solve soon, but I suggest that Griffin's account of religious experience and, more broadly, of experience does provide one important way to obviate an ambiguity that has lingered in the constructivist program since Kant. Strong constructivism holds that an experience is generated entirely out of prior concepts or thoughts; the cognitive component of an experience is constitutive of the experience itself. But now the question emerges whether a weaker form of constructivist theory is more adequate and more coherent. This would assert that concepts are in part, but not wholly, constitutive of experience. Also constitutive of experience is immediacy, spontaneity, or receptivity—in part, but not wholly. Indeed, whatever the verdict on Kant or Proudfoot's constructivism, I believe the weaker form is the position that Griffin either accepts or implies. His Whiteheadian approach might well argue, not that a pure, unvarnished "given" enters into religious experience, but that the interpretative aspect does not swamp the experiential aspect entirely. Furthermore, a Whiteheadian approach could acknowledge that beliefs and concepts are *a priori* conditions of religious experience, and still maintain that they are not entirely constitutive of it. In the case of "a feeling of permanent rightness," for example, one must have the concept of "permanence" and of "rightness" in order to have a feeling of permanent rightness, but the content of the feeling is not exhausted by the concepts.

If the experiential aspect is always specified under a certain description, and any description requires concepts and beliefs, then any questions about the nature of the experience apart from the interpretation of it are unintelligible.

There is nothing available to us that is independent of concepts and beliefs. In a Whiteheadian framework, therefore, we should be wary of placing the workings of perception in the mode of causal efficacy outside of the space of concepts, for the more we do so, the less clear we are as to how it can become available for awareness. We do not need to elide the distinction between experience and interpretation, which is the temptation of some constructivists. Yet we cannot say just how we should preserve and account for such a distinction. The intransigent tension is that the distinction can be preserved only at the cost of forfeiting any account of it. As soon as one develops an account of what "immediate experience" or "direct experience" is apart from interpretation, one slips into mediation, as Kant and Hegel each showed in different ways.

Since the time of Proudfoot's pioneering study almost thirty years ago, the constructivist agenda in religious studies, together with attribution theory, has evolved. In the hands most recently of Ann Taves in her book *Religious Experience Reconsidered* (2009), it has become a vital ingredient in what she calls a "building block" approach to the study of religious experience.[12] Taves offers the possibility of understanding that there are no antecedent facts of the matter when it comes to religious experience, other than what is produced through the shifting play of the ascriptions and attributions of socialized, embodied human beings. I suggest that her work also offers support to the way in which I have just portrayed David Griffin's philosophy of religious experience. Resisting the dichotomous either-or debate between perennialists and constructivists, Taves views both positions with partial sympathy. On the one hand, she recognizes that subjects cannot identify the object of religious experience as being the cause of it without at the same time losing the immediacy and passing into a conceptual, constructivist arena. At the same time, in research about religious experience, she seeks something that, if not exactly a common core, can be extrapolated across cultures as scholars employ a comparative method for understanding different traditions, times, and places. Attribution theory figures in this effort as a collection of theories developed by psychologists to explain the commonsense causal explanations that people offer for why things happen as they do. Taves uses attribution theory to shift our attention from "religious experience" to "experiences deemed religious." Deeming is an umbrella term that encompasses processes of ascription and processes of attribution. Ascriptions assign qualities or characteristics to some thing. Attributions assign causal explanations.

Several aspects of Taves' building block approach to the study of religious experience hold some promise for Griffin's road to re-enchantment. For example, the category of "specialness" or "special things" of one sort or another forms the building blocks for what we think of as religions or spiritualities. Focusing our attention on "special things" takes our attention away from "religion" in the abstract and refocuses it on the component parts or building blocks that can be assembled in various ways to create more complex socio-cultural formations, some of which people deem as "religious" or "spiritualities" or "paths." Furthermore, the turn to attributional theory illustrates (but does not provide the basis for) a claim that is implicit in Griffin's philosophy of religion and needs to be made explicit, namely: there is no specifically "religious" experience that is essentially so, or intrinsically so; that is, there is no independent *content* to experiences deemed religious that *makes* them religious. On my reading, Griffin could agree with Taves and Proudfoot that neither the felt quality alone nor its intentional object alone is sufficient to identify experiences as religious. What makes them religious is the deeming. And what motivates the deeming is bound up with beliefs about the cause of the experience.

How would Taves, in turn, characterize David Griffin's conception of religious experience? She might begin by noting that he thinks religious experience includes a noetic quality or epistemic element. Employing a constructivist approach, Taves could judge that the noetic component is best analyzed as an assumed claim about the proper explanation of the experience. Viewed attributionally, claims based on experience are not self-evident, and they are invariably contested. It is just this highly contested question of what constitutes "religion" that gives us no way to study "religious experience" *as such*. As a result, we are restricted to studying stipulated aspects of experience, some of which may be deemed by some people to be religious, according to Taves. Bringing together both constructivism and attribution theory, we could see Griffin's belief that "the Holy is given to experience" as representing an example of an endorsed proposition within the space of reasons with an attributed causal claim. Like everything else, it is subject to justification in terms of its explanatory value and its adequacy to experience.

Both Griffin and Taves unavoidably confront a particular constraint in designating any beliefs and practices *as religious*. In culture after culture, historically and in the present day, people report beliefs that the soul lives on after death, that rituals can change the physical world and divine the truth, and that illness and misfortune are caused and alleviated by spirits, ghosts, saints, fairies, angels, demons, devils, gods, and goddesses. Normally, we find that the intentional objects of belief are among the causes of ordinary beliefs, at least in the most basic of cases. But this condition is altogether lacking in the case of reports having to do with religious experiences involving—what I will call for lack of a better term—superhuman agents.[13] Interpreters are not in a position to traffic with gods, goddesses, ancestors, ghosts, water spirits or other superhuman agents. What they *can* discover is whether the people they are trying to interpret hold beliefs and attitudes concerning superhuman agents, and in that case it is statements and assertions about superhuman agents that are crucial to the interpretation of any particular practice or belief *as* religious. In the nature of the case, superhuman agents cannot be identified apart from people's beliefs about them. Defined in this way, "religion" comprises no particular subject matter of its own. It can be said to have a context—ritual—which itself has belief implicatures having to do with superhuman agents.

Of course, Griffin rejects the category of "superhuman agents" as an identifying description. He replaces it with the "Holy." I have some reservations about this term. Like "the Sacred" or "the Numinous," the term "Holy" is both an emic and an etic concept. For most scholars today, the term presents so many formidable methodological problems in the study of religion that it requires replacement by a new term that is not at once so opaque and so burdened by a phenomenological tradition of interpretation. This is where Taves' term, "specialness," supplies an identifying term as well as a second-order concept that engages a larger, more encompassing framework for incorporating whatever things, experiences, beliefs, and values people deem to be "religious." Extending Durkheim, Taves wants to use "specialness" or "special things" as a broad framework in which to situate various emic terms that can then be internally subdivided into different types, modes and methods and used as a bridge to other disciplines across the humanities and the sciences. This seems to me to have an advantage over the "Holy," a concept that does not admit of any subdivision in this way, and is in that respect limited. Ironically for a philosophy of process, a stipulative definition of religious experience in terms of the Holy, or the Sacred, or the Numinous will artificially stabilize the object of study, and obscure what scholars like Taves think we should study instead—i.e., the *processes* whereby people decide on the meaning of events and determine what matters most.

The two views, Whiteheadian and constructivist-attributional, are compatible. On my interpretation, both affirm that human experience is constituted in part by prior concepts and beliefs *and* in part by felt qualities in the perceptual mode of causal efficacy. These components are analytically distinguishable but concretely inseparable, so that one can never really say what is the experience and what is the interpretation, but neither can one collapse experience into interpretation, or interpretation into experience. In empirical studies, we see a constant fluctuation and a wide variation in the balance between neurological-physiological-causally efficacious components of experience and the conceptual-interpretive components. For example, drug-induced states can be more overwhelmingly causal than conceptual. In the continuum of experiences deemed religious, the same kind of fluctuation may occur, leading to greater or lesser emphasis on the receptive aspect, or on the conceptual aspect at any one time.

What is the sense in which experience reflects non-conceptual content? Having wrestled with this question quite a bit, both within a Whiteheadian context and a constructivist context, I want to say that we can recognize a formal, structural element of non-conceptuality in all judgments that depend on experience, without holding that it is possible to isolate the non-conceptual aspect of experience in the sense of entertaining it itself as a conscious state. In other words, we can "have" non-conceptual content without viewing it as non-conceptual *experience* or calling it "knowledge" in some sense. Griffin can avoid the contradiction involved in saying that religious experience is both intentional (*about* something—the Holy), *and* that it is independent of concepts and beliefs, by acknowledging the principal insight of constructivist-attributional theory: to say "the Holy" is already to specify something under a description and to make an inference to the best explanation. Indeed, for most people, the very act of distinguishing a *religious* experience *as* religious is due to the belief that the best explanation of what has happened is that it is due to non-natural causality of some sort; people *infer* that belief from other beliefs that they hold.

Likewise, Griffin can offer to constructivist-attributional theory the insight that the term experience cannot be exhaustively collapsed into interpretation or discourse. Some "space" needs to be open for the immediacy of experience in its receptive and non-discursive mode.

The related question, in addition to the one I called "the sense in which experience reflects non-conceptual content," is whether there can *be* non-inferential judgments; and where a Whiteheadian interpretation would want to go on this question. Griffin has stated that, on the basis of Whitehead's prehensive doctrine of perception, "there is no reason to deny, and many reasons to affirm, that we do directly perceive a Holy Actuality."[14] What is the meaning of "directly"? If "direct" experience is "immediate" in the sense of absence of self-awareness, it is unproblematic. But if it posits a pre-linguistic, non-conceptual contact with the Holy, it is problematic. The perception may be immediate, but as soon as one has judged that it is Holy or divine, concepts have come into play, inference occurs, and belief formation is well underway. A subject cannot both identify the object of religious experience *and* hold fast the immediacy without passing into a conceptual stage.[15] I am inclined to think that when we say, "we directly perceive a Holy Actuality," we are issuing a judgment. That judgment stands in inferential relations to other beliefs and concepts that we must have mastered in order to have any one concept. For me, that is one reason to deny that we do directly perceive a Holy Actuality, in any desired sense of immediacy.

It may be that Griffin needs a concept like *mediated immediacy* to do justice to the process view that experience has a non-conceptual aspect, in contrast to the constructivist view that concepts are constitutive of experience. Whether the two schools, Whiteheadian and constructivist, can themselves be mediated on this point will depend on whether one judges that Griffin's indefatigable defense of "givenness" has succeeded in rescuing Whitehead from the charge leveled against him, rightly or wrongly, that he succumbs to the "myth of the given," the mistaken idea that some object of experience can be given independently of concepts and beliefs.[16]

## A WORD ABOUT TRUTH

When it comes to the tricky question of truth, and how religious experiences might serve up truth, I suspect that Griffin and I diverge in more ways than I can delineate here. I follow Donald Davidson and others in elucidating truth in terms of semantics, not epistemology. This means that I take truth to be a primitive notion that does not stand in need of a theory or a definition, since all theories or definitions would have to be in terms of something more primitive. Truth is a concept we rely on to figure out our beliefs. To know the contents of beliefs is to have figured out the meaning of sentences, and that in turn presupposes the concept of truth. Indeed, truth and meaning and belief all presuppose one another. Tug on any one, and the other two swim into view. We understand the concept of truth as soon as we understand the meanings of sentences and acquire beliefs. It would be folly, however, as Davidson wrote in an influential paper, to try to define what *makes* a sentence true.[17]

Griffin has espoused a correspondence notion of truth, although he does not try to convert it into a full-blown theory.[18] Many of us don't have much use for the notion of truth as correspondence, and we have other, good reasons for rejecting relativism, as well as for wishing to get beyond the realist-antirealist arguments. One can have truth without correspondence, relativism, or realism (or anti-realism, for that matter), all by adopting a semantic conception of truth and distinguishing truth from the epistemic task of justification. The distinction between truth and justification is an important one, given up only at the cost of denying that we understand the difference between *what we think* and *what is true*. Without a distinction between truth and justification, we could not detect mistakes, lies, or pretenses. Perhaps it is justification that Griffin is really after, under the traditional banner of "truth."

If it pleases him, I think Griffin can keep the notion of truth as correspondence in the harmless sense of correspondence in which we say that true sentences correspond to the world. But we shouldn't assume this explains anything about the concept of truth. Nor should we think it gives us any traction in evaluating the vagaries of religious experience. Does it make sense to ask about "the truth of religious experience" or to claim, as tolerance inclines many to proclaim today, "all religions are true"? This strikes me as doubtful. On the assumption that truth pertains only to propositional attitudes expressed or uttered in sentential form, it is unintelligible to talk about the truth of religious experience or the truth of whole religious systems, as though there are sets of entities or facts that are just what they are independent of what we say about them.

Griffin has defended the notion of truth as correspondence on the grounds that it is impossible to reject without suffering "performative contradiction"; it is such a hard-core commonsense idea that we presuppose it, he says, even in the very act of criticizing it. Justly famous for the variety of ways in which he has recalled us to the wisdom of commonsense, Griffin may mislead us here. A lot of dualisms are deeply ingrained in commonsense, which is one reason process metaphysics comes across to many people as counterintuitive. An enduring dualism in philosophy of religion has long posited something "given" in experience, or in religious experience in particular, and something else that organizes, filters, fits, or copes with that givenness. My interest is in exposing that dualism as providing what Wittgenstein called "a picture that has held us captive," borne of a futile quest for an ultimate source of evidence whose character can be wholly specified without reference to what it is evidence for.

Even so, it is excellent advice, as Whitehead wrote, "to bow to those presumptions which, in despite of criticism, we still employ for the regulation of our lives."[19] I am deeply grateful to David Griffin for bringing this pragmatic theme to the foreground of our attention in his characteristically systematic way.

# 8. Psi Phenomena and a Whiteheadian Century

## Marcus Ford

In Whiteheadian circles, David Griffin is famous for his prediction, made at a 1998 conference, that the 21st century will be a Whiteheadian century.[1] It is too soon to know if his forecast is correct, but if it is, it will be, in no small measure, because he worked to make it so.

One of the ways in which Griffin has labored to make this the Whiteheadian century is by illuminating the metaphysical implications of psi phenomena, which are typically dismissed by philosophers and other well-educated people as simply impossible. Griffin's work in this area is less well-known than his work in other areas. This is both understandable and regrettable. It is understandable insofar it constitutes only a small part of his overall work and because it is a field of study that many people, including philosophers and theologians, shy away from. Even to be open to looking at the evidence in favor of parapsychological events is considered by many to indicate a lack of intellectual sophistication. It is, however, regrettable insofar as the reality of some types of parapsychological events provides empirical evidence in favor of panexperientialist metaphysics. Psi phenomena do not constitute the only empirical evidence in favor of such a worldview or even, as Griffin points out, the primary evidence. But it is evidence nonetheless and, for some people, it may prove to be decisive in how they understand the world.

There is an enormous body of scientific literature on the topic of mind-to-mind communication (mental telepathy), distant viewing (clairvoyance), psychokinesis (the ability to move objects using only the mind), out-of-body experiences, and the channeling of past lives.

Let me point to just one instance of reported clairvoyance. In her 2008 book, *Extraordinary Knowing: Science, Skepticism and the Inexplicable Powers of the Human Mind*,[2] Elizabeth Lloyd Mayer, a world-renowned psychotherapist with no previous interest in parapsychology, opens with this story. Her daughter was an accomplished harpist who as a young girl had her harp, which was very valuable, stolen after a performance. Mayer immediately contacted the Oakland police, local music stores, and the American Harp Association, all to no avail, in spite of the fact CBS News carried a story about the stolen harp.

A friend of hers then suggested that she contact a dowser. Mayer had no reason to believe that a dowser could provide reliable information about anything, but she agreed: What harm could it do? Her friend put her in touch with Harold Mc-Coy of Fayetteville, Arkansas, who at the time was the president of the American Society of Dowsers. Dr. Mayer called McCoy and asked if he could locate her daughter's harp. Saying that he would be glad to help, he—after focusing his attention—assured her that the harp was still in the Bay area, more specifically in Oakland. He then said if she would send him a map of the city he would do his best to locate the harp. She sent him a map immediately, and two days later he called back, reporting that he had located the harp. It was in the second house on the right of such-and-such street.

She could not get the police to go to that particular house with a search warrant (apparently having the word of a dowser is not considered "probable cause"). But she put up signs within a two-block area of the house offering a reward for the lost harp, and the harp was quickly returned to its rightful owner.

How does one make sense of this story? The neighborhood where she put up signs was many miles from where the harp was stolen, and it was the only neighborhood in which she put up signs. How could a man in Arkansas locate an object in Oakland, California, two thousand miles away? Most people assume that this is not an interesting or a meaningful question because the answer is obvious: Unless it was simply a lucky guess, the occurrence was simply impossible. Dr. Mayer was either mistaken in her belief in a causal connection between the dowser's information and the return of the harp, or she was lying.

It makes no sense to place much weight on this one example, but for over a hundred years the British Society for Psychical Research, and then the American Society for Psychical Research, have been scrupulously documenting these kinds of events and, for almost as long, researchers associated with universities have studied psi phenomena in laboratory settings. Tens of thousands of individual subjects have been involved in various well-designed and carefully monitored experiments. Currently, research on paranormal events is being conducted in over 30 countries. Griffin has summarized some of this research in his 1997 book, *Parapsychology, Philosophy, and Spirituality: A Postmodern Exploration.*[3]

In addition to the research that is being conducted for purely scientific purposes, there has also been psychic research carried out for its potential military applications. For twenty-four years, the CIA and the Defense Intelligence Agency teamed up with private researchers to explore the possible uses of remote viewing for military purposes. Some of these studies have been declassified. Physicist Harold Puthoff, who for several years was with military intelligence, was the founding director and researcher of such a project at the Stanford Research Institute, and he concluded that there was indisputable evidence for remote viewing. A fellow researcher at the Stanford Research Institute, Russell Targ, has presented an overview of some of the scientific evidence for types of ESP, especially distant viewing, in his 2012 book, *The Reality of ESP: A Physicist's Proof of Psychic Abilities.*[4]

What have philosophers said about these types of reported phenomena? In previous generations, there were several well-known philosophers—including William James, Henry Sidgwick, Henri Bergson, Alfred North Whitehead, C.D. Broad, F.S.C. Schiller, Gabriel Marcel and Leonard Eslick—who took these kinds of findings seriously, some of whom, James in particular, devoted a great deal of time exploring this aspect of reality and its metaphysical and social implications. But David Griffin is one of only a few contemporary philosophers who have written about these phenomena.[5]

The situation is somewhat different outside the area of philosophy. A number of prominent physicists, including Brian Josephson, David Bohm, and Freeman Dyson, as well as a few biologists and psychologists, have found the evidence for some kinds of paranormal events convincing.

But most physicists, biologists, and psychologists do not embrace the reality of paranormal phenomena. Most of them evidently reject the reality of these phenomena for exactly the same reason that philosophers do: psi phenomena are judged to be metaphysically impossible: There are no parapsychological occurrences because such events are impossible.

Here is one case in point. In a 1999 book entitled *Leaps of Faith: Science, Miracles, and the Search for Supernatural Consolation*, Nicholas Humphrey, a noted British theoretical psychologist and peace activist, dismisses the possibility of psi phenomena on the grounds that causation requires a "physical pathway." The only thing that our minds can affect directly, he says, is our bodies, and this is because our minds are connected to our bodies by "a set of fixed physical pathways, permanently in place, whose parameters are pre-established" by evolutionary history.[6] The relationship between our mind and our body is absolutely unique. Here is "the crucial point": "[O]f all the things in the world, our bodies are the *only ones* with which our minds can count on having a relationship anything like this."[7] "The truth is," he continues, "there is not, and we can safely say there never will be, this quasi bodily relationship between a human being and . . . the rain, or a human being and a spoon, or a human being and the seeds of a plant, or a human being and a random number generator . . . or even, sadly, a human being and another human being."[8] Psi phenomena are metaphysically impossible because there are no "physical pathways" connecting us to these other things, and causation requires physical pathways.[9]

Griffin agrees with Humphrey that a materialistic worldview that limits causation to mechanical interactions renders psi phenomena impossible. Unlike Humphrey, however, Griffin takes this as evidence for the inadequacy of a worldview that limits causation to mechanical interaction.

This is, to be sure, not the whole story. If the modern worldview were in every other respect internally consistent and completely adequate to all known facts, it would be an overreaction, it could be argued, to reject this worldview on the basis of psi events alone. But there are many reasons, in addition to the reality of psi events, to question the adequacy and coherence of the modern worldview. E.O. Wilson, one of the great champions of the materialist version of the modern worldview, is willing to admit this. In his 1998 book, *Consilience: The Unity of Knowledge,* Wilson lists what he considers to be the most important "gaps" in scientific understanding: "The gaps of greatest potential," he writes, "include the final unification of physics, the reconstruction of living cells, the assembly of ecosystems, the coevolution of genes and culture, the physical basis of mind, and the deep origins of ethics and religion."[10] What materialism cannot yet explain, in other words, is how the quantum world works and how it is compatible with relativity physics, how life emerged from dead matter, the inter-relatedness of living things and their environment, the relationship between the physical world and the world of free human beings, the physical basis of mind, and the material basis for ethical and religious experience and principles.

Moreover, one could easily add to this list of things that science has not yet explained, such as the metaphysical status of numbers and other abstractions, the directionality of time, and the existence of psi phenomena. Psi phenomena, then, are not anomalous in the sense that they are the one thing that modern science cannot explain (and therefore must dismiss). Instead, they are one of a long list of things that science, in its present form, cannot explain.

It is no accident that the modern worldview, in both its materialistic and its dualistic forms, cannot account for the reality of psi events. As Griffin makes clear in a number of places, the modern worldview was developed as an explicit rejection of a view of the natural world that allowed for the reality of "occult" powers, including action at a distance.[11] In both its dualistic and its non-dualistic forms, the modern worldview sees matter as dead, in the sense that it is unable to act and unable to be acted upon by any force other than direct physical contact. This view makes it *in principle* impossible for minds—if there *are* minds—to act on matter (other than the human body), and it makes it impossible for minds—if such there be—to interact over distances or to be affected by physical events that are spatially remote (with the possible exception of gravity). Although debates about these matters in the 17th and 18th centuries were primarily around religious and political issues that are largely irrelevant to the contemporary world, they have come to shape the way most modern individuals think about reality. Modern thinkers summarily dismiss the reality of psi phenomena because their worldview *requires* that they do so.

The importance of psi phenomena goes far beyond the apparent ability some people have to read another person's mind, "see" objects without using their eyes, move match sticks by thought alone, and so on. As Griffin notes in *Parapsychology, Philosophy, and Spirituality,* how we understand parapsychological events "could lead us to revise our views about the nature of the evolutionary process, the possibility of divine influence in the world, the relation between mind and body, the possibility of life after death, and the very meaning of life."[12] In other words, if we accept the evidence for the reality of psi experience and adopt a metaphysics that allows for these things, it is possible to address the very issues that Wilson has conceded have yet to be explained by scientific materialism.

The kind of metaphysics that is needed to account for psi phenomena, and the kind of metaphysics that psi phenomena suggests, is one that entails the existence of causally efficacious minds, a concept of efficient causation that is not limited to physical contact, and a theory of matter that is not altogether dead. Whitehead's philosophy of organism is just such a metaphysics. Whitehead did not argue for the need for a new metaphysics based on psi phenomena. Although he expressed his openness to the evidence on this topic and developed a metaphysics that allows for the possibility of most kinds of reported psi phenomena, his primary motivation lay in the need for theoretical coherence generally, seeking to reconcile our deep aesthetic, moral, and religious intuitions with the world as revealed by modern science. Griffin makes it clear that he, too, finds the arguments in favor of a process panexperientialist metaphysics quite convincing, independently of the evidence for psi phenomena. He writes:

> These parapsychology-based considerations are not, to be sure, the only or even the primary basis for accepting panexperientialism.... However, the prejudice in favor of the view of the elementary units of nature, and even living cells, as insentient is so great that the panexperientialist viewpoint can use all the help it can get. This evidence from parapsychology might be especially significant for data-led minds, for whom empirical evidence is more important than purely theoretical considerations.[13]

There are many good reasons to reject the metaphysics of scientific materialism that have nothing to do with psi phenomena. The reality is psi is just one more good reason.

It needs to be noted that there is at least one type of reported parapsychological event that Griffin rejects, almost completely on philosophical grounds: precognition. As the name denotes, precognition means knowing the future, knowing events before they happen. From a Whiteheadian perspective, the future is open and does not exist in the same way that the past and present exist. The problem with "knowing the future" is not merely a matter of affirming non-local causation. The main problem is the idea of *knowing* something that, if the future is really open, may not happen, so it could not possibly be *known*.

On this point, Griffin quotes philosopher Antony Flew: "Because causes necessarily and always bring about their effects, it must be irredeemably self-contradictory to suggest that (later) fulfillments might cause the (earlier) anticipations."[14] Apparent instances of precognition must be explained in some other manner, because, in Flew's words: "No amount of empirical evidence can turn nonsense into sense."[15] The only way that it would be possible for anyone to "know the future," literally, would be for the future already to exist, in which case it would not be *the future.*

Although one might say that Griffin's denial of literal pre-cognition for philosophical reasons is no different from Hum-phrey's denial of telepathy on philosophical grounds, *in fact it is quite different.* Flew, who rejected ESP and precognition, explained that these rejections were different in kind: ESP, he said, was "just plumb impossible," by which he meant: ESP was *contingently* impossible, so the claim that ESP occurs is at least intelligible. Literal precognition, however, is *logically* impossible, because the idea that an effect could precede its causes is a self-contradiction.[16] To affirm the reality of most kinds of parapsychological events, such as telepathy and tele-kinesis, does not require that one give up logic. To affirm the literal meaning of precognition *would* require this.

One might think that the parapsychological evidence against the adequacy of the modern worldview, which has rendered most religious beliefs metaphysically impossible, would be exceedingly welcomed by those individuals who understand the world in religious terms—who believe that there is a divine being at work in the world, in the efficacy of prayer, and who believe in life after death. Thus far, this has not proven to be the case. Many religious people have, more or less, made their peace with the modern worldview, rework-ing their understanding of religion to fit this worldview. In most cases this "reworking" of religion to fit with scientific materialism means rejecting the possibility not only of mira-cles but also of life after death, the efficacy of prayer, and God's ability to have any effect in the world. The "reworking" of their religious beliefs in light of scientific materialism has tended to leave many modern believers with a very thin set of religious convictions. For individuals who have adopted this strategy, psi phenomena cannot exist for the very same reason that life after death or divine influence cannot occur: it is metaphysically impossible.

Other religious people have somehow held to both materialism and their supernaturalistic religious views. Although this dual affirmation is contradictory, they are unwilling to give up or water-down their religious convictions or to reject modernity. For these individuals, psi phenomena are neither scientifically credible nor religiously legitimated. In fact, psi phenomena can be construed as a kind of threat to the miraculous status of religious miracles, because psi phenomena are held to be—if somewhat uncommon—purely natural. If it is possible for some people to "see" distant objects directly, without the use of their eyes, and if others can influence the growth of plants or manipulate match sticks using only their minds, it would be possible to explain the "miracles" reported in the Bible as natural—if unusual—phenomena. The miracles reported in the Bible (and in other religious texts) can only be seen as miraculous if they are naturally impossible. For these individuals, psi phenomena present a threat to religion as well as science!

Not all religious individuals fall into one of these two camps. There are some people who, like Griffin, see parapsychology as a "spiritual science" and who see psi phenomena as clear evidence that scientific materialism, with its implicit or explicit atheism, its mechanical view of causation, and its nihilism as inadequate to the facts of the world. Psi phenomena make it clear that the world is vastly more rich and complex, more alive, interconnected and valuable than scientific materialism permits.

Also, in rejecting scientific materialism, psi phenomena undercut the logic of supernatural theism. If reality is not made up largely of dead matter, and if causal relationships are not limited to mechanical interaction, then it is not necessary to think in terms of a divine being who occasionally breaks into the natural order of things. "On the one hand," according to Griffin, the reality of psi events "undermines one of the main traditional bases for supernatural theism [by undermining the materialistic form of naturalism]. On the other hand, it supports not only a naturalistic theism but also a spiritual life no less robust, challenging, and satisfying than that supported by supernaturalistic theism at its best."[17]

If the 21st century, following Griffin's prediction in 1998, does indeed become the Whiteheadian century, then the transition from a modern to a Whiteheadian postmodern worldview would likely bring with it a widespread acceptance of psi phenomena. That has not yet happened, not because there is any lack of empirical data but rather because the dominant worldview does not allow the evidence to be taken seriously. There are, as previously noted, a few physicists, biologists, philosophers, and psychologists who stand outside the dominant tradition. The recent publication of a book on parapsychology by Edward and Emily Williams Kelly, *Irreducible Mind: Toward a Psychology for the 21st Century,* provides some reason to think that, at some point, mainstream psychology might rethink its position regarding parapsychology. Here is how the authors describe their work:

> Current mainstream opinion in psychology, neuroscience, and philosophy of mind holds that all aspects of human mind and consciousness are generated by physical processes occurring in brains. Views of this sort have dominated recent scholarly publication. The present volume, however, demonstrates empirically

that this reductive materialism is not only incomplete but false. The authors systematically marshal evidence for a variety of psychological phenomena that are extremely difficult, and in some cases clearly impossible, to account for in conventional physicalist terms. Topics addressed include phenomena of extreme psychophysical influence, memory, psychological automatisms and secondary personality, near-death experiences and allied phenomena, genius-level creativity, and 'mystical' states of consciousness both spontaneous and drug-induced.[18]

This text is dedicated to the great psychic researcher, Fredrick Myers, and draws heavily on his thought, as well as that of William James. This text book also devotes several pages to David Griffin and his Whiteheadian explanation for psi phenomena. The fact that William James, Sigmund Freud, and Carl Jung, three of the most important psychologists of the past century, believed in the reality of psi, might also persuade some psychologists to take a fresh look at the evidence and then to consider the metaphysical implications.[19]

In terms of what has already happened, perhaps the most likely impetus to the development of a Whiteheadian century will come through the phenomenal interest in Whitehead, along with a constructive postmodernism influenced by Whitehead, that has emerged in China during the past two decades—a development in which Griffin has played an important role. Perhaps, just as Aristotle's writings were kept alive in the Islamic world until the Christian West rediscovered them, Whitehead's thought will be reintroduced to America and Europe by way of China.

But whatever the means, the movement from a modern to a Whiteheadian postmodern worldview would provide a framework in which the massive empirical evidence for psi events could be accepted as, in fact, *empirical* evidence. In other words, empiricism, which has been based on sensory experience, could be expanded to include non-sensory experience. This is what William James called "radical empiricism." Slightly over a century ago, James said: "Let empiricism once become associated with religion, as hitherto, through some strange misunderstanding, it has been associated with irreligion, and I believe that a new era of religion as well as of philosophy will be ready to begin."[20]

Much is at stake in ensuring that this new era comes into being. Quite apart from the intellectual inconsistencies and inadequacies of the dominant worldview—a worldview that dismisses the very possibility of psi phenomena, moral and aesthetic values, free will, life after death, a divine mind, causation at a distance, and intrinsic value in the nonhuman world—the modern scientific worldview provides a kind of intellectual justification for the ongoing destruction of the planet and the domination of the strong and powerful. If we are to survive as a species, we need a different way to make sense of the world. Griffin's work in psi experience does not constitute a radical break from his more general intellectual interests in metaphysics and religion. Rather, it is completely consistent with these wider philosophical and religious interests as well as his interest in a more just and sustainable civilization. The kind of worldview that we need, Griffin maintains, is

> one that would lead to a new sense of adventure, one replacing the modern adventure of unending economic growth based on the technological subjugation of nature and the military and/or economic subjugation of weaker peoples. Only . . . if we come to see human life as primarily a spiritual adventure . . . will we have a chance of becoming sufficiently free from destructive

modern motivations to effect a transition to a sustainable global order.[21]

Griffin's exploration of psi phenomena is part of this larger
project to make sense of the world, to protect the weak and
the powerless from the strong and powerful, to restore a sense
of meaning and purpose to human existence, and to protect
other species from annihilation in the name of "science" and
economic progress. It is not correct to say that the credibility
of this new world depends on the reality of psi; it does not.
The argument and the empirical evidence for this new
worldview go far beyond the evidence for parapsychological
events. However, this new worldview allows for the existence
of most types of psi occurrences and for some people it
is this evidence that will be decisive in accepting this new,
more adequate, worldview. This is why this much overlooked
portion of Griffin's work is important.

# 9. Life after Death and Parapsychology

## John Buchanan

Before starting my studies at an innovative under-graduate school, I signed up for a summer class in introduction to philosophy at a local two-year college. My recent adventures in non-ordinary states of consciousness had raised many questions related to philosophy, psychology, and religion—and to what appeared to be a region circumscribed by the integration or overlap of all three.

Near the end of the course, the professor presented his favorite philosophical orientation, which, as I recall, was this: philosophy should concern itself only with those questions that can at some point be decided with scientific certainly. Despite my still solid allegiance to the scientific enterprise, this position seemed wrong-headed in several ways. I did not bother to argue that the questions science cannot answer might be among the most interesting for philosophy; but I could not help asking just how one would determine in advance what questions science could not ever address. The example he offered was that science could never know whether there is life after death (thus making it, I presume, a non-question for philosophy). I objected, suggesting that for all we know some day a radio-like device might be invented that would allow clear, distinct, and reliable communication with the departed—a sort of electronic medium—and if this device became widely used and accepted, then life after death might come to be part of our scientific world-view.[1] My professor argued that this was impossible; I replied that I did not see why. But I did see my class grade drop from an "A" to a "B."

This is a long way around to saying how delighted I am that David Griffin has given me this opportunity to redress that injustice by discussing his fascinating philosophical investigation into the possibility of life after death, along with his analysis of how the evidence from parapsychology bears on the survival hypothesis.

David is perhaps the most rigorous researcher (not to mention thinker) that I know: when he undertakes an investigation of a subject, it will be careful and thorough. All of this was evident when I read through his papers on life after death and, in particular, his major work on this topic: *Parapsychology, Philosophy, and Spirituality*. Ironically, I had not yet read this book, even though it addresses my special area of interest, transpersonal psychology.

I went into this project without any strong opinions one way or the other about the possibility of life after death. Despite my extensive involvement with transpersonal psychology, nothing had struck me as persuasive either way. Even a class on para-eschatology at Claremont with John Hick, built around his monumental *Death and Eternal Life*,[2] seemed to provide nothing more solid than some moderately suggestive evidence from parapsychology and much thoughtful philosophical speculation—unfortunately with little metaphysical grounding. What a revelation to discover Griffin's exacting study of the evidence for the survival hypothesis, his unwavering commitment to examine alternative explanations fairly, and his overarching philosophical contextualization of the issue in all its historical, scientific, and metaphysical dimensions.

Griffin's writings on the survival hypothesis cogently address our culture's emotional and intellectual obstacles to accepting the possibility of life after death—or, conversely, uncritically assuming its existence—and thus being able openly and fairly to assess the relevant empirical evidence, which is considerable and impressive.

Through a revealing historical study, Griffin pinpoints the bases for the biases found in our contemporary intellectual clime that lead it to deny outright the very possibility of life after death. Griffin suggests an alternative philosophical vision that not only opens the door to the possibility of survival, but also addresses other related major problems within modern thought in such areas as mind-body relations, the nature of consciousness, the grounding of moral and aesthetic intuitions, and a realistic conception of causality and temporal order. Thus the same ideas that open the modern worldview to the possibility of parapsychological phenomena, including evidence for the survival of death, also provide a philosophical perspective that is much more coherent with the foundations of everyday experience, as well as the findings of modern science. Finally, Griffin suggests, rightly I believe, that the evidence for life after death strengthens the notion that our life and our world (and the Universe) is a spiritual adventure—a perspective that can prove difficult to entertain, or maintain, with the underlying belief that "this life is all I've got."

## PHILOSOPHY AND LIFE AFTER DEATH

The first surprise while researching this paper was the strength of the evidence supporting the reality of certain psi phenomena. For example, Helmut Schmidt's fully automated study of ESP produced positive results that would occur by chance only once in two billion times.[3] That is certainly a level of significance that most scientists would relish.

My second surprise was the deep-seated resistance to this evidence for psychical phenomena—nay, the outright denial of the possibility of their very existence—frequently exhibited by even highly educated and otherwise reasonable scientists, philosophers, and other leading intellectuals.

Early on in *Parapsychology, Philosophy, and Spirituality*, Griffin expertly deconstructs the historical antecedents of our modern worldview that cast the possibility of life after death, and all parapsychological phenomena, so severely into question. Until quite recent times, life after death was a commonly held belief throughout the world, and it is still a widely held belief in many parts of the globe. So why have things shifted so radically in the modern world? Griffin attributes this change to certain philosophical, scientific, and sociological transformations (and motives) starting around the time of Descartes and culminating in the 19th and 20th centuries. Setting the stage for the early modern worldview was the adoption of Descartes's mind/body dualism—surprisingly, for religious reasons to a large extent. Influential scientists, such as Newton, shared an interest with the Church in preserving a place for God to act in the universe. By delineating a realm of the soul not subject to the mechanistic causal laws of the new physics—Descartes' *res cogitans*—the immortality of the human soul, the possibility of miracles, and the existence of God could be preserved. Importantly for our considerations here, action at a distance was intentionally ruled out by this mechanistic philosophy.[4]

By the late 19th century, the revolution in thought springing out of Darwinism, along with other scientific and philosophical advances, led to the collapse of Cartesian dualism into a monistic mechanistic materialism and an inevitable trend towards atheism. This late modern worldview had no place for the soul or mind (except as "epiphenomenal"), and thus survival of death became irrational, an impossibility. Similarly impossible were all parapsychological phenomena that relied on action at a distance, which was ruled out even more thoroughly by late modernism, as there is no way for an epiphenomenon to exert any kind of influence.

Here, then, is the root of the problem of getting a fair hearing for parapsychological evidence, including evidence bearing on life after death, since action at a distance is impossible in both versions of modernism, and survival of death in the later version. In sum, "modern thought and sensibility discourage belief in life after death on the basis of three mutually reinforcing claims: life after death is impossible; there is no evidence for it; and it is a bad thing to believe in anyway."[5]

Having recently discussed the possibility of life after death with a number of people, I can see the wisdom of Griffin's point that, before one can effectively present the case for evidence of survival, it is first necessary to show that the existence of mind apart from the body is even conceivable. Both dualism and monistic materialism prove inadequate to this task. Materialism offers no possibility for survival whatsoever, while dualism provides no coherent way of conceiving of mind-body interaction even in life, and thus is in no position to offer a plausible theory of life after death.[6]

However, there is another metaphysical alternative. In addition to monistic materialism and dualistic interactionism, there is also nondualistic interactionism. This third option—based on Whitehead's panexperientialism—is crucial to Griffin's investigation into the possibility of life after death. Griffin is proposing a "nondualistic, neoanimistic, panexperientialist philosophy, in which experience and spontaneity are fully natural features of the world, characteristic of nature at every level."[7] In such a universe, parapsychological phenomena are a real possibility.

Materialism deems life after death impossible, since for this worldview the mind is at best epiphenomenal and is completely dependent on the brain/body for its existence. Thus survival of death becomes an absurdity. H.H. Price clarifies this point: If one equates life with "certain very complicated physio-chemical processes . . . then, of course, life after death is by definition impossible." But if the human psyche consists of a flow of occasions of experience in interaction with the body/brain—and the universe at large—it is no longer absurd to speculate about this flow of psychic experience continuing after the death of its bodily matrix. Life after death could be thought of instead as "the problem of after-death experience."[8]

## THE PARAPSYCHOLOGICAL EVIDENCE FOR SURVIVAL

Having briefly reviewed Griffin's position on the basic ontological question for survival—can the human soul exist apart from its body?—we can now turn to the basic epistemological question: Is there any strong evidence for this? Griffin makes the important, and inconvenient, point that Whitehead's philosophy "cuts both ways" on this central question: While his metaphysics allows for the possibility of survival of death, it also allows for types of psi phenomena that could offer credible alternative explanations for the evidence of such survival.[9]

It will quickly become evident to the neutral observer that the surprisingly strong evidence for survival requires some type of paranormal explanation—unless one clings to the idea that, since these phenomena are inherently impossible, fraud and gullibility and misinterpretation must account for all this evidence. Admittedly, phenomena suggestive of survival can be difficult to interpret, not to mention almost impossible to study under controlled conditions. But we do not need repeatable, irrefutable proof of life after death to take seriously the available evidence. As William James famously pointed out—and Griffin takes to heart—it takes only one white crow to prove not all crows are black.[10]

Regarding the scientific standard of repeatability, Griffin argues that there are four ways that the evidence from parapsychology can be claimed to be repeatable. Griffin's four kinds of "white crows" are: (1) trustworthy intellectuals who have carefully investigated psychic phenomena and become convinced of its significance, (2) individuals who have clearly demonstrated that they possess parapsychological powers, (3) the ubiquity of parapsychological phenomena across cultures and throughout history, and (4) the incontrovertible experimental confirmations from parapsychological research.[11] All these white crows exist.

Here is where Whitehead's philosophy complicates matters. In Whiteheadian metaphysics, the entire past is available to each new occasion of experience. This opens the door all the way for theories of "superpsi," according to which ESP of unlimited powers can be used to account for almost any paranormal phenomena. The difficult task, then, is to find evidence for survival that cannot just as easily be understood in terms of retroprehensive inclusion, super-psi, or other forms of ESP that are possible within a panexperientialist universe. Griffin uses the term "retroprehension" to refer to a "direct prehension of occasions of experience belonging to the life of another person," and could be used to account for how mediums gain knowledge from the deceased, and the living, along with other parapsychological phenomena.[12]

Going a step further, or deeper, it might be possible for these experiences from other human psyches to get synthesized within a receptive human mind in a mode that includes their original sense of self-identity: the other's experiences would feel like one's own. Griffin terms this retroprehensive inclusion and points out that it could contribute to, or even account for, the evidence from cases of possession and reincarnation. Sorting out explanations involving retroprehensive inclusion from those based on the survival hypothesis is one of the major challenges for parapsychological theory or, perhaps I should say, for parapsychological metatheory.[13]

Griffin considers five types of parapsychological evidence that bear on the possibility of life after death. I briefly discuss and summarize his conclusions for mediumistic messages and possession cases, then look more closely at the most suggestive evidence: cases of reincarnation, apparitions, and out-of-body near-death experiences.

## MEDIUMISTIC COMMUNICATIONS

Although today mediums are generally looked upon with derision, or at best indulgently as reflecting the romantic naiveté of another era, careful research into the material they have produced indicates that, in the best cases, powerful ESP at least would be needed to explain the information accessed, and mimicry demonstrated, during many séances.

Of particular interest for their evidential value are the so-called cross-correspondences and drop-in communications. "Cross correspondences" refer to some fascinating cases where unrelated mediums around the world received messages over a period of years that, upon being brought together and studied carefully, appear to have been intentionally designed to be decipherable in meaning only when viewed within a larger complex pattern. With "drop-in communications," a spirit appears that is unknown to anyone at the séance, often in an intruding manner, and reveals information of a paranormal nature. The critical point is that these cases seem to indicate contemporary purposes for these spirits, which is an important consideration when trying to evaluate this evidence for traces of life after death.[14]

There is not time here to do justice to the subtle analysis necessary to demonstrate the strength of this evidence. Let me simply present Griffin's conclusions: "Even the most impressive evidence from mediumistic messages would not, by itself, constitute sufficiently strong evidence for life after death. If that were all we had to go on . . . we should probably conclude that, as complex as the superpsi hypothesis must become to account for all the evidence, it is to be preferred to the survivalist hypothesis."[15]

## POSSESSION CASES

Cases of possession exhibit elements of reincarnation, or perhaps might be thought of as being on the same continuum, because the entity evidentially possessing another person is often identified as one or more individuals from the past. Giving possession cases more importance than they might seem to have at first blush—they usually bear little resemblance to their portrayal in films such as "The Exorcist"—is that information is often divulged and "possessed" that demands some kind of a parapsychological explanation.[16] Griffin concludes, however, that the evidence from possession cases alone is insufficient to establish life after death, because other parapsychological explanations, such as telepathy and retroprehensive inclusion, offer equally viable alternatives.[17]

Both possession cases and mediumistic communications, however, do provide definite evidence of paranormal knowledge and are suggestive of "postmortem agency," that is, influence from the dead.

## CASES OF THE REINCARNATION TYPE

In-depth investigation, by Ian Stevenson in particular, has established that the extraordinary knowledge demonstrated by many people claiming to be reincarnated regarding their previous lives, along with the exhibition of talents and abilities highly incongruent with their current life experience, demand some kind of parapsychological explanation.[18] The available options appear to be either literal reincarnation (the experiential center of a human psyche surviving death and incarnating into a new body) or a paranormal theory that bestows some individuals with almost unlimited access to the experiences of others' past lives.

Griffin's methodical consideration of objections to the survival hypothesis, in terms of the superpsi and retroprehensive inclusion alternatives, is worthy of Sherlock Holmes. Griffin argues that a "strong form" of superpsi could account for skills supposedly inherited through reincarnation and that retroprehensive inclusion could explain why only one past personality is accessed in cases of the reincarnation type, as well as why these experiences are felt as memories.

Requiring more careful analysis are two intriguing phenomena: "announcing dreams"—where someone has a premonition that a dead person will be reincarnating soon, usually as a new family or tribal member—and congenital deformities that correspond to physical characteristics of the individual supposedly being reincarnated. Griffin suggests that announcing dreams can be adequately understood through the powers of "superpsi combined with the creativity of dreams."[19] Paranormal birthmarks and deformities could be explained in terms of maternal psychokinesis and telepathy, with the mother's largely unconscious paranormal activities selecting and guiding the process of memory appropriation and physical mimicry for her fetus. (It is important to note that "maternal impressions," the mother's unconscious ability to create birthmarks, was at one time "widely accepted in the medical community.")[20]

Cases of "intermission memories"—memories of existence between incarnations—while difficult to verify and not abundant, are suggestive of literal reincarnation, although they can also be explained in terms of superpsi telepathy. The impressive evidence for out-of-body experiences offers more support for literal reincarnation, as superpsi theories would predict any kind of disincarnate existence to be impossible.[21]

At the end of his carefully reasoned analysis of the evidence relating to reincarnation, Griffin points out two phenomena that present particularly strong reasons for thinking that a literal approach to theories of reincarnation should be adopted over some kind of retroprehensive or super-psi strategy. Literal reincarnation is supported both by the fact that the same person (the same psyche) does not reincarnate in more than one body, and that only dead people reincarnate. Retroprehensive inclusion would make multiple reincarnations of the same person into different bodies a real possibility (which does not, in fact, seem ever to occur) and would also suggest that psyches of the living should at times be subject to reincarnation (which also does not appear to occur).[22]

## APPARITIONS

Apparitions represent fascinating and dramatic paranormal phenomena that should not be dismissed lightly, as they offer important evidence for the survival hypothesis. Apparitions are different from "hallucinations" of the insane: they are seen very rarely by any one individual, they are primarily visual, and they are not associated with an underlying mental illness. Furthermore, apparitions are common phenomena in cultures around the world and throughout the past. Griffin notes that apparitions are experienced as objective, that is, as really being present in many ways like normal objects, but as not having a physical presence in the sense of being able to be touched or being confined by the boundaries of other nearby objects.[23]

Collective appearances, that is, a number of witnesses to the same apparition, make it difficult to attribute apparitions simply to products of the observer's mind alone. Telepathic contagion—the idea that one observer telepathically implants an image of the apparition into the mind of other observers—has been used to try to explain some apparitions, but such superpsi explanations of apparitions are strained by these collective viewings.

There are three problems with the theory of telepathic contagion: there is little evidence that such a thing even exists; apparitions appear and disappear at the same time for multiple viewers; and the telepathic sender would have to make the apparitions appear in different perspectives for each viewer. Furthermore, collective appearances are not rare, but rather are very common when more than one person is present as a potential observer.[24]

The upshot of Griffin's analysis of the evidence of apparitions is that nonsurvivalist theories seem so overly complex and problematic that one is inclined to turn to explanations that rely on some type of "postmortem agency," that is, influence from the dead. Griffin believes that ultimately an adequate theory of apparitions would lie somewhere between Edmund Gurney's hypothesis, according to which apparitions are results of telepathic contact from the departed, supplemented by psychic contagion, and the literal interpretation, according to which apparitions are some type of spiritual or astral body.[25]

In sum, the evidence suggests that apparitions of the dead reflect the autonomy of still-conscious minds. Apparitions thereby offer surprisingly strong evidence for the reality of survival. However, this evidence is strengthened even more by the phenomena of OBEs, which support the idea that living persons are able to have experiences outside their bodies, and which provide a counterpart to the perception of apparitions of the living. Especially suggestive are reciprocal cases, in which the apparition and an observer are mutually aware of one another. Such occurrences lend credence to the idea that, when the apparition is observed, a real agent is actually present in some way.[26]

## OUT-OF-BODY EXPERIENCES (OBEs)

Griffin treats near-death experiences (NDEs) as a special case of OBEs, where during life-threatening trauma one seems to leave one's body and observe events as a disincarnate entity, or even leave this world entirely. While OBEs commonly occur during NDEs, they also take place under many other circumstances.The modern mind tends to interpret OBEs as "introsomatic" events, that is, as something going on in the brain that makes it seem like one is really out of the body. This bias arises naturally out of modernity's materialist metaphysics, which sees the mind at best as an epiphenomenon of the brain, so that to speak of the mind, psyche, or soul as "outside" the brain/body is nonsensical.

Let me offer a telling aside that bears on this point. Michael Sabom, a doctor who has carefully researched NDEs, took exception to Dr. Richard Blacher's skeptical comments about near-death reports in the *Journal of the American Medical Association*, where Blacher warned against "accepting religious belief as scientific data." Sabom responded that "equal caution should be exercised in accepting scientific belief as scientific data."[27] Blacher's rebuttal even more fully demonstrated the rigidity of the modern scientific worldview towards parapsychological phenomena:

> Dr. Sabom takes me to task for describing the episodes as "fantasy." By using this word, I locate the phenomenon with the patient's psyche. . . . The alternative to

the intrapsychic location would be one of something (the soul?) leaving the person in reality and hovering over the table. I do not think one has to apologize for scientific belief if one does not accept the ideas of spirits wandering around the emergency room.[28]

Griffin, as we have seen, is arguing for a panexperientialist option where psychic events are in a flowing interaction with their brain/body matrix; for this philosophy an "extrasomatic" interpretation—according to which psychic occasions of experience occur outside the body—is not a metaphysical impossibility. The question then becomes, what might be the best way to understand these phenomena?

The reality of OBEs and NDEs has been well documented. What is to be determined is the true nature of these experiences. Do people really leave their bodies and have experiences and perceptions that tell us something about the nature of reality, about our world, or even about the world beyond? Griffin runs through a number of the reductionist explanations for OBEs, including hallucination, depersonalization, oxygen deprivation, and dreaming and provides good reason to seriously doubt such psychological and physiological attempts to locate these phenomena intrasomatically as mere aberrations or as examples of known syndromes and categories.[29]

One strong piece of evidence that OBEs are extrasomatic in some important sense is that people frequently report a total lack of pain—indeed, often a powerful sense of well-being—during an out of body experience. This is true even in cases where extreme discomfort is experienced immediately before or after the OBE. The phenomenology of this pain-free state differs significantly from the pain relief offered by analgesics or from a heavy release of endorphins.[30]

In addition, according to Griffin, there are three further problems for any intrasomatic explanation of OBEs: (1) the strong and widespread similarities between cases; (2) the feeling that the OBE itself is an experience of literally being out of one's body; and (3) the occurrence of veridical perceptions, that is, impressions of the outside world that are objectively accurate.

With regard to the strength of the evidence for the first two phenomena, Sabom says: "All persons in this study who related an NDE described it as if it had taken place outside their physical body. They felt the 'essential' part of themselves had separated from their physical body, and that this part was able to perceive objects and events visually."[31]

With regard to the third type of phenomena: Sabom and others have documented cases where patients, who were at the time medically unconscious (and near death), later reported accurately many details pertaining to their specific medical care, the equipment used, and the staff involved in their treatment. More surprising—especially for those defending an intrasomatic explanation of OBEs—are those cases where subjects perceive events and objects beyond the range of their senses even if they had been fully conscious.

For example, according to Kimberly Clark—professor at the University of Washington's School of Medicine—a migrant worker named Maria reported that, while having a cardiac arrest, she left her body and viewed various features of the hospital, including a tennis shoe on a remote outside ledge. Its existence was verified eventually, with some difficulty, as the shoe was very hard to see even from the nearest window. More impressively, this patient had described certain details of the shoe's condition that were later confirmed, yet were impossible to see until the shoe was actually retrieved from its perch.[32]

This is a vivid example of what Griffin means when he states: "Probably the most difficult problem for intrasomatic theories . . . is that they cannot do justice to the veridical

perceptions reported in many OBEs," because these perceptions "show that something other than illusion is occurring."[33]
(Experiences and perceptions "happening outside" the body,
including ESP, would be viewed as illusory from the intrasomatic perspective, thus veridical perceptions present a major
anomaly for intrasomatic theories of OBEs.) These types of
veridical perceptions are found also in spontaneously occurring OBEs, but they seem to take on an especially powerful
character when accompanying NDEs.[34]

Griffin finds the evidence provided by veridical perceptions to be among the most important types of evidence bearing on the possibility of mind existing apart from the body,
that is, in support of an extrasomatic interpretation of OBEs.
Although the similar phenomenology reported by those who
have experienced OBEs provides significant evidence about
the nature of these experiences, these data rely on subjective reports that are largely recalcitrant to objective empirical verification. Veridical perceptions, on the other hand, are
able to offer such empirical support. This is why Griffin believes that some OBEs, namely those demonstrating veridical
perceptions, "present the most difficult cases for the various
intrasomatic theories."[35] Thus from the many cases of veridical perceptions, along with the uniformity of the phenomenological reports, Griffin concludes that the weight of the
evidence supports an extrasomatic interpretation of OBEs.
Although OBEs do not give direct confirmation for the reality of life after death, they "do provide experiential support
of an affirmative answer to the chief question at issue, which
is simply whether the person (the mind or the soul, with or
without some kind of nonphysical body) can exist apart from
the physical body."[36]

Along with his ideas on OBEs in general, Griffin offers
an intriguing theory of NDEs, the essence of which is: "the

transcendental dimensions of NDEs should usually be regarded as a creative synthesis of nonsensory, archetypal, cultural, and individual elements."[37] In short, the experience of the Void and God's love are seen respectively as mystical intuitions of creativity—Whitehead's ultimate of ultimates—and of, simply enough, a loving God. They are genuine spiritual experiences made far more accessible by the disembodied condition occurring in the NDE. Meeting departed loved ones and other guides are also seen as genuine intuitions of a more subtle reality. The other common features of the NDE—such as the tunnel, spiritual lights, heavens and hells—are understood as an amalgam of individual, cultural, and archetypal influences.

## GRIFFIN'S REVIEW OF THE EVIDENCE

The tension between the survival hypothesis and the superpsi hypothesis contains an important implication.[38] If one looks fairly at the evidence for life after death, one is confronted with this dilemma: either admitting the reality of survival, or having to resort to a superpsi theory to explain the paranormal evidence. Either way, the door to parapsychology has been opened.[39]

Regarding the significance of the five kinds of evidence for life after death, Griffin states: "four of them contained phenomena that were in themselves strongly suggestive of survival" (the exception being possession cases).[40] He goes on to argue that this evidence is much stronger when taken as a whole; it is mutually reinforcing for three reasons. The first is the "principle of parsimony": only one theory (survival) is called upon to explain many kinds of evidence and phenomena. Second, each kind of evidence strengthens the likelihood of the others; there are many kinds of evidence bearing on the same question, all of which demand explanation. Third, some of the phenomena "provide support for elements of the others."[41]

More particularly, OBEs provide good evidence that the mind can exist apart from the body. Apparitions and mediumistic communications offer evidence of postmortem agency. Cases of the reincarnation type are suggestive of a literal survival and continuing existence for the soul. And all five kinds of phenomena demand some kind of paranormal explanation.

Based solely on the metaphysical possibilities offered by panexperientialism, and the existence of ESP and psychokinesis, Griffin puts the odds of survival at fifty percent—"insofar as assigning a numerical figure makes any sense at all."[42] Once the evidence supporting life after death is factored in, which as we have just seen is quite striking, the odds must be even higher in favor of the survival hypothesis.

What is Griffin's final conclusion, you may ask? As we have seen, Griffin does believe that survival is metaphysically possible and that the evidence for it is strong. But perhaps there is a better way to frame this issue:

> One cannot prove either the truth or the falsity of the belief in life after death. The question should be posed instead in terms of the most plausible theory, Plato's "most likely account." In terms of this question, I have suggested that there is formidable evidence for life after death, some of which can be given a superpsi explanation at best with considerable difficulty and can be more naturally and simply explained in terms of a survivalist hypothesis.[43]

## GRIFFIN'S VISION OF POSTMODERN SPIRITUALITY

The final chapter of *Parapsychology, Philosophy, and Spirituality* focuses on the importance of being able to experience life as a spiritual journey, and the trilemma we face today. First, while supernatural theism still offers a robust religion, many problematic aspects make it "arguably as harmful as help-ful."[44] Second, naturalistic theism, which offers a promising alternative spiritual vision, has not had the power to engage widespread interest at a deep level. Third, our civilization is facing a set of unprecedented challenges that demand a major change of spiritual perspective—if we are to survive. Griffin concludes from this analysis that "we evidently need a spiritual reorientation that is both naturalistic and robust."[45]

Griffin makes a convincing and—for a theologian—a rather surprising case that the powers and possibilities for the soul that are found in parapsychology provide the necessary ingredients, when combined with a panexperientialist philosophy, for the kind of robust, naturalistic religion that is needed to face our world's unprecedented challenges.[46] These ingredients include a self-determining freedom, a psyche that can directly influence its world (for better or worse), the possibility of experiencing guiding values that arise from a universal center of power—understood not as an omnipotent God, but rather as a "Holy Reality that is perfect in goodness as well as supreme in power"[47]—and authentic mystical experiences of God in all their manifold dimensions. In other words, a religion empowered by spiritual adventure, an enchanted universe, a psychic soul, and a real loving God.

The final possibility offered by parapsychology is life after death. Experiences after death are vital to Griffin's notion of a spiritual journey, for "unless we can believe that lives lived as spiritual journeys will have time to reach their destination, we probably cannot believe that the universe in any sense intends them to be spiritual journeys."[48] Some of the benefits that could accrue from envisioning our lives as extended spiritual journeys include: relieving modernity's excessive fear of death; instilling courage for social action in the face of powerful resistance; reducing materialism; and reorienting society towards the creative pursuit of spiritual goals.[49] To face the challenges the future holds, our civilization will need all of these spiritual assets.

Having carefully studied Griffin's ideas on the possibility of life after death, I am surprised to discover that I, too, find survival to be the most plausible hypothesis. Despite my deep and longstanding interest in these topics, if asked about life after death six months ago, I would have felt agnostic and probably repeated the famous saying about why not to believe in an afterlife: "I would rather be pleasantly surprised than bitterly disappointed." Now I would rather lead my life believing what is more probably true, and my journey feels enriched because of it.

# PART TWO

# Moral and Political Perspectives

# 10. David Griffin on Morality

## Gene Reeves

Compared with his substantial total output of publications, David Griffin has not published much on ethics or morality. But he has hardly been silent, either. Much of what he has published in this area is within a conversation among philosophers and others interested in what many would term "meta-ethics," basically the attempt not to discern what is moral or immoral so much as to examine the grounds, or absence thereof, of any possible morality. Their concerns are not so much with substantive moral issues, such as assisted suicide, abortion, or assassination, but with how, or whether, moral judgments of any kind can be justified.

### THE GLOBAL CRISIS

One might gain an impression that such meta-ethical matters are Griffin's main concern. But I think this is not where Griffin's interest in moral theory begins, or ends. He begins, I believe, with a recognition, now quite common if not universal, that the world is in crisis. This crisis comes in many forms, including terrorism, environmental pollution and degradation, natural resource depletion, climate change, population growth and overpopulation, imperialism, the growing gap between rich and poor with increasing rule by the rich, idealization of economic growth, and so on.

For Griffin, this world in crisis constitutes "the present world order," an order that "not only allows billions of human beings to sink below 'the line beneath which no one [should] be allowed to sink,' it *pushes* them under."[1]

The present world order is a "war system," a system of global anarchy in which conflicts of interest can only be resolved through coercive power, typically military means.[2] This would include, I suppose, using drones to assassinate people suspected of being enemies of the state. It is a system of international anarchy because there is no recognized authority above that of individual nation states. The United Nations, far from qualifying or limiting state sovereignty, is *based* on it. It is not to the slightest degree a global government, but, rather, a treaty organization[3]—a treaty organization in which five nation states each have veto power over UN decisions.

What the world needs, or at the least needs to move toward, Griffin affirms, is real world government, a global democracy apparently patterned after the Western governments, with executive, legislative, and judicial branches. The "creation of a global democracy," says Griffin, is "a moral imperative," because it is "the only means by which we can hope to overcome the various problems threatening the very survival of civilization."[4]

But establishing such a global democracy depends on overcoming state sovereignty and the war system. And this overcoming must be impartial. Control of the world by a single empire, for example, will not do. Because it would not be democratic, it would be incapable of dealing *impartially* with any of the problems that constitute the world crisis.

Genuine impartiality requires objective, universal, moral principles, a "global ethic" in which moral norms are perceived as part of "the fabric of the universe." "Given the increasing globalization of human civilization, we need a global ethic, meaning a set of moral norms that are accepted by all societies."[5]

Such a global ethic requires overcoming contemporary *moral nihilism.* "If by nihilism one means a disbelief in the possibility of justifying moral judgments in some rational way, and if philosophers reflect the intellectual climate of the times"—wrote Paul Edwards—"then our age is truly nihilistic. At no period in Western history have so many philosophers regarded moral statements as somehow arbitrary."[6]

This moral nihilism, Griffin avers, constitutes a crisis in contemporary moral theory, a conviction that brings him into conversation with a wide variety of ethical or moral theorists. If doing the good of all, or anything else, is to be regarded as a universally valid moral principle, it has to be possible to provide a rational defense of such a principle and, beyond that, motivation for people to act on it.

Among the major issues in contemporary moral theory in the West is the idea of moral autonomy, the question of whether morality should be entirely independent of other discourses—in particular, independent of theology or religion and independent of metaphysics. "After two centuries of the attempt to develop an autonomous moral theory, however, this tradition is in crisis."[7] It can provide neither a credible defense of moral objectivity, or of doing the common good, nor any motivation to adopt a moral way of life. In addition, it cannot account for the ordinary moral thinking and feeling of human beings. Autonomous morality cannot, therefore, provide any basis for democratic world government, or for overcoming the global crisis.

Thus, it seems to me, Griffin does not enter the philosophical conversation primarily for philosophical reasons but rather because he regards overcoming certain philosophical issues as paramount to creating the needed kind of global ethic—

one that can provide a grounding for a world government that would be capable of effectively dealing with the global crisis. Thus, if overcoming the current world crisis through the creation of global democratic government is indeed Griffin's purpose, his moral theory, though certainly not purely utilitarian, may be more utilitarian than his emphasis on objective moral norms, principles, and rules might suggest. He writes, for example: "It is widely recognized that the creation of a global democratic government would be the only way to achieve several desirable results, such as overcoming the war-system, which makes imperialism possible, and protecting the human rights of all people."[8]

## THE SOLUTION: WHITEHEADIAN PHILOSOPHY AND THEISM

Whitehead's philosophy provides cosmological support for aesthetic, religious, and moral experience and intuitions, and thus for civilized life. In sharp contrast with those who seek an autonomous moral theory, Griffin insists that morals must be grounded in metaphysical and theistic ideas. But not just any metaphysical and theistic ideas will do. Traditional theism, for example, is no longer credible, and its valorization of power as divine omnipotence is morally objectionable. The advantages of a Whiteheadian-Hartshornean naturalistic theism are that it can both be supported on rational grounds and make sense of our basic human religious and moral intuitions.

Obviously, the theism relevant here is not traditional theism, with its notion of divine omnipotence and impassibility. In this context, I suppose there is no need to rehearse Griffin's account of Whitehead. Griffin's account is, in my view, both cogent and correct, reflecting his many years of close study of Whitehead. What Griffin does especially well I think, is to remind us of how profoundly concerned Whitehead was with morality, something that can be easily forgotten in the light of

Whitehead's emphasis on aesthetic values. And Griffin does this, appropriately in my view, by making use of both Whitehead's ideas of the primordial nature of God, as the source of felt ideals for every new occasion, and of the consequent nature of God, as that which gives everlasting importance to human actions—what Whitehead called "importance for the universe."[9]

It might, however, be useful to review Griffin's somewhat unique use of "theism" as grounds for morality. While a profoundly sophisticated Whiteheadian-Hartshornean account of God lies behind Griffin's appeal to theism as necessary for an adequate moral theory, often, for the sake of argument, "theism" is understood very, very minimally, for example as involving perception of "something holy"[10] or where "theos" is understood simply as the "place where moral norms exist"[11] or God is "simply the ideal observer regarded as actual."[12] This minimal "theism," Griffin holds, is both consistent with an ideal observer account of right and wrong that is needed for moral theory and is rooted in "a religious drive that is common to all people."[13] Of course this minimal theism has to be embedded in some richer version of theism, which for Griffin is process theism, but Griffin does not claim that process theism has to be adopted by all who seek a universal morality. This is why Griffin can rightly claim to be a religious "pluralist." But what is required for a universal morality is some minimal theism, some belief that moral principles are not all arbitrary but part of the nature of things.

And it is not only theism that makes Whitehead's philosophy especially useful for morals. His account of experience, particularly of non-sensory experience, making feelings of others basic to his metaphysics, is equally important for grounding morality. It is not enough that God makes ideals available to every occasion of experience: Such values have to be experienced in some way that is not a violation of what is known by science.

Whitehead advocated what Griffin calls a "reenchanted universe."[14] Given his account of non-sensory experience, especially his account of causal feelings, Whitehead "could regard the experience of moral ideals as involving genuine perception on our part, referring to our 'experiences of ideals—of ideals entertained, of ideals aimed at, of ideals achieved, of ideals defaced'—as our 'experience of the deity of the universe.'"[15]

At the same time, Whitehead's view of non-sensory experience provides a way of accounting for sympathy. "The primitive form of physical experience is emotional—blind emotion—received as felt elsewhere in another occasion and conformally appropriated as a subjective passion. In the language appropriate to the higher stages of experience, the primitive element is *sympathy*, that is, feeling the feeling in another and feeling conformally *with* another."[16]

By providing rational grounds for holding that an omniscient God could not be evil, Griffin finds Hartshorne's idea of God as "absolutely ethical" to be useful here. Hartshorne taught that divine experience should be thought of in analogy to our direct experience of our bodies, a kind of knowledge that is sympathetic. Divine omniscience, knowing all that can be known, rules out any need for divine altruism, as all interests are included within God's own. This lack of a need for altruism removes any basis for imagining that an omniscient being might not be sympathetic to interests of other sentient beings, since omniscience makes for a *"certain* and absolute coincidence of other-interest and self-interest."[17] If "ethical" means "being motivated by concern for the interests of others, then God alone is absolutely ethical; for to know interests, fully and concretely, and to share them are indistinguishable."[18] This means that God's goodness is not contingent, as some have claimed. "[T]he necessary connection between divine omniscience and impartial sympathy for all sentient beings is not an *ad hoc* assertion, but one which follows from a general analysis of the nature of direct perceptual knowledge of other sentient beings."[19]

Process theism also affirms the reality of limited human freedom. Self-determination, which in Whitehead's philosophy arises to some degree in every actual occasion as creativity or final causation, is a basic presupposition of moral life, required to make any sense at all of moral responsibility.

In sum, process theism provides support for the basic presuppositions of the kind of morality that can be used to support the creation of the kind of effective, democratic global government that can begin to deal with the global crisis.

To this point, I have simply tried to present Griffin's ideas on morality. What he has done, I think, is to identify a global crisis; argue that any effective solution to this crisis must include global democratic government; show that most contemporary ethical or moral theory does not affirm the reality of objective values and therefore cannot be used to support universal morality or world government; and, finally, make a case for the relevance of a Whiteheadian-Hartshornean process theism, for the kind of moral theory that could effectively contribute to creating the requisite world government.

Now I would like to turn to some limited, partially Buddhist, responses to Griffin's proposals. I should confess, I think, that so far as I can tell I have no substantive disagreement at all with what I have read of Griffin's moral and religious philosophy. What I sometimes have qualms about is his choice of terms. The meaning of terms is, of course, highly context-dependent, such that what is appropriate in one context may be inappropriate in another. One important context of Griffin's writing is Anglo-American philosophy. He has, in a sense, joined a particular conversation, albeit a conversation that points beyond itself to the matter of a universal ethics and overcoming the world crisis. I, on the other hand, have been living and working in East Asia for nearly 25 years, primarily involved in inter-faith and intercultural relations from a particular Buddhist perspective. I do not want to join the conversation to which Griffin has brought so much energy and wisdom. I do not think I have anything to contribute to that conversation, nothing to say that Griffin has not already said better than I possibly could. Thus our contexts, cultural, religious, and disciplinary, have been different. Here I want to hold up a few uses of language that I think, while appropriate in the contexts in which Griffin has used them, will not be as useful in promoting an international or intercultural approach to creating a universal morality that can overcome the world crisis.

## THE BODHISATTVA WAY

Part of what makes development of an effective universal morality nearly impossible is the typically assumed antithesis in the West between individual good and the general or common good. Christian teachers and theologians have long stressed that morality requires complete altruism, completely selfless behavior for the benefit of others. Thus, in the case of human beings, there is a total divide between the interests of the self and the interests of all others. Being complete and perfect, God is radically different from human beings. It is impossible for God to have any selfish interests. His love is perfect agape. Mortals should, of course, try to emulate divine love, love completely free of self-interest. But, of course, inevitable sin ensures that such completely selfless behavior is impossible for humans. For us, there is a radical disjunction between our individual interests and the good of others. What mortals

can do is to confess and atone for their inevitable shortcomings—their inevitable self-interest—through the instrumen-
talities of churches and other religious institutions.

Griffin, I think, like Whitehead and John Cobb, effectively
uses process philosophy to argue that genuine individual interest is part of the general good, and should be seen as such.[20]
Unfortunately such a position lacks strong religious support
in the West, as Western religious traditions have typically presupposed the correctness of an extreme antithesis between
individual interest and the common good.

Process thinkers can, however, move beyond inherited assumptions of the West, were they could find ample religious
support for their position in the Buddhist idea and ideal of the
bodhisattva, arguably the central ethical ideal of Mahayana
Buddhism. In some Western understandings of the bodhisattva, probably based on Christian assumptions, it said that the
bodhisattva is one who selflessly and sacrificially forgoes the
bodhisattva's own awakening in order to help others. But in
the Lotus Sutra and in much East Asian Buddhism, the bodhisattva is one who, based on the basic Buddhist understanding of interdependence (often misleadingly called "co-depen-
dent arising"), recognizes that no one can be saved unless all
are saved. The individual bodhisattva's own interest, in other
words, is in harmony with the interests of all living beings. Of
course any individual may have selfish individual interests,
but a bodhisattva is one who is wise enough to know that his
or her genuine interest is included within the common good.
The bodhisattva is not, therefore, required to be totally selfless
in order to help others.

The bodhisattva way is also entirely consistent with
Whitehead's, and Griffin's, notion of maximizing importance,
in which importance is understood to be a very general notion, applicable to religion, art, science, logic, morality and so

forth.[21] Buddhists speak of awakening and awakened behavior. Buddhist interpretations of their own tradition differ, but basic is the idea that the goal of Buddhist teachings is awakened life, the way of the bodhisattva, a life in which a variety of physical, mental (or spiritual), aesthetic, social, and ethical aims are realized in accord with the first vow of a bodhisattva to work for the salvation of all. And it is apparent that such a life is highly relative, relative both to the interests of those with whom one interacts and relative to one's own capacities, physical, social, and moral. The bodhisattva does the best that he or she can do in a particular situation that has arisen in a particular causal context. A moral code or a set of precepts may provide guidance for such a life, but adherence to precepts is not what is finally central to the way of the bodhisattva or an ideal way of life.

The bodhisattva's vow connects present life both with the past, often a mythical past or origin, in which the vow is made, and with the future, the not yet, into which the vow is projected, maximizing importance in the present. Bodhisattvas live with gratitude to the past that has formed them and with hope toward a largely unknowable future that they are in a process of using skillful means to create.

The bodhisattva is unusually aware of both his own buddha nature and of the buddha nature of others. In principle this is no different from being responsive to the divine element in experience—no different metaphysically and no different in terms of its behavioral consequence of identifying with the good of others and with the good of all others, the common good.

In other words, while the Mahayana Buddhist ideal of the bodhisattva is not normally taken to be a moral ideal, or at least not merely a moral ideal, it could provide a rich religious resource for the kind of moral life advocated in process thought.

## WESTERN PHILOSOPHY

My own training is in philosophy. I am still a member in good standing of the American Philosophical Association. I used to hope that philosophy could actually be of help to the world. I no longer think so, at least if what is meant by "philosophy" is what goes on for the most part in philosophy departments in American and British universities.

Griffin writes that the first of ten core doctrines of process philosophy is "The integration of moral, aesthetic, and religious intuitions with the most general doctrines of the sciences into a self-consistent worldview, as one of the central tasks of philosophy in our time."[22] Part of me wants to cheer, but I also react with a hope that we not leave this task to philosophy, at least not if by "philosophy" we mean what the majority of professional Anglo-American philosophers appear to mean by that term.

Like Whitehead, process thinkers, including Griffin of course, have a much broader conception of what philosophy is. I imagine that wide use of the term "process thought" rather than "process philosophy" by the Center for Process Studies points in this direction. And it is no accident that the Center has reached out to an enormously wide range of non-philosophers for the purpose of enriching process thought. Perhaps "philosophy" can be recovered for love of wisdom, but I fear that it has more and more come to mean the thinking of a very small group of people whose professional work is almost entirely a conversation among themselves.

While such philosophers may think that what they do is the whole of philosophy, Western hegemony in philosophy may not be the best way to pursue universal agreement on morality, at least not in a democratic way. Non-western peoples, and not just Asian peoples, know very well from their own experience that Western thinkers can be expected to assume the superiority of Western customs and habits of thought. It is not a surprise, then, that the only non-Western participant in the drafting of the very Western "Universal Declaration of Human Rights," P.C. Chang, was disappointed with the results. Being a pluralist who held, in Eleanor Roosevelt's words, "that there is more than one kind of ultimate reality," Chang suggested that, as she put it, "the Secretariat might well spend a few months studying the fundamentals of Confucianism!"[23]

Griffin has chosen to enter a conversation, a conversation which he deems very important for dealing with, or failing to deal with, what he properly sees as a global crisis. But I think, and I am sure Griffin agrees, there can be no hope at all of moving toward world government or ameliorating any of the components of the global crisis without inclusion of non-Western voices, with their own sensibilities, values, and habits of thought. A culturally and religiously wider conversation might also result in some significant changes in perspective among all participants.

## HUMAN RIGHTS

Griffin reminds us that Whitehead says that the "Gospel of Force," the idea that might makes right because there are no universally valid moral norms, "is incompatible with a social life."[24] And Griffin further argues that civilization needs to be based on reverence for—in Whitehead's language—the power in the universe that persuades us towards new ideals.[25]

Distinctions between universal values, basic moral principles or norms, normative ideals, and natural human rights are not important for Griffin's argument in favor of universal morality. So far as I can tell, he pretty much uses such terms interchangeably. But he often frames the discussion in terms of human rights, sometimes referring to the Universal Declaration of Human Rights adopted by the United Nations in 1948.

I suppose hardly anyone today wants to speak against human rights. They are something that just about everyone seems to regard as good. Without being very precise or even explicit about the meaning of the term, human rights can be, and have been, affirmed not only in the West, but also by East Asians and even by East Asian Buddhists. It probably is foolish of me to suggest that something may be amiss in use of such language.

Although such terms can be defined in other ways, the language of rights, I submit, is embedded in basically feudal assumptions or sensibilities. In normal parlance, rights are entitlements—they are granted, granted by some ruler or agency that stands above the recipient of such rights. Rights are inherently both authoritarian and hierarchical. The idea stems especially from feudalistic conceptions of God as king of kings or emperor, where God is the supreme ruler of the universe and provider of both rights and moral edicts or rules. On this I am with Jeremy Bentham—there are no human rights. And there are no human rights precisely because we do not have the kind of God who has the position and power to grant rights.

It can be, and has been, argued that this conception of human rights as granted by a higher power is not what is meant by advocates of human rights. I am sure that is generally correct. But it seems to me that some such connotation remains, making it quite feasible to talk about "civil rights," "constitutional rights," "legal rights," or even "states' rights." Such use of "rights" presupposes that rights are granted by some higher power or authority, usually a government or constitution. But an absence of human rights need not rule out divine values or divine persuasion. Griffin quotes Whitehead: "There is no one behavior system belonging to the essential character of the universe, as the universal moral ideal. . . . What is universal is the spirit which should permeate any behaviour system."[26]

Part of my qualm about human rights language has to do with connotations of the term "rights." But also giving me pause is something that I cannot properly discuss here because facts are so hard to come by. This is my perception of the way the language of human rights violations is widely used today, especially I think by Americans, to criticize others, perhaps especially to criticize the Chinese government. It's as though human rights language has become a central part of a growing propaganda war, a propaganda war that threatens to become a much more serious war.

Griffin writes: "To move forward, [Whitehead] is saying, civilization requires a sense of importance, based on a *reverence-evoking insight* into the nature of the universe."[27] This surely is correct, but such a sense of importance may not readily translate into human rights, especially not when such rights are interpreted not by American process thinkers but by the American government and CIA-funded organizations. Human rights talk, I believe, is being used to further exacerbate tensions between the two most powerful countries in the world and is often felt to be an example of American bullying.

I am not suggesting that all talk of human rights be abandoned, even by process thinkers. This language is a very important part of Western traditions. But we should not, I think, expect that in the long run such language can be part of what everyone agrees on, that is, of a universal morality. For that, I think we might better turn to Whitehead's notion of peace found in the final chapter of *Adventures of Ideas*, where there is a much stronger connection between Whitehead's philosophy and East Asian values.

### RIGHT AND WRONG

I think Griffin, following Whitehead, is correct in affirming that all people experience something "holy," some sense of importance and value in the very character of the universe. But, as he says, the religious sensibility common to all people and common to all religions is a desire for harmony with the Tao, or Brahman, or Buddha, or even the divine will.

A religious sense of the holy may be associated with a morality of right and wrong, but this is not always so. In Mahayana Buddhism, for example, one is much more likely to think in terms of better and worse than in terms of right and wrong. As Whitehead says, "The worth of men consists in their liability to persuasion. They can persuade and can be persuaded by the disclosure of alternatives, the better and the worse."[28] Thus Tiantai Buddhism asserts that even the Buddha, the best of living beings, includes an element of evil, and in Mahayana Buddhism we have story after story of bodhisattvas with very human failings, such as seeking fame and gain, who are nonetheless models for us. What's more, virtually all of Mahayana Buddhism now affirms that there is an element of the Buddha even in the most evil of living beings.

According to Mahayana Buddhism, others should always be respected both because they have buddha-nature and because doing so is most likely to produce good results, both for those being respected and those doing the respecting. Buddha nature is not something given, not even by the Buddha. Buddha-nature is, rather, a capacity or power inherent in all living beings; it cannot be granted or taken away. Good results are teleological and highly relative. Seldom if ever do we know what will produce the best fruit, but we do have ideas, based on centuries of human experience, about what is more likely to lead to good results. Thus, rules, such as rules against murder, lying or stealing are good common sense based on experience, including experience of what we hold to be holy. Similarly, perhaps human rights may be expressions of good sense about what is needed for human civilizations to advance or even survive.

## GOD THE CREATOR

Given a process conception of deity, it is no problem at all to agree with the idea that God participates in every creature's creation of itself.

My main concern here is a tendency for us to inadvertently resort to traditional, classical theistic notions without defending the appropriateness of their use. For example, at one point Griffin refers to God as "the creator who brought us forth."[29] Though we can make good sense of it, in process theism, whether Whitehead's or Hartshorne's or Griffin's, I submit, it is inappropriate to say that God brings us forth. We bring ourselves forth, with the help of our ancestors (our antecedents) and with the participation of God, or the Buddha.

Here I think that East Asian Buddhist emphasis on gratitude to our past, including not only to our blood ancestors but also to our teachers, near and remote, and even to the institutions that have contributed to our lives, might serve as a valuable corrective to Western tendencies toward individualism. This could be especially true I think when understood in the light of process philosophy. Whitehead wrote:

> God can be termed the creator of each temporal actual entity. But the phrase is apt to be misleading by its suggestion that the ultimate creativity of the universe is to be ascribed to God's volition. The true metaphysical position is that God is the aboriginal instance of this creativity, and is therefore the aboriginal condition which qualifies its action.[30]

Whitehead also said:

> [T]he initial stage of the aim is rooted in the nature of God, and its completion depends on the self-causation of the subject-superject. . . . If we prefer the phraseology, we can say that God and the actual world jointly

constitute the character of the creativity for the initial phase of the novel concrescence.[31]

I do not mean to suggest here that in the experience of God, and thus the inclusion of God in every experience, God is merely inert. For Griffin, God is indeed "actively present," part of the causation of every individual. Buddhists can agree that the Buddha is actively present in all of our moments of experience. The individual always creates itself out of its past, which is causal and efficacious, with suitable aims made available by God. If we focus on creativity or novelty, the real creator of an actual occasion is itself. If we focus on what is the dominant influence on any individual occasion, the real creator of an actual occasion is its past. If we focus on God's unique relation to all other occasions, we can say that God is the creator. The aims made available by God are necessary for there to be any creative advance, and creation.

Buddhism, at least some forms of it, is very compatible with Whitehead's and Griffin's understanding of the relationship of God to others as one of interdependence. Not only do we need the help of the Buddha and his bodhisattvas, the Buddha, we are told in countless ways, needs help, needs our help, to get his work done. In the Lotus Sutra for example, buddhas travel all over the universe, but no Buddha travels without having at least one bodhisattva to assist him. More importantly, our Buddha, the Buddha of this world, generally known as Shakyamuni Buddha, clearly needs—and emphatically says that he needs—the help of human bodhisattvas to do his work in this world. I think it would not be an exaggeration to say that without the help of others, the Buddha could not be the actual Buddha.

For me, this raises the question of whether "God's will" should be regarded as equivalent to initial aims.[32] Of course we can talk, as Griffin does, about being in harmony with divine will, and in some contexts that may be a very appropriate way of speaking, but the more natural connotation of divine will, even in East Asia, is that it is something to obey. Once again this language, it seems to me, comes from and is suggestive of a system involving obedience to a ruler. More consistent it seems to me, would be to say that initial aims are offered by or presented by God. We should not forget what Whitehead speaks of a concept of God in which the goodness of God replaces older emphasis on the will of God.

My reservations about use of the term "God's will" should not be taken to be against, in any way, what Griffin's purpose is in the argument, namely to show what with a properly reconstructed theism, that is, process theism, God is in some way the ultimate criterion of better and worse. My problem is with the language in which the argument is sometimes cast, a language that I think is not representative of Whitehead's or Hartshorne's thinking, nor likely to be accepted in truly interfaith and cross-cultural settings, that is, in settings in which Griffin's ideal of global democracy might be pursued.

I hope these contentious qualms will at least give us something to think about. As I am sure he would be quick to admit, David Griffin's ethics, which is both philosophical and theological, is not yet complete. What I have seen is a great beginning, but not yet a complete moral theory. I have tried to makes some suggestions as to how David Griffin and others might proceed with that larger project.

# 11. Postmodern Politics and Spirituality: Do We Need (or Want) World Government?

## Richard Falk

Whether in theology, philosophy, or politics, David Griffin has been dedicated to a search for truth reinforced by a strong ethical commitment to human well-being. In this respect, I find an organic consistency that links his explorations of the 9/11 attacks with investigations of the plausibility of life after death and paranormal psychological experience. In all these instances, Griffin's truth-seeking swims against the strong tides of conventional wisdom and societal consensus. It is no different in relation to world order, which Griffin finds ethically intolerable and geopolitically unsustainable.

Moving beyond critique, Griffin believes that the only way to respond to the dual challenge is by the establishment of a *democratic world government*. A satisfactory ethical solution could in principle be achieved within a system of global governance without any major centralization of political authority, for instance, by a redistributive global tax and drastic reform of the world trading and investment structure, but given ecological challenges and nuclear war dangers, such a world order would not be sustainable over time, in Griffin's view. Alternatively, it is possible that the American global state, a new form of empire, could impose limits on carbon emissions and control recourse to political violence sufficiently to establish a high probability of a sustainable future, but it would be ethically intolerable due to the need to subjugate most of the people in the world, so as to stabilize a regime of radical inequality in material benefits and human rights. On the basis of this rational assessment of world order alternatives, Griffin's advocacy of a democratic world government follows naturally.

In this chapter, my effort is to depict Griffin's approach, and then question the viability and even the desirability of his proposed solution, while endorsing the values and analyses informing his position. My view differs from that of Griffin because I believe we need to think more dialectically about the necessary and desirable form of future global governance. It is my belief that we need to seek the decentralization of power and authority to the extent possible while avoiding either empire or world government as preferential images of world order. Ideologically, my preferred image can be summarized on a bumper sticker: "anarchism without anarchy."[1] I will explain explicate this puzzling image in a concluding section.

The plan of the chapter is as follows. A first section on why, in Griffin's understanding, a democratic world government is needed and desirable. A second section is devoted to Griffin's rationale provided for his conceptions of a preferred plausible future world order. And finally, a brief set of suggestions based on globally constituted democratic values but without a comparable reliance on world governmentality.

It may be clarifying to ground this inquiry in a rejection of the "realist" frame of reference based on state-centric global governance as the end-point of world order. As Alexander Wendt observes in a trenchant and influential essay: "If Realists are right that anarchy is programmed for war, then it makes sense to define one's sovereignty in egoistic terms and act on that basis. International law is irrelevant or an impediment to the national interest, and one should pursue a unilateralist policy whenever possible."[2] It seems useful to acknowledge that despite some elements of empathy for the poor and vulnerable, behavior in world politics continues to be driven by policy elites seeking to maximize national or corporate interests in wealth, power, and prestige with very little deference to policies associated with the realization of global human interests. In an era of neoliberal globalization, corporate and financial orientations may be rather cosmopolitan in their outlook, although without overcoming their egoistic calculus in exerting influence.[3]

Such an acknowledgement helps us understand the limits on rational problem-solving at the global level, accounting for the inability to rid the world of war, or even of nuclear weaponry, and to address the multiple ecological challenges posed by climate change despite the near universal declared realization that the collective wellbeing of humanity requires at this stage of history that such steps be taken. In effect, as long as realist orientations guide the behavior of the most influential political and economic actors, the prevailing mode of global governance will remain catastrophe-prone, and the imperatives of realism and rationality will be locked in a dysfunctional embrace with one another.[4]

## WHY A DEMOCRATIC WORLD GOVERNMENT IS NECESSARY

Griffin is very clear about his point of departure with respect to the advocacy of democratic world government:

> If civilization is going to thrive or even survive much longer, I have long been convinced, the present system of global governance, which is based on power and wealth, must be replaced by global democracy, in which laws on all matters affecting the planet as a whole be

made by representatives from all the peoples of the
world. A transition to global democracy in this sense is
necessary, I believe, if we are to have a chance of solving
our problems of global scope, such as war, imperialism,
terrorism, international crime, global apartheid, climate
change, and the threat of nuclear annihilation.[5]

Griffin writes of "civilization" as the unit of concern, and posits that lawmakers of a global democracy need to be "representative"' of the "peoples" of the world. Such political language
completely bypasses the centrality of states and their leaders
in shaping laws and policies, and implies that the authority
structure of a global democracy will be legitimated by the con-
sent of peoples (not people) rather than through delegated
representatives appointed by the governments of sovereign
states (in the manner that ambassadors are currently des-
ignated). Griffin has a long list of global challenges that can
only be solved by a global mechanism, although some of these
would seem likely to persist, although undoubtedly in an altered form, even if such a global democracy came into being:
terrorism, crime, apartheid, and civil war have long flourished
within states, and might not be easier to address if some sort
of global government did indeed come into being. Arguably,
unless current levels of inequality were greatly reduced in
the process of transition to a global democracy, these kinds
of threats to human security could actually become worse as
some form of world government was being constituted. It is
this widely shared fear of worsening that helps explain the
persisting attachment to the sort of global pluralism that is the
structural part of the Westphalian heritage.

What gives great force to Griffin's argument for democratic world government is a combination of two essentially empirically grounded historical interpretations: firstly, that the
catastrophic risks of the present form of world order render

it unsustainable over time, and something of an unheralded miracle that it has so far avoided apocalyptic events; secondly, that despite the palpable menace of nuclear weaponry or the scientifically validated warnings about the dire consequences of trends toward global warming, there is little basis for believing that the present way in which global governance operates is capable of providing satisfactory solutions. In general, Griffin believes that despite centuries of what he calls "serious talk" about eliminating war "the globe remains more heavily militarized than ever before." Indeed, Griffin is convinced that all the world order problems of global scope are getting worse, not better, and that this situation reflects a structural deficiency that can only be solved by the establishment of a unified governmental structure that can establish and enforce law and policy globally. His belief in governmentality is asserted in confident language: "Just as no problem of national scope could be solved in a country without a central government, the problems of global scope cannot be solved without a global government."[6]

Griffin does acknowledge that there exists an unacceptable organizational alternative to a democratically constituted world government: empire. He rejects this alternative on both political and religious grounds. Griffin insists that the global structure of anarchy (that is, state-centric world order) is "demonic": Not only is it conducive to ceaseless warfare, but it necessarily produces domination by the strong of the weak, with resulting patterns of exploitation and waste, and it is incapable of taking sufficient account of either long-run considerations or global public interests.

Even beyond this problem of structure (which is almost synonymous with government in Griffin's formulations) is a fatal flaw embedded in human nature itself, which is at the root of most religious understandings of the human condition.

In Griffin's words,

> There is after all a deep truth in the testimony of the world's religions to the presence of a transcultural proclivity to evil deep within the human heart, which no new paradigm, combined with a new economic order . . . or any social arrangements, will suddenly eliminate.[7]

This view of the reign of the demonic is confirmed for Griffin by the teachings of the major world religions, especially their interpretation of the human condition. He points especially to the life and work of Jesus as expressing the need for a radical repudiation of "demonic control of the planet," which "has continued to increase during the past 2000 years, especially in the past four centuries, what we call the modern age." Despite this long trajectory Griffin insists that the dangers posed by the demonic have reached a circumstance of historical urgency:

> Even if we do avoid nuclear holocaust, furthermore, the present trajectory of civilization, with its increasing population, consumerism, and depleting-and-polluting technologies, promises unprecedented suffering through scarcity and climate change in the near future.

And these concerns are further magnified by "ethnic and cultural animosities, the proliferation of nuclear weapons, and arms sales" making "any realistic picture of the future based on present trends . . . completely terrifying."[8]

Significantly, Griffin acknowledges that there are influential advocates of the imperial solution to world government in the United States, and not only neo-conservative ideologues such as Richard Perle and William Kristol, but liberal internationalists such as Michael Mandelbaum.[9] Perhaps, the argument is best understood in its cruder forms as articulated, for instance, by William Kristol and Lawrence Kaplan, as quoted by Griffin: "The alternative to American leadership is a chaotic, Hobbesian world" in which "there is no authority to thwart global aggression, ensure peace and security, and enforce international norms."[10]

Usually such advocacy is hidden beneath a language that disguises its imperial character, and talks instead of "leadership" and "universal values," but the structural problems posed by state-centric anarchy are to be overcome by the projection of American power, a prospect that according to these thinkers should be welcomed. Griffin is politely skeptical of such pretensions, concluding that it would be unacceptable to most of the world's peoples and governments, especially given the declining respect for the American global role in many parts of the world and the post-colonial distrust of any world order scheme that is rooted in West-centric control.[11]

In this central regard, an American world state would be just one more phase in the long geopolitical narrative of demonic world order, and although responsive to the challenges posed by political fragmentation or anarchy would not be acceptable politically, morally, or spiritually. It is against such a background of analysis and assessment that Griffin believes that the only ethically acceptable political path for the future is the one that leads to *democratic world government.*

## WHY A DEMOCRATIC WORLD GOVERNMENT IS POSSIBLE

Griffin's views on the necessity of more centralized global governance seem rather widely shared. There are few careful students of the contemporary global setting who believe that the Westphalian framework can provide humanity with a sustainable future without drastic modification. Unfortunately, this consensus on the need for change is ignored by political leaders and their advisors who devote their energies and resources to the short-term and somewhat manageable challenges of the present. As far as the underlying challenges depicted by Griffin, and especially the reign of the demonic, is concerned, the current managers of world order are in total denial. There is no hint given that nationalism, statism, militarism—much less consumerism, patriarchy, and capitalism—exert a tightening stranglehold on human destiny. Although Griffin does not directly address this issue of severe alienation at elite levels, it implicitly shifts his hopes for drastic change away from the enlightenment of governments to a dependence on the activism of people, what I have called "globalization-from-below" or "moral globalization."[12]

Griffin does not adopt a utopian outlook that dispenses with the prospects for attaining his desired future. Following Hans Küng in affirming that the world religions share a universal adherence to a minimal morality encapsulated in the golden rule,[13] Griffin believes that such a moral commonality is sufficient to provide the basis for a survival-oriented transition to democratic world government. This idea of a moral foundation for universalism is only credible as the basis for political change if it informs the imaginary of ordinary people, and Griffin makes clear that part of his indictment of modernism is that it has detached ethics from its grounds in religion and nature, giving rise to "disenchantment." In reaction, and openly indebted to Whitehead's reenchantment of nature as repository of the sacred, Griffin and John Cobb responsively develop process theology as an antidote to this radical form of modern alienation and thereby reendow the reality of the human worldly presence in a manner that is spiritually uplifting without defying the strictures of science.[14]

In Griffin's introduction to his series on Postmodern Constructive Thought, there is written in italics the idea that his reorientation of perspective rests on the awareness that *"the continuation of modernity threatens the very survival of on our planet."*[15] Putting this thought in the pre-political terminology that Griffin employed in the 1980s and 1990s, the emergence of a postmodern consciousness involves a set of emancipatory ideas and norms to be encountered in religious and philosophical thought, but also in the lived experience informed by such normative ideals. Modernity has suppressed these ideals, but the challenges of the postmodern world are restoring their relevance to a sustainable human future that needs at some point to be translated into responsive political arrangements. Griffin believes, and argues repeatedly to this effect, that responsiveness presupposes democratic world government.

Griffin also finds confirming support for this confidence in a universal foundation for the establishment of a democratic world government even in the thought of such communitarian luminaries as Michael Walzer and Amitai Etzioni, as well as in the wide adherence to the Universal Declaration of Human Rights. There are no claims being made by Griffin of a full-fledged cosmopolitan ethos, and no evasion of the relevance of civilizational and religious differences, but only the minimalist assertion that under the various pressures of necessity and a shared "minimal morality supported by a minimal theism," world government is possible provided it is democratic.[16] If political centralization were to come about via unipolarity or imperial expressions of global responsibility, then its establishment would probably be impossible, because it would encounter strong resistance, and it could only be imposed by an extreme reliance on coercion and intimidation, and hence would be highly undesirable.

Arguably, the imperial possibility is more *probable* than the democratic government alternative and is already functioning as the vertical dimension of the current form of Westphalian world order. From an ethical perspective, Griffin rejects this merger of American grand strategy on a global scale with hyped claims of providing the world with benign global governance, but the projection of American military, diplomatic, and cultural influence on a global scale does create some of the components of a global state. It is, to be sure, dysfunctional in many respects and likely to be non-sustainable, but at the same time it seems durable when compared to present prospects for the emergence of global democracy. Unfortunately, at present, there exists scant evidence of the kind of mass popular support that is needed as a precondition making it possible to put forward as *a political project* a plausible transition from the doomed present to the preferred democratic future. By political project, what is meant is a conception of the desired transformation that cannot be easily discredited as an example of wishful thinking.

At present, there does not even exist a widespread understanding of what is meant by "global democracy." There is some limited attention given to democratic reforms of specific international institutions by way of making their operations more transparent, giving a wider range of stakeholders participatory roles, imposing mechanisms of accountability on officials, and de-Westernizing control over policy. The United Nations has been the target of such reformist campaigns as have been such institutions as the World Bank and International Monetary Fund. In addition, some speculations have suggested that the development of European institutions under the aegis of the European Union might provide some lessons for comparable developments in other regions, but no attention has been given to whether there is any reason to think of extending this European experience worldwide, and there is a fundamental difference. For states and regions there is an "outside" that exerts pressure for collective security and provides a basis for shaping an "inside" political identity. As experience in Europe during its period of economic crisis in the last several years has demonstrated, the development of

institutional regionalism has not produced a European identity strong enough to overcome divergent national interests
and rivalries.

World government in contrast is (mis)understood by
drawing an implicit analogy to well-governed territorial constitutional democracies, sometimes given greater specificity
by taking the shape of a greatly strengthened United Nations
or relying on the structure of the United States to provide a
model for governing the world according to federalist criteria.[17] Such ideas set forth as proposals have had three features
in modern times: they emanate from the West; they have
greatest political traction in the aftermath of major wars; and
so far they seem to be formulated by members of political and
social elites.[18]

Griffin has a different approach to the political plausibility of world government, relying on neither war, elites, nor
Western leadership. Instead, he pins his hopes on the extraordinary spread of nongovernmental organizations (NGOs) in
recent decades creating movement possibilities, that is, a bottom-up form of political action enacted on the new playing
field of world order that he and others characterize as "global
civil society." Griffin believes that global democracy would
provide this multitude of NGOs with the only common cause
that makes sense, given the various agendas being pursued.
In his words, "activists for global causes will come to realize
that, *whatever their cause, it is a lost cause without global democracy.*"[19] Griffin makes a plea for what he calls "moral NGOs"
(that is, those dedicated in some way to global justice and
ecological sanity) to join forces around global democracy as
a unifying goal that will enhance their overall leverage: "If a
majority of the moral NGOs of the world join forces, combining their money, expertise, and sheer numbers, they will be
able to wield tremendous influence. Out of these reflections

comes a recommendation: *Moral NGOs of the world unite! You have nothing to lose but your impotence.*"[20]

As yet, nothing that could be called responsive to Griffin's call has taken place. There have been impressive gatherings of NGOs at UN conferences devoted to global issues such as human rights, women, population, and environment, but the emphasis was a particular cause being addressed and networking among likeminded NGOs. The World Social Forum annual gatherings in Brazil and elsewhere were mainly unified by their hostility to neoliberal globalization and their demands for a more equitable and ecologically responsible world economy, with little focus on restructuring world order around democratic principles. Perhaps closest in spirit to the Griffin recommendation, was the 2011 Occupy Movement, itself taking inspiration from the Arab Spring and notable for its stress on democratic empowerment and learning how to act politically by mimicking challenges to the established order in the non-West, symbolized by the call in Occupy London for a "Global Tahrir Square." It is now uncertain whether the Occupy movement has the staying power to become a historical force, and if it does, whether it follows a locally driven set of priorities or unifies around an overarching theme such as the pursuit of global democracy. What was encouraging from the Griffin perspective was the spontaneous convergence on global democracy as the expression of their affirmative alternative to the status quo, but little effort was made to explain what that might mean, if anything, governmentally. In other words, the Occupy Movement, as far as is known, did not connect the dots in Griffin's manner of linking global democracy to world government.

This turn to global civil society as a site of struggle is overtly reinforced by Griffin's assessment of the compatibility of world religions and universal or naturalistic morality with a worldwide movement to promote democratic world government, creating a non-Western foundation for political action that draws upon religion and culture. Griffin makes the same recommendation to the religions of the world as he does to the moral NGOs: *"Religions of the world, unite! You have nothing to lose but your impotence."*[21] Creatively, Griffin posits a potential synergistic relationship between the domain of religion and that of the moral NGOs, the former benefitting from the knowledge and experience with substantive issues that the latter has accumulated, and the moral NGOs gaining leverage by the mobilization of the masses drawn to religion and by the practical wisdom embedded in religious traditions. This religious/secular orientation does lend an element of originality to the Griffin approach, as does his incorporation of non-Western thought and agency.

As far as the democratic nature of the world government that Griffin favors, not too much detail is provided beyond an insistence that democratic values pervade all governance structures from the local to the global and that the devolution of authority be shaped by deference to the principle of subsidiarity, that is, only as much centralization as is needed, with preference for maximum decentralization consistent with meeting material needs of people and the sustainability needs of the planet. In Griffin's words, "[g]enuine global democracy would not, therefore, consist entirely or even primarily of democracy at the global level."[22] To what extent such arrangements would challenge existing structures of inequality and hierarchy is not specified, nor is the need to moderate the consumerist ethos in this global democracy to come.[23]

The Griffin approach to democratic world government strikes me as coherent and comprehensive. Its arguments from necessity and possibility are thoughtful, and its ideal is depicted in a manner that seems responsive to both the survival imperatives of humanity and the justice ideals of religion and morality. It offers also a welcome shift of political emphasis away from West-centric top-down proposals and situates its hopes for the future on the mobilization and collective action of popular forces that combines the ongoing emergence of global civil society with the deep-rooted visions of human betterment and solidarity found in the world religions. Griffin does not make any effort to develop a credible scenario of transition or to assess the kinds of obstacles that would be placed in the path of the sort of movement he recommends, and thus in my view does not take sufficient account of the possible drawbacks of advocating world government within our present historical circumstances.

## WHY THE ADVOCACY OF A DEMOCRATIC GLOBAL GOVERNMENT IS NOT DESIRABLE

While sharing Griffin's concerns about the inability of the inherited structures and societal priorities of modernity to overcome the multiple crises confronting contemporary humanity, as well as the relevance of resting hope on the emergence of postmodern consciousness, visions, and initiatives, I remain skeptical about, and even opposed to pinning, hopes on the emergence of a democratic global government. At first glance, this skepticism may seem more semantic than substantive, as Griffin actually seeks to minimize the governmental presence at the global level via reliance on the subsidiarity principle to the extent practical, and we are both seeking to rely on values of democracy and nonviolence in responding to these challenges. Nevertheless, I believe that our divergences are significant both in relation to the goal being pursued and our shared commitment to democratization.[24]

The goal of world government seems to me ill-conceived, completely lacking in grassroots support throughout global civil society, including among those elements that are seeking to maximize democratization in international society.

In addition, there is no support for world government among political elites, and not even much interest.[25] If the language of world government is avoided, and the issues are put forth as distinct functional requirements for sustainability, there is removed the teleological concern that arises when "world government" is posited as a postmodern sequel to the modern politically fragments system of world order, but this weakens the Griffin tone of urgency in relation to the scope, gravity, and immediacy of the problems. The reason that postwar situations create a temporary willingness to consider centralizing world order alternatives, including world government for a fraction of the elite, is the reality of wartime suffering and hardship, and a realization that given technological advances in weaponry the future is likely to be worse. These feelings were sufficient after World War I to establish the League of Nations and after World War II the United Nations, but not enough to give such institutions the capabilities and independence they need to carry out the grandiose mission of war prevention.

My more substantive difficulties with the Griffin approach relate to issues of justice in a world that currently exhibits such drastic inequality as among and within existing political communities. In the United States we are experiencing the hollowing out of democratic political life as a consequence mainly of the effects of this inequality, and in global settings, where there is absent the sense of shared nationality, there is even less sense that those who are in privileged positions will be prepared to accept a leveling downward to create humane global governance. When such inequality exists, governmental coercion tends to increase with negative impacts on freedom and democratic liberties.[26] In this regard, it is highly unlikely that the universalist norms found in 'natural religion' or in human rights instruments of international law would be able to offset the political pressures mounted to preserve existing distributions of wealth and income.

Such a posture on my part does not intend to convey a sense of despair or the absence of an engagement with the work of human betterment under the darkening shadows of unresolved and neglected global challenges. I think there are various signs of potential surges of support for democratizing political movements at various levels of social organization. In this regard the upheavals associated with the Arab Spring and the widespread enthusiasm that accompanied the globally dispersed Occupy Movement, reinforced by high levels of youth unemployment and fiscal difficulties, reveal a fertile ground for the rise of a democratizing global political current.[27] In such an atmosphere, a condition of radical uncertainty exists that underscores the importance of the "black swan" phenomenon in which our sense of history is limited by our inability to anticipate the emergence of forces that alter trends in radical and unexpected ways.[28]

My own immediate preference would be to promote specific initiatives that move in a democratizing direction, exhibit sensitivity to moral globalization, and avoid any teleological pretension of a world order end-point that is the ultimate objective. Among those initiatives that seem to have significant democratizing potential, I would mention the establishment of a global peoples parliament, the imposition of a tax on international financial transactions and transnational air travel, strengthening of regional institutions along democratic lines, imposition of tax on carbon emissions, promotion of the scrapping of the nonproliferation treaty, and the establishment of a nuclear disarmament process to establish a world without nuclear weapons.[29]

# 12. Championing Truth and Justice: Griffin on 9/11

## Tod Fletcher

The distinguished authors of other chapters of this book have given many demonstrations of David Ray Griffin's exceptional scholarly achievements across a wide range of disciplines. Readers of this chapter will therefore not be surprised to see with what effect he has brought his unique intellectual tools and powers to the analysis and interpretation of the 9/11 events and the building of a 9/11 truth movement. Before proceeding, I would like to emphasize one quality that links his scholarly career, at the cutting edge of understanding in so many areas, with his 9/11 work. That is his courage. He has frequently tackled very difficult, "knotty" problems. As this book as a whole shows, Professor Griffin has repeatedly provided promising new solutions that were challenging to established academic views. He has never let the unreadiness of others to think in novel ways deter him. When he committed himself to unsnarling the "world-knot" of 9/11 he made yet another courageous decision, and not just in the intellectual sense. Griffin, who has argued for a realist understanding of truth and moral norms, including justice,[1] is a philosopher who takes his philosophy seriously, and who integrates his practice with his thought.

The subject of 9/11 may seem like a very significant departure from most of his earlier work. In fact, however, he had already undertaken major research and writing for a book on American imperialism, and it was in the course of this work that he realized that important questions had been raised about the official explanation of the events of September 11, 2001. As he examined the issue in more detail, he saw that its significance and complexity would require a separate treatment. This shift of focus, which he initially thought of as requiring an article, and then a book, has continued to the present (April 2012), with the writing of ten books and 40 articles on 9/11 and many other contributions to the growth of a global 9/11 truth movement.

After having not questioned the official account of 9/11 for some time after the events, Griffin began to look critically at the evidence in the spring of 2003. In March 2004, his first book on 9/11, *The New Pearl Harbor: Disturbing Questions about the Bush Administration and 9/11*, was published. Nothing comparable to it had been published previously. It displayed the typical virtues of Griffin's writings: precise identification of and focus on the core problem; mastery of the full range of available evidence bearing on it; careful discrimination between alternative interpretations of the evidence; due attention to and accurate statements of the arguments made by others; and the high level of argumentation, often with a compelling use of logic.

Right from this first foray, Griffin focused on the core issue for all of his subsequent research and writing on 9/11: the question of the truthfulness of the official account of the events. In *The New Pearl Harbor*, Griffin wrote:

> [T]he purpose of this book . . . is not to explain "what really happened" but . . . to summarize what seem to be the strongest reasons that have been given for considering the official account to be false (so as to show the need for a full investigation to *find out* what really happened).[2]

Thus, from the very outset, Griffin had identified his objective: a genuine investigation willing to go wherever the evidence leads.

Several other major emphases of Griffin's almost decade-long analysis of the 9/11 evidence were already present in *The New Pearl Harbor*. He initiated there critiques of the roles of the mainstream news media and of the left-leaning "alternative media," both of which appeared to be satisfied with the official account and actively avoided looking in a systematic way at the mounting evidence that it is false. He discussed, in a more intellectually rigorous way than had been done by anyone before him, important semantic issues, such as what the word "complicity" might mean in propositions that the Bush/Cheney administration was complicit in the 9/11 events, and the proper and improper uses of the terms "conspiracy theorist" and "conspiracy theory." Further, he discussed the cumulative type of argumentation appropriate to the complex issue of the truth about 9/11, which—unlike a purely deductive argument that is only as strong as each "link in the chain" of deductions—is like a cable of many strands, which is still strong even if some strands should fail.

Almost every strand *The New Pearl Harbor* identified has proven to be durable. Each chapter raised important questions challenging the official account: How could the alleged hijackers' missions have succeeded without a "stand-down" of the air-defense system, meaning that the pilots were ordered *not* to intercept the airliners? Did American Airlines Flight 77 under the control of al-Qaeda really strike the Pentagon? Was United Airlines Flight 93 shot down over Pennsylvania? Why did President Bush linger at the school in Florida for a half-hour after the second of the Twin Towers was struck? Did US officials block investigations into the activities of some of the alleged perpetrators prior to and after the attacks? Did US officials have strong reasons for allowing the attacks, or even planning them and carrying them out? Not one of these critical questions has ever been satisfactorily answered by authorities.

Griffin's second book on 9/11, entitled *The 9/11 Commission Report: Omissions and Distortions*,[3] was published in late November 2004, less than five months after the publication of *The 9/11 Commission Report*. Griffin saw that the *Report* lied about virtually all evidence raised by critics of the official account, either explicitly, by distorting it, or implicitly, by omitting to mention it at all. These lies suggested that one of the 9/11 Commission's purposes was to cover up the government's role in the attacks. The *Report*'s omission of the fact that a third major steel-framed skyscraper (in addition to the Twin Towers) collapsed on 9/11—World Trade Center 7—is only the most-famous of the more than 115 lies of omission or distortion that he identified.

In the first half of his book, Griffin systematically laid out these omissions and distortions of facts concerning a variety of issues, including the collapses of the buildings, the attack at the Pentagon, the alleged hijackers, the behavior of President Bush and the Secret Service during the crucial hours, advance warnings of the attacks, the long and intimate connections between the Bush family, the bin Ladens and the Saudi royal family, the flights of Saudis out of the country when all other flights were forbidden, the suspicious behavior of FBI headquarters before and after the attacks, the role of Pakistan's Inter-Services Intelligence (ISI) in the events, and the many motives the Bush/Cheney administration would have had for permitting or facilitating the attacks.

The impression of a cover-up given by the *Report* was especially strong with respect to its account of why the air-defense system failed to intercept any of the hijacked airliners.

The 9/11 Commission told a new story that contradicted all previous official claims regarding the sequence and content of communications between the FAA (the Federal Aviation Administration) and NORAD (the North American Aerospace Defense Command), blaming the FAA exclusively for the failure and exonerating the military. Griffin saw that the *Report's* assignment of blame on the FAA, charging it with repeated and unprecedented laxity and incompetence in failing to follow long-established standard procedures of notification to the military upon suspicion of in-flight emergencies, amounted to an unbelievable story. The second half of his book, therefore, was on the *Report's* attempt to explain away the appearance of a stand-down. Griffin's book has continued to provide the best analysis of the shortcomings of *The 9/11 Commission Report* and the process that created it, and remains a key document in the brief for a new, genuine investigation of 9/11.

*Christian Faith and the Truth Behind 9/11,*[4] published in July 2006, advanced Griffin's analysis of 9/11 in important ways. It is my personal favorite of his 9/11 books, because it combines a succinct overview of the primary evidence against the official account with a deep historical and philosophical interpretation of the special significance of American empire for Christians who seek to follow the teachings of Jesus. Part One presented the core of his increasingly powerful case against the Bush/Cheney administration. First, to show that an unprovoked attack on noncombatants by government leaders would not be unthinkable, he surveyed the history of modern false-flag operations, including Operation Gladio in Western Europe, in which the US government was responsible for the deaths of hundreds of innocent people. Then, to show that even an attack on US citizens would not be unthinkable, he discussed Operation Northwoods, a plan put forward by the

Pentagon's Joint Chiefs of Staff in 1962 to carry out a false-flag operation providing the pretext for a US attack on Cuba—a plan that included a scenario in which innocent US citizens would be killed.

In a line of evidence that Griffin was the first to investigate in detail, he analyzed—in a chapter called "Explosive Testimony"—the abundant testimony regarding explosions in the Twin Towers provided by firefighters and other first responders. In another chapter, he cataloged the many ways in which the collapses of the Twin Towers exemplified classic features of controlled demolitions. Griffin then argued that the case against the Bush/Cheney administration had progressed from a *prima facie* case to a conclusive case, because it had gone unrefuted by the 9/11 Commission.

Griffin's principal purpose in Part Two was to bring out the special significance of 9/11 for Christians. In the chapter "Jesus and the Roman Empire," Griffin, after describing the conditions imposed by Rome on the inhabitants of Palestine, argues that Jesus sought to persuade his followers to resist the terror, injustice, and idolatry of Rome. Then, in the philosophically profound following chapter, "The Divine and the Demonic," Griffin presents a sustained argument, based upon his understanding of God's power as persuasive rather than coercive, for the reality of demonic power. Presenting a critique of the traditional (but non-Biblical) doctrine of *creatio ex nihilo*, he shows that evil results from creaturely power, which God cannot unilaterally negate. Defining "the Demonic" as creaturely power exercised with indifference or hatred on a scale sufficient to threaten divine purposes, Griffin develops a concept of the Demonic as the "quasi-soul" of modern civilization, after which he argues that the US state has become the most powerful agency of the Demonic in the world, the "New Rome." He concludes that Christian faith, which in its essence is fidelity to divine values, calls upon US Christians to actively oppose the empire-building undertaken by their rulers, and especially to oppose the massive slaughter of innocents carried out in the wars of aggression triggered by the 9/11 false-flag operation.

As the fifth anniversary of 9/11 approached in 2006, four publications in August attempted to shore up the official version of the events by debunking the critical alternative account. The best-known of these was a book entitled *Debunking 9/11 Myths*, published by *Popular Mechanics* magazine (which had been supplied with a new staff, including a new editor-in-chief, by the president of Hearst Magazines). Griffin responded to all four of these debunking attempts in his next book, *Debunking 9/11 Debunking: An Answer to* Popular Mechanics *and Other Defenders of the Official Conspiracy Theory*,[5] which was published early in 2007. In my opinion, this book is his 9/11 magnum opus, best displaying his powers of argument and his mastery of all relevant evidence over the full range of issues. It definitively destroyed the pretensions of the debunking publications.

Griffin's Introduction prepared the ground by distinguishing between rational and irrational conspiracy theories, thereby pointing out that conspiracy theories are not irrational by definition. He also discussed the double standard used by the mainstream and even most of the left-leaning media, which discredits critiques of the official account on the grounds that they are "conspiracy theories," while ignoring the fact that the official story is itself a conspiracy theory. The Introduction concludes with a discussion of the role of scientific explanations in 9/11 conspiracy theories. The rest of the book demonstrates that science and reason are all on one side, that of the alternative, not the official, 9/11 conspiracy theory.

An especially important achievement of *Debunking 9/11 Debunking* was Griffin's compelling argument against the

authenticity of the so-called "NORAD tapes," which were the
focus of an article in *Vanity Fair* put forth by journalist Michael
Bronner, to whom the military had given exclusive access to
the "NORAD tapes." These tapes are purportedly selections
from audio tapes of conversations within the military that
were recorded by NORAD as the events took place. Bronner
claimed that the tapes provide the "authentic" story of the
military response to the hijackings.

But Griffin argues convincingly that the story told by
Bronner is unbelievable. First, the tapes, which only surfaced
in 2004, are contradicted by volumes of independent
evidence, which Griffin details. Then, on the basis of
interviews with a former FAA air traffic controller (Robin
Hordon), and with the military liaison at the FAA's Boston
Center (Colin Scoggins), Griffin argues that the tapes-based
story told by Bronner about the FAA's slow response to the
flight emergencies of all four planes is simply incredible. In
a compelling logical argument, Griffin concludes that the
"NORAD tapes" must be the product of fakery—by cherry-
picking key communications from a much larger body of
recorded material, by scripting new fictional communications
to be performed by the personnel involved, and/or by voice-
morphing technology.

In Chapter 3, Griffin takes up the online publication by
NIST (the National Institute of Standards and Technology) entitled "Answers to FAQs." This title refers to frequently asked
questions about NIST's earlier *Report* on the destruction of the
Twin Towers, which had failed to provide an explanation that
satisfied critical readers and had resulted in a flood of questions to the agency. In its "Answers to FAQs," NIST pretended
to set all such questions to rest. But Griffin demonstrates that
NIST had failed to debunk the controlled demolition theory of
the Tower's destruction, showing that:

- The planes could not have caused the extensive damage to the columns and fireproofing claimed by NIST; the fires were nowhere near as hot, long-lasting, and extensive as claimed; therefore, NIST's theory of "collapse" cannot be true.
- NIST fraudulently "tweaked" its computer models of the situations in the Towers, changing parameters until it generated the result it wanted.
- NIST, entirely unscientifically, did not consider alternative hypotheses, including the arguably most-likely hypothesis—that the buildings were brought down with explosives.
- Although Griffin and others had presented a massive amount of evidence that the Towers were brought down by controlled demolition, NIST claimed that there was no such evidence.

In the final chapter of *Debunking 9/11 Debunking*, Griffin took on the *Popular Mechanics* book, *Debunking 9/11 Myths*. Here Griffin explained the task facing *Popular Mechanics*:

It must show that every one of the key claims made by the leading critics of the official story is false. Why? Because each of these claims challenges one of the essential claims of the official story. If even one of those essential claims is disproved, then the official story as such is thrown into doubt.

By contrast, Griffin next points out:

Critics do not need to show the falsity of every essential element in the official account; they need to show only the falsity of one such element.[6]

Griffin then proceeded to demonstrate that the *Popular Mechanics* book utterly failed to accomplish its purpose with respect to even one claim made by leading critics of the official story, let alone all of them.

*9/11 Contradictions: An Open Letter to Congress and the Press*, published in March 2008, put a spotlight on contradictory statements made by members of the Bush administration, government departments and agencies, and official bodies such as the 9/11 Commission. Griffin asked why, if the government pronouncements are contradictory, have members of Congress and the mainstream media not launched investigations to determine which claims are true and which are false, and to ask why obvious falsehoods are being promulgated by official sources. As he explains in the preface: "If [Transportation Secretary Norman] Mineta said 'P,' that is a fact. If the 9/11 Commission said 'not P,' that is a fact. And it is a fact that 'P' and 'not P' cannot both be true."[7]

In 25 chapters, Griffin documented 25 of the most serious contradictions. The one referred to in the Preface involves the testimony of Secretary Mineta at a public hearing of the 9/11 Commission, in which he stated that he reached the Presidential Emergency Operations Center (under the White House) by 9:20 AM, to find Vice President Dick Cheney in charge there. Mineta described the interactions between Cheney and a young officer who was monitoring a radar screen and who repeatedly informed Cheney of the continuing approach of an aircraft toward Washington, D.C. Then, Mineta said,

> When it got down to "the plane is 10 miles out," the young man also said to the Vice President, "Do the orders still stand?" And the Vice President turned and whipped his neck around and said, "Of course the orders still stand. Have you heard anything to the contrary?"[8]

This testimony has been widely interpreted as evidence that a stand-down order had been given by Cheney—an order permitting the continued approach of the aircraft toward Washington without interception by NORAD. The approach by the aircraft alarmed the young officer, prompting his question ("Do the orders still stand?"). Griffin shows that the 9/11 Commission suppressed this evidence from Mineta, scrubbing the video of his testimony from its website, making no reference to it in its *Report*, and even replaced it with a distorted account of the incident. Some of the contradictions discussed in *9/11 Contradictions* show that the official story has changed over time, such as the new story about the chronology of FAA-NORAD communications told in 2004 by the 9/11 Commission. As criminal investigators know so well, when the story keeps changing, doubt is cast on all of its versions.

In *The New Pearl Harbor Revisited: 9/11, the Cover-Up, and the Exposé*,[9] published in September of 2008, Griffin examined significant developments in research into the events of 9/11 that had taken place since early 2004, when he had published *The New Pearl Harbor*. Griffin's account of the remarkable role that Philip Zelikow, Executive Director of the 9/11 Commission, had played prior to his appointment to that position—which Griffin began in *The 9/11 Commission Report: Omissions and Distortions* and continued in *Debunking 9/11 Debunking*—is concluded in this 2008 book with revealing facts about Zelikow's role in the writing of the Commission's *Report*.

Griffin's earlier accounts had treated Zelikow's working relationship with Condoleezza Rice, who had become Bush's National Security Advisor, and who had asked Zelikow to write *The National Security Strategy of the United States 2002*, in which the US government for the first time asserted the right of preemptive-preventive war (based on the pretext provided by the 9/11 attacks). Griffin had also examined Zelikow's co-authorship in 1998 of an article (in *Foreign Affairs*, the journal of the Council on Foreign Relations) entitled "Catastrophic Terrorism," which forecast in chilling detail the massive attack at the World Trade Center and many details of the government's "response" to the attack.

In *The New Pearl Harbor Revisited*, Griffin closed his treatment of Zelikow with a detailed examination of his complete control of the writing of *The 9/11 Commission Report*: He had (with a co-author) drafted a complete outline of the final report before the staff's research even began—complete with "chapter headings, subheadings and sub-subheadings"—which led Commission staff, when they learned of the outline, to circulate a parody entitled "The Warren Commission Report—Preemptive Outline," with a chapter entitled "Single Bullet: We Haven't Seen the Evidence Yet. But Really. We're Sure."[10]

In May 2009, Griffin published a very different book, *Osama bin Laden: Dead or Alive?*[11] Here Griffin examined the whole range of evidence bearing on the question whether Osama bin Laden was actually still alive. His conclusion was that bin Laden was almost certainly dead, and that in all likelihood he died in December 2001. Griffin surveyed in detail the many different indications published in the major media in late 2001 and early 2002 that bin Laden had been very ill and had died. These included a video from December 2001 in which he appeared to be at death's door (as admitted by a Bush administration spokesperson), analyses by medical experts of the grave state of his health, the sudden, total and permanent cessation in mid-December 2001 of any surveillance intercepts of communications from him, and even reports of his funeral.

Griffin argued that two videos that purportedly showed bin Laden taking credit for the attacks of 9/11 were faked. He then argued that if fake bin Laden videos were produced in this early period, when he was probably still alive, then there is even greater reason to be suspicious of "bin Laden videos" or other claimed "messages" that were released later. Griffin then presented reasons to be suspicious of the authenticity of the entire series of "messages from bin Laden" that had been released from 2002 to 2008.

Griffin's conclusion, that a massive amount of evidence indicated that bin Laden had likely died many years ago, probably in December 2001, has apparently been refuted by the media reports of the US Special Operations raid in Abbottabad, Pakistan, in May 2011, in which Osama bin Laden was reportedly killed. But many questions about this operation have been raised, including: why all the "evidence" comes from US officials; why bin Laden would have been killed rather than captured; why no photographic evidence has been released to support the claim that Osama bin Laden was killed; why the body was buried at sea, where no confirmation of its identity is possible;[12] why officials claimed that a pre-burial DNA report was given before there had been sufficient time, according to a DNA expert;[13] and why the US media have ignored an Abbottabad resident who said the man watching television was not bin Laden,[14] or the neighbor who told an account completely different from the story given by US officials about what happened the night of the raid.[15]

In *The Mysterious Collapse of World Trade Center 7: Why the Final Official Report about 9/11 is Unscientific and False*,[16] published in September 2009, Griffin provided a withering critique of NIST's treatment of the highly mysterious collapse of WTC 7, a 47-story steel-framed skyscraper about two blocks from the Twin Towers. This collapse was mysterious because, given NIST's insistence that explosives were not used, there was apparently no way to explain why this building came down. NIST could not even appeal to the faulty reasons it had used to explain the disintegration of Twin Towers, because WTC 7 was not struck by a plane and as a result had no big fires. Nevertheless, at 5:21 PM on 9/11, WTC 7 collapsed suddenly. NIST, after having delayed year after year, finally in 2008 issued a report on this building, claiming to present a scientific account of the causes of the building's collapse. But

Griffin demonstrated that NIST had produced only a pseu-do-explanation. Showing that NIST's report on WTC 7 is—as his book's subtitle says—"unscientific and false," Griffin even demonstrated that NIST's report committed scientific fraud.

Griffin considers *Mysterious Collapse* to be the one of his 9/11 books that most clearly demonstrates the falsity of the official story.[17] It is also the only one in which he quotes his principal philosopher, Alfred North Whitehead, who had said that a scientific frame of mind requires an "unflinching determination to take the whole evidence into account." You do not have that frame of mind, Whitehead added, if you adopt hypotheses that require you "to disregard half your evidence."[18]

Part I of the book, "NIST's Unscientific Rejection of the Most Likely Theory," examined the methods used by NIST to avoid considering controlled demolition as a possible explanation of the building's collapse. Controlled demolition is the most likely hypothesis because all previous instances of sudden, rapid collapse of steel-framed skyscrapers had been the result of intentional controlled demolition using explosives. Beginning by considering key indicators of scientific fraud, Griffin argued that scientific fraud in the strict sense was committed by NIST, because (a) it fabricated evidence to support its claims; (b) it even falsified evidence; and (c) it ignored relevant evidence. NIST also committed scientific fraud in a broader sense by violating additional scientific principles, including making claims implying that laws of nature had been violated.

In Part II, "NIST's Unscientific Arguments for Its Own Theory," Griffin shows in detail the failure of the authors of NIST's *Report* to adhere to standard scientific principles, including their failure to base their analysis on empirical facts and physical tests, and their distortion and fabrication of "data." After shredding the central pillar of NIST's account—its claim that thermal expansion of steel floor beams and girders caused "global collapse"—Griffin delivered the *coup de grace*. Having for years claimed that the collapse of WTC 7 was far slower than free fall (the gravitational rate), NIST had stated that fire could not possibly cause the free-fall collapse of a steel-framed building: Such a collapse would only be possible, barring a miracle, if all resistance to the fall had been eliminated by removal of the lower portion of the building by explosives. But then NIST was confronted with irrefutable evidence by physicists that the collapse of WTC 7 did in fact enter into free fall. Although NIST was thus forced to make this admission, it continued to maintain that the collapse had been caused by fire. Griffin demonstrated that the scientists at NIST, by maintaining these contradictory claims, had abandoned science by violating the scientific principles of non-contradiction and the impermissibility of claims implying that laws of nature have been broken. Unfortunately for NIST, Griffin is an expert on miracles!

*Cognitive Infiltration: An Obama Appointee's Plan to Undermine the 9/11 Conspiracy Theory*,[19] published in September 2010, was Griffin's response to writings concerning the 9/11 truth movement by Cass Sunstein, a Harvard law professor appointed by President Obama to the post of administrator of the White House Office of Information and Regulatory Affairs. Before his appointment in April of 2009, Sunstein had published an essay entitled "Conspiracy Theories: Causes and Cures,"[20] in which he argued that "conspiracy theories" are the expression of an ignorant state of mind caused by "informational isolation," and should be "cured" through secret "cognitive infiltration" by covert government agents of organizations the government deems "conspiracist." Because Sunstein painted a fantastic picture of the 9/11 truth movement as "harmful," "dangerous," and likely to resort to "terrorism," and he explicitly stated that "9/11 conspiracy theories" were his main focus, it was clear that his call for "cognitive infiltration" was directed specifically against the 9/11 truth movement.

But Griffin demonstrates that the case Sunstein made for what is essentially a new Cointelpro[21]—which was declared illegal by the US Congress—is deeply flawed. In illustration of the weakness of Sunstein's arguments and how thoroughly Griffin counters them, take Sunstein's thesis that, although people accept the alternative account of 9/11 "not as a result of a mental illness . . . or of simple irrationality," they do so "as a result of a 'crippled epistemology' in the form of a sharply limited number of (relevant) informational sources." He further clarified his term "crippled epistemology" by explaining that adherents of the alternative theory "know very few things, and what they know is wrong." Griffin simply points out that since knowledge is justified true belief, it is nonsense to say that what someone knows is wrong. Further, he shows that Sunstein's pseudo-philosophical term "crippled epistemology" is nothing but fancy dress meant to cover his threadbare claim that people who accept the alternative theory of 9/11 are simply ignorant, a charge that Griffin easily refutes by listing a large number of members of the movement with impressive scholarly or professional accomplishments.

On the tenth anniversary of the events, Griffin published *9/11 Ten Years Later: When State Crimes Against Democracy Succeed*,[22] which presented his latest analysis of a range of important issues: the lack of evidence that Muslims had attacked the US on 9/11; the multiple occasions on which, if the official account of the destruction of the World Trade Center is to be believed, the laws of physics were miraculously inoperative (Griffin documents nine such miracles); the extraordinary cover-up of WTC 7's classic demolition by the mainstream media and government agencies; Vice President Dick Cheney's changing account of his whereabouts and activities at key times during the morning of 9/11; the wide variety of evidence demonstrating that the official account of the events at the Pentagon, which claims that Flight 77 was flown by al-Qaeda hijackers into the building, cannot be true; and evidence that many nominally Christian Americans have subordinated their Christian faith to a "nationalist faith," which for them makes the suggestion that US leaders could have been responsible for 9/11 simply unthinkable.

In my view, Griffin's most important chapter in this book is his examination of evidence about the alleged phone calls from the 9/11 airliners, according to which passengers and flight attendants supposedly stated that the planes had been hijacked by Middle-Eastern Muslims. In Griffin's arguably strongest argument, he shows that calls to Deena Burnett, supposedly from her husband Tom Burnett from aboard United Flight 93, registered on her caller ID as calls from his cell phone. However, by 2003, it had become widely accepted that cell phones in 2001, given the technology then available, were not capable of completing calls from airliners at high elevation. Remarkably, the FBI then simply changed its account, saying that Tom Burnett had called home using a seatback phone—but without explaining how Deena's caller ID could have showed that the calls came from Tom's cell phone. Griffin also shows that the most famous of all the alleged calls—those from CNN reporter Barbara Olson to her husband, US Solicitor General Ted Olson—could not have occurred, and that the FBI also admitted that these alleged calls did not occur. Griffin then makes the logically compelling argument that if these two sets of claimed calls are demonstrably fake, *all* the reported calls must have been faked. In response to the question of how these calls could have been faked, Griffin points out that voice morphing was already a well-established technical capability by 2001.

The subtitle of the book indicates that the 9/11 attacks, in being a false-flag operation carried out by elements of the US government, were a "State Crime Against Democracy," or SCAD, through which the electorate of a supposedly democratic country is manipulated, so that it does not base its policies on a true understanding of the facts. The failure to carry out a genuine investigation, arrest the perpetrators, and reverse the policies undemocratically imposed by the government after 9/11 means that the operation has succeeded. Griffin argues, however, that the future is still open, and that the 9/11 truth movement, with its developed understanding of this reality, has a crucial role to play in reversing the course toward a global police state and endless war.

In conclusion, it is important to note that Griffin's devotion to the cause of 9/11 truth has not been restricted to his books on the subject. In addition to writing what I consider are the ten best books on 9/11, he has been a central figure in the movement in many other ways. Countless people who share his high scholarly and moral standards have been inspired by him to become active, and have formed an impressive array of professional organizations dedicated to 9/11 truth and to calling for a real, fully empowered investigation. For example, architect Richard Gage, who started Architects and Engineers for 9/11 Truth—which by now has over 1700 members—joined the movement after hearing a radio interview given by Griffin on his research, mentioned above, into the "Explosive Testimony" of first responders at the WTC.[23] In one of Griffin's most important roles, he has been an advisor to professionals in various fields for the development of their organizations, including Actors and Artists for 9/11 Truth, Political Leaders for 9/11 Truth, Religious Leaders for 9/11 Truth, and Scientists for 9/11 Truth.

Griffin has given many public addresses on 9/11 at universities, churches, and local venues organized by 9/11 truth activists, and has gone on several long lecture tours in the US, Europe and Japan. His radio and television interviews number in the hundreds, and include interviews on national television in Canada, the UK and other foreign countries. It seems to be only in the US that he has not been allowed to speak on national radio and television—with the important exception of the broadcast by C-SPAN of his 2005 lecture at Madison on "9/11 and American Empire," which did much to turn the 9/11 truth movement into a national, even a world-wide, movement. He has collaborated with other researchers on publications, including the important volume *9/11 and American Empire: Intellectuals Speak Out*, co-edited with Peter Dale Scott in 2006, which brought many academics and professionals into the movement. He has also advised film makers as a consultant on questions of fact. And he has been an advocate of building an inclusive movement, while at the same time seeking to develop the best evidence, as illustrated by his co-founding of the 9/11 Consensus Panel.

Professor Griffin is now widely recognized for his 9/11 work as one of the most influential people in the world: He received the Helios Foundation Award in 2006 for his first two 9/11 books; in November of 2008, his book *The New Pearl Harbor Revisited* was named by *Publishers Weekly* as "Pick of the Week"; he has been nominated for the Nobel Peace Prize four times; and in 2009 he was included by the British *New Statesman* in its list of "The 50 People Who Matter Today." As with his achievements in so many areas that have been surveyed and built upon in this volume, his productivity has been astounding, his standards exemplary, his example inspiring, and his impact historic.

# 13. 9/11, Deep Politics, and Spirituality

## Peter Dale Scott

I want to begin by saying how honored I consider myself to have been invited to this symposium, and more generally how fortunate to have known David, to have worked with him, and most recently, while preparing to write this essay, to have been forced to learn so much from and to reflect so much on his work.

I must also begin by confessing my inadequacies for this task. When I was invited to participate in this symposium, I believed that my exposure to David's book *Christian Faith and the Truth behind 9/11*, together with my personal collaboration with him on another 9/11 book, meant that I knew both David and his work well enough to handle the suggested topic: "David Ray Griffin on 9/11, Deep Politics, and Spirituality."

How wrong I was!

In the two months it took me to write this essay, I learned for the first time that Griffin has written or edited no fewer than 38 books, mostly in the cause of correcting what he sees as the twin modernist errors of atheistic materialism and mind-body dualism. Like, I am sure, other symposium members, I am humbled by the challenge of assessing this life work in a brief essay. I feel like the juggler in the chapel of Notre Dame. I cannot really rise to the task presented me. I can only juggle. (Remember that this is my first theological conference.

I could have presented you with a graduate essay on 9/11, but you will get instead a freshman essay on theology.)

## THE MERITS OF CHRISTIAN FAITH AND THE TRUTH BEHIND 9/11

Griffin's *Christian Faith and the Truth behind 9/11* sees America as suffering from a spiritual sickness, for which a needed remedy is truth. It is obviously risky to proceed in the same text from the destruction of the World Trade Center to a discussion of whether or not God created the universe out of nothing.[1] But Griffin's theodicy is dedicated to linking the two. His cosmology, like Whitehead's, is rooted in the indeterminacy, or what Griffin calls the self-determination, of all events in the universe, a vision of the world as process, rather than material substance, which Whitehead seems to have taken from the initial stages of quantum theory.[2] Griffin's summary exposition of this idea with examples from molecular biology is succinct and memorable:

> Whitehead's doctrine that all individuals embody creativity means that at least some iota of responsive, self-determining creativity, as well as some degree of outgoing, causal creativity, is exercised by all events, even those in the primordial chaos. . . . Such a view would have been ridiculed in the nineteenth century, when science was heavily committed to a strict determinism. But since the discovery of quantum indeterminacy, this idea is not ruled out. The idea is also increasingly supported by biologists who have discovered that bacteria make decisions. Likewise, the scientist Robert [Mulliken],[3] who was known as "Mr. Molecule" . . . once said that if molecules were as big as dogs, we would unhesitatingly attribute the power of decision-making to them.[4]

We often encounter the notion that deity itself is part of this process of cosmic creativity, not wholly under divine control, and evolving in time. But Griffin expands on the Whiteheadian notion of creativity latent in the world to see not only divine creativity but also what Griffin calls a "creaturely creativity" latent in God's creatures. This latter can be good or evil, but when evil becomes "powerful enough to threaten divine purposes" it becomes what Griffin calls demonic.[5] Griffin sees demonic power as both "rooted in something eternal (creaturely creativity) and . . . unlike Augustine's view of the demonic, not on a leash,"[6] rendering possible (for example) the Holocaust.

By discussing the demonic in recent historical and political developments, Griffin takes his place in a tradition dating back to Dostoevsky.[7] Dostoevsky's attacks on the demonic were first adapted by Reinhold Niebuhr into a *de facto* defense of the Cold War,[8] and then expanded by Aleksandr Solzhenitsyn into a condemnation of East and West alike. Solzhenitsyn's warnings about Russia as demonic were in turn adapted, in Reagan's "evil empire" speech, into a case for American global supremacy and "peace through strength."

The reactions of people like myself at the time was to respond, like the essayist Bernard Lee in Griffin's *Sacred Interconnections*, by saying "'Empire of evil' is not helpful."[9] But more recently many of us came to wonder if our moral equanimity was not perhaps too Laodicean in the face of today's quasi-apocalyptic events.[10] The perplexing challenge, again shared by many, is how to be morally clear without lapsing into hatred. Here Griffin has written something very helpful in *God and Religion in the Postmodern World*:

> Postmodern theology's . . . doctrine of the divine attitude portrays an essentially pluralistic, multilateral world. It says that every center of experience is loved for its own sake. No center of experience is hated, and none is viewed as having only instrumental value.[11]

Similarly, I was disinclined at first to believe Griffin's Dostoievskian implication that people with the wrong notion of God are more likely to misbehave.[12] But Griffin has helped me recognize that a culture promoting a textbook deity outside a quasi-scientific universe of inert matter, as well as shallow values of freedom and equality, is indeed more likely also to tolerate surrender to pressing impulses of greed than the quieter impulses of kindness and compassion. Thus Griffin's Whiteheadian theology corrects this cultural sickness by envisaging a panentheistic God consistent with a scientific reality that is a creative, indeterminate, evolving process.

Griffin's discussion of the divine and the demonic, of our own self-determination in a universal self-determining process, both separates and gives dimension to his chapters in *Christian Faith and the Truth behind 9/11* on the Roman and American empires. I accept his insight (following Richard Horsley) "that understanding the nature of the Roman Empire is crucial for understanding the message of Jesus."[13] Griffin then lists five features of the Roman empire that are also exemplified by the American empire: from "the sense that the empire is divinely authorized" to "the collection of taxes in order to enrich the empire's center and finance its imperial rule."[14]

His exposition of the parallels is very strong and very suggestive. I am tempted to add one more comparison: the imperial weakening of an earlier civic and republican society by its breakdown into classes of extreme wealth and extreme poverty. Griffin demonstrates very well how imperialism, then and now, enriches the metropolitan center at the expense of the impoverished provinces or the Third World. But the same disparity has increased at home as well, impoverishing not only the domestic poor but also the domestic state that once cared for them. What Sallust quoted about Rome—*privatim*

*opulentia publice egestas* (private wealth and public poverty)—
was in turn quoted by Matthew Arnold in his great cultural
critique, *Culture and Anarchy*, about 19th-century imperial
Britain and London.[15] It applies to America as well.

## The limitations of Christian Faith and the Truth behind 9/11

Griffin's comparison of the Roman and American empires is
both useful and evocative. At the same time, I consider it limited as presented, on three counts. First, it freezes both empires
in time as objects, ignoring the obvious and relevant fact that
both Rome and America evolved spectacularly in time from
progressive republics into oppressive empires. A second point
is that both empires contributed in a major way to the freedom
of some, even as they also contributed to the impoverishment
and virtual enslavement of others. The third point is that the
differences between Rome and America are if anything more
important than the similarities—especially when we are trying
to move, as Griffin's book does, beyond reflection to action.[16]

Inspired by Hegel, I agree that history is a process struggling towards emancipation, peace, and the progressive dis-
placement of violent power by persuasive power. In this process, empires play a dialectical role, when they are engines not
just of exploitation and oppression, but also of literacy and
law. Thus British law empowered Gandhi, and American law
empowered Martin Luther King Jr. (Furthermore Christianity
and Islam became world religions by spreading through the societies created by the Roman and Sassanid empires. One could
even make a case that all world religions, even Buddhism, began as dialectical reactions to excessive if not imperial power.)

American empire is not wholly evil: because of it
Germany is not like the former East Germany; South Korea
is not like North Korea. But in the late stages of American
empire we have seen insane doctrines of global domination

and unilateral violence. America's actions now violate the UN Charter it helped create. It is these specific actions that are evil, not empire *per se*.

In Christian terms, I believe we should judge America's sins, not the sinner. In practical terms, America's wrongdoings are scrutable but not predictable. Invading Iraq in 2003 was a crime. Sending US forces to East Timor in 1999 was not.[17] Will sending US forces into Uganda prove a crime?[18] When this essay went to press, it was too early to judge.

Thus Griffin's one-sided assessment of America explains what I consider to be the weakness of the book's final Call to Action. On an ethical level, it seems quite appropriate that Griffin, as a Christian theologian, would encourage fellow Americans to emulate the resistance of Dietrich Bonhoeffer and Karl Barth against Hitler. But in terms of political and social action, the two theologians' example seems much less relevant. The Confessing Church the two men founded achieved nothing and went exactly nowhere.[19] I much prefer Griffin's other example: the proclamation of the Lutheran World Federation in 1977 that the church had a duty to oppose apartheid in South Africa."[20]

As an example of mobilizing faith to speak in truth against evil, I also prefer the Civil Rights Movement of the 1960s, guided by heroic churchmen like Fred Shuttlesworth and Martin Luther King. But King is mentioned only once in the book, and even then not as a role model. The reason why would seem to be obvious, and symptomatic: King's political agenda, like Gandhi's before him, was to appeal to what was *good* in government and society, *against* what was evil. But what is good in the American society and government is not discussed in Griffin's book.[21]

In practice, Griffin is constantly appealing to the good in American society.[22] To give but one relevant example, the Civil

Rights Movement was ecumenical, and Griffin, one year before *Christian Faith*, edited another important volume, *Deep Religious Pluralism*, arguing for a "deep" pluralism with multiple paths to salvation. The word "ecumenical" is absent in *Christian Faith*—but only because the book is explicitly designed for a narrow purpose: to inspire Christian churches to take up the issue of 9/11.[23] I mention this only to illustrate that Griffin's overall contribution to the topic of spirituality and the truth of 9/11, on every level, goes far beyond the measure of this single book.

## GRIFFIN AND MERTON ON THE DEMONIC IN POLITICS: THE APODEICTIC VERSUS THE APOPHATIC

But before leaving *Christian Faith*, I would like to refer to the absence in it of Thomas Merton, another great theologian who described American imperial policies as demonic.[24] Griffin's call to reflect on "the church community [and] demonic power" would seem to echo Merton on the moral passivity of Christians in the face of "*Demonic* Activism."[25] Both men saw America's willingness to contemplate a nuclear first strike as proof of a demonic force in American government.

But their respective theologies are dramatically different. Griffin's approach to the conundrum of God and evil is to explain it, in a series of carefully argued conclusions that are almost Euclidean. Merton, by contrast, especially in his later life, spoke of God as Ineffable, and of evil as "the Unspeakable."[26] Merton's mature approach to God became characterized by what is called apophatic insight, an approach by negation to a realm of Unknowing beyond words.

Merton inspired James Douglass's important and relevant book, *JFK and the Unspeakable*. In some ways his book is like Griffin's, but on one central point it is different. Douglass sees the JFK assassination as an act inflicted *against* the state by an element within it.

Griffin also often blames such an element for 9/11, as when he concludes "that members of the Bush administration and the U.S. military orchestrated the attacks of 9/11 and that they did so in order to advance their imperial aims."[27] But Griffin also speaks repeatedly about what he calls "the *prima facie* case that the Bush administration [i.e. itself, rather than members of it] orchestrated the attacks of 9/11."[28]

In other words, where Douglass targets a demonic enemy within the state, Griffin sometimes attributes "demonic evil" to the American empire itself.[29] This simple condemnation is supported by Griffin's heavy reliance on structuralist epitomes of American wrongdoings by monochromatic writers like Noam Chomsky (an explicit anarchist) and Bill Blum.

Furthermore, where Merton and Douglass are trying to deal with a mystery, Griffin often writes as if the mystery has been conclusively solved. For example, he writes of the demonstrable coverup in *The 9/11 Commission Report* as "a decisive event: the moment at which the *prima facie* case against the Bush administration became a *conclusive* case."[30]

But in my opinion the predictable shortcomings of *The 9/11 Commission Report* prove very little more than that an initial cover-up was still being defended. It remains unclear to me whether this cover-up was to protect officials inside the Bush administration, allies like Saudi Arabia outside it, or (as I suspect) some combination of the two and perhaps others.[31]

To conclude: I applaud Griffin for courageously investigating and clarifying the mystery of 9/11. But I cannot agree that he has solved it.

KNOWING, UNKNOWING, AND DEEP POLITICS: CONFESSIONS OF AN IGNORANT JUGGLER

It is a mark of Griffin's open-mindedness and generosity that he invited me to participate in this symposium. He knows that

I do not endorse hard-edged and one-sided condemnations of the American empire, or his definitive explanations of 9/11.[32] Both in my prose and my poetry, I have repeatedly attacked monochromatic assessments of America's foreign influence.[33] I do see an evil force at work in America, and recently I have reproved myself, perhaps learning from David, for having been too reluctant in the past to use the term "evil." But to see evil in the American empire is very different from Griffin's flat judgment that "the American empire is evil."[34]

Griffin sees nothing particularly mysterious about 9/11: he presents what he calls a "conclusive case," blaming it on the Bush administration.[35] I in contrast believe that it was one of a series of "structural deep events"—of the sort I have defined elsewhere as

> mysterious events, like the JFK assassination, the Watergate break-in, or 9/11, which violate the American social structure, have a major impact on American society, repeatedly involve law-breaking or violence, and in many [perhaps most] cases proceed from an unknown dark force.[35]

With the passage of time, evidence about these events accumulates, but even so central mysteries remain.[36]

Thus I regard both Tonkin Gulf and 9/11 as deep events in which the question of ultimate causality and responsibility remains obscure. I see them as arising out of the murky substrate of "deep politics" which I see in all superstates with a surplus of power over what is needed for the security of their domestic society. I do, however, conclude that such surplus power is likely to lead to atrocities like 9/11, and that some of these atrocities are not the work of the public state itself, but committed *against* the legal structure of the public state.[38]

This recurring phenomenon, wherein part of the state acts against the public state as a whole, is what I have tried to explain as a "dark force" or "deep state" within, beyond, and above all against the public state. Griffin's explanation, in contrast, tends to ignore such duality.[39]

Thus David's political analysis of deep events is different from my deep political analysis. But the difference in our approach to political violence is symptomatic of a deeper difference in our approach to language and its limits, and indeed in our approach to God.

Merton and I both became poets, believing as we do that (as Czeslaw Milosz once suggested) language is like a bird thrashing against a glass windowpane, in a vain attempt to reach the realm of truth beyond it.[40] Clearly, David is wired differently: Where I am more likely to admit ignorance in the face of a mystery, he is more likely to seek out a truth to be explained. As a result, there is a difference in tone between us when we write about 9/11. More importantly, and in the same spirit, there is a difference in tone between us when we write about God.[41]

I believe that Whitehead gives far more prominence than does Griffin to the role of poetry and poetic intuition in the evolution of self-consciousness, and particularly in our evolution beyond Newtonian mechanism. In a memorable chapter of *Science and the Modern World*, Whitehead singles out the Romantic poets like Wordsworth for having expressed "deep intuitions . . . that nature cannot be divorced from its aesthetic values" transcending materialism.[42]

From my reading of Eliot, Milosz, and Merton, I believe that the veridical importance of poets like Wordsworth and Blake has to do with their awareness of the doubleness of the human condition. By "doubleness" (Eliot's word) I mean that we exist on two levels: normally in the world around us, but occasionally with access to what the poet Czeslaw Milosz calls a "second space" where we are more at home than in this world we normally inhabit.[43]

Caught in this doubleness, we have to deal not only with the present but also with an otherness (or what Lévinas has called "alterity") that is latent within it. As Adorno and others since Schiller have argued, this explains the importance of art: "Even in the most sublimated work of art there is a hidden 'it should be otherwise.'"[44]

Griffin does not quote the intuitions of poets as liberally as Whitehead. But he fully endorses Whitehead's respect for what both men call "non-sensuous perception" and defends the notion of intuition from the dogmatic criticisms of the British empiricist Bernard Williams.[45] And in *Reenchantment Without Supernaturalism*, he quotes Whitehead on our "intuition of holiness, the intuition of the sacred," or what I have called otherness.[46] There is the suggestion that the inclination to seek and to worship is as encoded in human DNA as the beauty of an oak tree is encoded in the DNA of an acorn.[47]

Griffin's openness to the extra-rational has also, I believe, had a practical consequence: his thinking was not afflicted with the firewall of denial causing so many post-Weberian social scientists to be blind to the extra-rational in modern society—more specifically, the realm of what is conventionally dismissed as conspiracy theory.

I am suggesting, in other words, that the importance Whitehead and Griffin give to intuition and non-sensuous perception ultimately helps explain Griffin's ability to respond so early and so fully to the events of 9/11. In a larger sense, I would say that Griffin exhibits what Keats called "negative capability"—the ability to think outside and beyond socially accepted assumptions—and that this poetic ability explains his courageous exploration of other unfashionable topics, from the parapsychological to the demonic.

SPANNING 9/11 AND SPIRITUALITY: THE OVERALL ACHIEVEMENT OF DAVID RAY GRIFFIN

The main point of this talk is that the dimensions of Griffin's contributions to spirituality and politics go far beyond the range of his book *Christian Faith*.

Together with John Cobb and Catherine Keller, and with assistance from his close friend Richard Falk, Griffin has devoted a lifetime to consolidating a postmodern spiritual *Weltanschauung*, one grounded in a community of postmodern theologians and others with a collective post-imperial vision.[48] They saw, long before 9/11, that the modern world was both in an age of spiritual crisis and also striving toward a more peaceful and communitarian age to succeed it.

Griffin did not just embody this thinking in his own writings: he assembled a number of like-minded thinkers from different faiths in the prodigious series of volumes he edited. He thus helped energize a realm of postmodern spiritual discourse, and in so doing became a spiritual leader long before 9/11.[49]

His long experience with unpretentious leadership carried over easily into the 9/11 truth movement. His graciousness and meticulous honesty have made him, of all the 9/11 critics, the most likely to gain access to the mainstream media.[50] However these qualities have not protected him from a flood of attacks, ranging from the severe to the deranged.

Here I cannot ignore the fact that some aspects of Griffin's 9/11 research have been criticized by researchers whom I consider responsible within the 9/11 truth movement.[51] But this has little bearing on the subject I am discussing today, especially when you consider that there are probably no two critics of 9/11 who can agree on everything.

I would rather close with the judgment that in my opinion David Ray Griffin is a great man. We see in the world today a retreat from the high tide of secularism that engulfed the 19th century, and Griffin has helped illuminate the cosmological and theological dimensions of that retreat. In addition, he is also a leader in the movement for truth about America, having to deal with all the special difficulties that fame and leadership can bring.

His qualities of modesty, compassion and good humor have been of great benefit to those of us who know him, and in a larger way to all his embattled followers who are dedicated to the cause of 9/11 truth, as a path towards greater peace and understanding in the world.

# 14. The Chinese Encounter with Constructive Postmodernism

## Zhihe Wang

More than 15 years ago, almost no Chinese heard the term "constructive postmodernism," which was coined by David Ray Griffin. But today, constructive postmodernism, which combines a study of Whitehead with a reclaiming of classical Chinese traditions—showing how such a creative synthesis can be applied to practical problems in China today—has become a large and influential movement in China. The last time I looked at google.com in Chinese (May 13, 2012), I found 4,430,000 results about constructive postmodernism.

### THE ORIGINS OF CONSTRUCTIVE POSTMODERNISM IN CHINA

In 2010, an article entitled "Constructive Postmodern Theory" was published in the official newspaper of the Central Higher Party School, *Studies Times* (March 1). Also in 2010, three papers on "constructive postmodernism" were published by the *Journal of China Executive Leadership Academy Pudong*, which is another national-level higher party school. In an article published more recently (2011) in *Wen Hui Bao*, Professor Yijie Tang of Peking University, a leading scholar in Chinese philosophy, wrote:

The influence of process thought or constructive post-modernism has kept increasing in China. Two broad intellectual trends are influential in China today: (1) The zeal for 'national essence' or 'national character, and (2) constructive postmodernism. These two trends can, under the guidance of Marxism, not only take root in China, but so develop that, with comparative ease, China can complete its 'First Enlightenment' of modernization, and also quickly enter into the 'Second Enlightenment,' becoming the standard-bearer of a postmodern society.

Tracing constructive postmodernism back to its beginnings in China, we find the work of Dr. David Ray Griffin—namely, the SUNY Series in Constructive Postmodern Thought, especially its first volume, *The Reenchantment of Science*, which he edited and which was translated and published in China in 1995. This book can be regarded as the origin of constructive postmodernism in China. Before the book's publication, the only kind of postmodernism with which Chinese scholars were familiar was the deconstructive postmodernism of French philosophers such as Derrida and Foucault. The translation and publication of *The Reenchantment of Science* made people aware of another kind of postmodernism, namely "constructive postmodernism."

*The Reenchantment of Science* has thus far been reprinted in China six times. At some universities, professors have assigned the book to their graduate students on their "must-read" list. In November 1996, *Studies in Dialectics of Nature* invited ten scholars to discuss the book. Comments were published (1997) in this national-level journal. With the publication of *The Reenchantment of Science,* it can be said, constructive postmodernism had officially stepped onto the Chinese academic stage. In addition, the following passage, addressed by Griffin to Chinese readers, has become very popular in China, being cited widely: "China can avoid the destructive impact of modernization by learning the mistakes the West made. In doing so, China will actually become postmodernized."[1]

In order to promote constructive postmodernism in China, Dr. Griffin and his main colleague, Dr. John Cobb, went to Beijing in 2002 to co-chair the International Conference on Whitehead and China, which made constructive postmodernism even more visible in China. There were 180 scholars participating in this historic event, roughly 120 of whom were from various parts of China, many of them being leading scholars of the Chinese academic world. Also, many national Chinese media personnel were present, including the *Peoples Daily*, *Guangming Daily*, *China Education Daily*, *Social Sciences Abroad*, and *World Philosophy*. A number of high government officials, including Guiren Yuan, the Vice-minister of Education, came to the conference to welcome the scholars. This conference was regarded in China as a historic event.

Also on this trip, Griffin delivered several lectures in some top Chinese universities, including Peking University, and in Wuhan he participated in a conference on Marxism and constructive postmodernism.

In 2005, Griffin helped establish the Institute for Postmodern Development of China (IPDC), a nonprofit organization whose aim is to create and promote new modes of development in China and the West. He has served as vice president of IPDC and has been deeply involved in many events the Institute planned.

In 2012 (shortly after having recovered from a 2010 heart operation), Griffin and his wife, Ann, took a trip to China to participate in a series of international conferences—in Harbin, Jinan, and Nanjing—on constructive postmodernism.

On this trip, he also cut the ribbon for the establishment of a new process center, the Nanking Center. In Nanking

(Nanjing), a leading school leader told the audience that he and his generation have grown up reading Griffin's books.

As a matter of fact, after the translation of *The Reenchantment of Science,* some other constructive postmodern books written or edited by Griffin have been translated into Chinese. These include *Spirituality and Society, Process Theology, Founders of Constructive Postmodern Philosophy, God and Religion in the Postmodern World,* and *Whitehead's Radically Different Postmodern Philosophy.* In addition, several books have been published by other process thinkers, preeminently John Cobb.

Furthermore, hundreds of writings on constructive postmodernism have been published by Chinese authors. These include books such as *On the Third Kind of Metaphysics: A Study of Constructive Postmodern Philosophy,* by Weifu Wu (2002); *Postmodern Ecological Science and Technology: A Constructive Perspective,* by Xianjing Xiao (2003); *Globalization and Postmodernity,* edited by Zhihe Wang (2003); and *A Dictionary of Postmodernism,* edited by Zhihe Wang (2004).

These writings also include articles directly discussing Griffin's ideas, such as "A Study of David Ray Griffin's Constructive Postmodern Thought," by Ping Zhang (2004); "The Inspiration of Griffin's Postmodern Thought to Creating a Harmonious Society in China," by Wenquan Wu (2009); and Junrui Cui's "Griffin's Constructive Post-Modern Thought and Its Inspiration" (2009).

## THE INFLUENCE OF CONSTRUCTIVE POSTMODERNISM ON CHINA

Is constructive postmodernism just a language game, or is it a serious movement with an impact on China? The answer is the latter, because constructive postmodernism has indeed become a big movement and its influence is regarded as "an unavoidable fact."[2] The influence of constructive postmodernism on China is reflected not only in the fact that the names of Griffin and

Cobb, as the leading constructive postmodern thinkers, appear on tests for graduate students in the Central Higher Party School's newsletter, but also in the following three ways.[3]

**1. Constructive postmodernism has changed people's view on postmodernism.** As mentioned before, prior to the encounter with constructive postmodernism, the Chinese understood postmodernism only as negative criticism and the deconstruction of modernity. This kind of view on post-modernism has influenced Chinese academia deeply. For ex-ample, *Philosophical Researches*, the top journal of philosophy in China, published an article in which the author argued that "Postmodernism views Humanism as an enemy" and "takes pleasure in turning traditional values upside down."[4]

However, the emergence of constructive postmodernism changed the picture. As Yuehou Qu pointed out in 2001:

> As the influence of constructive postmodernism has increased, the name of David Ray Griffin has increas-ingly become familiar to Chinese academia. The Chinese translation and publication of his books such as the *Reenchantment of Science, Spirituality and Society, Pro-cess Theology*, and *Founders of Constructive Postmodern Philosophy*, etc, has brought a share of fresh air to post-modernism studies in China, and challenged people to realize the integrativeness of postmodernism, which is different from deconstructive postmodernism.[5]

Also, Xiaohua Wang said: "Because of the appearance of *The Reenchantment of Science*, we have realized that it is too indiscreet of us to reject postmodernism since another kind of postmodernism has occurred and showed us a bright future. It is constructive postmodernism."[6]

A research report entitled "Toward Constructive Postmod-ernism" by the Philosophy Institute of the Chinese Academy of Social Sciences, states:

There is a gradual shift of attitude toward postmodernism in Chinese academia from rejection to affirmation
in some sense. Postmodernism shifted its direction from
'critical postmodernism' to 'constructive postmodernism.' It has, therefore, become an important way for
China to learn the trend of philosophical development,
to have direct dialogue with foreign philosophy, and to
pay attention to China's actual issues.[7]

Here are some examples of scholars' comments about constructive postmodernism:

- Before the report, Xinping Zhuo, Director of the Religion
  Institute (of the Chinese Academy of Social Sciences) had
  envisioned the fundamental transition in postmodernism
  from destructiveness to constructiveness, from negative-
  ness to positiveness, from pessimism to optimism, and
  recognizes the contribution by constructive postmodernism in this transition.[8]

- Constructive postmodernism is regarded by Yong Pei, Senior Official at the State Bureau of Religious Affairs, as "a
  very positive and constructive contemporary movement
  with farsighted vision."[9] For Shujin Huang, Director of the
  Philosophy Department of the National Defense University, constructive postmodernism is "a new attitude toward
  the relationship between humans and nature, individuals
  and society, individual and individual."

- To Zhong Chen, Philosophy Professor at Soochow University, "If the human history of ideas is a grand long picture, then the reflection and critique of modernity in the
  past half century is an important page. If the postmodern
  movements and streams such as deconstructive postmodernism and post-colonialism make this picture diverse and colorful, then it is constructive postmodernism
  that provides points of contact. Its emphasis on creative

transformation, organic plurality, the open self, and the common good, makes this picture full of genuine vitality and hope."[10]

- Even a leading scholar in deconstructive postmodernism, Xiaoming Chen, literature Professor at Peking University, has recognized the constructive side of postmodernism. He said: "Now we should focus our attention on more constructive postmodern theory and knowledge. The active presence of Constructive Postmodern theory and postmodern theology in the contemporary West has clearly shown that the postmodern is not against human nature and history. Postmodernism . . . is looking for the spiritual homeland for our time."[11]

- For Yong Xia, "many postmodernists have a positive and constructive side. In some sense, postmodernism aims at breaking the new iron chains the Enlightenment made for us. . . . What postmodernism pursues is a new liberation for humans."[12]

- Many postmodern points of view, especially the emphasis on diversity and plurality, have been accepted quite widely in China. In Yong Pei's words: "As a matter of fact, the Chinese people and China's government have unconsciously applied the postmodern idea."[13]

When we read China's leaders' talks such as Hu Jintao's speech at Yale University in 2006 and Wen Jiabao's in Paris in 2005, we can readily feel the postmodern tone. In his speech at L'Ecole Polytechnique de Paris, December 6, 2005, Wen Jiabao, Premier of China, said: "Cultural plurality is an important feature of human civilization. The cultural plurality in human society is an objective reality like the eco-diversity is in nature."[14] Sharing the same tone, Hu Jintao, President of China, said to Yale students and faculty: "A composer cannot write enchanting melody with one note, and a painter cannot paint a landscape with only one color. The world is a treasure house where the unique cultural achievements created by people of all countries are displayed."[15]

2. **Constructive postmodernism has challenged the Chinese to rethink modernization** by pointing out its negative consequences. Leaders are now talking about a new form of healthy modernization and "Green GDP," which bypasses the worst aspects of Western modernity. Healthy modernization is now understood to be "constructively postmodern" development.

Modernization has been a dream for China for almost one hundred years. After the Great Cultural Revolution, the Chinese government joined those of most developing countries in treating modernization as its goal. China's achievements on its path toward modernization such as its fast GDP growth have amazed the world. However, the price has been extremely high, including: environmental problems, an increasing gap between the rich and the poor, and the loss of faith among its people. Is there any alternative to the current form of modernization?

Constructive postmodern thinking proposes such an alternative. In his article entitled "The Weicheng (Fortress Besieged) of Modernization and Its Transcendence: On the Values Orientation of Constructive Postmodernism and its Inspiration," Kang Ouyang, a leading Marxist scholar in China and Vice president of Huazhong University of Science and Technology, explores the positive and negative sides of modernization. For him, the latter includes treating economic growth as the ultimate goal; neglecting ecology, the value of tradition, and aesthetic wisdom as complements to scientific knowledge; rejection of the positive role that religion can play in human life; and overemphasis on individuality at the expense of community. Constructive postmodernism has been successful in bringing up these issues to prevent us from repeating "the same mistakes the West made."[16]

Today more and more Chinese people are realizing that Westernized modernization is not the only way for China to develop. For Lanxian Xiang, regarding GDP growth as the main goal of a nation without considering social justice and morality is a typically mechanical understanding of development, which is a merely "Western notion."[17] More and more people have realized that China should offer the world "a unique model of development,"[18] and in doing so, China should "open up a new road to modernization," that is, move toward a "pos-modernization," whose aim is "for the common good."[19]

3. **Constructive postmodernism has colored and enriched contemporary Chinese academia by providing alternative views on the many issues with which Chinese intellectuals deal.** In particular, it has opened up discussions of postmodern education, sustainable agriculture, urban design, environmental economics, postmodern law, postmodern freedom, postmodern democracy, and even postmodern diplomacy and party-history studies. When examining the writings on constructive postmodernism and process thought, one can generally divide them into the following eight categories:

(1) *Philosophy:* Some Chinese scholars focus on the theoretical exploration of constructive postmodernism, process philosophy, or Whitehead. These topics are explored in writings such as *On The Third Kind of Metaphysics: A Study of Constructive Postmodern Philosophy* by Weifu Wu; Zhen Han's *The Value of Adventure: My Reading of Whitehead* (2002); Zhihe Wang's "Whitehead as a Postmodern Thinker" (2004); "Interpreting the Constructive Postmodern Notion of Creativity," by Lingling Luo and Song Zhang (2004); "Constructive Postmodern Holism," by Jinmei Chen (2000); "Could David Griffin's

Post-modern Science Be Tenable?" by Xianjing Xiao (2003);
"A Study on the Constructive Postmodernism Thoughts of
David Ray Griffin," by Ping Zhang (2004); "Toward a Postmodern Philosophy of Education: Whiteheadian Process
Philosophy of Education," by Yuehou Qu and Zhihe Wang
(2004); Yonghao Yuan's "Whitehead's Criticism, Correction
and Transcendence of the Traditional Metaphysics" (2005);
Yuehou Qu's "The Hard-Core Doctrines of Process Philosophy
and Its Theological Implication" (2007); and "On Freedom
with Deep Responsibility: Toward a Postmodern Freedom,"
by Zhihe Wang (2008).

(2) *Comparative Studies:* Some scholars are interested in
comparing constructive postmodernism with other systems
of thought, as illustrated by several articles: Linghong Kong's
"Constructive Postmodernism and Zhuang Zi Thought"
(1998); Zhong Cai, "Postmodern Science and Traditional Chinese Scientific Thought" (1999); Xuezhi Zhang's "The Concept of Event in Whitehead and Zhang Dainian" (2004); Lizhi
Wang's "Whitehead and Kant" (2007); Xiuao Tao's "Hegel and
Whitehead" (2007); Guihuan Huo's "Hegel, Marx, and White-
head" (2007); Shaojun Li's "Constructive Postmodernism and
Complexity Studies" *(2004)*; Lizhi Wang's "Process Philoso-
phy and the Dao of the University: A Comparison between
Whitehead's and Confucius' Creativity Principle" (2007);
"Process Psychology and Chinese Taoist Thought," by Ting
Jiao and Fengqiang Gao (2007); Shiping Chen's "Constructive
Postmodernism and Chinese traditional Confucian Values: A
Comparison" (2008); Meijun Fan's "The Notion of Harmony in
Whitehead and Chinese Philosophy" (2007); Zhaoming Dan's
"Labor, Freedom and Process Harmony: Viewing Marx from
Whitehead" (2008); and Wang Kun, "Xie Fuya's Absorption
of Whitehead's Philosophy of Religion: A Comparison with
Whitehead's View of God" (2012).

(3) *Application of Constructive Postmodernism to Social-Political Studies:* This may be the richest and fastest growing field in the constructive postmodern movement in China. Realizing the value of constructive postmodernism, Chinese scholars are trying to apply this new approach or way of thinking to the social-political field in order to solve the various pressing issues facing China. See, for example, "Hegel, Marx and Whitehead: Viewing the Conflicts between Sciences and Humanities from the Basic Transformation of Mode of Thinking in Western Philosophy Embodied by 'Process,'" by Guihuan Huo (a senior researcher of the Chinese Academy of Social Science),[20] and Xiuhua Zhang's "Science and Faith from Constructive Postmodern Perspective" (2005).

The following list of articles can provide readers with a relatively clear impression of this literature:

- "The Inspiration of Constructive Postmodernism for China's Higher Education," by Fei Li (2008).
- "The Inspiration of Constructive Postmodernism for Creating a Harmonious Society," Desheng Bu, Yi Ma, and Xiaohui Liu (2008).
- "The Inspiration of Constructive Postmodernism for Moral Education of Graduate Students," by Wei Zhang (2005).
- "The Inspiration of Constructive Postmodernism for Chinese Medicine," by Yuanzhao Wang (2006)
- "The Relationship between Science and Religion from a Constructive Postmodern Perspective," by Xiong Sun (2003.)
- Yunqiu Gao's "Analyzing the Economic Man from the Perspective of Process Philosophy" (2005).
- "On Constructive Postmodern Reconstruction of Postmodern Education," Jian Feng (2005).
- "Constructive Postmodernism and Chinese Party History Studies," by Chuanliang Shen (2006).

- "Promoting a Constructive Postmodern Culture of Birth," by Mingxing Zeng (2004).
- "Constructive Postmodernism and Chinese Jurisprudence," by Xuebin Liu and Yingjun Ma (2006).
- "Reflect on and Promote the Development of China's Modernization from a Constructive Postmodern Perspective," by Yougang Zhuang (2007).
- Zhihe Wang's "Chinese Constructive Postmodernism and the Construction of Ecological Civilization" (2009).

In addition, *Second Enlightenment,* by Zhihe Wang and Meijun Fan, published by Peking University in 2011, can be regarded as a systematic application and development of constructive postmodernism. Combining Chinese wisdom with process thinking and a constructive postmodern perspective, the authors propose a series of new concepts—such as Democracy with Dao, Science with Dao, Deep Freedom with Responsibility, Postmodern Law with Feeling, and Survival of the Harmonious—and also point out a constructive postmodern type of development with Chinese character. One scholar has said this book is able to "open up a way to chinalize constructive postmodernism."[21]

(4) *Education Reform:* Constructive postmodernism has promoted education reform in China by providing process-oriented experiments in education, developing a process-oriented curriculum, and bringing educators and philosophers together for dialogue.

The current education system in China is in crisis. More and more people have become dissatisfied with test-oriented and value-free education. Constructive postmodern education, based on Whitehead's process education, meets people's needs by offering a fresh, wisdom-oriented perspective. According to Dina Pei, education professor at Beijing Normal University and a leading figure in education reform in China:

"Whitehead's process education, its appreciation for co-creation, its emphasis on difference, and its regarding life as subject of education, have a very inspiring role to play in China's education innovation."[22] She and her colleagues have been applying process insights to China's education innovation. So far, ten Chinese universities, a hundred elementary and middle schools, seven local government education departments, and three educational institutions have joined this program.

Maybe it is not accidental that what Pei has said and done reminds us of another leading education reformer in China. Her name is Xiaoman Zhu, president of the National Central Institute for Education Studies and the head of the National Education Plan Office in China. Zhu, who identifies herself as a Whiteheadian, has, with her colleagues, been promoting curriculum reform in China. In her keynote speech entitled "A Whiteheadian Understanding of China's Curriculum Reform," which was presented at the International Conference on "Process Thinking and Curriculum Reform" in 2007, she emphasized the influence of Whitehead's education on curriculum reform in China. Explaining why Whitehead is so important to China, she said:

> Among all foreign philosophies, Whitehead's process philosophy is the way of thinking that is most convergent with the aim of China's education reform and with deep Chinese tradition. It has strong affinity with Chinese ideas such as organic thought, interrelationship, and concrescence. Also, it stresses harmony and balance. This is a philosophical way of thinking which is very helpful in the wide promotion of China's education reform and in dealing with various conflicts that appear during this process.[23]

Zhu stressed that Whitehead's concepts, such as value, feeling, personal experience, importance, and rhythm, have played a significant part in China's educational reform, after which she explained how these ideas have influenced the new curriculum that she and her colleagues have developed. This is especially noteworthy, because efforts at educational reform in China are now affecting 35 million students, who have used the new curriculum.

(5) *Ecological Civilization:* Constructive postmodernism has enhanced China's environmental movement and helped China begin creating an ecological civilization. As Griffin has argued, constructive postmodernism is ecological in the real sense because it "provides support for the ecology . . . movement."[24] There is, accordingly, an intrinsic connection between constructive postmodernism and the environmental movement in China. According to Yijie Tang, philosophy professor at Peking University and a top scholar in traditional Chinese philosophy and culture, "Process philosophy criticizes binary thinking and views nature and humans as an interrelated bio-community. This idea has important implications for the solution of the ecological crisis facing us today."[25]

This explains why Chinese environmentalists "prefer constructive postmodernism represented by David Griffin,"[26] said Fanren Zeng, former president of Shandong University, who is a founder of eco-aesthetics in China. For Xiujie Wang, Chair of Liaoning Literature Association, who is well known in China as an ecological feminist author: "Constructive postmodernism is the philosophical foundation of ecological literature." To Xiaohua Wang, "the fate of human beings and the whole eco-system will be determined by whether the postmodern turn succeeds."[27]

Among Chinese environmentalists, Sheri Liao has been most successful in putting constructive postmodernism into the practice of environmental protection. With a major in philosophy, Ms. Liao is China's best-known environmental activist and journalist. She founded the Global Village of Beijing in 1996, and has received commendations from the United Nations and the White House. The focus of her work has been on promoting a sense of individual responsibility and empowerment in relation to environmental issues in China.

Over the years, though, she became convinced that a genuine environmental movement in China must have a spiritual foundation that draws upon the intuitive wisdom from the Chinese past. She gradually found that constructive postmodern thinking or process thought can provide a philosophical grounding for the environmental movement. According to Sheri Liao's understanding, the constructive postmodern movement is a reflection on, and a correction of, modern fragmental and hegemonic thinking. "It places emphasis on wholeness, difference and uniqueness, while promoting ecological economy, organic agriculture, natural life cultivation, eco-architecture, spirituality, and simplicity of life—qualities that have sustained Chinese civilization for 5000 years."[28]

These efforts by environmentalists have not been in vain. In 2007, an idea with strong postmodern color was proposed by the Chinese government at the 17th National Congress of the Communist Party of China: "Ecological civilization." This concept reflects an important change in the Party's understanding of development. Rather than emphasizing economic construction as the core of development, as it did in the past, the Party authorities have come to realize that development, if sustainable, must entail a list of elements that includes the right relationship between humanity and nature.

Such a concept did not develop in a vacuum: constructive postmodernism has played a significant role. To be sure, many people with various points of view have been working in this direction. But a clear, intrinsic connection between constructive postmodernism and these social changes can be seen.

For example, Yue Pan, Vice-minister of China's Environment Department, wrote an essay entitled "On Socialist Ecological Civilization," in which he said: "Socialist Ecological Civilization is a critical absorption of environmentalism, eco-ethics and postmodernism." Likewise, Huibin Li, an official scholar of the Central Bureau of Compilation and Translation—a leading think tank of the Chinese government, said: "If ecological civilization is a civilization after industrialization and postmodern means after modern, then ecological civilization and postmodern civilization originally should be the same topic."[29] Li quoted John Cobb's lecture at the first International Forum on Ecological Civilization, in which he said: "Facing the ecological crisis, we need new wisdom. Marxist tradition may help stop the negative consequences of modernization in China." Li then said:

> In a sense, it is just this speech by Dr. Cobb that inspired our research on 'Marxism and Ecological Civilization.' After this speech was translated and published in Issue 2 of *Marxism and Reality*, it evoked widespread interest from Chinese readers and researchers. Ecological damage on China's way toward modernization has reached a very serious point, which has seriously influenced people's basic living condition. The Chinese Communist Party and Government have already made this issue a top priority.... The 17th National Congress of the Communist Party of China proposed 'ecological civilization.' In his political report, Hu Jintao regards 'ecological civilization' as a new goal of China.[30]

In addition, six international forums on Ecological Civilization we cosponsored in Claremont with the Central Bureau have further promoted and enriched the studies on ecological civilization. Shinan Fang's 2009 article, entitled "Constructive Postmodern Theory of Ecological Civilization in the West," has showed the influence. (Professor Fang is vice dean of Marxism School at Soochow University and the head of the expert consultant committee of the Soochow Government.)

(6) *Postmodern Agriculture:* Constructive postmodernism has helped promote postmodern agriculture in China. In Griffin's edited volume *Spirituality and Society: Postmodern Visions* (translated 1998, reprinted 2005 and 2011), there is a chapter on postmodern agriculture contributed by Dean Freudenberger. I suspect that neither Griffin nor Freudenberger expected this seed—the idea of postmodern agriculture—to grow in China. But it did. After a few conferences on postmodern agriculture were held, a paper entitled "China Should Develop Postmodern Agriculture," by Dean Freudenberger and his son David Freudenberger, was published by four Chinese journals, after which in 2009 it was republished (fully) in China's leading digest of publications, *Xinhua Digest.* Next year, a Chinese congressman stood up at an important meeting to propose that China should explore postmodern agriculture rather than modern industrialized agriculture. His arguments came exclusively from Freudenberger's chapter in Griffin's volume.

Now as a different voice and an alternative to modern agriculture, postmodern agriculture—that is, constructive postmodern agriculture in Chinese context—has begun to attract more and more Chinese scholars' interest. In an article entitled "Development Trend of World Agriculture and China's Postmodern Agriculture Development: A Suggestion," Wang Lingxiang and Sun Jinfu wrote that China, to make the best use of the advantages and bypass the disadvantages, should promote "the sustainable development of agriculture and rural-urban integration by developing postmodern agriculture."[31]

Some Chinese agronomists argue that "modernization is not the only way for farmers to eat well, to have books to read, and to be able to afford to see the doctor. . . . A postmodern ecological agriculture will be a better choice."[32]

Although some scholars criticize postmodern agriculture, saying it does not provide perfect solutions to remove the drawbacks of modern agriculture,[33] other scholars argue that postmodern agriculture indicates "the new direction of modern agriculture."[34] For Some Marxist scholars, "Postmodern agriculture is a new train of thought for building a socialist New Countryside."[35] Zhou Shu, a professor, even says: "For China, postmodern agriculture is the only way out of the predicament caused by imitating the western agriculture model."[36] The Taigu Conference on postmodern agriculture held in 2008 showed that many participating scholars and government officials were convinced that "postmodern agriculture is possible."[37] Since then, three conferences named "Constructive Postmodern Agriculture" have been held, and more and more Chinese people have shown interest in this unique approach and tried to apply it in practice. In a recent article published in the Journal of the Party School of the Central Committee of the C.P.C (the Party's top venue for training senior Party and government officials), the author states that "Chinese agriculture must make a shift" and "walk a postmodern agriculture road with Chinese characters."[38]

(7) *Reclaiming Ancient Traditions:* Constructive postmodernism has encouraged the Chinese to revalue their traditions and attempt to recover those aspects that will build a socially just, ecologically sustainable, and spiritually satisfying green China.

Beginning in 1919 with the May Fourth movement, which can be called "China's first enlightenment," China's ancient tradition was treated as something to be completely abandoned. "Down with Confucianism" was the most famous slogan of that time. The Chinese abandoned the spiritual resources of their tradition such as: respect for heaven, awe of the Dao, and "harmony with difference." We are now struggling to reclaim these traditions. Lacking any faith or sense of the divine, people easily worship the secular. That explains why scientism and worship of money are so popular today in China, as well as in the West.

However, constructive postmodernism helps the Chinese find the value and charm within their past because of its respectful attitude toward tradition.[39] This partly explains why the Chinese people would like to embrace postmodernism in its constructive rather than its deconstructive form. In a speech at Claremont, Kang Ouyang said:

> As a Chinese scholar, I especially noted that many constructive postmodernists are very friendly to Chinese people and Chinese culture. The Center for Process Studies has set a good example in this regard. Many postmodernists stress the importance of Chinese culture in overcoming modern problems and try to find enlightenment from traditional Chinese culture. This will certainly stimulate Chinese scholars to study their own traditional culture, to discover other possible resources, and to enlarge its influence in the further development of world culture.[40]

Today more and more people have realized the important role religion can play in promoting a harmonious society and an ecological civilization. In the words of Ye Xiaowen, chief of the State Administration for Religious Affairs of China: "Religion is a positive, valuable force in building a harmonious society."[41] Pan Yue says:

> From the Taoist view of the Tao reflecting nature, to the Confucian idea of humans and nature becoming one, to the Buddhist belief that all living things are equal, Chinese religion has helped our culture to survive for

thousands of years. Chinese religion can be a powerful weapon in preventing an environmental crisis and building a peaceful harmonious society.[42]

Inspired by constructive postmodernism, Dedong Wei, a researcher of the Chinese Academy of Social Sciences, expressed a convergence between constructive postmodernism and Buddhism, saying: "Buddhism is postmodern in the real sense. It is very possible and realistic for Chinese to cherish, study, and highlight the excellent elements in the Buddhist ecological outlook in order to avoid the detour of modernization."[43]

(8) *A Renaissance of Whitehead and Process Thinking:* Closely related to the resurgence of Chinese tradition, constructive postmodernism has stimulated a Renaissance of Whitehead and process studies in China. The study of Whitehead in China can be dated back to the 1930s. At that time, many leading Chinese philosophers were enthusiastic about Whitehead's way of thinking. Unfortunately, this encounter did not result in a long-lasting friendship, because the Sino-Japanese War and the war between the Communist Party and the Nationalist Party made struggle-thinking dominant and brought an end to Whitehead studies.

However, the emergence of constructive postmodernism in China in 1995 stimulated a new enthusiasm for Whitehead and process thought, thereby beginning a Renaissance of Whitehead and process studies in China. This is reflected not only in the fact that all of Whitehead's philosophy books have been translated and published in China. (There are even three different translations of *Process and Reality.*)

In addition, more and more Chinese writings on Whitehead came out in the past 15 years. A study conducted by Prof. Hengfu Wen and Li Yang shows the interest in Whitehead in China has rapidly increased in the past 15 years. When they input "Whitehead" into the "Reading Index," they found that

374 books are matched. Finding 29 additional books through other channels, they found that there are altogether 403 books dealing with Whitehead.

| Year | 1920-1950 | 1951-1960 | 1961-1970 | 1971-1980 | 1981-1990 | 1990-2000 | 2001-2010 | Total |
|------|-----------|-----------|-----------|-----------|-----------|-----------|-----------|-------|
| Toal | 9 | 2 | 9 | 13 | 71 | 119 | 180 | 403 |
| Percent | 2.2 | 0.5 | 2.2 | 3.2 | 17.6 | 29.5 | 44.8 | |

*Table 1: 403 Books Spread over 90 Years*

They also found 321 research papers on Whitehead.[44]

| Time period | 1920-1951 | 1951-1960 | 1961-1970 | 1971-1980 | 1981-1990 | 1991-2000 | 2001-2010 | |
|-------------|-----------|-----------|-----------|-----------|-----------|-----------|-----------|---|
| Total | 15 | 6 | 4 | 3 | 12 | 26 | 255 | 321 |
| Percent | 4.7 | 1.9 | 1.3 | 0.9 | 3.7 | 8.1 | 79.4 | |

*Table 2: 321 Research Papers over a Period of Time*

These two tables clearly show the growth of interest in Whitehead in China, with most of the growth coming after the publication of *The Reenchantment of Science* and other books in the SUNY Series in Constructive Thought.

Moreover, a journal was inaugurated called *China Process Studies*, which includes articles by Chinese as well as non-Chinese process scholars. Additionally, 22 centers for constructive postmodernism and process studies have been established in China, with foci ranging from postmodern philosophy, psychology, education, and religion, to science and values, sustainable urbanization, business ethics, theology, and ecology. Also, 60 international conferences have been held in China and in Claremont, 7 Summer Academies have taken place, and 30 Chinese visiting scholars have come to Claremont to study Whitehead and constructive postmodernism.

People have often asked: Why has constructive postmodernism been so well received in China today? An answer involves at least six factors:

- Constructive postmodernism meets the needs of China for fresh ideas and new alternatives to the modern development model.
- There are intrinsic affinities between constructive postmodernism and Chinese tradition.
- The emphasis on social responsibility by constructive postmodern thinkers resonates with the social concerns of Chinese intellectuals.
- "The most distinguishing feature of constructive postmodernism [according to one philosophy professor] is its character of practice, namely applying theory to practice."[45]
- The social and ecological concerns of constructive postmodernists resonate deeply with a Chinese intellectual commitment to "be the first to feel concern about the state affairs and the last to enjoy yourself."
- Zhihe Wang refers to character as "the backbone and morality of constructive postmodern thinkers."[46]

Although constructive postmodernism has become a fairly big movement in China, it must be admitted that constructive postmodernism is not yet mainstream in China. As Yong Pei pointed out, "the voice of constructive postmodernism is still not loud enough." Actualizing postmodernization in China is still "a huge undertaking."[47] The two major obstacles to its growth are linear thinking and worship of science.

1. Deeply influenced by the Hegelian-Marxist linear view of history, many people still believe that history must inevitably follow a linear model: namely, premodern, modern, and postmodern. They believe that China must become modern

before becoming postmodern, not realizing that postmodernism can be a contemporary alternative to unhealthy modernization, so that there can be a direct shift from the premodern to the postmodern.

2. Worship of science or scientism is still very powerful in China. For example, Nanyuan Zhao, Professor at Tsinghai University, argued against constructive postmodernism, saying: "Postmodern science is a pseudoscience through and through." For him, the ecological call to "revere nature" is unscientific.[48]

These obstacles are quite serious challenges. Chinese constructive postmodern thinkers must work very hard to overcome them if the movement is to continue to grow.

But this growth is the best hope for China and, ultimately, for a world that will inevitably be affected by China. As Griffin once stressed, "Only if China and India (as well as America) soon start to make the postmodern turn does our planet have hope."[48]

# PART THREE

# Responses and Reflections

# 15. Responses

## David Ray Griffin

I am keenly aware that I have been very fortunate: Only a relatively small number of thinkers have had symposiums of fellow thinkers presenting critiques of various dimension of their writings. Before beginning to engage these critiques, I want to express my deep gratitude to all of the colleagues who have written these critiques—which I have chosen to discuss individually.

### RESPONSE TO CATHERINE KELLER

It was appropriate for Catherine Keller to be asked to write about my writings on God and evil, because while still a graduate student in Claremont she took a class from me on this subject. It was during this class that I first realized that she is brighter than I. In the meantime, she has written with clarity and profundity about a range of issues, including the relation between God and evil (as exemplified especially in *The Face of the Deep and God and Power).*

Given the fact that, in addition, Keller has been "a member of [the] impassioned emancipatory collectivity," as she put it here, I especially appreciate her endorsement of a metaphysical—not a purely moral—argument for the claim that the universe supports goodness and justice.

*God and Gawd:* To introduce the central issue of theology, Keller uses the "ditty" in MacLeish's *J.B.*, "If God is God He is not good/If God is good He is not God."

Although one might think that MacLeish was making light of the problem, he actually, according to the E-Notes introduction, wrote this play as his response "to the horrors he saw during two world wars, including the Holocaust and the bombings of Hiroshima and Nagasaki." Using the Bible as a framework for this response, MacLeish explained, is sensible "when you are dealing with questions too large for you which, nevertheless, will not leave you alone."[1]

While agreeing that this is a sensible approach for a person such as MacLeish with dramatic and poetic talents, I would myself suggest a slight rewording. A staunch defender of traditional theism, I was told, once asked someone during a public discussion: "Are you talking about *Gawd*, or merely God?"[2] Appropriating this terminology, I would revise MacLeish's ditty to say: "If God is Gawd, God is not good/If God is good, God is not Gawd."

*The Necessity of Theodicy:* In any case, Keller has suggested that process theodicy is the linchpin of my "entire constructive postmodern theology." Whether it should be seen as *the* linchpin or one of several such pins, it is certainly central and essential: I agree with Keller that theology as such needs a rational theodicy to keep "the wheel of theism itself from falling off ... the cart of intellectual credibility."

It is unfortunate that, as Keller says, most recent types of progressive theology have suggested otherwise. Indeed, this has been true of most of the types of liberal theology over the past hundred years or so. One day during my 1965-66 year in Germany, I went to Tübingen for a discussion evening with Friedrich Gogarten, who had become well known in the 1930s as one of the leaders (with Karl Barth) of the "dialectical theology" movement. Something Gogarten said led me to ask: Did he deny that theologians need to explain why the existence of overwhelming evil does not contradict the existence of

God? Gogarten asked: "Do you mean apologetics?" When I replied affirmatively, he exclaimed: "Apologetics! The source of all atheism!"

*Mystery—Natural and Artificial:* Having expressed my agreement with almost everything in Keller's essay, let me point out that one of her statements about me is misleading. She said: "DG is no friend of 'mystery,' which he does not distinguish from the mystification that acquiesces in contradiction." *Au contraire.* For example, in discussing H.D. Lewis's treatment of the mind-body problem, I wrote:

> [Lewis] fails to distinguish between natural and artificial mysteries. The world is full of *natural* mysteries, such as how our universe began, how evolution proceeded . . . , and how spiders know how to spin their webs. These may be permanent mysteries, to which human beings will never know the answers. They are different in kind, however, from *artificial* mysteries, which are created purely by human conceptions or definitions. The traditional problem of evil, for example, is created purely by the human idea that the creator of our universe is not only perfectly good but also all-powerful, in the literal sense of essentially possessing all the power. The modern mind-body problem, likewise, is created by the conception of the physical world, including our physical bodies, as comprised of 'matter,' the ultimate units of which are devoid of experience and spontaneity. The fact that many natural mysteries may permanently exceed our capacities for understanding is no excuse for resting content with insoluble mysteries of the artificial type.[3]

Believing that there is a very long list of genuine mysteries, I simply cannot understand how a philosopher could say: "Human consciousness is just about the last surviving mystery."[4]

When I make negative comments about "mystery," I mean the artificial type, or the type that, as I have put it, "should be called 'Contradiction.'"[5] To criticize these is fully compatible with seeing divinity as extremely mysterious. For example, in an essay of 1941—which was long after he had developed his doctrines of the primordial and consequent natures of God—Whitehead wrote:

> Of course we are unable to conceive the experience of the Supreme Unity of Existence.... The various attempts at description are often shocking and profane. What does haunt our imagination is that the immediate facts of present action pass into permanent significance for the Universe.[6]

## RESPONSE TO GARY DORRIEN

While I was listening to Gary Dorrien's lecture at the conference, I was very impressed—so much so that, if I were still a professor, I would have given the paper an A⁺. My response was likely influenced by the fact that Dorrien has a very engaging presentation style—which, after all, should be expected of the Reinhold Niebuhr Professor of Social Ethics at Union Theological Seminary.[7]

However, needing to write a response, I realized that there are three points with which I would take issue—one of which is relatively unimportant.

*Whitehead or Hartshorne:* To begin with the least important point: Referring to the fact that I have discussed several issues on which Whitehead and Hartshorne had different views, Dorrien said: "Griffin usually sides with Hartshorne when there is a difference." This assessment surprised me, as I have never thought this about myself. I describe myself, for example, as a "Whiteheadian," never a "Hartshornean." When the issue has arisen, I have referred to myself as a "Hartshornean

Whiteheadian," but never as a "Whiteheadian Hartshornean."[8] This fits with the fact that, in my view, Hartshorne was a very good philosopher, but Whitehead was a genius—albeit a genius who, like all geniuses, had some blind spots and made some errors.

The most important issue on which Whitehead made a philosophical error, in my view, was his reference to God as a single actual entity. This is the main issue on which I have agreed with Hartshorne, who said that, to avoid making God an exception to Whiteheadian metaphysical principles, God must be characterized as a "living person" (meaning an everlasting personally ordered society of divine occasions of experience).

But this is not contrary to my thinking of God as having a "primordial nature," through which God leads the world with a "vision of truth, beauty, and goodness."[9] My treatment of evolution, for example, depends on siding with Whitehead on this issue. With regard to the "divine dipolarity," this means that I hold a "double dipolarity"—as Dorrien rightly says— which affirms not only the dipolarity associated primarily with Hartshorne (God as having both an abstract essence and concrete states), but also the primordial-consequent distinction associated primarily with Whitehead.

With regard to the other six of seven differences discussed in my 1973 article to which Dorrien refers,[10] I also do not clearly endorse Hartshorne's position against Whitehead's on any of the others, and on three of them (eternal possibilities, secondary qualities, and perishing), I endorse Whitehead's view against Hartshorne's.

*Foundationalism:* I also disagree—to move to a more important issue—with Dorrien's characterization of my position, by virtue of its acceptance of hard-core commonsense notions, as "foundationalist." He says, in fact, that I "make an aggressively foundationalist claim." Dorrien's claim here is important, because foundationalism is now considered discredited by almost all philosophers, including me: In the introduction to the final chapter of *Reenchantment without Supernaturalism*, I wrote: "I explain how the appeal to hard-core commonsense notions avoids relativistic historicism without returning to foundationalism."[11]

In appealing to "hard-core common sense," I thereby distinguish it from the way in which "common sense" has come to be widely used, that is, to refer to ideas that have become widely accepted at a certain time and place. These can be called "soft-core commonsense ideas," because they do not have the characteristics of hard-core commonsense ideas, namely, ones that are (1) inevitably presupposed in practice, therefore (2) common to all human beings at the presuppositional level, and (3) cannot be denied verbally without self-contradiction.[12]

These hard-core commonsense notions provide a universal criterion for philosophy. "[T]he metaphysical rule of evidence," said Whitehead, is "that we must bow to those presumptions, which, in despite of criticism, we still employ for the regulation of our lives."[13] Hartshorne, calling this the "pragmatic principle," said: "[W]hat we have to be guided by in our decision-making, we should not pretend to reject theoretically."[14]

Dorrien takes issue with at least some of the ideas I have included, saying, for example: "Immanuel Kant was notoriously perplexed about causality, freedom, [and] time." But Dorrien thereby misses the central feature of hard-core commonsense ideas: They do not necessarily involve people's explicit beliefs, about which philosophers may debate, but are, instead, "those presumptions, which, in despite of criticism, we still employ for the regulation of our lives."

In any case, Dorrien says that the endorsement of a universal criterion for philosophy makes me (along with Whitehead and Hartshorne) a foundationalist. But whether I exemplify or reject foundationalism depends entirely on the meaning of "foundationalism." In explaining why this term should not be used for my position, I wrote:

Foundationalism is the epistemological view (1) that a system of beliefs is distinguishable into basic and nonbasic beliefs, (2) that basic beliefs are known immediately to be true, (3) that in a rational system basic beliefs form the starting points, from which all nonbasic beliefs must be derived, and (4) that the relation between basic and nonbasic beliefs is an entirely one-way relation, with basic beliefs supporting, without in any way being supported by, nonbasic beliefs.[15]

According to foundationalism, I added: "A rational system of beliefs is assumed to be like a building, in which the super-structure is supported by a solid foundation. As Thomas Reid put it, 'that all knowledge got by reasoning must be built on first principles . . . is as certain as that every house must have a foundation.'"[16]

"[A]s distinct from Reid's philosophy, which has been called 'common-sense foundationalism,'"[17] I continued, my view says: "One does not begin with [hard-core common-sense ideas], then try to infer all other ideas from them. The philosophical enterprise is more like a journey than a building. We start wherever we happen to be. The set of hard-core commonsense notions serves not as a foundation but as a compass, letting us know when we have gotten off course."[18]

Accordingly, I "reject half of the defining principles of foundationalism (namely, the third and fourth principles)."[19] Given this background, I added a paragraph that applies directly to Dorrien's charge. Pointing out that foundationalism as originally understood can be called "foundationalism$_{om}$," (with "om" standing for "original meaning"), "one could redefine foundationalism so that it includes any position that affirms universally valid criteria—which we could call foundationalism$_{UC}$ (for 'universal criteria')." However, given the fact that foundationalism$_{om}$ came into disrepute because of its third and fourth features, why should one use the term "foundationalism"—with its odious connotations—for a position that has only the first two features? But yet this is what Dorrien does, saying:

> I fail to see how [Griffin's advocacy of a universal criterion] is not a type of foundationalism, even if it is not the type that builds a house on distinct first principles. Certainly, there is a meaningful difference between saying, as Thomas Reid did, that every house needs a foundation, and saying, as Griffin does, that thinking must begin wherever we happen to be. But to say that commonsense universalism is the only worthwhile way to do philosophy is to make an aggressively foundationalist claim.

One caveat: I have never suggested that "commonsense universalism is the only worthwhile way to do philosophy." I have merely said that any philosophy, whatever its approach, will be better to the extent that it avoids, in Whitehead's words, "negations of what in practice is presupposed."[20]

In any case, the main point is that, while explicitly recognizing that I reject the third and fourth characteristics of foundationalism, Dorrien nevertheless says that I make a "foundationalist claim," even "aggressively."

To make my point in different words: To use foundationalism$_{UC}$ as a charge, one would need to explain why any position that advocates a universal criterion is *ipso facto* bad. It seems to me, however, that the only reason that could be given for this evaluation would be the claim that there are

not, in fact, any notions that are universally presupposed—
and this would beg the question.

3. *A Highly Ramified Holy Reality?* I disagree, finally, with
Dorrien's treatment of my criticism of Alvin Plantinga's claim
that his belief in God can rightfully be regarded as "properly
basic"—that is, as rational even though it is not based on
evidence. Such a belief can be considered basic, Plantinga
says, just as we are rational to believe in the reality of the
past, the external world, and freedom, without any evidence
for these beliefs.

I do hold that the belief in a very generalized notion of
divinity, understood simply as the belief in a holy reality, can
arguably be considered basic, insofar as it can plausibly be
argued that everyone in fact—in spite of perhaps verbally denying any and all doctrines of divine realities—presupposes
that there is something about life or the universe that is holy,
something that is *felt* to be of ultimate intrinsic value, which
gives a derivative sense of value to other things.

However, Plantinga wants to regard as basic his belief in a
highly ramified doctrine of deity—"God as conceived in traditional Christianity, Judaism, and Islam: an almighty, all-know-
ing wholly good and loving person who has created the world
and presently upholds it in being."[21] This doctrinal belief is not
at all analogous to our beliefs in the past and the external world.

Dorrien does not disagree with my criticism of Plantinga.
But he suggests that the same criticism applies to my own
position. He begins by saying: "The sense of a Holy Reality
is," according to Griffin, "properly basic to human experience;
thus, a generic form of the Holy Reality experienced by people
from various traditions would be, and is, universal." That is
fine. But then Dorrien mixes this generic form with a very
different view, saying:

Griffin's early version of this claim described God as the supreme, nonderivative, Holy Power that is alone worthy of worship and ultimate concern; the purposive creator of the world, perfectly good, and source of moral norms; and the ultimate guarantee of life's meaning and hope of ultimate victory of good over evil." Dorrien then says: "I fail to see how this is not a quite specific God . . . a specific version of belief in a Holy Reality. "

But that is because this discussion, which occurred elsewhere, was not a statement about a holy reality in a generic sense, but about biblical theism in particular.

*Conclusion:* Gary Dorrien is a master interpreter of other people's thought, as I know from his interpretation of my thought in *The Making of American Liberal Theology: Crisis, Irony, and Postmodernity,* 1950-2005.[22] His accuracy is demonstrated by the fact that, in his essay for the present volume, I could find only three issues with which to take issue.

RESPONSE TO DANIEL DOMBROWSKI

I wish to begin my response to Dan Dombrowski by expressing amazement at the fact that, although he had not previously written about the philosophy of mind, he wrote for this symposium an essay surpassing in clarity and profundity the work of many philosophers who have spent virtually all of their careers on the mind-body problem.[23]

Part of the value of Dombrowski's essay is due to the unique approach he took, dealing with my book in the context of not only the current discussion but also the "perennial" tradition rooted primarily in Plato. He emphasized, therefore, that although the Whiteheadian position I articulated is new (at least in the sense that it had been almost completely ignored in mainstream philosophy), it is also old (although it was always a subdominant motif, even in Plato himself, whose passages suggesting a panexperientialist approach were outweighed by ones supporting dualism).

*A Family Quarrel:* In relation to the recent discussion, Dombrowski emphasizes the fact that, by taking a panexperientialist position, one can see that the long-standing debate between dualists and materialists is a "family quarrel." This is the case because both of them accept the Cartesian view that the "matter" composing the human body is, like all other "matter," devoid of characteristics that would prevent it from being completely different from our own experience: Although some dualists and materialists now regard the components of matter as active, rather than inert, they usually do not speak of them as *self*-moving, and they certainly insist that they have no experience. That is the belief that makes the "mind-body problem" a *problem*.

*Panexperientialism in Analytic Philosophy:* Rather recently, Dombrowski points out, some philosophers in the analytic tradition have been moving in a panexperientialist direction (while still using the term "panpsychism"). The first of these was Thomas Nagel, who included a chapter entitled "Panpsychism" in a 1979 book.[24]

David Chalmers began moving toward panexperientialism in his 1995 essay, "Facing Up to the Problem of Consciousness,"[25] which has attracted considerable attention (sometimes under the title "The Hard Problem of Consciousness"). Given the fact that the conference for which *Unsnarling the World-Knot* had been written occurred in 1994 (although the book was not published until 1998), Chalmers and I had evidently written our works at about the same time. Since that time, the interest in panexperientialist (panpsychist) approaches has grown, thanks significantly to Chalmers, who has published three books and over 20 papers on this issue.

Galen Strawson—whose first book on this topic, *Mental Reality*, appeared in 1994—was treated (next to Whitehead himself) as the hero of my book. Two years later, a special issue of the *Journal of Consciousness Studies* was devoted to discussions of Strawson's article "Realistic Monism: Why Physicalism Entails Panpsychism."[26] This symposium was then turned into a book, *Consciousness and Its Place in Nature*.[27]

William Seager attended our 1994 conference. A year later, he published an essay entitled "Consciousness, Information, and Panpsychism,"[28] then published several more articles in the following decade.[29] Most important for our purposes is his latest essay, "Whitehead and the Revival (?) of Panpsychism." Pointing out that mainline philosophers have ignored Whitehead's metaphysics, Seager "suggest[s] in the face of the evident difficulty of the problem of consciousness and the apparent convergence of several lines of argument towards some of Whitehead's most fundamental ideas, that it is time to have a serious look at Whitehead's approach to the mind-matter problem."[30]

Finally, although Thomas Nagel in his earlier-mentioned discussion of panpsychism did not refer to either Whitehead or Hartshorne, he mentions them both in his 2012 book, *Mind and Cosmos*.[31] Having referred in a footnote to Galen Strawson's *Consciousness and Its Place in Nature*, Nagel describes as an "acute and historically informed discussion" Hartshorne's "Physics and Psychics: The Place of Mind in Nature" (which was in the book that Cobb and I edited from the Center for Process Studies' first conference[32]). With regard to Whitehead, Nagel says: "Whitehead argued that to identify the abstractions of physics with the whole of reality was to commit the fallacy of misplaced concreteness, and that concrete entities, all the way down to the level of electrons, should all be understood as somehow embodying a standpoint on the world."[33] Nagel sees that a fully naturalistic worldview requires some version of panpsychism, according to which "organisms with mental life are not miraculous anomalies but an integral part of nature."[34]

*Panexperientialism v. Panpsychism:* Finally, besides putting my book in the context of other authors sympathetic to pan-experientialism, Dombrowski also points out that "Griffin's view is not panconsciousness, but panexperientialism"—a term that is less likely than "panpsychism" to be understood to imply that all things are conscious. Although some philosophers friendly to panexperientialism have considered this change of terminology unhelpful, even thinking that retaining the older term will help people recognize "the distinctiveness of process philosophy within, and therefore by means of, the broader category of panpsychism,"[35] I still affirm the reasons I gave for preferring "panexperientialism" in the 1977 publication in which I coined the term.

Noting that Whitehead himself "never uses the term 'panpsychism,'" I suggested probable reasons for his avoiding it: "He uses the term 'soul' (the translation of 'psyche') only for the series of dominant or presiding occasions in the higher vertebrates. There are hence three differentiating characteristics implied by his use of the term 'psyche' which make it inapplicable even to all individuals. A psyche is a series of (1) very high-grade occasions which (2) are dominant occasions in an orqanism and (3) are ordered into a personally ordered society."[36] This suggestion fits with the report that Whitehead avoided the term "panpsychism" because he saw it as implying the all-pervasiveness of consciousness.[37]

In recent years, incidentally, the term "panexperientialism" has become more widely used. For example, in a book entitled *A Place for Consciousness,* analytic philosopher Gregg Rosenberg says he has "a panexperientialist view very reminiscent of the sort proposed by Whitehead, in which the fundamental entities are processes composed of internally linked, experiential events."[38] And an entire issue of the *Journal of Consciousness Exploration & Research* was devoted to the writings on panexperientialism by Gregory Nixon.[39] Finally, there is now even a website entitled "Panexperientialism."[40]

*Conclusion:* I wish to conclude by thanking Dombrowski for quoting an important passage in Whitehead's *Concept of Nature*—"The mutual structural relations between events are both spatial and temporal. If you think of them as merely spatial you are omitting the temporal element, and if you think of them as merely temporal you are omitting the spatial element. Thus when you think of space alone, or of time alone, you are dealing in abstractions"[41]—which I wish I had had in mind while writing my book.

## RESPONSE TO JOHN COBB

John Cobb and I have written some things together, and we have together organized a few conferences on evolution. It is not surprising, therefore, that there is not much in his essay with which I would take issue.

*Lynn Margulis, Neo-Darwinism, Experience, and Platonic Realism:* One of the many things on which we agree is that, while accepting an evolutionary view of life, we do not accept the neo-Darwinian interpretation of it. Our confidence in this rejection was recently strengthened by developing a friendship, which began at a 2003 conference organized by Cobb, with Lynn Margulis. A longtime opponent of neo-Darwinism, Margulis especially rejected its view that (1) evolutionary novelty comes about exclusively by means of natural selection of random mutations, which entails that (2) evolutionary change always comes about gradually. These were two of the core doctrines of neo-Darwinism I discussed in my contributions to Cobb's *Back to Darwin*.[42]

Our friendship was aided by the fact that, besides sharing our rejection of neo-Darwinism, Margulis—who had also
been a long-time opponent of theism—was surprised to learn
about what she called our "science-friendly philosophical
outlook," in which "[t]ruth, especially scientifically/empiri-
cally established truth, seemed intrinsic to [our] Christianity."
My point here is that our theism proved to be no barrier to
our friendship and cooperation; what had made her seem so
hostile to religious people and ideas was "the usual authori-
ty-pleasing consensus."[43]

Having only recently formed our friendship and cooperation, it was with great sadness that John and I learned (in
November 2011) that Lynn had suddenly died. Having also
become friends with her son Dorion Sagan, who had likewise
come to the conference, we were asked by him to write an
essay for a book he was editing on her life and legacy.[44] It was
only in writing my part of this essay that I became aware of
the bearing of her thought on the topic with which my response to Dombrowski ended: panexperientialism.

I learned of her emphatic assertion that awareness (she
said "consciousness") goes all the way down, at least to prokaryotic cells. She affirmed "the perceptive capacity of all live
beings"[45] and that "consciousness is a property of all living
cells," even the most elementary ones: "Bacteria are conscious.
These bacterial beings have been around since the origin of
life."[46] With allusion to the way in which this perspective can
dissolve the mind-body problem, Margulis said: "Thought
and behavior in people are rendered far less mysterious when
we realize that choice and sensitivity are already exquisitely
developed in the microbial cells that became our ancestors."[47]

Her support for this point of view is very valuable, given
the fact that, after her central claim—that the eukaryotic cell
is a *composite individual* resulting from a symbiotic union of

primitive prokaryotic cells[48]—had long been ridiculed, it came to be seen as "one of the great achievements of twentieth-century evolutionary biology" (Richard Dawkins), even "probably the grandest idea in modern biology" (Niles Eldredge).[49] Due partly to this achievement, she became regarded as "one of the great living American scientists" (Lee Smolin), as "one of the heroes of twentieth-century biology" (Daniel Dennett).[50]

One of my great regrets is that I had not talked to Margulis about this issue. I would have wanted to ask her whether she would affirm experience all the way down, below living cells.

Also, I wish I had been more conversant with her argument that most evolutionary novelty comes about through symbiogenesis.[51] Had I been aware of this, I may have not felt the need—in order to account for the apparent evolutionary facts—for the rather strong form version of Platonic realism I had suggested.

In any case, Lynn Margulis has provided us powerful support against neo-Darwinism and the mechanistic interpretation of science more generally.

Additional support has recently been provided in Thomas Nagel's aforementioned book, *Mind and Cosmos*, which is subtitled: *Why the Materialist Neo-Darwinian Conception of Nature Is Almost Certainly False*. Whereas objections of Margulis were primarily empirical, Nagel's objections are mainly philosophical. Materialistic neo-Darwinism, Nagel argues, cannot explain ourselves as human beings: our consciousness, our rationality), and our values (moral realism). Arguing similarly to my appeal to hard-core common sense, Nagel says—against neo-Darwinism's "heroic triumph of ideological theory over common sense"[52]—that we need "a way of understanding ourselves that is not radically self-undermining."[53]

*Purpose, Truth as Correspondence, and Hard-Core Common Sense:* In discussing various ways in which thinkers who endorse religious and/or moral ideas have responded to the unfriendly worldview provided by modern science, Cobb points out that I try to identify ideas that are based more on questionable metaphysics than on empirical evidence.

The most effective way, I have suggested, is often to show various doctrines to involve "performative self-contradictions," in which the doctrine contradicts the act of stating it. Whitehead himself used this approach with regard to the idea that our bodily behavior is to be explained in purely mechanistic terms, not in terms of purposes. He wrote: "Scientists animated by the purpose of proving that they are purposeless constitute an interesting subject for study."[54] Whitehead thereby illustrated the fact that the denial of hard-core commonsense ideas, such as human freedom and purposive behaviour, presupposes their reality.

Taking notice of hard-core commonsense ideas can also be used against an approach to avoiding conflicts between scientific and religious-or-moral notions that, as Cobb comments, is not helpful. This approach involves the claim that "truth" does not mean "correspondence with reality." On that basis, one cannot criticize various moral or religious notions, such as freedom or divine influence, by pointing out that the scientific worldview has no room for such notions. If scientific doctrines are not meant to correspond to reality—to state the way things really are—then these notions do not threaten moral and religious notions—which are also not meant to correspond with reality. I reject this approach because, I argue, the idea that truth *means* "correspondence to reality" is one of our hard-core commonsense ideas.

I have illustrated this fact by quoting Richard Rorty, who rejected the intuition that "some nonlinguistic state of the world . . . makes a belief true by 'corresponding' to it."[54] Rorty admitted that we have this intuition, but urged us to "do our best to *stop having* it."[56] Rorty himself, however, was not able to do so. For example, having advocated the Romantic view that truth is *made* rather than *found*, he admitted that it was difficult for him "to avoid hinting that this suggestion gets something right, that my sort of philosophy corresponds to the way things really are."[57] Rorty illustrated the self-contradiction by referring to "what was true in the Romantic idea that truth is made rather than found."[58]

Gary Dorrien, in response to the fact that I have included "truth as correspondence to reality" among the hard-core commonsense ideas, said that "the correspondence theory of truth is widely disputed." The question, however, is not whether it is disputed, but whether, as Rorty illustrated, it is always presupposed, even in the act of denying it.

Cobb says that I (rightly) consider the "yielding of authority to scientific experts as a mistake." Like Cobb, I generally accept the authority of experts on theories "that stay close to the scientific evidence." But when they do not, I feel free to challenge them, most definitely when a theory contradicts one of our hard-core commonsense presumptions.

*Darwin v. Neo-Darwinism:* I obviously failed to make clear to Cobb my reasons for objecting to "Back to Darwin" as the proposed title of his book. He evidently believed that I objected to this title because it ignored "aspects of Darwin's beliefs and assumptions that the book as a whole rejected" and that I in particular "had gone to the trouble of pointing out." Cobb even thought he owed me an apology! But I merely thought that the title was an unwise choice because Darwin endorsed supernaturalistic deism, and this fact had recently been emphasized in a book of that title, *Back to Darwin,* the subtitle for which was *The Scientific Case for Deistic Evolution.*[59] I was especially aware of this book because its author, Michael Corey, had written his dissertation under my supervision, and I even—although I, of course, did not agree with his position—suggested the title.

Cobb is certainly correct that his title draws attention to a major way in which neo-Darwinism differs from Darwin's own approach, because the neo-Darwinian "constriction" (as William Provine characterizes it) limits the source of evolutionary change to natural selection and random mutations, whereas Darwin himself had a more pluralistic view. But because Corey's book already existed and, in any case, the phrase "Back to Darwin" could easily suggest a return to Darwin's omnipotent (albeit deistic) creator—who had arranged all the details of the evolutionary process in advance[60]—I would have chosen a different title.

Nevertheless, Cobb's title served to draw attention to the important distinction between neo-Darwinism and Darwin himself, which is often blurred. For example, in *Darwin's Dangerous Idea*, Daniel Dennett described this idea as the notion "that Design can emerge from mere Order via an algorithmic process that makes no use of pre-existing Mind." Whereas John Locke thought design inconceivable without Mind, claimed Dennett, Darwin's idea "that evolution is a mindless, purposeless, algorithmic process" allowed him "to overthrow Locke's Mind-first vision."[61] In a few passages, however, Dennett admitted that Darwin himself, being a deist, believed in divine design as the basis of the laws of nature behind the evolutionary process.[62] Darwin had, therefore, a "Mind-first vision." A more honest title for Dennett's book would have been *Neo-Darwinism's Dangerous Idea*—but this title, of course, would not have sold as well.

## RESPONSE TO PHILIP CLAYTON

I had very much hoped that Philip Clayton would participate in this symposium, but I feared that he would be too busy—

besides being a professor, he is the dean of the Claremont
School of Theology and the provost of Claremont Lincoln
University. So I was very pleased that he managed to work it
in. As he indicated, during our one year of overlap—his first
year in Claremont and my last—we became good friends, with
weekly discussions in the late hours of the evening, during
which we discussed a wide variety of topics. Our discussions
were great fun, because we discussed everything—from God,
the mind-body relation, and evolution to 9/11—with good
humor and no holds barred. The present exchange reflects that
same approach. I have organized my response in terms of his
five questions (plus one more, which I discuss only in a note[63]).

*Are Science/Religion Walls Lowered by Griffin's "Naturalism"?*
Asking whether "Griffin's use of 'naturalism' really lower[s]
the walls of division between religion and science," Clayton
suggests that it would not. I have explained how it *would* if
the needed changes occur in both the religious and scientific
communities.

On the one hand, religious thought must not violate what
has long been a basic scientific conviction: that interruptions
of the world's most fundamental causal principles are impossible. This means the acceptance of naturalism in the sense
of the rejection of supernaturalism, according to which there
is a supreme being with the power to interrupt the world's
cause-effect relations. An example of supernaturalism is provided by ultra-conservative theologian Millard Erickson, who
says that his religious community "operates with a definite supernaturalism—God resides outside the world and intervenes
periodically within the natural processes through miracles."[64]

The rejection of such supernaturalism is *generic* naturalism,
the form of naturalism that all more specific types of
naturalism have in common. Naturalism in this generic sense
I call *non-supernatural naturalism* (abbreviated *naturalism$_{ns}$*),

by which I mean "naturalism" that affirms nothing other than the denial of supernaturalism.

On the other hand, conflict between science and religion will be created if the scientific community construes an atheistic-materialistic version of generic naturalism, thereby making religion impossible.

Therefore, there will never be harmony between science and religion unless these two conditions—the religious community not presupposing supernaturalism, and the scientific community not presupposing an atheistic-materialistic naturalism—are fulfilled. Although these two conditions may not be *sufficient* for harmony, they *are* necessary. I do not understand why Clayton thinks that naturalism in this twofold sense would not be helpful.

*Does Griffin Have a Naturalistic Methodology?* Stating that I do not employ "a 'naturalistic' methodology" as employed in physics, chemistry, or biology, Clayton points out that I do not deal with the question of whether religious practices are "adaptive" (in the Darwinian sense). That is correct. I do not claim to adopt any such "naturalistic methodology" (except in the sense that supernatural interruptions are ruled out). In endorsing naturalism, I am dealing only with *ontology* or *worldview* (not methodology). For example, in the first chapter of my *Religion and Scientific Naturalism*, I wrote that unless discussions of the relation of science and religion can "contribute to overcoming the perceived conflicts between the worldview presupposed by the scientific community and that presupposed by the religious communities, they are largely irrelevant. One reason I wrote this book was to try to drive home this point—that the overriding issue is that of *worldview*."[65]

In viewing the issue this way, I am following Whitehead, who wrote that philosophy "attains its chief importance by fusing the two, namely, religion and science, into one rational scheme of thought."[66] This means, I added, that harmony between science and religion can be achieved only *"by integrating them into a philosophical worldview."*[67]

This is all I have advocated with regard to naturalism. Surely to use "naturalism" in this sense does not imply that I must be a naturalist in other possible senses of the term.

*Trying to Redefine "Naturalism"?* If it is agreed that harmony between religion and science means that the religious community must, like the scientific community, presuppose generic naturalism and hence naturalism$_{ns}$, the next question is whether there is a more specific type of naturalism$_{ns}$ that, if adopted by the scientific community, would prevent conflict. I have already mentioned that it would need to reject an atheistic-materialistic type of naturalism. Getting more precise, I have suggested that anti-religious naturalism has usually involved three dimensions: a *sensationist* doctrine of perception, an *atheistic* view of the universe, and a *materialist* view of human beings—which I have abbreviated *naturalism$_{sam}$.*

Most fully compatible with religion, I have suggested, would be a type of naturalism that, being the opposite of naturalism$_{sam}$, could be called *naturalism$_{ppp}$,* meaning a *prehensive* doctrine of perception (which involves nonsensory perception), a *panentheistic* view of the universe, and a *panexperientialist* view of the world and hence human beings. (Of course, if naturalism$_{ppp}$ is accepted by the scientific community, this will not be because it is compatible with religion, but only because it comes to be seen as good for science itself.)

Clayton, speaking of "dangers in attempting to redefine previously existing terms," believes that I have done this "with the term naturalism," because "most philosophers who use the term [do not] mean to include views that are 'prehensive, panentheistic, and panexperientialist'—if anything, they mean to *exclude* such views!"

That is, of course, true.[68] But I do *not* redefine "naturalism" to mean a prehensive-panentheistic-panexperientialist worldview. Rather, I suggest that the generic meaning of "naturalism"—at least with regard to worldview questions—is naturalism$_{ns}$. However, because most recent thinkers who have called themselves "naturalists" have, while presupposing the rejection of supernaturalism, given naturalism a sensationist-atheistic-materialistic gloss, it is often forgotten that this is a specific type of naturalism$_{ns}$. It is still possible, however, to distinguish generic naturalism from the specific type of it that is currently fashionable.

As an example of generic naturalism, philosopher Sterling Lamprecht said, in a 1944 essay entitled "Naturalism and Religion," that naturalism sees the world as "an interrelated whole without intrusions from some other 'realm.'"[69] Exemplars of naturalism in this generic sense include, of course, Whitehead, as shown—in the same volume, entitled *Naturalism and the Human Spirit*—by John Hermann Randall, who referred to Whitehead as "one of the pioneers of contemporary naturalism."[70] Likewise, James Bissett Pratt, in a 1939 book entitled simply *Naturalism*, also referred to Whitehead as expressing a naturalist worldview.[71]

Accordingly, there is nothing unprecedented about my use of "naturalism." Virtually everyone agrees that naturalism rules out supernatural interruptions of the world's normal processes. For example, William Drees, in his 1996 book, *Religion, Science and Naturalism*, says that naturalism rejects the belief "that God intervenes occasionally in the natural world."[72] Then, once it is realized that this is the generic meaning of "naturalism," we would expect at least two species. I have proposed that naturalism$_{sam}$ could be replaced by naturalism$_{ppp}$.

*Do Chinese Intellectuals Accept This "Naturalism"?* In light of the fact that some of my books have become well known in academic circles in China, Clayton asks whether I "understand 'naturalism' to mean the same thing as the many Chinese scholars and leaders who use the term?" I believe that what lies behind this question is Clayton's mistaken belief that I have defined "naturalism" in terms of a prehensive-panentheist-panexperientialist worldview. Given the fact that by "naturalism" (in the generic sense) I mean the rejection of supernaturalism, most Chinese intellectuals and I are clearly on the same page.

*Too Negative toward Mainline Science?* Clayton suggests that I, in advocating naturalism, have been guilty of equivocation, so that I should drop this term. This would mean that I would be left with *sam* and *ppp,* and this would entail "a battle to the death," because "*sam* and *ppp* share virtually no common ground." Again, the problem envisaged by Clayton is of his own making: A sensationist-atheistic-materialist worldview has, of course, nothing in common with a prehensive-panentheist-panexperiential worldview. But there is common ground between naturalism$_{sam}$ and naturalism$_{ppp}$ because they share their rejection of supernaturalism.

Having eliminated this common ground, so that only opposition remains, Clayton is "disappoint[ed] . . . that the stance of process thinkers toward the mainline science of our day . . . is so consistently negative." But insofar as this is true, it is not surprising, given the fact that the Center for Process Studies was created to formulate, in various fields, an alternative to what Clayton himself calls "the dehumanizing reductionism that rules scientific circles." Given the fact that "the mainline science of our day" in virtually all fields— from evolutionary theory to physiological psychology—is materialistic, reductionistic, and ultimately nihilistic, the Center's very *raison d'être* is to present a reasoned alternative. (Our science conferences, however, do not consist of denunciations of mainline science. Rather, they consist of conversations, aimed at trying to nudge scientists to pursue facts that could lead to more positive conclusions.)

Clayton admits that the Center "has generally found some allies from within the sciences on each topic that has been studied." But this statement makes it sound as if these positive relationships were with minor people, whereas the reality is that we have had very positive relationships—both personal and professional—with major thinkers in various fields, such as biology (Theodosius Dobzhansky, William Thorpe, C.H. Waddington, Sewall Wright, Lynn Margulis), chemistry (Ilya Prigogine), and physics (David Bohm, Reginald Cahill, B.J. Hiley, Henry Stapp).

Continuing his call for the Center to be less oppositional toward mainline thinking, Clayton says: "Prophets challenge norms and push back against the establishment. But they usually do this by making contact with that establishment and speaking to it in effective ways." He then seeks to illustrate this point with my *God, Power, and Evil.* "That book had such a significant impact," Clayton said, "because it spoke to Christians and Jews whose assumptions had led them to an unanswerable problem of evil. Its more adequate model of God allowed them to solve inconsistencies in their own position while remaining Christian or Jewish in thought and practice. *The genius of the book is that it made contact.*" But insofar as that is true, it was because the book made contact with *people,* not with mainline theologians who endorse some version of traditional theism. My approach to those theologies—those of Augustine, Luther, Calvin, Barth, Hick—was almost entirely negative.

From my perspective, process thinking has been most effective with issues on which we have been simply prophetic, making contact *with people,* some of whom are scientists, by expressing a clear alternative to mainstream orthodoxy, not only in theodicy but also in feminism, economics, religious pluralism, and (especially in China) constructive postmodernism.

I see no reason, therefore, to soften my two-fold approach on the question of overall worldview: complete agreement with mainstream thinkers on naturalism (vs. supernaturalism), complete opposition to the *ppp-type* of naturalism.

## RESPONSE TO SANDRA LUBARSKY

*Cobb and Hick on Religious Pluralism:* The conference from which *Deep Religious Pluralism* was created—which was organized in honor of Marjorie Suchocki—focused on John Cobb's position on religious pluralism, showing its superiority to the best-known type of religious pluralism. I was pleased that John, after seeing my two introductory essays for the conference, said that I had articulated his position better than he himself had done. I can now say that Sandra Lubarsky, putting these two essays in the context of other writings of mine, has articulated my position better than I myself had done.

Lubarsky says that my work has "done much to raise the profile of the pivotal work of John Cobb, and . . . to save genuine religious pluralism from a premature end." Insofar as that is true, the same can be said for Paul Knitter, who edited a book of Cobb's essays on religious pluralism,[73] providing a much fuller explanation and defense of the position he had first laid out in *Beyond Dialogue*.[74]

Religious pluralism needed to be saved "from a premature end," Lubarsky points out, because it had become equated with an "identist pluralism," according to which all the religions "affirm the same ultimate reality and the same final goal." As a result, religious pluralism came to be seen as not "really pluralistic at all" and as leading to a "debilitating relativism."

Given the fact that identist pluralism had been most influentially articulated by John Hick, my chapters for *Deep Religious Pluralism* took the form of (a) explaining how Cobb's version of religious pluralism differs from Hick's and, therefore, (b) why Cobb's version does not have the consequences that were threatening to lead religious pluralism to a premature end.

Lubarsky points out that "the urge to find common ground between [religions]"—to see them all as oriented toward the same ultimate—"seems irrepressible." I have illustrated this urge (in a long footnote in *Deep Religious Pluralism*) with one of our best theologians, David Tracy. In spite of Cobb's argument that the biblical God and Buddhist Emptiness are (very) different ultimates, Tracy insisted that there can be only one ultimate reality, so that what Buddhists call "Emptiness" must be the same reality that Christians call "God."[75] As a Christian, Tracy realized that this equation is very threatening. Given his commitment to liberation theology and his faith in God as the one by whom "hope is granted" for "acts of resistance to the status quo,"[76] Tracy found trying to think of ultimate reality as emptiness, as simply another name for God, to be "a deeply disorienting matter." It led him to experience, in fact, "the full terror of otherness."[77] This psychic disorientation experienced by Tracy was due entirely to the fact that he, like Hick, could not relinquish the metaphysical assumption that there can be only one ultimate reality.

Most interesting on this issue is the report by Gene Reeves (see his essay) that P.C. Chang, according to Eleanor Roosevelt, said that "there is more than one kind of ultimate reality."

*Naturalism:* Turning to what Lubarsky calls my "unique contribution," she focuses on my treatment of "naturalism," especially the question of how scientific naturalism is related to religious naturalism, which is a precondition for religious pluralism.

Central to this treatment, Lubarsky correctly emphasizes, is my effort (against great resistance) to get people to understand that scientific naturalism in the *generic* sense, and hence naturalism *as such*, is simply the doctrine that, contrary to supernaturalism, there is no being that can violate the normal causal processes of the world. Insofar as there was a "battle between science and religion" in the 18th and 19th centuries, it was oriented around the battle about naturalism in this sense.

In the English-speaking world, this battle was essentially won in the middle of the 19th century (it had been won earlier in France), significantly through the work of Charles Darwin. His great predecessor, Charles Lyell, had become famous for espousing "uniformitarianism," according to which nature had always followed the same physical laws followed today. And yet Lyell made an exception for the human mind, saying that "the moral and intellectual faculties of the human race [have been added] to a system of nature which had gone on for millions of years without the intervention of any analogous cause." This suggestion meant, Lyell added, that we must "assume a primeval creative power which does not act with uniformity."[78]

However, being unable to tolerate this exception, Darwin wrote: "If I were convinced that I required such additions to the theory of natural selection, I would reject it as rubbish. . . . I would give nothing for the theory of Natural Selection, if it requires miraculous additions at any one stage of descent."[79] Richard Dawkins commented: "This is no petty matter. In Darwin's view, the whole *point* of the theory of evolution by natural selection was that it provided a *non*-miraculous account of the existence of complex adaptations."[80]

So, this is what the battle for scientific naturalism—for a consistent uniformitarianism—was about. There is nothing inherent to this naturalism that dictates that perception must be limited to *sensory* perception: For thousands of years, human beings have held that we can also get information in non-sensory ways.

There is, likewise, nothing inherent to scientific naturalism entailing that there could not be, beyond all the finite existents constituting the universe, an inclusive whole that can influence its' parts—as long as this influence is part of, rather than an occasional exception to, the normal processes of the universe.

Finally, there is nothing inherent to scientific naturalism that dictates that the fundamental constituents of the world must be understood as material in Descartes' sense, according to which it is devoid of experience and spontaneity.

This seems elementary: Naturalism arose as a rejection of supernatural interruptions of the world's normal processes. Therefore, "naturalism" in the generic sense should be understood to be limited to the rejection of supernatural interruptions. This can be understood, in Lubarsky's helpful term, as "non-supernatural naturalism," meaning naturalism limited to the rejection of supernaturalism (which is what I had called "naturalism$_{ns}$").

Given this generic meaning, there can then be more specific types of naturalism, some of which might accept sensationism, atheism, and materialism (which I have abbreviated "naturalism$_{sam}$"), and others of which might reject them.

And yet most philosophers of science have thus far assumed sensationist-atheist-materialist naturalism to be the one and only valid meaning for "naturalism." Most of them evidently accept this view simply because this is the kind of naturalism into which they had been socialized. Insofar as some of them offer a defense, it is that this has been the dominant way naturalism has been understood, so it would be confusing—perhaps a misuse of words—to use the term in a different way (such as naturalism$_{ns}$).

If they are social liberals, these philosophers would likely heap scorn on the claim that, because marriage has traditionally been "between a man and a woman," the word "marriage" cannot be used for a union of two people of the same sex. But they will use the same kind of argument to defend the view that "naturalism" means (1) not only a rejection of supernatural interruptions (2) but also the three-fold doctrine that there is no perception except through the physical senses, there is no divine influence in the world, and the world is composed entirely of entities devoid of experience.

Insofar as even philosophers of religion and theologians accept this definition, they force people into a dilemma: If they reject naturalism, they thereby affirm supernaturalism, which brings with it an anti-science stance and an insuperable problem of evil. But if they, to avoid these problems, affirm naturalism, they have thereby ruled out the possibility of religious experience and even a divine reality.[81]

But this dilemma has been created by an artificial definition of naturalism. An increasing number of people since the 18th century have held a religious worldview compatible with science's rejection of miraculous interruptions of the world's normal causal processes. The dilemma—one must affirm a materialist, non-religious worldview, or one must reject science's most basic principle—is entirely artificial. I have been trying to get religious people not to fall for the definition that has created this. I am thankful to Lubarsky for adding "non-supernatural naturalism" to the arsenal.

*The Ecology in which Religions Evolve:* I will close with gratitude for her statement that God is "part of the ecology in which religions evolve," implying that, just as we have come to understand our lives as living in "the ecology," meaning the total complex of elements and forces—such as the atmosphere, sunlight, and rain—on which our individual lives and our societies are entirely dependent, we should see ourselves as within an even more inclusive ecology—the one in whom we as religions and cultures, as well as individuals, "live, move, and have our being."

Evidently many theists—especially Protestant Christians, now that "faith" has come to be widely understood as belief—do not think of God as shaping their religious lives, except perhaps occasionally in response to prayer. Much less do they think of God as shaping Christianity. Still less do they think of Judaism, Islam, Hinduism, Buddhism, Confucianism, and other religious traditions as living within, and thereby being shaped by, God. Religious pluralists, Lubarsky points out, should think in these "ecological" terms.

## RESPONSE TO NANCY FRANKENBERRY

I wish to begin my response to Nancy Frankenberry by congratulating her on coming up with such a clever title for her essay. Beyond that, I wish to thank her for her appreciative assessment of my work on giving reasonable theism a hearing. My task, however, is to respond to her critique of my treatment of religious experience. Although she raises many issues, I will respond in terms of the five issues that seem most central.

*Is God "Given"?* Frankenberry asked "what [Griffin] means by 'givenness' when he writes that God is given to experience." It is true that, if I had said this, it would imply that my position is similar to Alvin Plantinga's, as discussed in my response to Dorrien—except that I would consider the process deity, rather than the deity of traditional theism, as *given*.

However, Frankenberry was evidently misled by my criticism of Samuel Preus's claim that academic students of religion should explain the existence of religion on the assumption that "God is not given." In saying this, Preus meant the academic study of religion should operate in terms of a "naturalistic paradigm," understood to mean "an altogether nonreligious point of view." In being critical of Preus's claim, therefore, I was not saying that "God *is* given." I was merely arguing that the academic study of religion need not be carried out from "an altogether nonreligious point of view." It would be at least equally valid, I have suggested, to assume that all human communities have had religion because of a universal awareness of a holy reality.

*Is Anything "Given" to Experience?* Even after this clarification, Frankenberry would be critical of my view that an awareness of a Holy Reality is given, because she has evidently accepted the view that *nothing* is given: Expressing her acceptance of Wilfrid Sellars' critique of what he called "the myth of the given," she referred to this as "the mistaken idea that some object of experience can be given independently of concepts and beliefs." I, however, consider this idea only partially mistaken. To explain why will require a somewhat technical discussion of Whitehead's epistemology—in particular, his "reformed subjectivist principle."

Whitehead accepted the view that our conscious experience is *largely* constructed. He, in fact, praised Kant as "the great philosopher who first, fully and explicitly, introduced into philosophy the conception of an act of experience as a constructive functioning."[82] Whitehead rejected, however, the view that nothing at all is given to a moment of experience, so that it is *wholly* constructed. Rather, he said that each moment of experience is an act "of self-production arising out of some primary given phase."[83] The importance of this insistence was stated by Whitehead's Harvard colleague C.I. Lewis, who wrote: "If there be no datum given to the mind, then knowledge must be contentless and arbitrary; there would be nothing which it must be true to."[84]

Whitehead's insistence on givenness is the *reformed* part of the "reformed subjectivist principle." The subjectivist principle as such is the *subjectivist bias* of modern philosophy, according to which actualities that are "subjects enjoying conscious experiences provide the primary data for philosophy." The subjectivist principle thus understood was considered by Whitehead to be "the greatest philosophical discovery since the age of Plato and Aristotle."[85] But modern philosophy's subjectivist bias led much of it to faulty philosophy, because it accepted a solipsistic version of subjectivism, according to which "the datum in the act of experience can be adequately analysed purely in terms of universals."[86] To accept this view implies that our experience includes no experience of other actualities, which in turn implies that we have no experiential knowledge of the existence of actual things beyond ourselves.

Needed to overcome this faulty interpretation of experience is Whitehead's *reformed* subjectivist principle, which involves the "doctrine of the objectification of one actual occasion in the experience of another actual occasion."[87]

Now for the difference between my Whiteheadian position and the claim that a given is a "myth": Sellars, as I wrote in *Reenchantment without Supernaturalism*, "argued cogently that sensory data are *constructed* by the perceiver, not passively received." Whitehead said the same. But to move from that point of agreement to the conclusion that, in Wayne Proudfoot's words, "[w]e have no access to any uninterpreted given,"[88] would follow, I wrote, "only on the assumption that sensory perception is our primary mode of perception." Proudfoot's conclusion, moreover, would be self-stultifying, because he "is intending to tell us how experience really works, thereby presupposing that he [has] some direct access to it, but his account implies that no one has such access, that we can only give interpretations of interpretations."[89]

In explaining how a moment of experience begins with a pre-interpreted given, Whitehead says that sensory perception, which he calls "perception in the mode of symbolic reference," is constructed out of two prior modes of perception: "perception in the mode of causal efficacy," which involves the perception of other actualities (which are *given* to the mind, from beyond itself), followed by "perception in the mode of presentational immediacy," the data of which do not point beyond the present experience. The data of presentational immediacy, which arise only in a later phase of a moment of experience,[90] are "data"—that is, *given* elements—not in the sense of being given to the occasion of experience from beyond itself, but only in the sense of being given to perception in the mode of presentational immediacy *by the prior functioning of that occasion* of experience itself."[91]

Consciousness, moreover, tends to light up the data of presentational immediacy while leaving the data of presensory perception in the mode of causal efficacy largely in the dark.[92] Whitehead fully agrees, accordingly, that the prominent data of *sensory* perception are constructed by—not given to—a moment of experience. But this fact is fully consistent with the insight that the data of sensory perception are constructed *out of data that are given from beyond* itself to the primary phase of an occasion of experience.

The data of perception in the mode of causal efficacy include God and other human psyches. Just as our prehensions of other human psyches may occasionally rise to consciousness, leading us to speak of telepathy, our prehensions of God may occasionally arise to consciousness, leading to an awareness of a Holy Reality.

*The Distinction between Experience and Interpretation*: In rejecting "strong constructivism"—according to which experience is interpretation all the way down—in favor of a weaker form, Frankenberry says: "We do not need to elide the distinction between experience and interpretation. . . . Yet we cannot say just how we should preserve and account for such a distinction." Whitehead's doctrine, according to which each moment of experience is an act "of self-production arising out of some primary given phase,"[93] explains how we can preserve the distinction.

*From "Religious Experience" to "Experiences Deemed Religious":* Recommending the "attribution" theory of Ann Taves, Frankenberry suggests that I should replace my account of "religious experience" with Taves's reference to "experiences deemed religious." If I understand Taves correctly, however, her proposal is similar to that of Wayne Proudfoot, according to which no experiences are inherently religious. William James believed religion to be rooted in a *sense*, which is distinct from thoughts. Proudfoot, however, insisted that "what James refers to as a sense is actually a thought that carries conviction."[94] This correction of James, in Proudfoot's view, illustrates the fact that "the distinguishing mark of religious experience is the subject's belief that the experience can only be accounted for in religious terms."[95] Unless I have misunderstood, Taves's idea of "experiences deemed religious" is not essentially different—that is, it is the deeming that makes an experience religious.

If so, I could not consider her suggestion, according to which religious experience is built up out of "special" experiences, adequate. Certainly specialness is a necessary condition of experiences we would classify as religious. But it is not sufficient.

*Truth as Correspondence:* In Frankenberry's "word about truth," she says that she and I diverge because she "follow[s] Donald Davidson . . . by adopting a semantic conception of truth and distinguishing truth from the epistemic task of justification." Frankenberry thereby evidently understands me to have described truth in terms of epistemology. However, my chapter on truth in RWS was based largely on the views of William Alston, who "opposed all *epistemic* conceptions of truth" and said, simply, that a statement "is true if and only if what the statement says to be the case actually is the case."[96]

While speaking against the "correspondence theory of truth," Frankenberry acknowledges that I, rather than defining truth in terms of a correspondence *theory* of truth, simply speak of "truth as correspondence." However, she says: "Many of us don't have much use for the notion of truth as correspondence.... One can have truth without correspondence." But she does not explain how this would be possible. Frankenberry, moreover, presupposes the notion of truth as correspondence on every page of her essay. Take this statement: "Gary Dorrien has depicted theological liberalism as a third way, rationally and experientially, between 'authority-based orthodoxies,' on the one hand, and 'secular disbelief,' on the other hand." What could it mean to say that this statement is true, but not in the sense that it corresponds to what Dorrien has depicted?

Perhaps recognizing that she cannot really have truth without correspondence, Frankenberry then adds: "Griffin can keep the notion of truth as correspondence in the harmless sense of correspondence in which we say that true sentences correspond to the world." But why should this be called "harmless," given the fact that this notion has been rejected by many recent philosophers, such as Richard Rorty, who rejected the idea that "some nonlinguistic state of the world ... 'makes a belief true' by 'corresponding' to it"?[97]

Why call the insistence on truth as correspondence harmless, given the fact that, over the past century, philosophers of many different stripes have tried to replace the notion of truth as correspondence with some epistemic notion of truth, such as the idea that a true proposition is one that promotes human affairs, has pragmatic usefulness, coheres with other propositions, has warranted assertability, or is good to steer by? As Paul Horwich has said in his book *Truth*, all such definitions have been problematic because "they don't accommodate the 'correspondence' intuition."[98]

These epistemic definitions of truth have recently been rejected by Donald Davidson, who has observed that the main "complaint against correspondence theories is not sound [because] it depends on assuming that some form of epistemic theory is correct."[99]

Davidson also observed that the motivation to debunk truth arose from the long-time tendency to represent truth "as something grander than it is," or as having "powers it does not have."[100] However, truth should be understood not as something grand but merely, as Horwich has said, as a "common-sense notion"—namely, that "truth is a kind of 'correspondence with the facts.'"[101]

Consider also Harvard's Hilary Putnam, who was partly responsible (when he held an anti-realist, epistemic theory of truth) for Rorty's rejection of truth. Later affirming a "common-sense realism," Putnam took issue with Rorty's claim that "certain commonplace notions about representation—in particular, 'the whole idea that our words and thoughts sometimes do and sometimes do not "agree with" or "correspond to" or "represent" a reality outside themselves'—ought to be rejected as entirely empty."[102]

Finally, Frankenberry graciously concluded her essay by calling it "excellent advice, as Whitehead wrote, 'to bow to those presumptions which, in despite of criticism, we still employ for the regulation of our lives.' I am deeply grateful to David Griffin for bringing this pragmatic theme to the foreground of our attention." She evidently did not notice, however, that I include "truth as correspondence" as one of those presumptions. In the first sentence of my section, "The Notion of Truth as Correspondence," I said: "It belongs to our hard-core commonsense notions, I have suggested, that to say that a proposition is true is to say that it corresponds to the reality to which it refers."[103]

In short, as far as I can see, Frankenberry has no good grounds for rejecting or even belittling the notion of truth as correspondence. However, I thank her for taking my work seriously enough to provide a vigorous response.

## RESPONSE TO MARC FORD AND JOHN BUCHANAN

I am responding to Marc Ford and John Buchanan together, because there is some overlap between their essays (with Ford dealing with parapsychology in general and Buchanan focusing on life after death in particular).

*Parapsychology and a Whiteheadian Century:* Ford suggests that Whitehead's capacity to integrate parapsychology—which is sometimes called "paranormal science"—with "normal science" might contribute to making this a Whiteheadian century. That might seem far-fetched. But there are people who believe that this integration would be comparable in importance to the integration of quantum and relativity physics.

For example, the Center for Process Studies' first conference, which took place at the Rockefeller Foundation's conference center in Bellagio (Italy), was on evolution. During a break, Arthur Koestler told John Cobb and me: "It will be great if Whitehead's philosophy can show how to integrate the evidence accepted by the orthodox position with all the evidence that does not fit. But if you can show how Whitehead can unify parapsychology with the rest of science, then you would really have something!"[104]

*The Widespread Dismissal of Parapsychological Interaction as Impossible:* As Ford said, psi phenomena are "typically dismissed by philosophers and other well-educated people as simply impossible." John Buchanan likewise commented on the "outright denial of the possibility" of the existence of psychical phenomena, adding that "the root of the problem of getting a fair hearing for parapsychological evidence" is the idea that the alleged phenomena are "impossible."

Ford quotes, for example, a philosopher who says that these alleged types of interaction are impossible, because "our bodies are the *only ones* with which our minds can count on having a [causal] relationship."

Of course, to say that "such-and-such interactions are impossible" means: Given *our present dominant understanding, they could not occur.* But if the these phenomena are well-attested, it would make sense to muse: *Perhaps our present dominant understanding is false.* But that is seldom done. Most philosophers simply continue to repeat, decade after decade: *Such things are impossible.*

That dismissal might be rational, if parapsychological phenomena were the only putative interaction that philosophers have been unable to understand. But, as both Ford and Buchanan have pointed out, there is a long list of things that there is no way to understand, *given the present dominant understanding,* including:

- Various questions about the relation between our minds and our brains, such as: How can physical changes in our brain cause us to see colors? How can decisions in our minds produce changes in our brains and hence our larger bodies? How can psychosomatic illness occur?
- Various questions about epistemology, given the accepted view of perception, such as: On what basis can the employment of the principles of causation and induction be

justified? (In Whitehead's words, although Hume showed that, given the accepted view of perception, there is no justification for induction, philosophers of science have been content "to base it upon our vague instinct that of course it is all right."[105]) How do we justify speaking about time, the past, and even the external world (beyond our minds)? How could we possibly know the existence of ethical norms, mathematical objects, and logical principles?

However, while continuing to presuppose all of these things on the basis of "the vague instinct that of course it is all right," they single out putative parapsychological phenomena to reject because they are "impossible." The irrationality of this practice demonstrates the wisdom of Ford's suggestion: If some studies (such as the ones by clearly "respectable" people he mentioned) were to convince the scientific and philosophical communities that (a) paranormal interactions must be accepted, that (b) they could be integrated with "normal" science only if the latter's principles of causation and perception were revised, and that (c) Whitehead has provided the best way to do this, then we might indeed have a "Whiteheadian century."

*The Possibility of Psi, the Impossibility of Precognition:* My main attempt to show how Whitehead's philosophy could bring about this unification was in my 1993 essay, "Parapsychology and Philosophy: A Whiteheadian Postmodern Perspective" (which was long available only in a rather obscure journal, but is now available online).[106]

I devoted considerable time in this essay to the question of how Whitehead's philosophy can explain the possibility of the three main types of parapsychological phenomena, often simply called "psi":

- *Receptive* psi (including telepathy, clairvoyance, and retrocognition);

- *Expressive psi* (including psychokinesis, levitation, and psychic photography);
- Out-of-body experiences and life after death.

Most discussions include precognition a fourth type. As Ford points out, however, I reject this alleged type, "almost completely on philosophical grounds." This rejection has been the source of the main criticism I have received from members of the parapsychological community. Critics say, in Ford's words: "Griffin's denial of literal precognition for philosophical reasons is no different from [other philosophers'] denial of telepathy on philosophical grounds." But *"in fact it is quite different,"* Ford points out, citing Anthony Flew. Rejecting ESP as well as precognition, Flew put it this way: ESP is "just plumb impossible"—merely *contingently* impossible—whereas literal precognition is *logically* impossible, because it would mean that a person knows an event before it happened, and this would mean that an effect (the knowledge) had come before the cause (the event). We can rightly disagree with Flew's judgment that ESP is (contingently) impossible, but he was absolutely right that denying the possibility of precognition is *different in kind* from denying the possibility of ESP.

However, although Flew was correct to say that "[n]o amount of empirical evidence can turn nonsense into sense," there has been *an enormous amount* of empirical evidence that has seemed to many people to show the reality of precognition. Rather than simply pointing out that it is impossible, therefore, it is important to show that there are alternative interpretations of the evidence. In "Parapsychology and Philosophy," therefore, I provided 13 alternative interpretations of *spontaneous* events that have been taken to be precognitive.[107]

In any case, I endorse the view, held by J.B. Rhine among others, that parapsychology is a *potentially revolutionary* science,[108] but by virtue of rejecting true precognition, I reject the idea that it is *ultra*-revolutionary, because it does not undermine the very notions of time and efficient causation. As psychoanalyst Jule Eisenbud said: "The radical assumptions about time that have been suggested to account for 'precognitive' phenomena are irreconcilable on all fronts with all other correspondences known to science."[109]

*Life after Death:* Buchanan's discussion of my treatment of life after death, it seems to me, is excellent. I was interested to learn that writing his study of the various types of evidence moved him from agnosticism to the view that survival is the "most plausible hypothesis." I think that this would be the response of most intellectuals if they, not being absolutely certain that this would be impossible, were actually to look at the evidence.

## RESPONSE TO GENE REEVES

Gene Reeves has done a remarkable job of providing an overview of my ideas about morality and ethics drawn from various essays of mine here and there.

*The Centrality of Morality:* As Reeves indicates, my writings about these issues have been more central to my thought than would appear from my bibliography. Much of my work in the 1990s was for an intended book on global democracy, chapter titles of which included "Moral Commitment," "The War System," "Global Imperialism," "Human Rights," "Subsistence Rights and Global Apartheid," "The Trajectory Toward Ecological Collapse," and "From Global Plutocracy to Global Democracy." The 9/11 attacks sidetracked me from this book. But had it appeared, the centrality of morality to my thinking would have been more obvious.

Another indication of this centrality is the fact that the original manuscript for *Reenchantment without Supernaturalism* concluded with Chapter 8, "Religion, Morality, and Civilization."

But my manuscript was being written for a series of books dealing with various types of philosophy of religion, and every book, I learned, had to cover the same topics, so I added the ninth and tenth chapters. Later, having learned that an enormous price was to be put on my book, I withdrew it from that series (and had it instead published by Cornell University Press). But I retained those final two chapters because, besides enjoying writing them, I decided they were pretty good. But without them, the book's structure would have indicated more clearly that Chapters 1-7 were meant to lead up to the discussion of morality in the final chapter.

*Theism: Minimal and Whiteheadian:* Reeves rightly says that theism is central to my ethical position. But his treatment of my "minimal theism," which I first presented at a 2009 conference in Japan as a moral basis for a global ethic,[110] is misleading. He discusses this notion under the heading of "Whiteheadian Philosophy and Theism" and hence sees it as part of my "case for the relevance of a Whiteheadian-Hartshornean process theism." But my "minimal theism," which is not simply a stripped-down version of process theism, is part of my case for a global ethic—an ethic equally acceptable in principle to all peoples.

My minimal theism is partly analogous to Michael Walzer's "minimalist morality,"[111] which consists of "principles that are *reiterated* in all the maximalist moralities."[112] This minimalist morality, by consisting only of principles that the moralities of all people have in common, is universal. A minimal theism is likewise universal, but not by containing principles common to all the positions normally described as theistic.

Rather, my minimal theism is formulated as the opposite of philosophical atheism with regard to the issue of the status of moral norms or principles. The atheism defended by recent philosophers is not simply the denial of "God" as understood in the Abrahamic traditions and analogous theistic positions. Rather, it is the assertion "there is simply *no place* in the universe for moral norms, that moral norms are not—in the phrase employed by [Bernard] Williams and [John] Mackie— "part of the fabric of the world."[113]

On the principle that atheism and theism should be opposites, I propose an either/or dividing line: "Either there is a 'place' in which moral norms can and do exist, so that they are part of the fabric of the universe, or there is no such place." Defining theism as the idea that there *is* such a place means that, for example, Hinduism, Buddhism, and Native American traditions, are theistic in this extremely minimal sense.

As to why this notion is important: Although there are people who desire a theocracy based on the maximal moralities of their own tradition—people wanting a Christian America, a Jewish Israel, a Hindu India, or a Muslim Egypt— the deepest concern of such people is that their governments be based on moral values understood to be divinely rooted. None of these visions could become the basis for a global ethic. But this basis could be provided by the suggested minimal theism, which could also be endorsed by more moderate members of such religious traditions and even by people who normally describe themselves as non-religious but nevertheless do not believe that their moral values are totally without cosmic support.

The minimal theism I have proposed, therefore, is not a version of process theism and is not identical, as Reeves suggested, with an "ideal observer regarded as actual."

*Human Rights:* Regarding human rights as rooted in an authoritarian "king of kings," Reeves says that "there are no human rights . . . because we do not have the kind of God who has the position and power to grant rights." By contrast, while not endorsing the same kind of deity Reeves is denying, I am a strong advocate of human rights. There seem to be two bases for our different views here.

First, those who discuss rights usually distinguish between *having* rights—"Human rights are commonly understood *as inalienable fundamental rights to which a person is inherently entitled simply because she or he is a human being*"—and being able to *enjoy* them by having them as *legal* rights—which presently depends on living in a state in which they are protected. Reeves is referring primarily to *legal* rights, as shown by his statement that "rights are granted by some higher power or authority, usually a government or constitution." But I am discussing, in Whitehead's language, "the idea of the essential rights of human beings, arising from their sheer humanity."[114]

Second, I do not believe the idea of human rights as such is dependent on any a legalist, authoritarian worldview. The US Declaration of Independence, which spoke of "certain inalienable Rights," certainly had no such conception. It did say that people's inalienable rights were "endowed by their Creator." But this Creator was "Nature's God," and Thomas Jefferson, the primary author, was a deist. Also, given Reeves' use of the P.C. Chang quotation to suggest that proposing a rights-centric global ethic would be to continue Western hegemony, I will mention that Tu Weiming wrote an essay entitled "Human Rights as a Confucian Moral Discourse," in which he said: "Human rights discourse . . . specifies the minimum requirements and basic conditions for human flourishing." And, far from thinking of human rights discourse as tied to any form of western theism or individualistic secular humanism, Tu Weiming portrayed this discourse as fully compatible with, and even strengthened by, the Confucian view of the unity of Heaven and humanity.[115]

*God as Our Creator:* Worried that process thinkers may "inadvertently resort to traditional, classical theistic notions," Reeves objects to my reference to God as "the creator who brought us forth." Certainly, this phrase would be inappropriate if it implied anything even remotely verging on "*creatio ex nihilo*," which made Whitehead warn against any suggestion that "the ultimate creativity of the universe is to be ascribed to God's volition." But my reference to God as creator does not imply this.

However, beyond rejecting *creatio ex nihilo*, Reeves suggests that we cannot correctly use *any* notion of God as creator, saying that "it is inappropriate to say that God brings us forth." Rather, he says, "We bring ourselves forth, with the help of our ancestors (our antecedents) and with the participation of God."

It seems to me, however, that these statements by Reeves give the wrong emphasis. He says: "If we focus on creativity or novelty, the real creator of an actual occasion is itself. If we focus on what is the dominant influence on any individual occasion, the real creator of an actual occasion is its past. If we focus on God's unique relation to all other occasions, we can say that God is the creator." Reeves suggests that these three—myself, God, and the past—are equally important to the fact that I was brought forth.

However, whereas our self-determination is generally the central factor with regard to the particular shape of a moment of my conscious experience, the very fact that I exist—the fact that I was "brought forth"—is due overwhelmingly to God. That is, my existence is due not only to my parents, grandparents, great-grandparents, and so on back, but also to the evolutionary developments that brought forth human beings hundreds of thousand of years ago. God's role, in initiating the present cosmic epoch and then in guiding the evolutionary process in the billions of years is, hence, what I primarily had in mind by referring to the Whiteheadian God as "the creator who brought us forth."

*4. The Buddha in Us:* Citing with approval my position that all people have in common "a desire for harmony with the Tao, or Brahman, or Buddha, or even the divine will," Reeves says that "virtually all of Mahayana Buddhism now affirms that there is an element of the Buddha even in the most evil of living beings." There is an analogous notion in Quakerism, which speaks of "that of God in everyone." Both of these are similar, in turn, to Whitehead's statement, quoted by Reeves, that "the initial stage of the [subjective] aim is rooted in the nature of God." So on this, the most important point, Reeves and I are one.

## RESPONSE TO RICHARD FALK

Richard Falk has given an excellent account of many of the ideas in my thinking about global government—a project on which I got started under the inspiration of a talk he gave on "global anarchy" in late 1992. Although Falk and I agree on most issues, we have different views on the idea of global democracy.

I will respond to four objections Falk raises to my view. I will then raise four questions about his suggestion as to a better way to respond to the global dangers human civilization now faces. Finally, I will point out that, despite his explicit rejection of global democracy, his honest, realistic assessment of the state of civilization implies the need for a shift to some type of global democracy.

### 1. Falk's objections to the alleged need for global democracy

*Global Democracy and Global Apartheid:* Falk argues that even if a global government were to be created, many problems would still persist. That is certainly true. But Falk mentions "apartheid" as one of those and even added that "unless current levels of inequality were greatly reduced in the process of transition to a global democracy, [this threat] to human security could actually become worse." In a parallel argument, Falk says he has difficulty with my approach because of "issues of justice in a world that currently exhibits such drastic inequality as among and within existing political communities."

But overcoming the gross and increasing inequality would be one of the main purposes of global democracy as I conceive it: One of the chapters of my still unfinished book manuscript on global democracy is entitled "Subsistence Rights and Global Apartheid," with "apartheid" understood as a system of enforced socioeconomic disparity along largely racial terms. As the first major article on this issue, by Gernot Köhler, said: "[G]lobal apartheid is even more severe than South African apartheid."[116] Titus Alexander in *Unravelling Global Apartheid* adds this fact: "The West ... has a sixth of the world's population and commands over three-quarters of global resources."[117]

Falk, of course, knows about global apartheid well, having reprinted Köhler's article and written wisely about it himself.[118] Given the fact that I never got my book manuscript published, he cannot be blamed for not knowing that I intended to have an entire chapter on this issue, which was to begin by "showing how [the global economy] supports global apartheid so severe that a significant percentage of the human race lives in poverty, much of it so abject that millions die of starvation each year," and to conclude with the observation that, "if we are to . . . regulate global corporations and global finance, end corporate welfare, enforce subsistence rights, institute a global tax and/or put a cap on income inequality, and, more generally, overcome global apartheid, we need to create a multilevel global democracy, complete with a democratic government at the global level." This chapter was then to be followed by one on "global plutocracy."

*Why the Westphalian Structure Has Remained:* Falk has suggested that, in spite of all the problems created by the

Westphalian structure of global relations, which could arguably be overcome by the creation of global democracy, the continued attachment to the Westphalian structure is partly explained by fear—the fear that with the creation of a body above the individual states, some "threats to human security could actually become worse." However, the real fear of any change in the global structure has been the fear by imperialist powers, the USA most of all, that their freedom to do what they wish might be constrained. Given the fact the that the USA has been the global hegemon since the end of WW II, American economic, political, and military leaders, and even most academics, have heaped scorn on any idea of a global organization that would lessen US supremacy.

Falk remarks that "the reality of wartime suffering and hardship" created "a temporary willingness to consider centralizing world order alternatives," and "[t]hese feelings were sufficient after World War I to establish the League of Nations and after World War II the United Nations, but not enough to give such institutions the capabilities and independence they need to carry out the grandiose mission of war prevention." But what caused these movements to fail was not the weakness of the people's "feelings," but the self-interest of the business, political, military, and media elites.

The First World War led to the creation of the League of Nations in 1920. Although the people wanted an organization that would be able to prevent war, leading thinkers in the United States would not approve this, said Senator Sharp Williams, because of their "stupid selfishness"—that they "want [their] nation left free and untrammeled to do whatever it please." The subtitle of Alan Cranston's book on this failure, *How the Will of the People Was Thwarted After World War One*, made clear that the desire for a new structure of international relations was not blocked by the people.[119]

The same thing happened after World War II. In planning a successor to the League, the idea that inspired the allied forces was that the League had failed because it was not a super-state, and that "something like a super-state would have to be created if aggressor states as strong as Nazi Germany were going to be halted."[120] But eventually, the political leaders of "the United States, Great Britain, and the Soviet Union decided that their own, individual interests were too important to entrust to a world body," that the wartime dream of an international peacekeeping agency might interfere with their own nationalistic dreams of hegemony."[121] So they opted for "an organization that they could control, at least where their own vital interests were concerned."[122]

This same self-interestedness, rather than any fear by the people, would be the primary obstacle today to creating global democracy.

*Prospects for the Emergence of Global Democracy:* Falk writes: "[A]t present, there exists scant evidence of the kind of mass popular support that is needed as a precondition making it possible to put forward as *a political project* a plausible transition from the doomed present to the preferred democratic future," so the proposal for global democracy can "be easily discredited as an example of wishful thinking."

It seems to me that this—that we must wait for "mass popular support"—has it backwards. The abolitionists did not wait for mass support before they suggested that slavery should be abolished; rather, they argued for abolition on moral, religious, and political grounds, and thereby created a mass movement. The same for the civil rights movement: Rather than waiting for a mass movement, civil rights leaders, such as Rosa Parks—who had taken a ten-day workshop on nonviolent resistance before refusing to go to the back of the bus—*created* the movement. In these cases, the creation of these movements depended on events as well as ideas, but the ideas were essential.

"Senseless agencies and formulated aspirations cooperate in the work of driving mankind from its old anchorage," wrote Whitehead.[123] Neither one by itself will do the trick—the "senseless agency" for the abolition of slavery was "the growth of technology ... which weakened the necessity for slavery."[124] But the technology would not have brought about the abolition without the Methodists, Quakers, and others who argued that slavery was morally wrong.

A "senseless agency" presently working, perhaps the rise of carbon dioxide in the atmosphere and the resulting climate change, may turn out to be decisive for the creation of global democracy. But unless the idea has already been widely accepted, it will not be there in people's minds as a possible solution to the crisis.

Falk also holds it against the proposal for global democracy that "there does not even exist a widespread understanding of what is meant by 'global democracy.'" But unless intellectuals have been explaining this idea, one can hardly expect the public to understand it. "Engaged intellectuals" should be ready to explain and argue for presently unpopular ideas. Falk himself has done this, of course, with regard to various issues, such as Palestinian rights.

Falk also commented on the fact that "there is no support for world government among political elites." In response to this, I can only reply: What a surprise! (Elites almost by definition are people who like things the way they are. It would be very rare members of the American elite—those rare persons called "traitors to their class"—to promote global democracy, which would move the world toward greater equality.)

*Ultimate and Penultimate Problems:* Given the fact that there is presently little support for global democracy, Falk considers this goal "ill-conceived." Instead, he says—while recognizing "the darkening shadows of unresolved and neglected global challenges," his "own immediate preference would be to promote specific initiatives that move in a democratizing direction."

I find this response surprising. Falk knows that I see the emergence of global democracy as necessary for dealing with a number of what Falk calls "unresolved and neglected global challenges," including global climate change, which threatens the very existence of human civilization, according to an increasing number of climate scientists and journalists. For example, climate journalist Elizabeth Kolbert wrote: "It may seem impossible to imagine that a technologically advanced society could choose, in essence, to destroy itself, but that is what we are now in the process of doing." National Medal of Science Winner Lonnie Thompson, having stated that climate scientists had always avoided crying "the sky is falling," said: "Why then are climatologists speaking out about the dangers of global warming? The answer is that virtually all of us are now convinced that global warming poses a clear and present danger to civilization."[125]

Falk knows that, if the percentage of $CO_2$ in the atmosphere continues to increase, human civilization will simply become impossible, and he knows that I favor the creation of global democracy in part to deal with this crisis. Indeed, in the chapter in my manuscript on "ecological suicide," I wrote: "a continuation of the present economic-technological trajectory of human civilization will lead to a catastrophic environmental collapse—one that will involve the extinction of many forms of life, a miserable premature death for billions of human beings, and possibly the collapse of human civilization as such," but that the creation of a global democracy could "provide the framework in which the human race could conceivably prevent ecological suicide." I added: "A good case can be made for considering this argument to be the most compelling of [my seven arguments for global democracy]." I would say this even more strongly today.

I have argued that, given the competitive nature of the (anarchic) state-centered system, it will be very difficult to reverse the build-up of $CO_2$ in the atmosphere. It might be thought that there could simply be created a *global authority* with the mandate and power to bring the $CO_2$ emissions down to the level deemed necessary by the Intergovernmental Panel on Climate Change. Authorities to eliminate nuclear weapons and to regulate the global economy should also be created. But these authorities would amount to a minimal global government (which, we would think, should be democratic).

As far as I know, Falk does not disagree with the threat to civilization posed by climate change. Also, as far as I know, he has not explained how this threat could be overcome apart from an at least minimal global government.

I am, therefore, puzzled by Falk's dismissal of the idea of global democracy, which, if created, could deal with most of the "unresolved and neglected global challenges," including the ultimate challenge: climate change. Certainly the creation of a global government would be exceedingly difficult, but is that a good reason not to even try—to focus instead on penultimate problems? Certainly Falk's "support for democratizing political movements" is a good thing. But whatever successes of this nature are achieved will be short lived, if human civilization as such disappears.

### 2. Four questions about Falk's alternative suggestion
*Who Could Authorize a Global Tax?* Falk says that a "redistributive global tax" could be levied "without any major centralization of political authority." Given the present structure, who

would authorize the tax? Who would enforce its payment? The USA? That would be simply treating this country as the de facto global government. NATO? Same problem. The UN? Perhaps the Security Council could authorize the tax and also the enforcement. But it has not been authorized to do such things.

*Who Would Lead the Effort to Prevent Ecological Collapse?* According to Falk, "we need to seek the decentralization of power and authority to the extent possible while avoiding either empire or world government." But surely we need to complete the sentence to say: "while avoiding either empire or world government, while preventing ecological collapse." How would that be done?

*How Could Anarchism Prevent Ecological Collapse?* Falk's bumper-sticker motto, he says, is "anarchism without anarchy." I can understand this slogan, assuming that "anarchy" refers to the popular image of anarchy as chaos and of anarchists as bomb-throwers. But I have trouble with the title of the essay to which Falk refers the reader, "Anarchism without 'Anarchism.'"[126] In any case, given either slogan, how would anarchism work with regard to a city? How, for example, does the garbage get collected? With regard to a nation: Who does the things necessary for the health, safety, and general welfare of the citizens? And with regard to civilization, we come back to the question above: How could anarchy (or anarchism) deal with global climate change?

*Should We Pin Hopes on a Black Swan?* Near the end of his essay, Falk says: "I remain . . . opposed to pinning our hopes on the emergence of a democratic global government." Presumably, however, Falk must pin his hopes, with regard to "the unresolved and neglected global challenges," on *something*. In this essay, he suggests that he pins his hopes for the survival of civilization on a "Black Swan"—on, in Taleb's words, something that is a real "outlier," because "nothing in the past can convincingly point to its possibility." If arguing in favor of global democracy is "wishful thinking," as Falk says, what would we call relying on a Black Swan to save us? Given the dire straits the planet is now in—that the $CO_2$ parts per million (ppm) is already far past the point that the leading climatologists consider safe; that the ppm have been increasing faster every year; and that climatologists say that if we continue with "business as usual," the planet will soon reach a "tipping point," at which no reversal will be possible—would it be wise to pin our hopes on the occurrence of an event that, as far as past experience teaches, is not even possible?

### 3. Falk's implicit recognition of the need for global democracy

Falk, of course, does not expect any truly impossible occurrence, such as the $CO_2$ ppm spontaneously declining, even while we keep pumping fossil fuels into the atmosphere, or the cancelation of any physical laws. We can, therefore, dismiss any idea that he would expect us to be saved from an ecological tipping point by a *deus ex machina*.

Furthermore, Falk has made statements expressing great pessimism about the future of civilization, given its present incapacity for problem-solving. He says, for example: that "behavior in world politics continues to be driven by policy elites seeking to maximize national or corporate interests in wealth, power, and prestige with very little deference to policies associated with the realization of global human interests." He also speaks of "the limits on rational problem-solving at the global level, accounting for the inability to . . . address the multiple ecological challenges posed by climate change despite the near universal declared realization that the collective wellbeing of humanity requires [that serious steps be taken]." Finally, he seems to accept the view that, "despite the . . . scientifically validated warnings about the dire consequences of trends toward global warming, there is little basis for believing that the present way in which global governance operates is capable of providing satisfactory solutions."[127]

In light of these statements, it would seem that Falk, in spite of his negative comments about the idea of global democracy, recognizes that some form of it is necessary if civilization is to survive the ecological crises, especially climate change.

## Response to Tod Fletcher and Peter Dale Scott

As I did with John Buchanan and Marc Ford, I am combining my responses to Tod Fletcher and Peter Dale Scott, each of whom dealt with my work on 9/11.

I am very grateful to Fletcher for the summary he provided of my ten 9/11 books, which is a better summary than anyone else could have provided—including myself.

I am also grateful for Fletcher's pointing out that my work on 9/11 has been part and parcel of my work on American imperialism (which has thus far appeared only in some chapters of *The American Empire and the Commonwealth of God* and Chapter 9 of *Christian Faith and the Truth behind 9/11*), which in turn is part and parcel of my work on global democracy.

However, although 9/11 began as a sub-point of a sub-point, it consumed most of my time and energy for almost a decade. One could say—not without reason—that I let the tail wag the dog, thereby allowing it to distract me from these two more important issues (global democracy and American imperialism), not to mention the even more urgent task of finding ways to prevent climate change from doing us in.

But I became convinced that getting the truth about 9/11 exposed would be of great revelatory value for all three of these projects.

When I began working on American imperialism, the fact that America is an empire was still seldom admitted and was often even denied (even though America had become the most extensive empire the world has ever seen). In the first decade of the 21st century, the claim changed: Although America is an empire, it is a *good* empire. My view was (and is) that if the American people as such could be led by evidence that 9/11 was an inside job, orchestrated for imperialist purposes, the claim that America is a "good empire" would become laughable.

Likewise, the conceit of "America the good" has led many Americans to believe that the rest of the world could rightly allow *this* superpower to serve as the de facto global government (a position for which, as Richard Falk points out, some US intellectuals have actually argued). By contrast, insofar as 9/11 is taken as a revelation of the true nature of American imperialism, 9/11 and its consequences provide one of the strongest arguments for the need for a global government— but a *democratic* one, through which the rest of the world can be protected from America's seemingly insatiable quest for control.

Finally, I argued that there would be little chance of the world's turning itself wholeheartedly to solving the ecological crisis unless it sees the truth about 9/11.[128] If this truth were to be seen, the world could turn its attention away from terrorism (which, if the USA would quit provoking it, would be a rather minor threat), and turn its attention to the real threat. As it turned out, the 9/11 Truth Movement, which is convinced that any genuine investigation would show 9/11 to have been an inside job, has been unable to get any such investigation— at least one with any official status—established. And so, as the subtitle of my 2011 book indicates, 9/11 is now in the category of *State Crimes Against Democracy [That] Succeed.*

But that does not mean that we have given up—see Consensus 9/11 (online).[129]

Whereas Fletcher limited himself to exposition, showing the development of my evidence and arguments for the conclusion that the 9/11 attacks were planned and carried out by some leading members of the Bush administration (most obviously Dick Cheney and Donald Rumsfeld), Peter Dale Scott engaged in critique, focusing on the second half of what turned out to be my most controversial book, *Christian Faith and the Truth behind 9/11*.[130]

Much of Scott's critique is positive. A feature of my work that he treats especially well is my notion of the "demonic." Unlike critics who, upon seeing this word, assume that I am affirming the idea of a literal Devil—critics who evidently miss the fact that I am proffering a "nonmythological notion of demonic power"[131]—Scott sees that I understand the demonic as creaturely creativity that, besides being diametrically opposed to divine creativity, is also powerful enough to threaten divine purposes. In the world today, there is no better example of demonic power than fossil-fuel corporations, preeminently Exxon Mobil, using their riches for propaganda to convince people that there has been no human-caused climate change.[132]

However, although Scott (like Fletcher) gives me excessive praise, he also raises some criticisms. I will deal with six issues.

*America and the American Empire.* He says, against me: "American empire is not wholly evil," regarding this as a "one-sided assessment of America." However, Scott is conflating the American empire and America itself: I have never said that America is wholly evil. There is much about America that has been wonderful—especially the pre-9/11 America. But insofar as America is an empire, it is evil (some empires are, to be sure, more evil than others).

*Martin Luther King on America:* Contrasting me with Martin Luther King, Scott says: King's political agenda, like Gandhi's before him, was to appeal to what was *good* in government and society, *against* what was evil. But what is good in the American society and government is not discussed in Griffin's book."

I have not discussed what is good because my topic has been American imperialism, not America as such. An intended book, *America: Divine or Demonic?* will, if I get to it, discuss both sides.

As for King: When he discussed America in relation to Vietnam, he portrayed it as simply evil. Calling the United States "the greatest purveyor of violence in the world today," he said:

[W]e increased our troop commitments in support of governments which were singularly corrupt, inept and without popular support. All the while the people . . . languish under our bombs and consider us—not their fellow Vietnamese—the real enemy. They move sadly and apathetically as we herd them off the land of their fathers into concentration camps where minimal social needs are rarely met. They know they must move or be destroyed by our bombs. . . .

They watch as we poison their water, as we kill a million acres of their crops. They must weep as the bulldozers roar through their areas preparing to destroy the precious trees. They wander into the hospitals, with at least twenty casualties from American firepower for one "Vietcong"-inflicted injury. So far we may have killed a million of them—mostly children. They wander into the towns and see thousands of the children, homeless, without clothes, running in packs on the streets like animals. They see the children, degraded by our soldiers as they beg for food. They see the children selling their sisters to our soldiers, soliciting for their mothers.

So yes, I have described the American empire as demonic, just as King described the American empire as demonic—even if, as far as I know, he did not employ "demonic" as a technical term (although he did say that "adventures like Vietnam . . . draw men and skills and money like some demonic destructive suction tube").

*9/11 and the JFK Assassination:* Saying that James Douglass in his book on the JFK assassination regarded it as "an act inflicted *against* the state by an element within it," Scott suggests that the same analysis applies to 9/11. "[T]hese atrocities are not the work of the public state itself, but committed *against* the legal structure of the public state."

But I wonder about this, even with regard to the JFK assassination. The conspirators involved the CIA, the FBI, the Secret Service, the Joint Chiefs of Staff, and (according to considerable evidence) the Vice President (LBJ) and two future presidents (Richard Nixon and George H.W. Bush). If these men and organizations were acting *against* the state, how much of "the state" was left? Certainly the attorney general, RFK. But even if one says that not all of the above list of men were involved, the needed elements for the assassination—the preparation of a "patsy," the assassination itself, and the organization of the cover-up (with LBJ appointing to the Warren Comm ission the fired CIA director Allen Dulles, who became the *de facto* head of it—were certainly not organized by rebels within the state.

With regard to Scott's statement that the assassination was "committed *against* the legal structure of the public state," this appears to be a tautology, insofar as by definition the assassination of a president would be illegal. The important point is that the assassination was organized (or at least allowed) and covered up by people in charge of the national security state.

*9/11 and the State:* With regard to the 9/11 attacks, the case is at least equally clear. Scott thinks I am wrong to say that "the Bush administration [i.e. itself, rather than members of it] orchestrated the attacks of 9/11." But although I can understand the distinction between *an administration* and *some of its members,* I cannot see how it applies here. The conspirators included the Vice President (as well as *probably* the President, who was *definitely* involved in the cover-up), the National Security Advisor, the Secretary of Defense, the Acting Chairman of the Joints Chiefs of Staff, the US Solicitor General, and the Mayor of New York City. Once these members are taken out, there was not much of the public state left for this operation to act *against.* To be sure, just as RFK was in 1963 a member of the cabinet who did not know about the assassination plans, Norman Mineta, the secretary of transportation in 2001, did not know about the 9/11 plans. But it would be hard to show that there were enough senior members of the Bush Administration, the Congress, the Supreme Court, and the military to constitute the "public state" against which 9/11 was committed.

Scott's line between the public state, on the one hand, and 9/11 and the JFK assassinations, on the other hand, is further called into question by the title of the best book on the King assassination, *An Act of State: The Execution of Martin Luther King.*[133] Whereas Scott says that, in these events, "part of the state acts against the public state as a whole," it would be more accurate to say that a part of the state was not involved in the acts of the public state.

*Mystery and Clarity:* 9/11 and the JFK assassination belong to a class of events that Scott calls "deep" or "mysterious," because "the question of ultimate causality and responsibility remains obscure." He criticizes me, therefore, for often writing "as if the mystery has been conclusively solved."

In saying that "the *prima facie* case against the Bush administration became a *conclusive* case," I was using language from criminal cases. If the judge declares that the prosecution has presented a *prima facie* case for the accused's guilt, the defense attorney must then rebut the various elements in the prosecution's case. If this attorney fails to present a convincing rebuttal, the *prima facie* case is presumed to be conclusive. In writing *The New Pearl Harbor*, I had summarized the main elements in the 9/11 Truth Movement's argument against the official theory. At that point, I assumed that the 9/11 Commission might provide satisfactory answers to the *prima facie* case for government complicity that had been alleged. But when I saw *The 9/11 Commission Report*, I saw that the Commission—which had multiple copies of *The New Pearl Harbor*—did not provide a rebuttal: While distorting a few points, it simply omitted the rest. That is when I concluded that the case was conclusive (although developments in the following years made the case, in my mind, even more conclusive).

This is far from thinking there is no mystery left about "the question of ultimate causality and responsibility." I have long pointed out that, although we know some of the people who were in operational control of the 9/11 attacks, we do not know who was paying the bills. A likely clue into the kinds of people in charge at that level was provided by a report that, a year before the 9/11 attacks, Nicholas Rockefeller laughingly said (in a private conversation) that a year later we will have troops going through caves in Afghanistan looking for terrorists. But while this report suggests that the ultimate causality and responsibility for the 9/11 attacks lay in very elite circles, it gives us no more than a hint. Beyond this hint, essays have been written suggesting the most likely suspects among the elite class—one such essay was, in fact, included in the 9/11 book that Scott and I co-edited.[134] But these essays are based on speculation, not hard evidence. There is plenty of mystery left.

I disagree, however, with Scott's suggestion that events such as 9/11 and the King and Kennedy assassinations "proceed from an unknown dark force." It seems to me that this force is known, and greedy plutocracy is its name.

*Bad Theologies, Bad Ethics:* I conclude with a point on which Scott, Fletcher, and I agree: That bad theologies—atheistic as well as traditionally theistic—tend to lead to bad ethics. This issue has been brought into America's public discussion currently (Summer of 2012) by the fact that Paul Ryan, chosen to be the Republican vice-presidential candidate, had long praised Ayn Rand, whose atheism was combined with her free-market ideology and her praise for selfishness and the rich.

## Response to Zhihe Wang

Dealing with the influence of my work—primarily the SUNY Series in Constructive Postmodern Thought—Zhihe Wang has written an amazing essay. Although I have been with him in China twice, meeting various professors and students influenced by this kind of thought and seeing how easy it has been to attract fairly large audiences to my lectures (an experience that John Cobb has also had), I did not really understand, until reading Wang's essay, just how broad and deep Constructive Postmodernism has become in China.

It appears, in fact, that starting the SUNY series may, thanks primarily to its influence in China, turn out to be the way in which I exert my greatest influence. The impact that Constructive Postmodernism has had in China thus far has, in any case, been quite a surprise.

To say it has been a surprise is not, however, to say that I had not dreamed of it. When I was getting ready to write the introduction to *Spirituality and Society*, my wife and I went to China, and while there we thought how great it would be if China, being introduced to the agricultural-economic-ecological-scientific ideas that had just been articulated in our first Santa Barbara conference ("Toward a Postmodern World"), would move directly from a premodern to a postmodern society—that is, without going through the modern way of life, which has turned out to be deadly in every respect. So, upon returning home, I wrote the introduction to *Spirituality and Society* with China very much in mind. Primarily for that reason, I included a discussion of Marxism, presenting it as a half-modern, half-postmodern type of thought.

However, the fact that I had high hopes for Constructive Postmodernism in China meant very little, by itself. After all, I have hoped that my books on many topics—such as physics and time, parapsychology, scientific naturalism, process philosophy of religion, and religious pluralism—would become game-changing books. But they did not. The route from my introduction for *Spirituality and Society* to the implantation of Constructive Postmodernism in China required six lucky breaks.

The first such break was that my introduction, because of its discussion of Marxism, was translated for a journal in Poland, from which it found its way to China. The second lucky break was that Wenyu Xie, having learned about this introduction, translated it (from the English) in 1992 for *Social Sciences Abroad*, after which Xie came to Claremont in 1994 to begin a Ph.D. program. The third lucky break was that he had a very energetic and persuasive friend named Zhihe Wang, who persuaded a colleague to translate *The Reenchantment of Science* into Chinese. The fourth break was that Wang soon decided that he, too, wanted to come to Claremont to earn a Ph.D. The fifth piece of luck was that, although Wang's wife, Meijun Fan, already had her Ph.D., she was willing to give up her teaching position to join Wang in Claremont. The sixth lucky break was that Meijun Fan, a good organizer, was also very energetic, and together she and Zhihe initiated the Center's China Project, which commissioned the translation of several of my books, along with some by John Cobb, and also started organizing conferences in China, through which, along with the books, many scholars and students learned about Constructive Post-modernism.

When we are in China, my wife is repeatedly told, "Your husband is very famous in China." The reason for this is—as this brief history shows—due to a lot of luck plus a lot of hard work by Zhihe Wang and Meijun Fan.

## CONCLUSION

To continue the theme of luck: I am very lucky that 14 colleagues have been willing to the take the time, which was considerable, to write these essays—the time for which included attending a three-day conference at which the first drafts of these essays were discussed. Some of these essays have consisted primarily of positive evaluations of my work, while others have vigorously expressed criticisms. I cherish both equally, and those who offered criticisms knew that I would give equally vigorous responses—indeed, they would have been disappointed if I had not. So I wish to thank these colleagues, along with all the people who made possible the conference and this book.

# 16. Late Afternoon Remarks

## Beth Johnson

What can you really say about the person who gives you back God, empowers a vision of a value-laden world, and inspires you to acts of justice on behalf of that world? In 7 minutes? Having had the Deep Innerness of God that I'd experienced as a small child taught out of me, I subsequently *thought* my way out of any notion of a god other than that associated with pantheism. By the time I got to Claremont, I was an ecofeminist who had contented herself with that lovely but really, for me, inadequate notion of the Divine.

I had heard of process theology before coming to Claremont and had taken a short course here when I first arrived, but it was in David's "Backgrounds of Contemporary Theology" class in my second semester that the process God and the constructive postmodern process vision claimed me.

David persuasively unfolded a vision of God and the world that not only did not *offend* my sensibilities, but awakened them further; that not only described my experiences but allowed me to theorize them, that led to both a recovery and a transformation of the traditions that shaped me.

There occurred a harmonizing of the past that was aesthetically and emotionally satisfying, along with a coherent worldview that was consistent with the unfolding revelations of science, equipping me with a robust faith as well as fidelity to reason. I discovered a language to communicate that radical love of God, the depth of the interrelatedness of all things, and the wonder of the complexity of life, which deepened my call to justice-love.

I was fortunate to have been able to take all of my electives and a good number of required courses in my M.Div. with David, and some with Marjorie Suchocki and John Sweeney. David encouraged me to go into the D. Min. program. He was my mentor, and with John Sweeney as my reader, I applied postmodern process thought to animal advocacy and rights.

It was exhilarating to be a student of David's. As we all know, David's mind is so sharp, his thinking so precise, his writing so clear, and his ideas so helpful and relevant (to me) that I was swept away by his discipline and rigor, enlivened by his incisive critiques, and emboldened by his ecological vision of a re-enchanted world.

David had high expectations his students. He expected us to think clearly and to write persuasively and well, and he taught us how to do that.

There was, of course, the famous red pen—feared or disdained by some, anticipated and appreciated by others: A paper returned saturated in red ink was a sign of David's engagement with the paper, with the ideas, with us, his students—he took us seriously and expected us to take our writing and thinking seriously. He even corrected footnotes! Who does that? I was offended when other professors returned my papers with nary a red mark.

David's enlightened religious pluralism made this Unitarian Universalist feel at home here and provided inspiration for what was possible in my ministry. His good humor was (and still is) a joy to experience.

Once, when I expressed my enthusiastic appreciation of the notion of three Ultimates, David leaned back, his eyes danced, and he suggested that I had "Trinity envy."

David inspired me with his empathy and passion for justice.

I recall sitting in our religious pluralism and global ethics class. It was after the invasion of Iraq. A plane flew overhead loud and low, shaking the windows. David fell silent, cocked his head—we could feel the emotion that David embodied in that moment, as he said, "and they are living with that every day." We knew what he meant—a world away, but as present as the breath, bombs were being dropped on innocents in that illegal and immoral occupation that shaped us all.

Then I witnessed David's courageous turn toward 9/11 truth and he made me brave.

David's constructive postmodern process thought addressed with clarity every area that I, in preparing for UU ministry, was concerned with: theology, philosophy, feminism, morality, religious pluralism, science and religion, evil, social justice, and as an added bonus for me, my own personal interest in Jungian and depth psychology.

In all of what we've heard presented at this conference, with such skill and expertise related to David's influence in the academy, we, who trained with David for ministry, felt supremely equipped to engage in our ministries.

I feel I can offer something substantive to my folks as we grapple with imagining new possibilities, for us as a spiritually diverse and justice-seeking religious community, and in the wider world.

As I prepare sermons, worship, and do pastoral care, David's influence is with me.

As I defend and protect animals and the earth, David's influence is with me.

In the possibilities that emerge from the multiplicity of voices in the Occupy space, I see the constructive postmodern vision pulsing.

David has shaped me as a thinker, a minister, an activist. I live from what he taught and exposed me to. I am still continually enriched in fresh ways by his engaged and compassionate teaching, rigorous thinking and writing, and by his brave example of speaking truth to power.

And, of course, I'm not the only one. When I posted on facebook that I was attending this conference and speaking about David as my teacher, J.R. Hustwit wrote: "Please tell him I send my thanks for his influence on my own adventure!"

Siri Celine Dale Erickson, a Lutheran pastor and contemporary of mine in the M.Div. program, wrote: "The clarity of his mind is a rare gift in a world where so many default to being vague and unclear. David always strove for precision and clarity, and I SO appreciated it."

Patricia Farmer sends her and her husband Ron's blessings.

And when I posted on facebook yesterday afternoon that I was "loving the discussion of religious naturalism," Siri responded, "Would that be naturalism ppp?"

I, we all, continue to live from the influence of David Ray Griffin, and I, we, and the world, are better for it.

David, thank you for the grand adventure that you have boldly led us on.

# 17.

# My Intellectual Journey

## David Ray Griffin

At the time of my retirement, John Cobb suggested that he would organize a volume in my honor. I expressed my thanks but said that, if there was ever to be one, it should wait until I had done something worthy of this honor. I still feel that way. But coming within a whisker of dying two years ago made me aware that this was an opportunity that should not be put off indefinitely. So when Richard Falk and his fellow conspirators—Catherine Keller and John Buchanan as well as John Cobb—came up with the idea of an event like this, I agreed. My own contribution, they said, should be an account of my intellectual journey.

Having never considered the idea of writing an autobiography, I had never thought about how I would structure an hour-long summary of my intellectual life. But as I started jotting down ideas, I decided to explain how my intellectual journey was influenced by various external events.

### HIGH SCHOOL

With regard to my high school life, one incident stands out. Church was always an important factor in my life, and the youth group of my church was always a big part of my social life—I served as its president during my final two years of high school. But I did not think of making the church my life's work. At least not immediately: In the summer before my first year of college, I asked my girl-friend, whom I assumed I would marry, whether it would be OK with her if I were to go into the ministry when I was 40—by which I meant: After my life would be essentially over anyway!

## COLLEGE

I started college as a music major. But I soon changed my plans for several reasons, including my first and only fraternity party. It was truly gross (this was at the University of Oregon, mind you, where "Animal House" was filmed). That party evoked in me a there-must-be-more-to-life type of experience. Later that night, I told my roommate that I was going to go into either psychology or the ministry.

So the next two terms, I signed up for psychology classes and a class across the street at NCC—Northwest Christian College—a Bible college of my own denomination, the Disciples of Christ. The following year, wanting to test out the idea of going into the ministry, I transferred to NCC, and I ended up going there for four years. Although this experience instilled some evangelical fervor, much of what I learned there I later had to *unlearn*. But this experience meant that, when I went to seminary and graduate school, I seemed to value the classes there more strongly than did students who had attended secular colleges.

My favorite classes at NCC had been in pastoral counseling, so I was considering going into this. However, instead of leaving for seminary right after college, I needed to wait a year, because my fiancé was already committed to go on a drama troupe tour. So I went back over to the University to get a master's degree in counseling. But my plans were changed by some visits to California.

Having read some of Paul Tillich's sermons, I learned that he was going to give the Earl Lectures at the Pacific School of Religion in Berkeley. My fiancé and I, along with our best friends, drove down to attend the lectures. Tillich was magnificent. Between his books and these lectures, I started telling my friends that I was going to go into *philosophical theology*—which usually led to the query: "What's that?"

Having made this decision, the next question was: Where should I go? PSR had a professor who taught Tillich, so this seemed a natural choice. But a preacher in Eastern Oregon told me—while we were bowling—that Yale was the best school. So I applied to these two schools and got accepted by both. PSR even gave me the entrance scholarship, which was worth $1,000— which in today's terms amounted to real money. I had a terrible time deciding between them, but I eventually decided on PSR. I was very relieved about having that choice behind me.

But almost the next day, I was invited into the office of John Boosinger, NCC's one liberal professor, who showed me the catalogue from a school of theology named Claremont. It had never been mentioned by any of the professors at NCC, even though the School of Theology at Claremont was an official seminary of the same denomination. In any case, although I told Boosinger I was not interested—I had made my decision—he encouraged me to take the catalog home. The next day, I called my parents, telling them that the catalog made the school look a lot more exciting than either PSR or Yale, but I didn't think I should make such a big decision on the basis of a good catalog. They agreed, and I planned to fly down to southern California the following week.

However, the morning I was planning to leave, I told George Nordgulen—he and I were taking a class at the University on various religious thinkers—that I was going down that day. George, who had studied Whitehead and Hartshorne at Phillips Seminary in Oklahoma, got very excited, saying that if I would drive down, he would come with me. I agreed, and we drove down—along with a couple of my friends who just wanted to see some sun. While we were there, George arranged to meet a professor I otherwise might not have met, Dr. John. B. Cobb, Jr. In response to George's question whether he had written anything recently, Dr. Cobb gave him a little paper entitled "A Personal Christology."

At that point, I had decided that, although I liked Cobb and the other professors I met, I would stick with PSR. But on the trip home, when it was my turn to sit in the back seat, I picked up Cobb's little paper, and after reading only four or five pages, I had decided that I would go to Claremont. I saw that Cobb was not only dealing with the kinds of questions I had been struggling with but also that he was dealing with them *with clarity* (a book on philosophical theology I had read by one theologian was so maddeningly unclear that I threw it across the room). So I was set to study philosophical theology with John Cobb.

However, my decision to focus on philosophical theology was not as final as I had thought. After a friend and I heard Aldous Huxley lecture at the University on *The Doors of Perception,* my friend sent to Texas for some peyote. Having ground it up in my blender and put in some Kool-Aid—no one had told me to squeeze out the mescaline—I had to throw up, but I then had a very interesting time. Huxley had said that under mescaline, he had stared at a rose for an hour. I thought, "C'mon Aldous: Maybe five minutes, but not an hour." Soon after throwing up, I walked across the street and stared at a 24-Hour Martinizing sign for an hour—hence the origin of the saying, "drinking the Kool-Aid."

Although I did not ingest many more such things, I did become increasingly interested in mystical literature. This path was importantly influenced by an unusual philosophy professor at Oregon, who told us about Flying Father Joseph of Cupertino, about whom, the professor pointed out, there was an article in the *Journal of Psychical Research*.

Having moved to a new residence at the beginning of the 1963 summer—I had gotten married—I discovered that only a block away there was a library of the Theosophical Society. Besides having the American and British journals of psychical research, this library had many fascinating books, including one about Edgar Cayce. He gave people "readings" in which he, in trance, reportedly told them various things about themselves that he should not have known—even where they could find needed medicines. The mystical literature in the Theosophical library, heavily influenced by Hindu and Buddhist ideas, led me to think that perhaps I should focus on these religions at Claremont.

## CLAREMONT

As fate—or God—would have it, the class in Eastern Religions that I had to take was at the same time as a seminar by Dr. Cobb called "Whitehead's Philosophy and Its Religious Relevance." I soon found myself skipping out of the Eastern Religions course to attend Cobb's seminar. I still remember a simile he used. In opposing the traditional view of divine action—according to which God miraculously intervenes here and there—much liberal theology seems to assume, Cobb said, that the only alternative is to think of God as acting like a cosmic hydraulic jack, exerting the same pressure always and everywhere. Cobb thereby implied that Whitehead provided a third view. This and other suggestions made me anxious to learn more about process theology.

During my first two years at Claremont, I read some books by Charles Hartshorne, who had been Cobb's professor at

the University of Chicago. However, I spent most of my time
learning German and studying for several entrance exams.
One of these was over my dissertation proposal, which was to
develop a process christology. After completing these exams,
I would be ready to study with Cobb, along with New Testa-
ment scholar and theologian James Robinson, who was the
leader of the "new quest for the historical Jesus," which I had
planned to make central to my dissertation.

However, Cobb and Robinson, I learned, were both to be
away the following year. With little reason to remain in Claremont, and having learned that our best friends were planning
to go to Germany for the year, my wife and I decided to go with
them. It turned out that our friends were unable to go, but my
wife and I went anyway, having realized that Cobb would be
at the University of Mainz with Wolfhart Pannenberg, who
was to be the subject of the third volume of a series edited by
Cobb and Robinson called "New Frontiers in Theology," and
about whom Robinson taught a course that I audited.

GERMANY

My year in Mainz, where I heard Pannenberg's lectures and
participated in his seminars, was extremely valuable. Pannenberg was a brilliant lecturer who, unlike my professors in
Claremont, simply announced the truth on issue after issue.
This style forced me, especially when I disagreed with him, to
start a notebook, in which I worked out my own ideas: Insofar
as I disagreed with Pannenberg, I had to ask: Why? That was
when I started becoming a theologian.

While being appreciative of Whitehead, Pannenberg
was working out a different type of process theology, one
based more on Hegel. The contrast was made clearest with
his provocative notion of the *retroactive* effect of the future
on the past. The provocative nature of this notion was most

important with respect to the doctrine of the resurrection of Jesus: This doctrine, said Pannenberg, will be true if, and only if, there is an end of history containing a general resurrection of the dead. This future event will make it true that Jesus had been, in first-century Palestine, raised from the dead. This was the crucial example of what Pannenberg called the backward working, or retroactive effect, of the future on the past.

Coming out of a lecture one day, I overheard a student say: "Pannenberg's entire theology is based on a notion that *gar nicht stimpt*"—that is *absolutely not true*—because the future cannot affect the past. What this student evidently did not understand was that Pannenberg presupposed Hegel's Absolute Idealism, according to which nothing is truly settled until history has reached its goal.

Analogously, there is no time, as we normally understand it, within a single Whiteheadian actual entity, or actual occasion. Rather, each actual occasion is a self-determining whole, so that nothing is finally settled until the occasion reaches "satisfaction." But time exists because of the transition from actual occasion to a subsequent actual occasion, and there are many occasions in each second. Whitehead's type of thought, he said, involved "a transformation of some main doctrines of Absolute Idealism onto a realistic basis."[1] I later did receive confirmation from Pannenberg, in response to a question from me, that he regarded the whole universe as like a single Whiteheadian actual entity.

I also became critical of Pannenberg for another reason. After Cobb first arrived in Mainz, he and Pannenberg had private discussions once a week. Marveling at the comprehensiveness of Pannenberg's thought, Cobb told me after several weeks that he had not yet brought up an issue that Pannenberg had not already worked out. But in a seminar one day, a German student, taking note of Pannenberg's definition of

God as the "power over everything,"[2] asked how that view of God fit with the reality of evil. Pannenberg started explaining that God gave human beings freedom, and that terrible things happen because of the sinful misuse of this freedom. But the student said that he was not asking about *böse*—sin—but about *"übel,"* which includes *natural* evil. Given this clarification, Pannenberg replied that he had not yet dealt with this issue. I could hardly believe my ears. It seemed to me that theologians should not deal with anything else before working out their positions on the relation of God to evil, especially natural evil. One of the benefits of my year in Germany was that it cured me of a then-common malady among American theologians: having an inferiority complex in relation to Germans.

Another benefit was due to the fact that Cobb and Pannenberg co-taught a seminar on Hegel, Teilhard, and Whitehead. While studying for this course, I finally came to understand Whitehead's philosophy.

## CLAREMONT AGAIN

However, my self-congratulation was premature, for it was really only after I was back at Claremont that I, for the first time, came to understand Whitehead's philosophy. This understanding came about through three means. First, I helped Cobb with publications as his assistant—unofficially in Germany, and officially after returning to Claremont. Second, I took Cobb's Whitehead class, for which I wrote a paper on perhaps the most difficult feature of Whitehead's thought, which was central to understanding Pannenberg's doctrine of retroactive causation: the first phase of an actual entity. Third, I employed Whitehead in my dissertation, especially the chapter that had already become my first published article: "Schubert Ogden's Christology and the Possibilities of Process Philosophy."[3]

The unhappiest feature of my time in Claremont was that it was bookended by political assassinations. I had been in Clare-mont only two months when one day, upon returning to the School of Theology campus, a fellow said, "The president has been shot." I exclaimed: "Why would anyone have shot President Colwell?" I was assuming that the reference was to Ernest "Pomp" Colwell, the first president of CST—who had brought Cobb and Robinson to Claremont from Emory. Learning that it was President *Kennedy*, I was in a daze the rest of the week, and the assassination shaped the rest of my time in Claremont. In 1967, my best friend at NCC, who had come down to Claremont at the same time as I, started coming over every week to watch a TV show in which Mort Sahl and others discussed the Warren Report's lies. And then in 1968, Martin Luther King was assassinated in April. Then in June—when my parents were visiting as I was getting ready to defend my dissertation—we learned of the assassination of Bobby Kennedy, whose progression through the presidential primary contests I had been following intensely. Like many other people, I was hoping for a president who would bring the end of America's barbaric war in Vietnam—in which my then-wife's brother was soon to die in one of those stupid search-and-destroy missions.

## DAYTON

After completing my dissertation, I took a position in the theology department of the University of Dayton, a Roman Catholic school. Besides teaching required classes, I was able to teach Whitehead for M.A. and honors students, and it was by actually teaching Whitehead's philosophy that I came, really, to understand this philosophy.

Soon after coming to Dayton, I met Gene Reeves, who was living in Yellow Springs, about 20 miles away. Knowing that

Cobb and Lewis Ford were planning a journal called *Process Studies*, we produced the first fairly complete "Bibliography of Secondary Literature on A.N. Whitehead."[4] Through that work, which consumed hundreds of hours over a couple of years, I developed an awareness of the extensiveness of the articles, books, and reviews that discussed or employed Whitehead's thought (we located over 1900 of them).

I had another project with a more senior author, the death-of-God theologian Thomas J.J. Altizer. Cobb, considering the thought of Altizer very important, had co-edited a book on his theology.[5] Thinking that Cobb's theology was equally important, Altizer and I decided to co-edit a book on *his* theology, which we called—with a double entendre, if not originality—*John Cobb's Theology in Process*.[6]

Considering Cobb's two most important essays until then to be "From Crisis Theology to the Post-Modern World" and "Christian Natural Theology and Christian Existence," I entitled my introduction to the volume "Post-Modern Theology for a New Christian Existence."[7] This was my first use of the term "post-modern," which I would later come to use *ad nauseum*.

During that Daytonian period, I wrote a fateful letter to Cobb: I outlined some ideas I had developed for an "institute of Whitehead studies" and asked Cobb if he had ever thought of such a thing. He wrote back immediately, saying that he had been thinking almost exactly the same thing. We both wondered, of course, if such a dream was realistic. But shortly thereafter, Cobb was invited to give lectures at the Candler School of Theology at Emory University, and the dean, James Laney, asked Cobb what it would take to bring him there. Cobb replied, "an institute of Whitehead studies." Asked by Laney how much this would require, Cobb, telling Laney about me, replied that I had said we would need $100,000 a year, but that Cobb thought we could get by with somewhat less. Laney said: "I'll get it." Nothing happened immediately, but the following year, Cobb, who was in Hawaii, where he was on sabbatical, wrote that Laney had come up with $52,000 and asked if I considered that enough. Although this was about half as much as I considered necessary, I knew that this would open other opportunities that would never have been possible at Dayton. I was invited for a visit at Candler, all went well, and Laney sent a contract to Cobb, who was on sabbatical in Hawaii.

But Cobb received a letter from Claremont saying: "Don't sign anything. We're working on a plan to keep you here." Pretty soon, I received an invitation to come to Claremont to interview. Fortunately, there would be a position for me, as the professor of philosophy of religion was only one year away from retirement. Some of the faculty were less than enthusiastic about my coming, because I had performed less than brilliantly in some of their classes, having worked hard only on topics that were central to my project. But this obstacle was overcome by the fact that, as soon as I had completed my dissertation, I had begun publishing. Besides turning my dissertation into a book, I had published a dozen journal articles. Tom Trotter, the dean of the School of Theology, told me that after he handed out my bibliography, there was no more grumbling.

## CLAREMONT ONE MORE TIME

*Beginning the Center for Process Studies:* One of the greatest stimuli for my intellectual development was my work for the Center for Process Studies (which was what we decided to call our institute of Whitehead studies). The school allowed me to teach only half time so that I would have time for this work, which primarily involved—besides supervising the Center's staff—organizing conferences and then sometimes arranging publications of the papers. Our first conference, which was on evolutionary theory, had been arranged by Cobb and Australian biologist Charles Birch to take place at the Rockefeller Foundation's study and conference center in Bellagio, Italy. This conference gave me the opportunity to participate in discussions involving biologists who had helped create neo-Darwinism, such as Sewall Wright and Theodosius Dobzhansky; philosophers such as Charles Hartshorne, Milic Capek, and Arthur Koestler; and the physicist David Bohm. This conference resulted in the Center's first book, *Mind in Nature* subtitled *Essays on the Interface of Science and Philosophy,* which I co-edited with Cobb and which appeared in 1977.[8]

*Process Theology and Other Publications:* Thanks to our trip to Italy, Cobb and I published another book at about the same time. Prior to the Bellagio conference, Cobb had been contacted by an Italian publisher about writing a book explaining process theology. Cobb told me that he could do it only if I co-authored the book and, in fact, outlined it. Telling him that I also did not have time—I was starting my theodicy book—I said I would meet with the publisher after the Bellagio conference and, after confirming our suspicion that his publishing house was quite minor, I would suggest an alternative author for the book on process theology. I discovered, however, that this publishing house was Italy's major publisher of American and European theological books. I still suggested, nevertheless, that because most of his readers would be Catholics, he should get Bernard Lee to write the book. The publisher, however, said that he wanted "*Claremont* process theology." So I agreed that we would squeeze it in.

Working out an outline on the flight home, I assigned the first four chapters to myself and the last five to Cobb. After writing my four chapters in two weeks, Cobb—having gone by himself to his cabin in Wrightwood where he could work 20 hours a day—wrote his five chapters in a week. But each of his chapters was primarily an exposition of the thought of other process theologians, after which Cobb allowed that he, too, had some ideas about the topic. Having assumed that Cobb would simply summarize the books he had written on these topics, I reminded him that the Italian publisher wanted "*Claremont* process theology." So he went back up to Wrightwood and, in another week, came back with a new version of his five chapters. When I ran into Jean Cobb in the library, where she was working, she said (with her southern accent): "Now don't you make John rewrite those chapters again." I found this quite humorous: Only a few years earlier, I had been Cobb's student assistant, and here was his wife suggesting that I could have given him an order.

I was able that same year—1976—to do what I had vowed to do as soon as I had turned my dissertation into a book: write a book on the problem of evil. *God, Power, and Evil*, in which I showed that Whitehead's philosophy provides the basis for a solution to the problem of evil that had scarcely been noticed in the mainline discussions (in which the relative merits of atheism and traditional theism have been endlessly debated).[9]

At the same time, I began working with still another senior scholar—Vanderbilt philosopher Donald Sherburne—on the corrected edition of Whitehead's *Process and Reality*.[10] By editing this book, I rather belatedly learned the English language.

## Year-long Sabbatical Leave

The next phase of my intellectual development occurred in the 1980-81 year. The previous year had been the worst year of my academic life, because the president had asked me—

that is, *ordered* me—to serve as the acting dean, while Dean Joseph Hough was on sabbatical for the year in Cambridge. That entire year I got only one essay written—which I was able to do only thanks to a long weekend in Santa Barbara. Because of the terrible year the president had inflicted on me, he allowed me to extend my sabbatical leave to an entire year, and so, having learned from Joe how wonderful Cambridge was, I went there.

I had two topics to work on there. First, having learned from a literary friend in 1976 that postmodernism was becoming quite important in her field, I wanted to study the origins of distinctively *modern* thought, so as to understand what distinctively *postmodern* thought would be.

Second, having been invited to make a presentation to Cambridge University's theology society, I gave a critique of John Hick's book *The Myth of God Incarnate*.[11] In this critique, I explained how I, as a process theologian, use the mind-body relation as an analogy for understanding the interaction between God and the world. Afterwards, a philosopher told me that philosophers and neuroscientists no longer think of the mind as distinct from the brain, but instead hold the position called "identism," according to which the mind is identical with the brain: The mind and the brain are not two distinct things, and hence cannot "interact." I began reading around to see if there really was any good evidence for identism—a study that would eventuate, almost two decades later, in my *Unsnarling the World-Knot: Consciousness, Freedom, and the Mind-Body Problem*, in which I showed how Whitehead's philosophy provides the basis for a solution to the mind-body problem that had scarcely been noticed in the mainline discussions (in which the relative merits of dualism and materialism have been endlessly debated).[12] (Yes, the parallel with my earlier discussion of the problem of evil is deliberate.)

Near the end of my semester at Cambridge, I decided to spend the second half of my sabbatical in Berkeley, partly because it would be warmer, but mainly because it was the location of a first-rate physicist, named Henry Stapp, who was influenced by Whitehead. I learned about Stapp through a 1979 book called *The Dancing Wu Li Masters*, about which I was told by David Bohm, whom I had gone to Birkbeck College in London to visit. (On the way back to Cambridge, incidentally, I learned that John Lennon had been shot.)

Shortly before ending my tenure in Cambridge, I found in the library a book on the mind-body problem by a Scottish philosopher who argued that, although the evidence can be seen as supporting either mind-brain identism or the contrary view, the evidence from psychical research tips the balance in favor of the view that the mind is different from the brain. This Scottish philosopher assumed that the rejection of identism entails the acceptance of mind-brain *dualism*, meaning Descartes' view that the mind and the brain are different in kind, according to which the mind is a mental or spiritual substance, whereas the brain is composed of physical stuff.[13] Although I as a Whiteheadian rejected this kind of dualism—which has never been able to explain how, apart from miraculous intervention, the mind and the brain could interact—I was intrigued by the fact that a sophisticated philosopher was appealing to psychical research—a subject I had left behind almost two decades earlier.

When I got to Berkeley, I began studying physics and biology during the day while in the evening reading books on psychical research—by then generally called parapsychology. I soon decided, however, that in addition to the fact that parapsychology had been less milked than physics and biology for philosophical and theological purposes, it was also, in some respects, more important. Through this study,

I greatly expanded my appreciation of the senses in which Whitehead's philosophy is postmodern. Whitehead not only said that telepathy provides empirical evidence in favor of influence at a distance—which, I had learned, was the idea that had been most severely scorned by distinctively modern philosophers, such as Descartes and Newton[14]—Whitehead also said that his philosophy allows for the possibility of life after bodily death.[15]

Readings in parapsychology came to fill most of my days as well as my evenings. When I returned to Claremont, where I had been asked to give the lecture at the Center for Process Study's annual banquet, I spoke on "Parapsychology and the Need for a Postmodern Philosophy,"[16] which Joe Hough called "Griffin's talk on the spook world."

## THE CENTER FOR A POSTMODERN WORLD

Two years later, having moved to Santa Barbara to escape Clare-mont's smog—which was quite bad in those days—I started the Center for a Postmodern World in Santa Barbara along with Ann Jaqua, who was soon to become my wife. This was to be a community-based, rather than academy-based, center. (More about it later.)

## PHYSICS AND TIME

Only a couple of years later, the relationships Cobb and I had established with Bohm and Stapp led to a conference in Claremont on the relation of physics to time, which featured, in addition to Bohm and Stapp, also Ilya Prigogine, the Nobel Prize-winning chemist. In a visit with Bohm in Ojai at the Krishnamurti Foundation (which kept a permanent apartment for him), I suggested that the conference be called *Physics and the Ultimate Significance of Time: Bohm, Prigogine, and Process Philosophy*, and he readily agreed. My discussion of Prigogine in the introduction to the resulting volume was greatly aided by a visit I had while in Paris with Isabelle Stengers (the co-author of Prigogine's most well-known book, *Order Out of Chaos*[17]), who has since become one of Europe's most respected philosophers of science and interpreters of Whitehead, relating him to leading European philosophers.

It was while writing this introduction to the volume that I came to my fullest appreciation of the appropriateness of the term "process philosophy" for Whitehead's cosmology. Most science-based philosophy argues that time, with its distinction between the past and the future, is not rooted in basic physics—that time only became real when the universe developed processes that could suffer entropic decay. If there were nothing but simple enduring objects, such as electrons and photons, this view holds, there would be no time. For Whitehead, however, each of these enduring objects is constituted by a rapidly repeating series of momentary events—of electronic, protonic, or photonic events. Each such momentary event inherits from previous events and influences future events. Accordingly, time as we experience it, with its irreversible direction from the past to the future, exists for electrons and photons, even quarks.

It was also by writing this introduction that I came to a full appreciation of Whitehead's doctrine that the things that are actual entities in the fullest sense are momentary events, whereas things that endure are *societies* of actual entities.[18] They are, to be sure, not societies as we normally think of them: They are societies that are purely temporal, having only one member at a time. Whitehead called them "serially-ordered societies."

## The SUNY Series in Constructive Postmodern Thought and the China Project

I was able to get this book—*Physics and the Ultimate Signifi-cance of Time*—published by SUNY Press, which luckily was headed by William Eastman, who had studied with Charles Hartshorne. The following year, moreover, Eastman accept-ed my proposal for a book series called the SUNY Series in Constructive Postmodern Thought. During its existence from 1988 to 2004, this series published 32 volumes, ten of which I wrote or edited.

The first two, entitled *The Reenchantment of Science* and *Spirituality and Society*, arose out of the Santa Barbara center's first conference, *Toward a Postmodern World*. They illustrated the purpose of that center: providing a new *vision* of the world and also prescriptions for *changing* the world. Although process philosophy remained at the core, we brought in many people who, while sharing our values, were not card-carrying Whiteheadians—people such as Richard Falk, Matthew Fox, Joanna Macy, Brian Swimme, and Rupert Sheldrake.

These two edited volumes created considerable interest in China, and shortly thereafter Zhihe Wang came to Claremont to get his Ph.D. under my supervision and to establish—with his wife Meijun Fan, who already had her Ph.D.—the China Project of the Center for Process Studies and, later, the Institute for Postmodern Development of China. Thanks to their indefatigable energy—including their supervision of the translation of many of our books into Chinese—process philosophy, under the title of constructive postmodernism, is now as important in China as the deconstructive type of postmodernism, perhaps more so. John Cobb and I have become much better known in China than we are in America.

GLOBAL ANARCHY, BELLAGIO, AND PATMOS

At that first Santa Barbara conference, I met Richard Falk and Charlene Spretnak. The three of us, together with postmodern architect Charles Jencks, established a postmodern "gang of four," which started holding conferences in Santa Monica, London, and "Portrack House" in southern Scotland. In a conference at Portrack House in 1992, we focused on global politics, at which Falk made a presentation on global anarchy, meaning a situation in which there is no global authority by which disputes between states can be peacefully settled.

For many years, I had been trying to develop a "post-nuclear theology," aimed at finding a way to  eliminate nuclear weapons. There were three main positions. Some people advocated "nuclear pacifism," according to which nuclear weapons would be ruled out, but I could see no way in which a system allowing for war in general could rule out *nuclear* war. A second position was complete pacifism, but I agreed with Reinhold Niebuhr's argument that it would be unworkable. The third position was Niebuhr's, according to which there was no way to get rid of nuclear weapons: we would have to continue living with nuclear weapons, relying on mutual deterrence, hoping that it would hold indefinitely. But I agreed with pacifists that the reliance on mutual deterrence to prevent the first use of nuclear weapons was unchristian, immoral by *any* ethical standard, and too risky. Explaining in several chapters of a projected book why all of these standard approaches were inadequate, I assumed that in this process an answer would emerge. But it did not. So in the mid-1980s, I simply put these chapters away and began focusing on other aspects of a postmodern worldview and world-order.

Falk's 1992 discussion of global anarchy, however, implied that there might be a fourth approach—one that was suggested in two books that I had taken with me for five weeks of study at Bellagio: *The Parable of the Tribes*, by Andrew Bard Schmookler, and *The Pursuit of Power*, by University of Chicago history professor William McNeill.[19] This fourth approach had actually been suggested by several thinkers, including Einstein: the idea that war could be outlawed, and rendered unnecessary, by the development of a global government. This government could be made just, I argued, by instituting democracy and ruling out any influence of money—the feature that has increasingly destroyed American democracy by turning it into plutocracy.

After my time at Bellagio was up, Ann and I had planned to go to one of the Greek islands. But which one? Because the idea of global democracy had hit me with the force of revelation, I suggested that we should go to the Isle of Patmos, where there was some precedent for writing down revelations.

## GLOBAL DEMOCRACY AND A GLOBAL ETHIC

Deciding that global democracy would probably be the only way to overcome the ecological crisis as well as war, I started, upon returning to Claremont, teaching a graduate seminar called "Theology, Ecology, and Peace"—which was, as Joe Hough correctly stated, "Griffin's course on global government." At first, the students were extremely skeptical. One student even admitted, during a class party at the end of the semester, that for the first few weeks he had thought I must be crazy. But as the students worked through the readings, they came to believe that, without the emergence of a global democratic structure, there was no hope for overcoming plutocracy, war, and the nuclear and ecological crises. During the final decade of the 20th century and the first part of the next decade, I taught this course every other year, coming closer each time to completing a book manuscript on global democracy.

At the same time, recognizing that global democracy would require a universal bill of rights, I began working on this issue, challenging the assumption that cultures have such different moral standards that a global ethic, sufficient to ground a universally acceptable bill of rights, would be impossible. In relation to a 2002 conference (on "Democracy, Globalization, and the Law") at the Hamline University Law School (which Hamline law professor Howard Vogel and I, with assistance from Richard Falk, organized), I wrote a quite long paper (with a quite long title: "Natural Law, the Ideal Judge, Communitarian Cosmopolitanism, and Global Democracy")—which was only one draft away from being publishable as a little book. (There seems to be a pattern here.)

Religious pluralism

Closely related to the question of a global ethic is, of course, the issue of universalism and pluralism in the various religions. In my 2001 book *Reenchantment without Supernaturalism*, I had a chapter entitled "The Two Ultimates and the Religions," in which I built on Cobb's writings on religious pluralism. The occasion for a further treatment of this issue arose when, on the occasion of the retirement of Marjorie Suchocki from her position as the academic dean of the Claremont School of Theology, I volunteered to organize a Center conference in her honor on religious pluralism, which had become the greatest passion of Marjorie, who, like me, had studied with Cobb. Writing introductory chapters for the resulting book, I gave a threefold argument: First, although John Hick had provided the best-known type of religious pluralism, this type had led many theologians and religious philosophers to say that religious pluralism should be rejected. Second, Cobb's type has none of the problems in Hick's position that led religious pluralism into ill-repute. Third, although it was wrong to say, as did several critics, that Hick's position was not really pluralistic at all, his pluralism *is* shallow, compared with Cobb's. Accordingly, I— with the aid of the participants at the conference—named the resulting edited volume *Deep Religious Pluralism*.[20]

FOUR SCIENCE-BASED BOOKS

This period, during which I was working on global democracy, global morality, and religious pluralism, was also the period in which I wrote four science-based books: In addition to *Unsnarling the World-Knot*, I also, having written a major paper on parapsychology for a conference in Santa Barbara I had planned with Esalen-founder Michael Murphy, wrote a book entitled *Parapsychology, Philosophy, and Religion*,[21] arguing that Whitehead's philosophy allows for the possibility of the three major subjects of parapsychology: telepathy, psychokinesis, and phenomena suggestive of life after death.

I also wrote *Religion and Scientific Naturalism*,[22] in which I pointed out that atheism and supernaturalistic theism do not exhaust the options. There is also naturalistic theism, of which Whitehead is arguably the outstanding exemplar. In this book's longest chapter, which deals with evolution, I argued that Whitehead's philosophy provides an alternative beyond the standard alternatives of neo-Darwinism and intelligent design.

Finally, this same period brought forth my most extensive treatment of philosophy of religion, *Reenchantment without Supernaturalism*, which argued that Whitehead's philosophy provides the basis for a response to Max Weber's disenchantment thesis, according to which modernity has permanently destroyed the idea that philosophy can provide the basis for public morality.[23]

AN INTERRUPTION TO DEAL WITH AMERICAN IMPERIALISM

To return to my developing manuscript on global democracy: Although it was three-fourths written by the beginning of the 21st century, a funny thing happened on my way to press. Actually two things. The first thing was 9/11. Accepting the standard liberal interpretation, I had regarded the 9/11 attacks as vengeance by Muslims on America for its imperialist foreign policy, especially in the Middle East. But although American imperialism played a central role in every chapter of my intended book, I had not thematized US imperialism as such. So I set out to correct this oversight by writing a chapter on it.

But as a colleague said, once you get into American imperialism, you find that there is no end to it—certainly not a *short* end. So my intended *chapter* on American imperialism soon became my intended *book*, after which I would write a summary to serve as a chapter in the book on global democracy. By the beginning of 2003, I had my intended book on American imperialism about three-fourths finished.

## An interruption to deal with 9/11

But at that point, the second funny thing happened: I became aware of evidence that 9/11 was an inside job. I had been told about this by a visiting scholar a few months earlier, but, after looking at the suggested websites, I found it unconvincing and went back to my work on American imperialism. Early in 2003, however, I became aware of a website and a few books that presented a much stronger case. I decided that, if this was true, it was of utmost importance not only to the questions of war and ecological survival but also to theology. So I needed to drop other matters long enough to determine whether it was true.

Shortly after the Iraq war started, I was asked by School of Theology students to speak about this war. Rather than speaking about the Iraq war as such, I spoke about 9/11 as the precondition for that war. Afterwards, I decided I should turn my outline into an article, perhaps to be sent to *Harpers*. But as before, my intended essay soon became a proposed book—which I decided to call "The New Pearl Harbor."

As for publishing it, I assumed that this would be no problem, given the fact that I had already published over 20 books.
I quickly found, however, that publishers would not answer
my letters, even if Richard Falk would tell them—friends of
his—that he recommended that they look at my manuscript.
I did get a response from one publishing house called "Common Courage," which gave me a three-word email: "Not for
us." At least this publisher, I told Ann, was not guilty of false
advertising: It did not call itself *"Uncommon* Courage."

Thanks to Richard, however, I finally found a publisher. Being aware that Richard had published a little book on
the US war in Afghanistan, I asked him whether this book's
publisher might take mine. Saying it was worth a try, Richard
gave me the email address of Pam Thompson, the editor, and
soon we had a deal. She later revealed how this decision came
about—a revelation relevant to the oft-asked question whether my being a theologian had helped or hurt my 9/11 work.
Pam had felt torn: On the one hand, Richard had told her that
I was sensible and my book was well written. On the other
hand, she said to herself, Griffin was a *conspiracy theorist.* So
she called her father, a Presbyterian clergyman, and asked
whether he had ever heard of a theologian named David Ray
Griffin. "David Ray Griffin," her dad exclaimed, "I have all of
his books." So my being a theologian has helped more than it
has hurt, because apart from being a theologian, I might never have published a single book about 9/11.

Another question I have often been asked is how, given
my background, I started writing about 9/11—a question
often meaning: Why is a nice theologian like you dealing
with an issue like this? I answer: If 9/11, in which American
political and military leaders arguably orchestrated 9/11 as a
pretext to attack Islamic countries, to give even more money
to the already bloated military budget, and to further enrich

the already rich, is not a theological issue for those who see themselves as standing in the tradition of Amos, Isaiah, and Jesus, then what *would be* a theological issue?

Sometimes the question has been stated with a more hostile meaning: How could you, being a theologian, possibly have anything relevant to say about 9/11? I answer: That my education at Claremont and my writing during my teaching years dealt with history, religion, theology, philosophy, science, and global politics, and a background in these field was exactly what was needed to deal with the various aspects of 9/11.

For example, my work in the philosophy of science gave me much of the background I needed to deal with the destruction of the World Trade Center; I even employed Whitehead in my book on the destruction of World Trade Center 7.[24] In addition, my extensive treatment of evil helped me avoid the fallacy that has led many Americans to refuse to look at evidence that 9/11 was an inside job—the belief that American political and military leaders simply would not have done such a heinous thing.

## What next?

My interruption to work on 9/11—an interruption that has resulted in ten books and 65 articles—has certainly prevented me from doing many things I had planned. I now hope, besides completing the still unfinished books on American imperialism, global democracy, and ethics, to write a systematic theology. Back when I was a graduate student, I asked John Cobb when he was going to write his systematic theology. He replied that this would have to wait until he had retired. Some years after he had retired, he said to me: "Do you remember when you asked when I would write my systematic theology and I said, 'After I had retired'? Now my answer is 'Never.'"

He gave several reasons to justify this decision. But I did not accept those reasons. In any case, I planned to write my own systematic theology. Indeed, when I said that a conference or volume on my thought should not be planned until I had done something worthy of this honor, I primarily had in mind a systematic theology. Because of my close brush with death, I did accept the idea of the present conference, even though I have not even started my systematic theology. But I still plan to do it—God and my heart doctors willing.

I also hope to write some other books that I have had in mind for some time. One of those would be called "America: Divine or Demonic?" Another book, replying to the growing number of books advocating the so-called new atheism, would be called "Gawd Does Not Exist, but God Does"—here following the terminology employed by a conservative British philosopher who, during a debate, asked: "Are you referring to God, or *Gawd*?" Employing "Gawd" to mean the deity of Augustine, Thomas, and Calvin, I will explain that virtually all arguments for atheism point out that there are many reasons to deny the existence of "Gawd," whereas God as portrayed in process theism is supported by very strong considerations, and contradicted by none.

Let me conclude by saying that—like people who have received the Nobel Peace Prize on the assumption that they will sometime do something to be worthy of it—I thank you for participating in this conference, celebrating the worthy work that I plan to do.[25]

ADDENDUM: *The above was my after-banquet lecture at the close of the conference. The banquet itself was a grand affair, enjoyed by all, thanks to witty talks by Philip Clayton (who served as the master of ceremonies) and John Cobb, and to the perfect planning by my wife, Ann Jaqua.*

# Notes

CHAPTER 1. CATHERINE KELLER: GOD, POWER AND EVIL

1. Archibald MacLeish, *JB: A Play in Verse* (1958; New York: Houghton Mifflin, 1989).

2. David Ray Griffin, *God, Power, and Evil: A Process Theodicy* (Philadelphia: Westminster, 1976; reprinted with a new preface, University Press of America (Lanham, Md.), 1991; reprinted with a newer preface, Westminster John Knox (Louisville), 2004).

3. Ibid., 9.

4. David Ray Griffin, *Evil Revisited: Responses and Reconsiderations* (Albany: State University of New York Press, 1991).

5. David Ray Griffin, with Joseph A. Deegan and Daniel E.H. Bryant, *How Are God and Evil Related?* Claremont: Process & Faith Booklet, 1988, rev. 2001, 2088.

6. *God, Power, and Evil,* 16.

7. John B. Cobb, Jr., and David Ray Griffin, *Process Theology: An Introductory Exposition.* Philadelphia: Westminster, and Belfast: Christian Journals, 1976. Also published in German (1979), Japanese (1976), Italian (1978), and Chinese (1999).

8. *God, Power, and Evil,* 268.

9. Ibid.

10. Ibid., 269.

11. Ibid., 269-70.

12. Ibid., 291-97.

13. Ibid., 293.

14. Ibid., 284-85.

15. Anna Mercedes, *Power For: Feminism and Christ's Self-Giving* (London: T & T Clark, 2011).

16. Henry P. Stapp, *Mind, Matter, and Quantum Mechanics*, 2nd ed. (Springer, 2009); *Mindful Universe: Quantum Mechanics and the Participating Observer*, 3rd edition (Springer, 2011).

17. See Griffin, *Evil Revisited*, 108-14.

18. Ibid., 161.

19. Whitehead, *Process and Reality*, 4.

20. Ibid., 259.

21. See ibid., 5.

22. *Evil Revisited*, 212.

23. Ibid., 209-10.

## CHAPTER 2. GARY DORRIEN: RATIONALISTIC PANEXPERIENTIAL PANENTHEISM

1. David Ray Griffin, *God, Power, and Evil: A Process Theodicy* (Philadelphia: Westminster Press, 1976), 239-50, 275-310, quotes, 276-77; Alfred North Whitehead, *Adventures of Ideas* (New York: Macmillan, 1933), 213.

2. Griffin, *God, Power, and Evil*, 297-300, 311-13, quotes, 298, 312; Charles Hartshorne, *The Divine Relativity* (New Haven: Yale University Press, 1948), 41; Charles Hartshorne and William L. Reese, eds., *Philosophers Speak of God* (Chicago: University of Chicago Press, 1953), 277.

3. David Ray Griffin, *Evil Revisited: Responses and Reconsiderations* (Albany: State University of New York Press, 1991), 5-6, 23-26.

4. David Ray Griffin, *Unsnarling the World-Knot: Consciousness, Freedom, and the Mind-Body Problem* (Berkeley: University of California Press, 1998); Karl R. Popper and John C. Eccles, *The Self and Its Brain: An Argument for Interactionism* (Heidelberg:

Springer-Verlag, 1977); Geoffrey Madell, *Mind and Materialism* (Edinburgh: Edinburgh University Press, 1988); W. D. Hart, *The Engines of the Soul* (Cambridge: Cambridge University Press, 1988); Daniel E. Dennett, *Consciousness Explained* (Boston: Little, Brown, 1991); Paul M. Churchland, *Matter and Consciousness: A Contemporary Introduction to the Philosophy of Mind* (Cambridge, MA: MIT Press, 1988); Colin McGinn, *The Problem of Consciousness: Essays Towards a Resolution* (Oxford: Basil Blackwell, 1991); Thomas Nagel, *Mortal Questions* (London: Cambridge University Press, 1979); John Searle, *The Rediscovery of the Mind* (Cambridge: MIT Press, 1992); Searle, "Minds and Brains Without Programs," *Mindwaves: Thoughts on Intelligence, Identity, and Consciousness,* ed. Colin Blakemore and Susan Greenfield (Oxford: Basil Blackwell, 1987), 209-33.

5. Griffin, *Unsnarling the World-Knot,* 92-98, quote, 96; Alfred North Whitehead, *Science and the Modern World* (New York: Free Press, 1925), 79; see David Ray Griffin, *Religion and Scientific Naturalism: Overcoming the Conflicts* (Albany: State University of New York Press, 2000), 137-78.

6. Griffin, *Religion and Scientific Naturalism,* 90-93, 107-33; see David Ray Griffin, *Two Great Truths: A New Synthesis of Scientific Naturalism and Christian Faith* (Louisville: Westminster John Knox Press), 2004.

7. Thomas Reid, *An Inquiry into the Human Mind: On the Principles of Common Sense,* 3rd ed. (Dublin: R. Marchbank, 1779); abridged edition in Reid, *Inquiry and Essays,* ed. Ronald E. Beanblossom and Keith Lehrer (Indianapolis: Hackett Publishing Co., 1983), 118; Whitehead, *Process and Reality,* 151.

8. David Ray Griffin, *Reenchantment Without Supernaturalism: A Process Philosophy of Religion* (Ithaca: Cornell University Press, 2001), 29-35, 352-53; Charles Sanders Peirce, *Collected Papers of Charles Sanders Peirce,* 6 vols., ed. Charles Hartshorne and Paul Weiss (Cambridge: Harvard University Press, 1931-1935), 5:376, 416; Griffin, "Process Theology as Empirical, Rational, and Speculative: Some Reflections on Method," *Process Studies* 19 (Summer 1990), 116-35.

9. Griffin, *Reenchantment Without Supernaturalism,* 356-58.

10. Ibid., 169-203.

11. Alvin Plantinga, *God and Other Minds* (Ithaca, NY: Cornell University Press, 1967), quote 271; Plantinga, "The Reformed Objection to Natural Theology," *Rationality in the Calvinian Tradition,* ed. Hendrik Hart, Johan van der Hoeven, and Nicholas Wolterstorff (Lanham, Md: University Press of America, 1983), 363-83; Plantinga, "Advice to Christian Philosophers," *Faith and Philosophy 1* (July 1984), 253-71; Plantinga, "Is Belief in God Properly Basic?," *Philosophy of Religion: Selected Readings,* 2nd ed., ed. William L. Rowe and William J. Wainwright (Fort Worth: Harcourt Brace, 1989), 417-26; Nicholas Wolterstorff, "Can Belief in God Be Rational if It Has No Foundations?" *Faith and Rationality: Reason and Belief in God,* ed. Alvin Plantinga and Nicholas Wolterstorff (Notre Dame: University of Notre Dame Press, 1983), 135-86; Griffin, *Reenchantment Without Supernaturalism,* 367-92.

12. David Ray Griffin, "Hartshorne's Differences From Whitehead," *Two Process Philosophers: Hartshorne's Encounter with Whitehead,* ed. Lewis S. Ford (Tallahassee, Fl: American Academy of Religion, 1973), 35-57; see Griffin, "Charles Hartshorne," in Griffin, et al., *Founders of Constructive Postmodern Philosophy* (Albany: State University of New York Press, 1993), 197-231.

13. Griffin, *Reenchantment Without Supernaturalism,* 148-50.

14. Ibid., 150-52; Whitehead, *Process and Reality,* "a mere factor," 34; H. A. Johnson, "Whitehead as Teacher and Philosopher," *Philosophy and Phenomenological Research* 29 (1969), 351-76, quote, 370; John B. Cobb, Jr., *A Christian Natural Theology* (Philadelphia: Westminster Press, 1965), 180-81.

15. Griffin, *Reenchantment Without Supernaturalism,* 151-52; Charles Hartshorne, "Interrogation of Charles Hartshorne," *Philosophical Interrogations,* ed. Sydney Rome and Beatrice Rome (New York: Holt, Rinehart & Winston, 1964), 321-54, "a new Consequent," 323.

16. Griffin, *Reenchantment Without Supernaturalism, 156-61; Cobb, A Christian Natural Theology,* 187.

17. Griffin, *Reenchantment Without Supernaturalism,* 161-62; Charles Hartshorne, *Creative Synthesis and Philosophic Method* (La Salle, Il: Open Court, 1970), 233.

18. Griffin, *Reenchantment Without Supernaturalism,* 392; Griffin, *Religion and Scientific Naturalism,* 107-08.

19. David Ray Griffin to author, 12 March 2003.

20. David Ray Griffin, "Professing Theology in the State University," *Theology and the University: Essays in Honor of John B. Cobb, Jr.* (Albany: State University of New York Press, 1991), 3-34, quote, 12.

21. David Ray Griffin, conversation with author, 5 October 2002.

22. Griffin to author, 14 December 2002; Marjorie Suchocki, conversation with author, 20 June 2002; Gary Dorrien, *The Making of American Liberal Theology: Crisis, Irony, and Postmodernity, 1950-2005* (Louisville: Westminster John Knox Press, 2006).

CHAPTER 3. DANIEL DOMBROWSKI: GRIFFIN'S PANEXPERIENTIALISM AS *PHILOSOPHIA PERENNIS*

1. David Ray Griffin, *Unsnarling the World Knot: Consciousness Freedom, and the Mind-Body Problem* (Berkeley: University of California Press, 1998), 1, 4-6. Numbers in parentheses in the text refer to page numbers in this book. I should add that, as Griffin indicated, Seager and Strawson, having moved toward panpsychism, do not now regard the mind-body relation as totally inexplicable.

2. Josiah Royce, *The Philosophy of Loyalty* (New York: Macmillan, 1908), 11.

3. Alfred North Whitehead, *The Concept of Nature* (Cambridge: Cambridge University Press, 1920), 229.

4. Daniel Dennett, *Consciousness Explained* (Boston: Little, Brown, 1991), 37.

5. Griffin, *Reenchantment without Supernaturalism.*

6. Whitehead, *The Concept of Nature,* 187.

7. Ibid., 168.

8. Whitehead, "Immortality," in *The Philosophy of Alfred North Whitehead,* ed. P.A. Schilpp (LaSalle, IL: Open Court, 1941), 695.

9. See Whitehead, *Adventures of Ideas* (New York: Free Press, 1961), 5-6, 25, 83, 118-22, 129, 166-69, 179, 197; *Modes of Thought* (New York: Free Press, 1966), 119. Also see Daniel Dombrowski, "Hartshorne and Plato," in *The Philosophy of Charles Hartshorne,* ed. Lewis Hahn (LaSalle, IL: Open Court, 1991); and *A Platonic Philosophy of Religion: A Process Perspective* (Albany: State University of New York Press, 2005), ch. 2.

10. Charles Hartshorne, *Whitehead's Philosophy* (Lincoln: University of Nebraska Press, 1972), 100. Also see Dombrowski, *Rethinking the Ontological Argument: A Neoclassical Theistic Response* (New York: Cambridge University Press, 2006).

11. See Hartshorne, *Creative Experiencing: A Philosophy of Freedom* (Albany: State University of New York Press, 2011), 68.

12. Once again, see Dombrowski, "Hartshorne and Plato" as well as *A Platonic Philosophy of Religion.*

13. See William Christian, *An Interpretation of Whitehead's Metaphysics* (New Haven: Yale University Press, 1959), ch. 5, regarding what is living and what is dead in Aristotle's concept of substance.

14. See James Felt, *Coming to Be: Toward a Thomistic-Whiteheadian Metaphysics of Becoming* (Albany: State University of New York Press, 2001); and W. Norris Clarke, *The Philosophical Approach to God,* revised ed. (New York: Fordham University Press, 2007).

15. See Hartshorne, *Creative Experiencing,* 58.

16. Ibid., 113-19.

17. Whitehead, *Process and Reality,* corrected ed. (New York: Free

Press, 1978), xi.

18. Ivor Leclerc, *The Nature of Physical Existence* (New York: Humanities Press, 1972), ch. 21.

19. Whitehead, *The Concept of Nature,* 26.

20. Whitehead, *Process and Reality,* 39.

21. Also see Griffin, *Religion and Scientific Naturalism: Overcoming the Conflicts* (Albany: State University of New York Press, 2000), ch. 5.

22. Leclerc, *The Nature of Physical Existence,* ch. 21.

23. Hartshorne, *Whitehead's Philosophy,* 39.

24. Hartshorne, *Creative Experiencing,* 60.

25. Immanuel Kant, *Dreams of a Spirit-Seer,* tr. and ed. Emmanuel Goerwitz and Frank Sewall (New York: Macmillan, 1900), part I, ch. 1. Also see Hartshorne, *Whitehead's Philosophy,* 158-59, 206.

26. See Catherine Wilson, "Kant and Leibniz," Stanford Encyclopedia of Philosophy <http://plato.stanford.edu>.

27. Hartshorne, *Creative Experiencing,* 55.

28. Whitehead, *Process and Reality,* 27.

29. See John Cobb, *A Christian Natural Theology: Based on the Thought of Alfred North Whitehead,* 2nd ed. (Louisville: Westminster John Knox Press, 2007), 8, 149.

30. Hartshorne, *Creative Synthesis and Philosophic Method* (LaSalle, IL: Open Court, 1970), 4-6.

31. David Skrbina, *Panpsychism in the West* (Cambridge: MIT Press, 2005).

32. Hartshorne, *Creative Experiencing,* 3.

33. Ibid., 4, 13.

34. See Marcus Ford, ed., *A Process Theory of Medicine* (Lewiston, NY: Edwin Mellen Press, 1987).

35. Hartshorne, *Creative Experiencing,* 39, also 16, 38.

36. Ibid., 40-41, 75, 100, 140.

37. Ibid., 14-15, 17, 51, 62, 129-30.

38. Whitehead, *The Concept of Nature,* 160.

39. Nathaniel Barrett, "The Perspectivity of Feeling: Process Panpsychism and the Explanatory Gap," *Process Studies* 38 (2009), 189-206.

40. Whitehead, *The Concept of Nature,* 29; Hartshorne, *The Philosophy and Psychology of Sensation* (Chicago: University of Chicago Press, 1934), 94; and Dombrowski, *Divine Beauty: The Aesthetics of Charles Hartshorne* (Nashville: Vanderbilt University Press, 2004), ch. 5.

41. Barrett, "The Perspectivity of Feeling," 200.

42. Ibid., 204.

43. See Hartshorne, *Creative Experiencing,* 23-24, 71, 101, 115.

CHAPTER 4. JOHN B. COBB, JR.: GRIFFIN ON EVOLUTION

1. The final and longest chapter of Griffin's major science-religion book, *Religion and Scientific Naturalism: Overcoming the Conflicts* (2000), was entitled "Creation and Evolution."

2. I first learned of Griffin's research in this area in 1983 from an essay, called "Theology and the Rise of Modern Science," which was written as a background paper for a book by Joe Hough and me, *Christian Identity and Theological Education* (Chico: Calif.: Scholars Press, 1985), which was supported by a grant from the Association of Theological Schools. A revised and updated version of Griffin's essay, entitled "Religion and the Rise of the Modern Scientific World," appeared as Chapter 5 in his 2000 book, *Religion and Scientific Naturalism: Overcoming the Conflicts.*

CHAPTER 5. PHILIP CLAYTON: SCIENTIFIC AND RELIGIOUS NATURALISM

1. See Robert S. Brumbaugh, *Whitehead, Process Philosophy, and Education* (Albany: State University of New York Press, 1982); Brumbaugh and Nathaniel M. Lawrence, *Philosophical Themes in Modern Education* (1973; Lanham: University Press of America, 1985).

2. Timothy E. Eastman and Hank Keeton, eds., *Physics and Whitehead: Quantum, Process, and Experience* (Albany, NY: SUNY Press, 2004); Michael Epperson, *Quantum Mechanics and the Philosophy of Alfred North Whitehead* (New York: Fordham University Press. 2004); John B. Cobb, Jr., ed., *Back to Darwin: A Richer Account of Evolution* (Grand Rapids: William B. Eerdmans Pub. Co., 2008).

3. For an overview of the literature in process philosophy and theology, see the online bibliographies at the Center for Process Studies, <http://www.ctr4process.org/publications/Biblio/Thematic/>, accessed July 4, 2012.

4. This and other parenthetical instances of *"PR"* stand for Alfred North Whitehead, *Process and Reality: An Essay in Cosmology,* corrected edition, ed. David Ray Griffin and Donald W. Sherburne (1929; New York: Free Press, 1978).

5. John B Cobb, Jr., *A Christian Natural Theology, Based on the Thought of Alfred North Whitehead* (Philadelphia: Westminster Press, 1965); Cobb, ed., *Back to Darwin;* David Ray Griffin, ed., *Deep Religious Pluralism* (Louisville: Westminster John Knox Press, 2005).

6. For a useful summary of process philosophers, see Douglas Browning and William T. Myers, eds., *Philosophers of Process,* 2nd ed. (Bronx, NY: Fordham University Press, 1998). The best single summation of process philosophy of religion is still David Griffin's *Reenchantment without Supernaturalism: A Process Philosophy of Religion* (Ithaca: Cornell University Press, 2001).

8. Joseph Bracken and Marjorie Hewitt Suchocki, eds., *Trinity in Process: A Relational Theology of God* (New York: Continuum, 1997), 21, 25-27, 36.

9. David Ray Griffin, *God, Power, and Evil: A Process Theodicy* (Philadelphia: Westminster Press, 1976); *Evil Revisited: Responses and Reconsiderations* (Albany: State University of New York Press, 1991).

10. Marjorie Hewitt Suchocki, *The End of Evil: Process Eschatology in Historical Context* (Albany: State University of New York Press, 1988).

11. Joseph Bracken, ed., *World without End: Christian Eschatology from a Process Perspective* (Grand Rapids, MI: William B. Eerdmans, 2005).

12. Examples include Lewis Ford, *The Lure of God: A Biblical Background for Process Theism* (Minneapolis: Augsburg Fortress, 1979); John Cobb and David J. Lull's process interpretation of Romans, *Romans (*St. Louis, MO: Chalice Press, 2005); and Catherine Keller's *Face of the Deep: A Theology of Becoming* (London: Routledge, 2003). One can find over a dozen volumes on process and prayer; see e.g. Norman Pittenger, *Praying Today* (Grand Rapids, MI: William B. Eerdmans Publishing Co., 1974).

13. See, for example, Clark Pinnock and others in *The Openness of God: A Biblical Challenge to the Traditional Understanding of God* (Downers Grove, IL: InterVarsity Press, 1994); John Sanders's *The God Who Risks: A Theology of Divine Providence,* 2nd ed. (Downers Grove, IL: IVP Academic, 2007); and David Basinger's *The Case for Freewill Theism: A Philosophical Assessment* (Downers Grove, IL: InterVarsity Press,1996). Process and free will theism are both represented in Cobb and Pinnock's collection, *Searching for an Adequate God: A Dialogue between Process and Free Will Theists* (Grand Rapids, MI: Eerdmans, 2000).

14. Cobb and Pinnock, eds., *Searching for an Adequate God.*

15. See, for example, Thomas Jay Oord, ed., *Creation Made Free: Open Theology Engaging Science (*Eugene, OR: Pickwick Publications, 2009).

16. Charles Hartshorne, *Reality as Social Process* (Glencoe, IL: The Free Press, 1953), 147.

17. Lewis Ford worked out the layers of composition in *The Emergence of Whitehead's Metaphysics, 1925-1929* (Albany, NY: State University of New York Press, 1984).

18. Donald W. Sherburne, "Whitehead without God," *The Christian Scholar* 50/3 (1967): 251-72.

19. Gordon Kaufman, *In the Beginning—Creativity* (Minneapolis: Fortress Press, 2004). The role of a process agnosticism in the philosophy of religion should also be mentioned. Sometimes this agnosticism represents a transition point for philosophers who are disillusioned with classical theism and the arguments on its behalf, yet who have reasons not to settle into a doctrinaire atheism. Sometimes agnosticism attracts naturalists who have become disillusioned with reductive materialist naturalism but who are skeptical about the metaphysical commitments necessary for full-fledged theism. For others, however, it becomes a resting place, a settled via media between an untenable traditional theism and an untenable reductionist naturalism. A brilliant example of this process agnosticism can be found in "On 'Wide Sense Agnosticism' and Process Theism" by Mary Herczog, whose tragic death from cancer a few years ago cut short her dissertation work on this topic. It is important to remember that this response is a live option in the debate. See Mary Herczog, "On 'Wide Sense Agnosticism' and Process Theism" (2008), published online at <http://www.ctr4process. org/publications/Articles/HerczogM-On_Wide_Sense_Agnosticism.shtml>, accessed July 4, 2012.

20. Griffin, *Reenchantment without Supernaturalism: A Process Philosophy of Religion* (Ithaca, NY: Cornell University Press, 2001).

21. Richard Rorty famously made a similar point in *Philosophy and the Mirror of Nature* (Princeton: Princeton University Press, 1979).

22. For a briefer exposition of this view, see David Ray Griffin, *Two Great Truths: A New Synthesis of Scientific Naturalism and Christian Faith* (Louisville: Westminster John Knox Press, 2004).

23. See Clayton, *Adventures in the Spirit: God, World, Divine Action* (Minneapolis: Fortress, 2008), e.g. chapter 11, "Open Panen-

theism and Creation as *Kenosis.*"

24. Again, the most significant authors in this area are Roland Faber and Catherine Keller. See Roland Faber, *God as Poet of the World: Exploring Process Theologies* (Louisville: Westminster John Knox Press, 2008); Keller, *Face of the Deep* (cited above); and Keller, *On the Mystery: Discerning Divinity in Process* (Minneapolis: Fortress Press, 2008). Keller has also organized and edited an important series of anthologies under the title "Transdisciplinary Theological Colloquia."

25. William Dean, *American Religious Empiricism* (Albany: State University of New York Press, 1986), x.

26. See Robert Walter Bretall, *The Empirical Theology of Henry Nelson Wieman* (New York: Macmillan, 1963), 4.

27. Pascal Boyer, *Religion Explained: The Evolutionary Origins of Religious Thought* (New York: Basic Books, 2001); Scott Atran, *In Gods We Trust: The Evolutionary Landscape of Religion* (Oxford: Oxford University Press, 2002).

28. For example, Nancey Murphy, *Anglo-American Postmodernity: Philosophical Perspectives on Science, Religion, and Ethics* (Boulder, CO: Westview Press, 1997).

29. See Clayton, *Adventures in the Spirit,* Section 1.

Chapter 6. Sandra B. Lubarsky: Non-Supernatural Naturalism and Deep Religious Pluralism

1. Alfred North Whitehead, *Science and the Modern World* (New York: Free Press, 1967), 185.

2. Ibid.

3. David Ray Griffin, *Religion and Scientific Naturalism: Overcoming the Conflicts* (Albany:  State University of New York Press, 2000), xv.

4. Personal notes from conference.

5. Religious Tolerance: Ontario Consultants on Religious Tolerance <http://www.religioustolerance.org/rel_plur1.htm> [accessed March 15, 2012]. Rabbi Laemmle served for many years as Dean of Religious Life at the University of Southern California.

6. Robert Wuthnow, *America and the Challenges of Religious Diversity* <http://www.carnegiecouncil.org/resources/transcripts/5234.html/:pf_printable> [April 1, 2012].

7. David Ray Griffin, "Introduction to SUNY Series in Constructive Postmodern Thought," see, for example, *Religion and Scientific Naturalism: Overcoming the Conflicts* (Albany: State University of New York Press, 2000), xi.

8. David Ray Griffin, *Religion and Scientific Naturalism: Overcoming the Conflicts*, xv.

9. Gary Dorrien, *The Making of American Liberal Theology: Crisis, Irony, & Postmodernity, 1950-2005* (Louisville: Westminster John Knox Press, 2006), 246.

10. David Ray Griffin, *Two Great Truths: A New Synthesis of Scientific Naturalism and Christian Faith* (Louisville: Westminster John Knox Press, 2004), 98-115.

11. Griffin's book, *Deep Religious Pluralism* (Louisville, Westminster John Knox Press, 2005), grew out of a conference with Whiteheadians from Christian, Jewish, Islamic, Hindu, Buddhist, and Chinese traditions, all of whom found a Whiteheadian-based approach to be of much value.

12. *Deep Religious Pluralism*, 20.

13. Ibid., 14; Griffin, *Whitehead's Radically Different Postmodern Philosophy: An Argument for its Contemporary Relevance* (Albany: State University of New York Press, 2007), 31.

14. Paul J. Griffiths, "Beyond Pluralism" (review of S. Mark Heim's *"Salvations: Truth and Difference in Religion)*, *First Things*, January 1996: 50-52.

15. "Given the non-coercive nature of divine influence plus

the radical freedom and thereby historicity of human beings, we have no basis for assuming that all the religious traditions would teach essentially the same thing" (Griffin, *Reenchantment Without Supernaturalism* [Ithaca: Cornell University Press, 2001], 259).

16. See Griffin, "Process Theodicy, Christology, and the *Imitatio Dei,"* in *Jewish Theology and Process Thought,* ed. David Ray Griffin and Sandra Lubarsky (Albany: State University of New York Press, 1996).

17. Griffin, *Deep Religious Pluralism,* 24.

18. Griffin, *Reenchantment without Supernaturalism,* 273-77.

19. Ibid., 277.

20. Griffin, *Deep Religious Pluralism,* 63; quoting Cobb, *Transforming Christianity and the World: A Way beyond Absolutism and Relativism,* ed. Paul F. Knitter (Maryknoll, NY: Orbis Books, 1999), 137.

21. Griffin, *Deep Religious Pluralism,* 63.

22. Ibid., 65.

23. Griffin, *Reenchantment without Supernaturalism,* 360.

CHAPTER 7. NANCY FRANKENBERRY: THE VAGARIES OF RELIGIOUS EXPERIENCE

1. Gary Dorrien, "American Liberal Theology: Crisis, Irony, Decline, Renewal, Ambiguity," *Cross Currents* 55(4), Winter, 2006. See also his three-volume work: Gary Dorrien, *The Making of American Liberal Theology: Imagining Progressive Religion* (Louisville: Westminster John Knox Press, 2001); Dorrien, *The Making of American Liberal Theology: Idealism, Realism & Modernity* (Louisville: Westminster John Knox Press, 2003); Dorrien, *The Making of American Liberal Theology: Crisis, Irony & Postmodernity* (Louisville: Westminster John Knox Press, 2006).

2. Alfred North Whitehead, *Religion in the Making* (New York,

The Macmillan company, 1926), 74. For Griffin's most important works on the question of theodicy, see *God, Power, and Evil: A Process Theodicy* (Philadelphia: Westminster, 1976) and *Evil Revisited: Responses and Reconsiderations* (Albany: State University of New York Press, 1991). I agree with Catherine Keller's assessment in this volume that Griffin's signature work is found in his books on the problem of evil and the need for a revisionist conception of omnipotence. Space prevents me from expounding the constructive details of process theism or considering any of the issues that bedevil even the process model, especially the choice between an entitative or a societal model of "God."

3. David Ray Griffin, "Kai Nielsen, *God, Scepticism, and Modernity*," in *Journal of the American Academy of Religion* 59/1 (Spring, 1991), 189-90.

4. Kai Nielson, *Naturalism and Religion* (Amherst, NY: Prometheus Books, 2001), 424.

5. See Jeffrey Stout, *Ethics After Babel: The Languages of Morals and Their Discontents* (Boston: Beacon Press, 1988), 163-64.

6. Henry Samuel Levinson, in conversation, June 1995. See also his comments on Whitehead and the Chicago School in his entry on "Religious Philosophy" in the *Encyclopedia of the American Religious Experience: Studies of Traditions and Movements, Volume II*, ed. by Charles H. Lippy and Peter W. Williams (New York: Charles Scribner's Sons, 1988), at 1203-04.

7. See especially Griffin, *Reenchantment Without Supernaturalism*, 52-93.

8. *Reenchantment*, 71. Equivalent terms Griffin uses are "Cosmic Mind" (73) and "a loving, holy actuality" (83). I find that the way in which he employs the term "genuine religious experience" tends to beg the question.

9. Ibid., 69.

10. Ibid., 69. Griffin's analysis states only one half of Proudfoot's actual two-step methodology with its useful distinction

between descriptive and explanatory forms of reduction. Proudfoot cautions *against* "descriptive reductionism," that would discount or redescribe the subject's own report in ways the subject would not recognize; and he advises *in favor of* explanatory reductionism, in which the scholar, rather than being strictly bound by the subject's own report, offers an explanation in light of historical, sociological, and psychological considerations that can be attributed to the subject(s). Griffin says he wants a "religious explanation" for reports about religious experiences. What would that be, apart from inference to the best explanation using natural causes as these are understood through the arts and humanities, the social sciences, and the physical sciences?

11. *Reenchantment,* 54-68; 76-77; 338-42.

12. See Ann Taves, *Religious Experience Reconsidered: A Building Block Approach to the Study of Religion and Other Special Things* (Princeton: Princeton University, 2009). Readers of her earlier study, *Fits, Trances, and Visions: Experiencing Religion and Explaining Experience from Wesley to James* (Princeton: Princeton University Press, 1999), will appreciate how the latter book grew out of a set of questions generated by the former.

13. Rather than engage disputes about the meaning of "supernatural," I prefer the term superhuman, which simply designates putative beings who can do things that you and I cannot do. "Superhuman" amply covers the exploits of religious founders such as Moses, Krishna, Buddha, Jesus, and Mohammad, as narrated in myths and legends.

14. *Reenchantment,* 348.

15. Griffin has analyzed much of what I am discussing here in the highly technical language of Whitehead's "stages of concrescence." I am willing to forgo that precision for the sake of seeking some simplicity, which devout Whiteheadians will no doubt distrust.

16. For the "myth of the given," see Wilfrid Sellers, *Empiricism and the Philosophy of Mind* (Cambridge: Harvard University Press, 1997).

17. Donald Davidson, "The Folly of Trying to Define Truth," in *Dialogue and Universalism* 6 (1996): 39-53; reprinted in *Journal of Philosophy* 94 (1997): 263-78.

18. See, in particular, the case Griffin makes in "Truth as Correspondence, Knowledge as Dialogical: On Affirming Pluralism without Relativism," in *Truth: Interdisciplinary Dialogues in a Pluralist Age,* ed. Christine Helmer and Kristin De Troyer with Katie Goetz (Leuven: Peeters, 2003), 233-50 (also in Griffin, *Whitehead's Radically Different Postmodern Philosophy).* See, also, *Reenchantment,* Ch. 9. Griffin commented (2003) on what he took to be Davidson's change of heart about rejecting correspondence theories, citing a 1990 paper in which Davidson said that the usual "complaint against correspondence theories [that it makes no sense to suggest that it is somehow possible to compare one's words or beliefs with the world] is not sound [because] it depends on assuming that some form of epistemic theory is correct." In context, it is clear that Davidson was refining, rather than withdrawing, his complaint to correspondence theories, as he went on to state two pages later: "The correct objection to correspondence theories is not, then, that they make truth something to which humans can never legitimately aspire; the real objection is rather that such theories fail to provide entities to which truth vehicles (whether we take these to be statements, sentences or utterances) can be said to correspond" (cf. Davidson, "The Structure and Content of Truth," *Journal of Philosophy* 87/6 (June 1990), 279-328, at 304. What Davidson called a "mistake" was his having said that a Tarski-style truth theory was a form of correspondence theory. For the record, he also deplored his having appeared to endorse (1983) "coherence" as a theory of truth when he only meant it could serve as a *test* of knowledge. See Davidson, "A Coherence Theory of Truth and Knowledge" (with "Afterthoughts", 1987) in *Reading Rorty,* ed. A. Malachowski (Oxford: Blackwell, 1990), 120-38.

19. Alfred North Whitehead, *Process and Reality,* corrected edition, ed. David Ray Griffin and Donald Sherburne (New York: Free Press, 1978), 151.

CHAPTER 8. MARCUS FORD: PSI PHENOMENA

1. David Ray Griffin, "Being Bold: Anticipating a Whiteheadian Century," *The Journal of Whitehead Studies* (Seoul: The Whitehead Society of Korea) 1 (1998): 15-34. Also in *Process Studies* 31/2 (2002) and in *Process Studies in China* 1 (2004): 226-44.

2. Elizabeth Lloyd Mayer, *Extraordinary Knowing: Science, Skepticism, and the Inexplicable Powers of the Human Mind* (New York: Bantam Books, 2008).

3. David Ray Griffin, *Parapsychology, Philosophy, and Spirituality: A Postmodern Exploration* (Albany: State University of New York Press, 1997).

4. Russell Targ, *The Reality of ESP: A Physicist's Proof of Psychic Abilities* (Wheaton: Quest Books, 2012).

5. For some of these philosophers (beyond Griffin), see Stephen Braude, *The Limits of Influence: Psychokinesis and the Philosophy of Science* (New York: Routledge & Kegan Paul, 1986 (rev. ed. 1996); *Immortal Remains: The Evidence for Life After Death* (Lanham: Rowman & Littlefield Publisher, 2003); and *The Gold Leaf Lady and Other Parapsychological Investigations* (Chicago: University of Chicago Press, 2007); Patrick Grim, ed., *Philosophy of Science and the Occult,* 2nd ed. (Albany: State University of New York Press, 1990); Antony Flew, "Parapsychology Revisited: Laws, Miracles, and Repeatability," in Jan Ludwig, ed., *Philosophy and Parapsychology* (Buffalo: Prometheus Books, 1978), 263-69, and "Parapsychology: Science of Pseudoscience?" in Paul Kurtz, ed., *A Skeptic's Handbook of Parapsychology* (Buffalo: Prometheus Books, 1985), 519-36.

6. Nicholas Humphrey, *Leaps of Faith: Science, Miracles, and the Search for Supernatural Consolation* (New York: Copernicus, 1996), 216.

7. Ibid., 216-17.

8. Ibid., 217.

9. It is interesting to note that, in an earlier book, Humphrey admitted that "the evidence that has accumulated over the ages [for ESP] is undeniably impressive" (*Soul Searching: Human*

*Nature and the Supernatural Belief* (London: Chatto & Windus, 1995), 115).

10. E.O. Wilson, *Consilience: The Unity of Knowledge* (New York: Alfred Knopf), 268.

11. See especially Griffin, *Religion and Scientific Naturalism: Overcoming the Conflicts* (Albany: State University of New York Press, 2000), Chapter 5. For a less detailed account by Griffin, see *Parapsychology, Philosophy, and Spirituality,* Chapter 1: "Parapsychology and Postmodern Philosophy."

12. Griffin, *Parapsychology, Philosophy, and Spirituality,* 8.

13. Ibid, 277.

14. Ibid., 91, quoting Antony Flew, "Parapsychology: Science of Pseudoscience?" in Paul Kurtz, ed., *A Skeptic's Handbook of Parapsychology* (Buffalo: Prometheus Books, 1985), 519-36, at 533.

15. Ibid., 91.

16. Flew, "Parapsychology Revisited: Laws, Miracles, and Repeatability," Jan Ludwig, ed., *Philosophy and Parapsychology* (Buffalo: Prometheus Books, 1978), 263-69, at 264.

17. Ibid., p. 272.

18. *Irreducible Mind: Toward a Psychology for the 21st Century,* by Edward Kelly, Emily Williams Kelly, and others (Lanham: Rowland & Littlefield, 2006). The quote is both on the jacket cover of the hardback edition and on the Amazon.com website.

19. For a collection of James' essays, reviews, and articles written over the course of twenty-five years on this topic, see *Essays in Psychical Research,* The Works of William James, ed. Frederick H. Burkhardt (Cambridge: Harvard University Press, 1986), with an introductory essay by Robert A. McDermott. Freud's thoughts concerning mental telepathy are found in "Psychoanalysis and Telepathy "(1921), and "Dreams and Telepathy" (1922), and a note on "The Occult Meaning of Dreams" (1925), published in the *New Introductory Lectures on Psychoanalysis* (1933). For Jung's thoughts about psi, see *Jung*

*on Synchronicity and the Paranormal* (Princeton: Princeton University Press, 1998), ed. Roderick Main.

20. William James, *A Pluralistic Universe* (1908; Cambridge: Harvard University Press, 1977, with an introduction by Richard J. Bernstein), 142.

21. Griffin, *Parapsychology, Philosophy, and Spirituality,* 292.

CHAPTER 9. JOHN BUCHANAN: LIFE AFTER DEATH AND PARAPSYCHOLOGY

1. If this sounds absurd to some readers, I am not alone in entertaining such notions. Robert Thouless wrote: "It would be a big breakthrough if anyone could devise methods of communication that did not involve a human medium, but there is no hint yet of how such a development could take place." See Robert H. Thouless, *From Anecdote to Experiment in Psychical Research* (London: Routledge & Kegan Paul, 1972), 164.

2. John H Hick, *Death and Eternal Life* (1976; New York: Harper and Row, 1980).

3. Thouless, *From Anecdote to Experiment,* 87.

4. David Ray Griffin, *Parapsychology, Philosophy, and Spirituality: A Postmodern Exploration* (Albany: State University of New York Press, 1997), 18-21.

5. David Ray Griffin, "Life After Death, Parapsychology, and Post-Modern Animism," in Stephen T. Davis, ed., *Death and Afterlife* (London: MacMillan, 1989), 94.

6. Griffin, *Parapsychology, Philosophy, and Spirituality,* 110, 108.

7. David Ray Griffin, "Parapsychology and Philosophy: A Whiteheadian Postmodern Perspective," *Journal of the American Society for Psychical Research* 87/3 (July 1993) <http://www.anthonyflood.com/griffinparapsychology.htm>, 217-88, at 223.

8. H.H. Price, "Personal Survival and the Idea of Another World" (1964), in John Hick, ed., *Classical and Contemporary Readings in the Philosophy of Religion,* 2nd ed. (New Jersey: Prentice Hall,

1970), 370-93, at 375.

9. Griffin, "Parapsychology and Philosophy," 276.

10. Griffin, *Parapsychology, Philosophy, and Spirituality,* 24, 57.

11. Ibid., 42.

12. Ibid., 95.

13. Ibid., 155-56.

14. Ibid., 161-68.

15. Ibid., 168.

16. A dramatic exception to this caveat is found in a dev-il-possession case unearthed during LSD therapy and finally recounted by Stanislav Grof in a recent book. In this case, "Flo-ra," being treated through an experimental program for the criminally insane, demonstrated paranormal knowledge and powers that shocked even a seasoned psychedelic researcher like Grof. See Stanislav Grof, *When the Impossible Happens: Adventures in Non-ordinary Reality* (Boulder, CO: Sounds True, Inc., 2006), 288-94.

17. Griffin, *Parapsychology, Philosophy, and Spirituality,* 182-83.

18. Ian Stephenson, *Twenty Cases Suggestive of Reincarnation* (New York: American Society for Psychical Research), 1966.

19. *Parapsychology, Philosophy, and Spirituality,* 200.

20. Ibid., 201.

21. Ibid., 197-204.

22. Ibid., 204-07.

23. Ibid., 211-12.

24. Ibid., 220.

25. Ibid., 223.

26. Ibid., 227-28.

27. Michael B. Sabom, *Recollections of Death: A Medical Investigation* (New York: Harper and Row, 1982), 152.

28. Ibid., 238.

29. Griffin, *Parapsychology, Philosophy, and Spirituality*, 239-43.

30. Sabom, *Recollections of Death*, 172.

31. Ibid., 20-21.

32. Griffin, *Parapsychology, Philosophy, and Spirituality*, 250-51.

33. Ibid., 243.

34. In *Life at Death: A Scientific Investigation of the Near-Death Experience* (New York: Coward, McCann and Geoghegan, 1980) and *Heading Toward Omega: In Search of the Meaning of the Near-Death Experience* (New York: William Morrow, 1984), noted NDE researcher Kenneth Ring addressed NDEs and the related veridical perceptions occurring during OBEs. In *Mindsight: Near-Death and Out-of-Body Experiences in the Blind* (Palo Alto: William James Center for Consciousness Studies, 1999), Ring and coauthor Sharon Cooper made an extensive effort to find objectively verifiable evidence of visual perception during near-death experiences in the blind (who report being able to "see" during NDEs). Ring and Cooper's conclusions from their study were: NDEs do occur in the blind and are similar to NDEs in general; 80% of the blind have visual impressions during their NDEs; and there is some suggestive evidence that these visual perceptions are objectively authentic (121-22) Their explanation for such visual impressions in the blind is "a complex form of synesthetically modulated awareness with clairvoyant aspects" (167). This description fits well with a Whiteheadian understanding, and could equally well be applied to how perception might function after death in the sighted. Ring's own speculations about a theoretical contextualization for "mindsight" are based on the kind of Eastern philosophy/quantum physics amalgams (171-73) that rarely seem helpful to me.

35. Griffin, *Parapsychology, Philosophy, and Spirituality,* 232.

36. Ibid., 263.

37. Ibid., 262.

38. Ibid., 152.

39. Ibid., 262.

40. Ibid., 264.

41. Ibid., 266-67.

42. Ibid., 150-51.

43. Ibid., 264.

44. Ibid., 271-72.

45. Ibid., 272.

46. Ibid., 272-87.

47. Ibid., 282.

48. Ibid., 287.

49. Ibid., 290-91.

CHAPTER 10. GENE REEVES: DAVID GRIFFIN ON MORALITY

1. David Ray Griffin, "The Moral Need for Global Democracy," 9; Griffin, "Moral Values and Global Democracy," *Creative Transformation,* 15/1 (Winter 2006), 25-35, at 27.

2. Griffin, "Moral Values and Global Democracy," 6-7.

3. Griffin, "The Moral Need for Global Democracy," 11.

4. Ibid., 7.

5. David Ray Griffin, "Ethics and the Fabric of the Universe," in Haruo Murata, ed., *Whitehead and Ethics in the Contemporary*

*World: For Sustainability and the Common Good* (Tokyo: The Japan Society for Process Studies, 2010), 7-17, at 1-2.

6. Quoted in Griffin, *Reenchantment without Supernaturalism: A Process Philosophy of Religion,* 286.

7. Griffin, "Theism and the Crisis in Ethics: Rethinking Modern Autonomy," 4.

8. Griffin, "Moral Values and Global Democracy," 21.

9. Whitehead, *Modes of Thought,* 86.

10. Griffin, "The Holy, Necessary Goodness, and Morality," *The Journal of Religious Ethics,* 8:2 (Fall 1980), 330-49 (http://anthonyflood.com/griffinholygoodnessmorality.htm), at 331.

11. "Ethics and the Fabric of the Universe," 10.

12. *Reenchantment without Supernaturalism,* 315.

13. "The Holy, Necessary Goodness, and Morality," 333.

14. "Saving Civilization: Straussian and Whiteheadian Political Philosophy," in Michel Weber and Will Desmond, eds., *Handbook of Whiteheadian Process Thought* (Frankfurt: Ontos Verlag, 2008), 521-32, at 525.

15. Ibid., 525; citing Whitehead, *Modes of Thought,* 103.

16. "The Holy, Necessary Goodness, and Morality," 340, quoting Whitehead, *Process and Reality,* 162.

17. Ibid., 341 (quoting Charles Hartshorne, *Reality as Social Process: Studies in Metaphysics and Religion* [Glencoe: Free Press; Boston: Beacon Press, 1953]), 141.

18. Ibid., 342.

19. Ibid.

20. See, for example, David Ray Griffin, "Feeling and Morality in Whitehead's System," in *Schleiermacher and Whitehead:*

*Open Systems in Dialogue,* ed. Christine Helmer, with Marjorie Suchocki, John Quiring, and Katie Goetz (Berlin and New York: Walter de Gruyter, 2004), 265-94, at 29-94.

21. *Reenchantment without Supernaturalism,* 305.

22. Ibid., 5.

23. Reported in *The Autobiography of Eleanor Roosevelt* (1961; New York: Da Capo Press, 1992), 317.

24. "Saving Civilization," 527; citing Whitehead, *Science and the Modern World,* 206.

25. Whitehead spoke of "the growth of reverence for that power in virtue of which nature harbours ideal ends, and produces individual beings capable of conscious discrimination of such ends. This reverence is the foundation of respect for man as man" (*Adventures of Ideas,* 86).

26. *Reenchantment without Supernaturalism,* 304-05; quoting Whitehead, *Modes of Thought,* 14.

27. Ibid., 288.

28. Whitehead, *Adventures of Ideas,* 83; quoted in "Feeling and Morality in Whitehead's System," 291.

29. *Reenchantment without Supernaturalism,* 312.

30. Whitehead, *Process and Reality,* 225.

31. Ibid., 244.

32. Griffin, "The Holy, Necessary Goodness, and Morality," 334-35.

## CHAPTER 11. RICHARD FALK: POSTMODERN POLITICS AND SPIRITUALITY

1. See Richard Falk, "Anarchism without 'Anarchism': Searching for Progressive Politics in the Early 21st Century," *Millennium: Journal of International Studies* 39/2 (2010): 381-98.

2. Alexander Wendt, "Why a World State is Inevitable," in Luis Cabrera, ed., *Global Governance, Global Government: Institutional Visions for an Evolving World System* (Albany, NY: SUNY Press, 2011), 27-64, at 56. In *The Anarchical Society* (New York: Columbia University Press, 1977), Hedley Bull presents a much more optimistic view of the normative potential of a world of sovereign states, including the significant role played by international law.

3. On neoliberal globalization see Richard Falk, *Predatory Globalization: A Critique* (Cambridge, UK: Cambridge University Press, 1999). For the de-democratization of governmental leadership in the United States see Sheldon Wolin, *Democracy Incorporated: Managed Democracy and the Specter of Inverted Totalitarianism* (Princeton, NJ: Princeton University Press, 2008).

4. Realism is understood as an ideology based on Westphalian consciousness, not on a practical assessment of the real, and what can and should be done about it.

5. Griffin, "Is a Global Ethic Possible?" in Cabrera, ed., *Global Governance,* 101 n. 2.

6. Ibid., 101.

7. Griffin, "Introduction to SUNY Series in Constructive Postmodern Thought," in David Ray Griffin and Richard Falk, eds., *Postmodern Politics for a Planet in Crisis* (Albany: State University of New York Press, 1993), xi-xiv, at xiv.

8. Griffin, "Moral Values and Global Democracy," *Creative Transformation* 15/1 (2006): 25-35.

9. The least overtly imperialistic, yet self-serving and insensitive to the historical situation, is Michael Mandelbaum's elaborate argument that America already provides world government as a global public good; see *The Case for Goliath: How America acts as the World Government in the Twenty-First Century* (New York: Public Affairs, 2005).

10. Griffin, "Global Empire or Global Democracy," in David Ray Griffin et al., *The American Empire and the Commonwealth of*

*God* (Louisville: Westminster John Knox, 2006), 103-19, at 107; the quotation is from Lawrence Kaplan and William Kristol, *The War Over Iraq: Saddam's Tyranny and America's Mission* (San Francisco: Encounter Books, 2003), 121.

11. See Griffin "Is a Global Ethic Possible?" 102.

12. Falk, "Anarchism without 'Anarchism,'" n. 1.

13. Hans Küng, *A Global Ethic for a Global Politics and Economics* (New York: Oxford University Press, 1998).

14. See Griffin, "Is a Global Ethic Possible?" n. 2, 107-111, explaining the religious grounding of lived morality.

15. Griffin, "Introduction to SUNY Series in Constructive Postmodern Thought," n. 7.

16. Griffin, "Is a Global Ethic Possible?" n. 2, at 122. Griffin explains that he is there using "minimal theism" as "the opposite of atheism, understood as the belief that moral norms are *not* part of the fabric of the universe."

17. See Grenville Clark & Louis B. Sohn, *World Peace Through World Law* (Cambridge: Harvard University Press, 3rd ed., 1966), and more generally, Cornelius F. Murphy, Jr., *Theories of World Governance: A Study in the History of Ideas* (Washington, D.C.: Catholic University of America Press, 2001).

18. See G. John Ikenberry, *After Victory: Institutions, Strategic Restraint, and the Rebuilding of Order after Major Wars* (Princeton: Princeton University Press, 2001); Thomas Weiss, "What Happened to the Idea of World Government," *International Studies Quarterly* 53(2): 253-271; see also Campbell Craig, "Why World Government Failed After World War II: A Historical Lesson for Contemporary Efforts," in Cabrera, n. 2, 77-99.

19. Griffin, "Global Empire or Global Democracy," 114, n. 10.

20. Ibid., 115.

21. Ibid., 118.

22. Ibid., 113.

23. See Jacques Derrida's remarks in Giavanna Borradori's *Philosophy in a Time of Terror: Dialogues with Jürgen Habermas and Jacques Derrida* (Chicago: University of Chicago Press, 2003), at 118, 120-21, 130.

24. My perspective on these issues can be found in a number of essays, including Richard Falk in Daniele Archibugi and David Held, eds., *Cosmopolitan Politics* (Cambridge, UK: Polity), 163-79, and Falk in Deepak Nayyar, *Governing Globalization* (Oxford, UK: Oxford University Press, 2002), 177-208.

25. Often to legitimate reformist advocacy of liberal internationalism, authors make explicit their opposition to world government. For instance Anne-Marie Slaughter, *The New World Order* (Princeton: Princeton University Press, 2004).

26. See David Cole and Jules Lobel, *Less Free, Less Secure: Why America is Losing the War on Terror* (New York: New Press, 2007); Nathan Goetting, "The National Defense Authorization Act for Fiscal Year 2012: Battlefield Earth," *National Lawyers Guild Review* 68 (No. 4): 247-55 (2011).

27. See Michael Hardt and Antonio Negri, *Multitudes: War and Democracy in the Age of Empire* (New York: Penguin, 2004); Falk, "Anarchism without 'Anarchism,'" n. 1.

28. See Nassim Nicholas Taleb, *The Black Swan: The Impact of the Highly Improbable"* (New York: Random House, 2007). Many important transformative events in recent international history were unanticipated by pundits and experts: collapse of the Berlin Wall; release of Nelson Mandela from jail after 27 years; 9/11 attacks; Arab Spring."

29. Richard Falk and Andrew Strauss, *Global Parliament* (Berlin, 2011); Richard Falk and David Krieger, *The Path to Zero: Dialogues on Nuclear Dangers* (Boulder, CO: Paradigm, 2012); President Barack Obama, Prague speech on nuclear disarmament, April 5, 2009.

CHAPTER 12. TOD FLETCHER: CHAMPIONING TRUTH AND JUSTICE

1. See, for example, his chapters "Truth as Correspondence, Knowledge as Dialogical: Pluralism without Relativism" and "Whitehead and the Crisis in Moral Theory: Theistic Ethics without Heteronomy," in David Ray Griffin, *Whitehead's Radically Different Postmodern Philosophy: An Argument for Its Contemporary Relevance* (Albany: State University of New York Press, 2007), 86-105 and 139-64.

2. David Ray Griffin, *The New Pearl Harbor: Disturbing Questions about the Bush Administration and 9/11,* updated edition (Northampton: Olive Branch Press, 2004), 209n32.

3. David Ray Griffin, *The 9/11 Commission Report: Omissions and Distortions* (Northampton: Olive Branch Press, 2005).

4. David Ray Griffin, *Christian Faith and the Truth Behind 9/11: A Call to Reflection and Action* (Louisville: Westminster John Knox, 2006).

5. David Ray Griffin, *Debunking 9/11 Debunking: An Answer to* Popular Mechanics *and Other Defenders of the Official Conspiracy Theory* (Northampton: Olive Branch, 2007).

6. Ibid., 214.

7. David Ray Griffin, *9/11 Contradictions: An Open Letter to Congress and the Press* (Northampton: Olive Branch, 2008), viii.

8. Ibid., 22.

9. David Ray Griffin, *The New Pearl Harbor Revisited: 9/11, the Cover-Up, and the Exposé* (Northampton: Olive Branch, 2008).

10. Ibid., 239.

11. David Ray Griffin, *Osama bin Laden: Dead or Alive?* (Northampton: Olive Branch, 2009).

12. Richard Lardner, "After bin Laden's Death: A Different Kind of Hunt," Associated Press, March 16, 2012.

13. Russ Baker, "Doubts on 'Official Story' of Bin Laden Killing," Original Investigations, August 17, 2011.

14. "Bin Laden—Abbottabad Residents "It's All a Fake, Nothing Happened," YouTube, May 9, 2011 (http://www.youtube.com/watch?v=b1JWpgAWKEU).

15. "The Mysterious Death of Osama bin Laden: Creating Evidence Where There Is None," Global Research, August 4, 2011.

16. David Ray Griffin, *The Mysterious Collapse of World Trade Center 7: Why the Final Official Report about 9/11 Is Unscientific and False* (Northampton: Olive Branch, 2009).

17. Personal communication, March 2012.

18. Alfred North Whitehead, *Science and the Modern World* (1925; New York: Free Press, 1967), 187.

19. David Ray Griffin, *Cognitive Infiltration: An Obama Appointee's Plan to Undermine the 9/11 Conspiracy Theory* (Northampton: Olive Branch, 2010).

20. This article was published in *The Journal of Political Philosophy* in June 2009, and hence after Sunstein's appointment, which was made in April of that year. However, this essay had been posted online in August 2008.

21. Cointelpro (sometimes written COINTELPRO), or "Counter Intelligence Program," was the FBI's name for its operations to infiltrate, provoke, undermine and disable civil rights, socialist, antiwar, black power and Native American movements during the late 1950s and the 1960s.

22. David Ray Griffin, *9/11 Ten Years Later: When State Crimes Against Democracy Succeed* (Northampton: Olive Branch, 2011).

23. "Explosive Testimony: The 911 Oral Histories," *Guns and Butter,* March 29, 2006, Bonnie Faulkner and Yarrow Makho (producers) and Tod Fletcher (co-producer); KPFA-FM, Berkeley, CA <http://www.kpfa.org/archive/id/19969>.

## CHAPTER 13. PETER DALE SCOTT: 9/11, DEEP POLITICS, AND SPIRITUALITY

1. There is not time in this essay to discuss the book's contribu-

tion to 9/11 studies. But the 9/11 section contains an original and valuable discussion of the oral histories from the Fire Department of New York, important evidence that, inexcusably, was not released until 2005 (David Ray Griffin, *Christian Faith and the Truth Behind 9/11* [Louisville: Westminster John Knox Press, 2006], 21-33).

2. Timothy E. Eastman and Hank Keeton, *Physics and Whitehead: Quantum, Process, and Experience,* 165.

3. The text of Griffin's book has "Millikan," but it should have been—he has told me—"Mulliken."

4. Griffin, *Christian Faith,* 131-32: "The idea that freedom goes all the way down might seem to be obviously false. There is surely no freedom in a rock or a pile of sand. But ... the idea that some degree of freedom goes all the way down applies only to individuals—both simple and compound. This doctrine is not falsified, therefore, by the fact that things such as rocks and styrofoam cups have no freedom."

5. Griffin, *Christian Faith,* 137.

6. David Ray Griffin, personal communication, April 5, 2012.

7. "Dostoevsky ... predicted that 'the world will be saved only after it has been possessed by the demon of evil.' Whether it really will be saved we shall have to wait and see: this will depend on our conscience, on our spiritual lucidity, on our individual and combined efforts in the face of catastrophic circumstances. But it has already come to pass that *the demon of evil, like a whirlwind, triumphantly circles all five continents of the earth"* (Aleksandr Solzhenitsyn, "Godlessness, the First Step to the Gulag," Templeton Prize Address, London, May 10, 1983 [http://www.roca.org/OA/36/36h.htm], emphasis added). Dostoevsky's warnings reached the West through writers like Soloviev, Shestov, Nicolas Berdyaev, and—perhaps most notably—Czeslaw Milosz (Nicolas A. Berdaev, "The Revelation about Man in the Creativity of Dostoevsky" <http://www.berdyaev.com/berdiaev/berd_lib/1918_294.html>; Czeslaw Milosz, *The Land of Ulro).*

8. "At the start of the Cold War, Niebuhr gave another set of lectures, this time in Fulton, Missouri; they served as the starting point for a book called *The Irony of American History* (1952). He began the book by making his position against Communism clear: 'We are defending freedom against tyranny and are trying to preserve justice against a system which has, demonically, distilled injustice and cruelty out of its original promise of a higher justice.' Niebuhr would have chosen the word "demonically" with care; in effect, he dubbed the Soviet Union an evil empire thirty years before Ronald Reagan did" (David Brooks, *Atlantic Monthly,* September 2002 <http://www. theatlantic.com/past/docs/issues/2002/09/brooks.htm>).

9. Bernard Lee, S.M., in David Ray Griffin, *Sacred Interconnections* (Albany: State University of New York Press, 1990), 56.

10. A noted example was when the late Susan Sontag commented that *Reader's Digest* had done a better job than *The Nation* of conveying the reality of Communism ("Susan Sontag Provokes Debate on Communism," *New York Times,* February 27, 1982 <http://www.nytimes.com/books/00/03/12/specials/ sontag-communism.html>). I myself was influenced by a series of painful discussions with Czeslaw Milosz, who responded to my defense of coexistence and détente with the simple statement, "You treat the Soviet Union as if it was a state. It is not. It is a cancer" (Peter Dale Scott, *Listening to the Candle: A Poem of Impulse* [New Directions, 1992], 131). More recently, I have translated a sonnet by the German resistance leader Albrecht Haushofer, and used three lines of it as an epigraph to a recent unpublished essay on 9/11: "Yes! I am guilty, but not the way you think,/I should have recognized where duty called, *more harshly named as evil what was evil"* (Albrecht Haushofer, *Moabit Sonnets,* #39, emphasis added).

11. David Ray Griffin, *God and Religion in the Postmodern World* (Albany: State University of New York Press, 1989), 144.

12. David Ray Griffin, "Process Theodicy, Christology, and the Imitatio Dei," in *Jewish Theology and Process Thought,* ed. Sandra B. Lubarsky and David Ray Griffin (Albany: State University of New York Press, 1996), 95-125.

13. Griffin, *Christian Faith,* 107; citing Richard A. Horsley, *Jesus and Empire: The Kingdom of God and the New World Disorder* (Minneapolis: Fortress, 2003), 13.

14. Griffin, *Christian Faith,* 108.

15. Cf. Peter Dale Scott, "The Tao of 9/11," in *Mosaic Orpheus* (Montreal: McGill-Queens University Press, 2009), 66-67.

16. One significant difference is that, under the emperor Hadrian, the Roman empire retreated from excessive expansions into Mesopotamia and settled within fixed limits. This stability became the key to Rome's relative longevity. As of this writing under Obama, the American military presence is still expanding.

17. "U.S. Support Increases to East Timor 'Operation Warden,'" American Forces Press Service, September 29, 1999 <http://www.defense.gov/news/newsarticle.aspx?id=42858>.

18. Cf. "US on 'KONY 2012': No plans to remove advisers," MSNBC News, March 8, 2012 <http://worldnews.msnbc.msn.com/_news/2012/03/08/10613108-us-on-kony-2012-no-plans-to-remove-advisers>.

19. Bonhoeffer was actually martyred because of his association with an Abwehr assassination plot against Hitler, while Barth sat out the war in exile in his native Switzerland.

20. *Christian Faith,* 192; cf. David Ray Griffin, in Griffin et al., *The American Empire and the Commonwealth of God: A Political, Economic, Religious Statement* (Louisville: Westminster John Knox, 2006), 155. Cf. Dirkie Smit, *Essays in Public Theology: Collected Essays,* Vol. 1: 416-17.

21. In other books edited by Griffin, process theologians have made it clear that they see King, along with Gandhi, Dorothy Day, and others, as a model of the efficacious power that comes from the "true spirituality . . . unleashing divine powers in us all." Richard Falk acknowledges his debt to Gandhi, King, Tolstoy, "and all others who insist that moral concern is serious only if it includes active participation in ongoing struggles

against injustice and suffering." However, without access to all of Griffin's prodigious bibliography, I did not find any significant published references by Griffin himself to the work of King. (When I mentioned this to David, he then forwarded to me his 4500-word unpublished essay on King, making essentially the same argument for King's importance.)

22. Recognizing that the *New York Times* helped achieve the release of previously suppressed details about 9/11, Griffin appeals to the *Times* to play an even bolder role in exposing the truth (*Christian Faith,* 54).

23. Griffin, *Christian Faith,* ix.

24. Griffin has since advised me that he once contemplated a book comparing King, Merton, and Rabbi Abraham Heschel, but (in his words) "this was one of many plans that didn't get past the drawing board stage."

25. Griffin, *Christian Faith,* 188; Thomas Merton, "Moral Passivity and Demonic Activism," in Thomas Merton, *Peace in the Post-Christian Era,* ed. Patricia A. Burton (Maryknoll: Orbis, 2004), 102-08.

26. Thomas Merton, *Raids on the Unspeakable,* 4-5; quoted in James Douglass, *JFK and the Unspeakable* (Maryknoll, NY: Orbis Books, 2008), xv.

27. Griffin, *Christian Faith,* ix. Cf. pages 54 and 184: "9/11 was a false-flag operation carried out by forces within our own government in order to advance the American empire."

28. Griffin, *Christian Faith,* 82. Cf. 105: "9/11 was orchestrated by the Bush-Cheney administration.

29. E.g. *Christian Faith,* 175: "how can we withhold the judgment that it [the American empire] ... is an evil, even demonic, empire?" In correspondence with me, Griffin has clarified his position, reaffirming that the U.S. global dominance project is indeed wholly antithetical to Christian faith, while the United States itself is not. This was an important distinction in the era of the George W. Bush administration, which generated

documents in support of its doctrine of "Full Spectrum Dominance" (U.S. Space Command, *Vision for 2020, quoted in Griffin, The 9/11 Commission Report: Omissions and Distortions,* 119). But the Obama interventions—first in Libya, and now increasingly in Syria and Uganda—have been in the name of the more benign-sounding "responsibility to protect" (R2P) doctrine of the United Nations. Does Griffin condemn this doctrine as well? Or only (as I do) when it is a pretext for something else, such as regime change in the case of Libya?

30. Griffin, *Christian Faith,* 82, emphasis added.

31. See my recent essay, "Launching the U.S. Terror War: The CIA, 9/11, Afghanistan, and Central Asia," The Asia-Pacific Journal: Japan Focus, March 15, 2012 <http://japanfocus. org/-Peter_Dale-Scott/3723>.

32. Cf. Scott, *Road to 9/11,* 179: "Much of the debate over 9/11 has been focused on what I have called a false dilemma: whether it was Islamists or the U.S. government who were responsible for the disaster. We should at least contemplate the possibility that it was a global meta-group, working as 'an unrecognized Force X operating in the world,' that had the various resources and far-reaching connections necessary for the successful plot." I was referring in context to "the shadowy Texas-Saudi-Geneva milieu" surrounding the Bush family and the Saudi prince known as "Bandar Bush," about whom more suggestive evidence has since accumulated. See Scott, "Launching the U.S. Terror War."

33. E.g., Peter Dale Scott and Jonathan Marshall, *Cocaine Politics,* 179; Peter Dale Scott, *The Road to 9/11,* 307.

34. Griffin, *Christian Faith,* 176. Griffin assures me that he has "never stated, implied, or believed . . . that American foreign influence has been wholly evil." But if this is true, then I believe his statement ("the American empire is evil"), and more importantly the argumentation in support of it, should perhaps be restated in a more balanced assessment.

35. Griffin, *Christian Faith,* 82, emphasis added.

36. Peter Dale Scott, "The Doomsday Project and Deep Events: JFK, Watergate, Iran-Contra, and 9/11," The Asia-Pacific Journal: Japan Focus, November 21, 2011 <http://japanfocus.org/-Peter_Dale-Scott/3650>. Another recurring feature is a public cover-up (Scott, *American War Machine,* 3; cf. 193-203).

37. In the case of the second Tonkin Gulf incident, for example (an obvious precedent for 9/11), it remains uncertain whether the master manipulator was ultimately Lyndon Johnson, or whether (as Gareth Porter and Jared Goldstein have argued) Johnson was manipulated by his advisers.

38. Thus, for example, the British massacre at Amritsar in 1919 was designed in part to frustrate the planned reforms of a Liberal colonial secretary, and the French shelling of Haiphong in 1946 was designed in part to forestall the negotiations proposed by a weak coalition government in Paris. Even the false-flag "Mukden incident" engineered in 1931 by the Kwantung Army of Japan (the first incident discussed in Chapter 1 of *Christian Faith*) was an act in conspiratorial subordination of the guidelines set by a weak civilian government in Tokyo, and ineffectually enforced by a vacillating Imperial General Headquarters.

39. Scott, *American War Machine,* 20-21. In all three incidents, I see also a possible third factor: a dominant overworld (including for example the Japanese imperial family in the case of Mukden). Take, for example, Griffin's explanation of Mukden: "In 1931, Japan, which had been exploiting Manchuria for resources, decided to take over the whole province. To have a pretext, the Japanese army blew up the tracks of its own railway near the Chinese military base in Mukden, then blamed the sabotage on Chinese solders" (David Ray Griffin, "9/11, American Empire, and Christian Faith," lecture, March 25, 2006 <http://davidraygriffin.com/articles/911-american-empire-and-christian-faith/>; cf. *Christian Faith,* 4, where the incident is attributed to "Japanese leaders."

40. Czeslaw Milosz, "Treatise on Theology," *Second Space: New Poems,* trans. Czeslaw Milosz and Robert Hass (New York: Ecco, 2004), 47. Cf. Peter Dale Scott, "Changing North America," Asia Pacific Journal: Japan Focus, June 27, 2011 (http://japanfocus.

org/site/view/3553).

41. In response to an earlier draft of this paper, David asserted that process theologians today would never claim to "know" things about God. He admits that "Charles Hartshorne was a full-fledged rationalist. But [John] Cobb and I and most other theologians find Hartshorne's certainty as somewhat embarrassing."

42. Alfred North Whitehead, *Science and the Modern World* (New York: Macmillan, 1925), 122. Cf. Nikki Curtis, "English Romantic Poetry and A.N. Whitehead," *Simulacra: The University of Reading Online Journal of Philosophy, Poetry & Literature,* October 30, 2010. Milosz attributes similar powers to Blake in *The Land of Ulro* (New York: Farrar, Straus and Giroux, 2000).

43. Czeslaw Milosz, "Second Space," *Second Space: New Poems*, 3.

44. Theodor W. Adorno, "Commitment," *New Left Review* I/87-88, September-December 1974; in Terry Eagleton and Drew Milne, *Marxist Literary Theory: A Reader* (Oxford: Blackwell Publishers, 1996), 202.

45. David Ray Griffin, *Reenchantment Without Supernaturalism: A Process Philosophy of Religion* (Ithaca, NY: Cornell University Press, 2001), 300.

46. Griffin, *Reenchantment Without Supernaturalism,* 89; quoting Alfred North Whitehead, *Modes of Thought,* 120.

47. At the conference at which an earlier version of this essay was presented, I jokingly suggested that David should add to his bibliography a book on process theology and poetry. I learned later that he had in fact already helped to organize a conference on process theology and the arts, including poetry. This conference featured a major and often republished essay by the poet Robin Blaser, showing how Whitehead influenced Charles Olson's poetic efforts to "build the measure of ourselves within the process to stand against the wreckage which the human order has become"; see Robin Blaser, "The Violets: 'A Cosmological Reading of a Cosmology,'" *Process Studies,* 13:1 (Spring 1983), 8-37, reissued in Robin Blaser, *The Fire: Collect-*

*ed Essays of Robin Blaser* (Berkeley: University of California Press, 2006 [http://writing.upenn.edu/library/Blaser-Robin_ The-Violets.html]).

48. In researching for this essay, I was amazed how many of my acquaintances and role-models had already appeared in anthologies edited by Griffin. Among them are writers like Michael Lerner, Charlene Spretnak, Joanna Macy, Huston Smith, and Rosemary Ruether (to name only my friends and neighbors in Berkeley).

49. This expansion has been truly global: his books have been translated into thirteen languages, including French, German, Dutch, Danish, Swedish, Italian, Japanese, Chinese, Indonesian, Korean, Persian, Turkish, and Arabic.

50. As Robert Lockwood Mills wrote in *Conscience of a Conspiracy Theorist,* "Griffin's obvious sincerity helped him pierce the mainstream media's conspiracy of silence in re 9/11. This makes him a rare exception among skeptics. His Madison speech was nationally televised by C-SPAN, and even more significantly, an article about his work appeared in *The Washington Post* on 2006. It's notable that even those who don't necessarily agree with Griffin appreciate him" (Robert Lockwood Mills, *Conscience of a Conspiracy Theorist,* 198).

51. See, e.g., Griffin, *Christian Faith,* 20. See also e.g. Paul Zarembka, "Critique of David Ray Griffin regarding Calls from 9-11 Planes," October 14, 2011 <http://ithp.org/articles/davidray-griffincritique.html>. For Griffin's response, see David Ray Griffin, "A Response to Paul Zarembka about Phone Calls from the 9/11 Planes," October 25, 2011 <http://ithp.org/articles/davidgriffinresponse.html>. Cf. also Erik Larson <http://911blogger.com/news/2011-02-10/critique-david-ray-griffin-s-911-fake-calls-theory>; "loosenuke" <http://911blogger.com/news/2011-02-10/critique-david-ray-griffin-s-911-fake-calls-theory#comment-245663>; David Ray Griffin, *9/11 Ten Years Later: When State Crimes Against Democracy Succeed* (Northampton MA: Olive Branch Press, 2011), 105-06. Kevin Ryan has written a response to Larson <http://911blogger.com/news/2011-02-10/critique-david-ray-griffin-s-911-fake-calls-theory#comment-245987>.

CHAPTER 14. ZHIHE WANG: THE CHINESE ENCOUNTER WITH CONSTRUCTIVE POSTMODERNISM

1. David Griffin, "Preface to Chinese Translation of *Reenchantment of Science*."

2. Xiangping Shen, "Process Philosophy and the Scientific Outlook of Development, *Journal of Theory* 12 (2008): 70-73.

3. Zhihe Wang, "The Second Handshake: Constructive Postmodernism in China Today," in *Tattva: Journal of Philosophy,* 2009: No. 1.

4. Youzheng Li, "On The Strategy and Consequence of Postmodernism," *Philosophical Researches* 2002: No. 2.

5. Yuehou Qu, "On Griffin's Postmodern View of Human Rights," *Theory and Modernization* 2001: 3.

6. Xiaohua Wang, "A Real Postmodern Postmodernism: Comments on *The Reenchantment of Science*" <http://www.xici.net/b325795/d17596730.htm>.

7. *Newsletter of Chinese Academy of Social Sciences* (Philosophy Institute of Chinese Academy of Social Sciences), April 15, 2003.

8. Xinping Zhuo, "Postmodern Movement and the Response of Theology," *Journal of Chinese Academy of Social Sciences Graduate College,* 1997: 3.

9. Yong Pei, "Postmodern Issues in China's Modernization," February 9, 2006 <http://blog.sina.com.cn/s/blog_5380a309010001ze.html>.

10. Zhong Chen, "Development Ethics in Constructive Postmodern Context," *China Process Studies* Vol. 2 (2007).

11. Xiaoming Chen, "After Critique: The Hard Process of Chinese Postmodernism," *China Book Review* No. 3 (2006).

12. Yong Xia, "The Right of Philosophy and Localism," *Reading* No. 6 (2002).

13. Yong Pei, "Why China? The Significance of China to the Postmodern Movement," *Process Studies* 35/2 (Fall-Winter, 2006), 359.

14. Wen Jiabao, Speech at Ecole Polytechnique de Paris, December 6, 2005 <http://news.xinhuanet.com/english/2005-12/07/content_3886424.htm>.

15. Speech by Chinese President Hu Jintao at Yale University, April 21, 2006 <http://www.mfa.gov.cn/eng/zxxx/t259224.htm>.

16. Kang Ouyang, "The Weicheng [Fortress Besieged] of Modernization and Its Transcendence: On the Values of the Orientation of Constructive Postmodernism and its Inspiration," *Seeking Truth* 1 (2003).

17. Lanxian Xiang, "China's Reform Should Get Rid of Western Dogmas," *Global Times.* February 4, 2008.

18. Jay McDaniel, "The Greening of China: The Constructive Postmodern Movement in Contemporary China," *Worldviews: Global Religions, Culture, and Ecology,* 12: 2-3 (2008), 270-90.

19. Shui Yi, "Constructive Postmodernism and China's Postmodernization," *People's Daily* [Oversea Edition], March 2, 2012.

20. Guihuan Huo, "Hegel, Marx and Whitehead: Viewing the Conflicts between Sciences and Humanities from the Basic Transformation of Mode of Thinking in Western Philosophy Embodied by 'Process,'" *Journal of Jiangsu Administration College* No.5 (2006).

21. Hongri Shang, "Exploring the Philosophy with Impossible Worlds: A Dialogue with *Second Enlightenment,* by Zhihe Wang and Meijun Fan" (unpublished).

22. Deina Pei, "Viewing China's Education Innovation from a Process Perspective," paper for the "International Conference Themed Process Thinking and Education Innovation," Claremont, California, January 27-29, 2008.

23. Xiaoman Zhu, "Viewing China's Curriculum Reform from

the Standpoint of Process Philosophy," *Culture Communication,* No. 29 (2007).

24. David Griffin, "Introduction to SUNY Series in Constructive Postmodern Thought," In *The Reenchantment of Science,* ed. David Griffin (Albany: State University of New York, 1988), xi.

25. Yijie Tang, "Reflective Western Scholars View Traditional Chinese Culture," *The People's Daily,* February 4, 2005.

26. Fanren Zeng, "Ecological Aesthetics: A Brand New Ecological Aesthetics in the Postmodern Context," *Journal of Shanxi Normal University,* No. 3 (2002).

27. Xiaohua Wang, "China's Environment Movement and Constructive Postmodernism," lecture at the Center for Process Studies, Claremont, May 7, 2002.

28. "Liao Xiaoyi: A Thinker in Action," *Finance Times,* October 28, 2007.

29. Huibin Li, "Postscript to *Ecological Civilization and Marxism,"* *Ecological Civilization and Marxism.* eds. Huibin Li, Xiaoyuan Xue, and Zhihe Wang (Beijing: Central Compilation and Translation Press, 2008), 227-28.

30. Huibin Li, "Ecological Right and Ecological Justice," *New Horizon* 5 (2008).

31. Wang Lingxiang and Sun Jinfu, "The Development Trend of World Agriculture and Developing China's Postmodern Agriculture," *Modern Agriculture* 7 (2011): 369-370.

32. Tang Yong Dou Ying, "Farming System Innovation in the World and the Development of Post-Modern Agriculture," *World Agriculture* 7 (2010): 25-28.

33. Tan Xuewen and Du Zhixiong, "Viewing Postmodern Agriculture from the Angle of Sustainable Food Supply Chains," *Journal of China Agricultural University* 1 (2010): 156-65.

34. Zhu Qizhen, "Clarifying Some Misunderstandings of Modern Agriculture," *Farmers Daily,* December 2, 2011.

35. Li Mingyu and Li Li, "Postmodern Agriculture—Ecological Agriculture in the View of the Scientific Concept of Development," *Journal of Wenzhou Vocational and Technological College* 4 (2009; 49-52.

36. Zhou Shujing, "The Transformation of Agriculture Development Strategy and Post Modern Agriculture," Research on *Financial and Economic Issues* 11 (2004): 74-76.

37. Dong Hui, "Postmodern Agriculture is Possible." *Marxism and Reality* 5 (2008): 124-27.

38. Zhuang Rongsheng, "A Study on Transforming Chinese Agriculture into Postmodern Agriculture," *Journal of the Party School of the Central Committee of the C.P.C* 1 (2012).

39. David Ray Griffin, "Introduction to SUNY Series in Constructive Postmodern Thought," *The Reenchantment of Science,* ed. Griffin (Albany: State University of New York, 1988), xi.

40. Ouyang Kang, "Contemporary Marxism in China and Process Thought" (lecture at the Center for Process Studies, Claremont, August 21, 2001).

41. Ye Xiaowen, "Religion and Social Harmony," *People's Daily,* November 28, 2006.

42. Pan Yue, "Marxist Notion of Religion Must Catch Up with the Times," *Huaxia Times,* December 15, 2001.

43. Dedong Wei, "Buddhist Ecological Outlook," *China Social Sciences,* 1999: No. 5.

44. Hengfu Wen and Li yang, "Whitehead Philosophy of Organism Studies in China for 85 years," *Seeking the Truth* 4 (2011).

45. Weifu Wu, "A Brand New View of Philosophy: A Preliminary Exploration of Constructive Postmodern Philosophy," *China Process Studies* Vol. 2 (2007).

46. Zhihe Wang, "Postmodern Spirit and the Backbone and Morality of Postmodern Thinkers: Taking Griffin as a Case," *Journal of Zhejiang Gongshang University* 2; 2009.

47. Yong Pei, "Why China? The Significance of China to the Postmodern Movement," *China Process Studies* Vol. 2 (2007).

48. Nanyuan Zhao, "Anti-Scientism is a Antiscientific Slogan," *Science and Society* No. 3, 2003.

49. Cited in the brochure of the Institute for Postmodern Development of China.

## CHAPTER 15. DAVID RAY GRIFFIN: RESPONSES

1. "J.B. by Archibald MacLeish," E-Notes <http://www.enotes.com/j-b/>.

2. It has been suggested that this philosopher was likely Peter Geach.

3. H.D. Lewis, *The Elusive Self* (London: Macmillan, 1982), 33; quoted in Griffin, *Religion and Scientific Naturalism,* 147.

4. Daniel E. Dennett, *Consciousness Explained* (Boston: Little, Brown & Co., 1991), 21.

5. *God, Power, and Evil,* 89.

6. "Immortality," in Alfred North Whitehead, *Essays in Science and Philosophy* (New York: Philosophical Library, 1947), 94.

7. The theological lectures by Niebuhr were surely the most exciting ones in the country.

8. I do, to be sure, refer to myself as belonging to the "Whiteheadian-Hartshornean school of thought."

9. Alfred North Whitehead, *Process and Reality,* corrected edition, ed. David Ray Griffin and Donald W. Sherburne (1929; New York: Free Press, 1978), 346.

10. Griffin, "Hartshorne's Differences From Whitehead," in Lewis Ford, ed., *Two Process Philosophers* (American Academy of Religion, 1973), 35-57.

11. David Ray Griffin, *Reenchantment Without Supernaturalism: A Process Philosophy of Religion* (Ithaca: Cornell University Press, 2001), 353.

12. Ibid., 32

13. Whitehead, *Process and Reality,* 151.

14. Charles Hartshorne, "A Reply to My Critics," in *The Philosophy of Charles Hartshorne.* The Library of Living Philosophers Vol. 20, ed. Lewis Edwin Hahn (LaSalle, Ill.: Open Court, 1991), 569-731, at 676, 624.

15. Griffin, *Reenchantment Without Supernaturalism,* 362-63.

16. Ibid., 363.

17. Paul Helm, "Thomas Reid, Common Sense and Calvinism," in *Rationality in the Calvinian Tradition,* ed. Hendrik Hart, Johan van der Hoeven, and Nicholas Wolterstorff (Lanham, Md.: University Press of America, 1983), 71-89. at 78.

18. *Reenchantment Without Supernaturalism* 364.

19. Ibid.

20. Whitehead, *Process and Reality,* 13.

21. "Reformed Epistemology," in Philip L. Quinn and Charles Taliaferro, eds., *A Companion to Philosophy of Religion* (Cambridge, Mass.: Blackwell, 1997), 383-89, at 383.

22. Gary Dorrien, *The Making of American Liberal Theology: Crisis, Irony, and Postmodernity, 1950-2005* (Louisville: Westminster John Knox, 2006).

23. The organizing committee had originally invited Jorge Nobo (of Washburn University) to deal with *Unsnarling the World-Knot,* because he, besides having written an excellent review of this work (*Process Studies,* 28/1-2 [Spring/Summer 1999], 139-41), had been Griffin's table-tennis partner during a summer conference on American philosophy they had attended in 1966. But Nobo, having recently learned that he has

Parkinson's Disease, declined. At this point, the organizing committee—having formed a list of possible alternatives in case one of more of the original invitees could not be able to make it—turned to Dan Dombrowski, having made him the "first alternative" on the grounds that "Dombrowski can do almost anything." Besides expressing my appreciation to Dan, who fulfilled this expectation in spades, I also want to use this opportunity to express best wishes to Jorge, who has been a fine philosopher and good friend—as well as an excellent table-tennis player.

24. Thomas Nagel, *Mortal Questions* (Cambridge: Cambridge University Press, 1979), 181-92. Rather than embracing panpsychism in this chapter, however, he merely flirted with it. Although Nagel concluded that it must be true, he said he could not see how it *could* be.

25. David Chalmers, "Facing Up to the Problem of Consciousness," *Journal of Consciousness Studies* 2/3 (1995): 200-19.

26. *Journal of Consciousness Studies* 13/10-22, October/November 2006 <http://www.imprint.co.uk/jcs_13_10-11.html>.

27. Galen Strawson et al., *Consciousness and Its Place in Nature: Does Physicalism Entail Panpsychism?*

28. William E. Seager, "Consciousness, Information, and Panpsychism," *Journal of Consciousness Studies* 2/3 (1995): 272-88.

29. William E. Seager, "Panpsychism," *Stanford Internet Encyclopaedia of Philosophy,* 2001 (http://plato.stanford.edu/ entries/ panpsychism); "The 'Intrinsic Nature' Argument for Panpsychism," *Journal of Consciousness Studies* 13/10-11 (2006)): 129-45; and Seager "Panpsychism," *Macmillan Encyclopaedia of Cognitive Science.*

30. William E. Seager, "Whitehead and the Revival (?) of Panpsychism," in Franz Riffert and Michel Weber, eds., *Searching for New Contrasts* (Peter Lang GmbH, 2003); Seager's essay is also available online <http://www.scar.utoronto.ca/~seager/ whitehead.htm>.

31. Thomas Nagel, *Mind and Cosmos: Why the Materialist Neo-Darwinian Conception of Nature Is Almost Certainly False* (Oxford and New York: Oxford University Press, 2012), 57-58 n. 16.

32. Charles Hartshorne, "Physics and Psychics: The Place of Mind in Nature," in John B. Cobb, Jr., and David Ray Griffin, eds., *Mind in Nature: Essays on the Interface of Science and Philosophy* (Washington, D.C.: University Press of America, 1977), 89-96.

33. Nagel, *Mind and Cosmos,* 58 n. 16.

34. Ibid., 15.

35. Nathaniel Barrett, "The Perspectivity of Feeling: Process Panpsychism and the Explanatory Gap," *Process Studies* 38 (2009), 189-206, at 205.

36. David Ray Griffin, "Some Whiteheadian Comments on the Discussion," in John B. Cobb, Jr., and David Ray Griffin, eds., *Mind in Nature: Essays on the Interface of Science and Philosophy* (University Press of America, 1977), 97-100, at 97.

37. A.H. Johnson, "Whitehead as Teacher and Philosopher," *Philosophy and Phenomenological Research* 29: 351-76, at 354. Charles Hartshorne, when asked about the term "panexperientialism," said he saw "advantages in that terminology'"; Robert Kane and Stephen Phillips, eds. *Hartshorne, Process Philosophy and Theology* (Albany: State University of New York Press, 1989), 181.

38. Gregg Rosenberg, *A Place for Consciousness* (Oxford: Oxford University Press, 2004), 229; there are chapters on both the "possibility" and the "probability" of panexperientialism. In a more recent writing, Rosenberg began by saying: "Two cornerstones of Whitehead's process philosophy are his rejection of 'vacuous actuality' and his acceptance of panexperientialism." See "The Carrier Theory of Causation," in Michel Weber and Anderson Weekes, eds. *Process Approaches to Consciousness in Psychology, Neuroscience, and Philosophy of Mind* (Albany: State University of New York Press, 2009), 273-91, at 273.

39. *Journal of Consciousness Exploration & Research* 1/3, April 2010

<http://www3.telus.net/public/doknyx/pubs/JCER_V1(3). pdf>.

40. "Panexperientialism: Exploration of the Philosophical and Scientific Implications of a Panexperientialist Worldview" <http://panexperientialism.blogspot.com/>.

41. Alfred North Whitehead, *The Concept of Nature* (Cambridge: Cambridge University Press, 1920), 168. This statement reflected Whitehead's awareness that physics, both quantum and relativity, implied—assuming the rejection of dualism—that even the most elementary components of nature must have experience, because there is no way of conceiving of events being temporal, and hence having duration, apart from conceiving them as experiential.

42. John B. Cobb, Jr., ed., *Back to Darwin: A Richer Account of Evolution* (Grand Rapids: William B. Eerdmans Publishing, 2008).

43. Lynn Margulis, "Two Hit, Three Down—The Biggest Lie," *Rock Creek Free Press,* January 24, 2010 <http://rockcreekfreepress. tumblr.com/post/353434420/two-hit-three-down-the-biggest-lie>.

44. David Ray Griffin and John Cobb, "Lynn Margulis on Spirituality and Process Philosophy," Dorion Sagan, ed., *Lynn Margulis: The Life and Legacy of a Scientific Rebel* (Chelsea Green, 2012).

45. Lynn Margulis, "Gaia and Machines," in Cobb, *Back to Darwin,* 167-75, at 172.

46. Dick Teresi, "Lynn Margulis Says She's Not Controversial, She's Right," *Discover Magazine,* April 2011 issue, published online June 17, 2011 <http://discovermagazine.com/2011/apr/16-interview-lynn-margulis-not-controversial-right/article_view?b_start:int=0&-C>.

47. Margulis, "Gaia Is a Tough Bitch," Chap. 7 of John Brockman, *The Third Culture: Beyond the Scientific Revolution* (New York: Simon & Schuster, 1995); also online <http://www.edge. org/documents/ThirdCulture/n-Ch.7.html>. For more on the relation of Margulis to process thought, see David Ray Griffin,

"Lynn Margulis: Scientist, Scholar, and Friend," *Process Perspectives: News Magazine of the Center for Process Studies* 34/1 (Winter 2012), 9; and Griffin and Cobb, "Lynn Margulis on Spirituality and Process Philosophy."

48. Margulis, "Serial Endosymbiotic Theory (SET) and Composite Individuality: Transition from Bacterial To Eukaryotic Genomes," *Microbiology Today* 31 (2004): 172-74 <http://www.sgm.ac.uk/pubs/micro_today/pdf/110406.pdf>.

49. Margulis, "Gaia Is a Tough Bitch."

50. Ibid.

51. See ibid., and Dick Teresi, "Lynn Margulis Says She's Not Controversial, She's Right," *Discover Magazine,* April 2011.

52. Thomas Nagel, *Mind and Cosmos: Why the Materialist Neo-Darwinian Conception of Nature Is Almost Certainly False* (Oxford and New York: Oxford University Press, 2012), 128.

53. Ibid., 25.

54. Whitehead, *The Function of Reason* (1929; Boston: Beacon Press, 1968), 16.

55. Richard Rorty, *Contingency, Irony, and Solidarity* (Cambridge: Cambridge University Press, 1989), 5.

56. Richard Rorty, *Consequences of Pragmatism* (Minneapolis: University of Minneapolis Press, 1982), xxix-xxx.

57. Rorty, *Contingency, Irony, and Solidarity,* 3, 8.

58. Ibid., 7.

59. Michael A. Corey, *Back to Darwin: The Scientific Case for Deistic Evolution* (University Press of America, 2004).

60. See Chap. 8 of my *Religion and Scientific Naturalism.*

61. Daniel Dennett, *Darwin's Dangerous Idea: Evolution and the Meaning of Life* (New York: Simon & Schuster, 1995), 83, 320.

62. Ibid., 67, 149-50, 164, 180.

63. In addition to Clayton's critique of my position, he makes five misleading statements about Whitehead: (1) Clayton suggests that the "starting point for [Whiteheadian process philosophy] is the metaphysical framework advanced in *Process and Reality";* but actually, Whitehead's metaphysical writings began earlier, with *Science and the Modern World* and *Religion in the Making*. (2) Clayton states that "many features of Whitehead's theism were only introduced in the final stratum of the composition of *Process and Reality";* but this statement relies on Lewis Ford's views, which exaggerate the degree to which Whitehead's theism in *Process and Reality* differed from *Religion in the Making*—as I argued in reviews of Ford's *Emergence of Whitehead's Metaphysics (Process Studies* 15/3 [Fall, 1986], 194-207) and his *Transforming Process Theism (Journal of Religion* 81/4 [October 2001], 668-70 <http://www.anthonyflood.com/griffinreviewsford.htm>). (3) Clayton says that theism plays little to no discernible role in *Modes of Thought and Adventures of Ideas;* but this is wrong, especially with regard to *AI*: It contains Whitehead's one theological essay, "The New Reformation," in which Whitehead makes some of his most important statements about God; and although elsewhere the word "God" is not used much, Whitehead used "Eros" (alternatively, "the Eros of the Universe," "the Divine Eros," "the supreme Eros") for God as primordial, and "the Unity of Existence" for God as consequent. John Cobb, in fact, has said: "In many ways, *Adventures of Ideas* is Whitehead's most religious book" (*A Christian Natural Theology* [Philadelphia: Westminster, 168n]). (4) Clayton says: "Atheist process philosophers . . . argue that Creativity has as much claim to ultimacy in Whitehead's writings as does the notion of God." This is not in question: Whitehead himself classified "creativity" (along with "many" and "one") as the "category of the ultimate," and Cobb has famously argued that for Whitehead, God and Creativity are equally ultimate (see Cobb's *Beyond Dialogue*). (5) Clayton then, suggesting that Creativity can "be taken as a basic metaphysical principle independent of God," says: "If this argument is successful, the notion of God becomes optional for, if not actually counter-indicated by, Whitehead's notion of Creativity. Sherburne made this argument in 1967." Yes, Donald Sherburne (my co-editor

for the corrected edition of *Process and Reality*) briefly suggested 45 years ago that this argument could be successfully made. But he—in spite of prodding from me and others—has never worked it out, so there is no basis for suggesting that it *could* be successful.

64. Millard J. Erickson, *Christian Theology* (Grand Rapids: Baker Book House, 1985), 304.

65. Griffin, *Religion and Scientific Naturalism*, xv.

66. Whitehead, *Process and Reality*, 15.

67. Griffin, *Religion and Scientific Naturalism*, 5.

68. However, as I mentioned in my response to Dan Dombrowski, there has recently been some movement in mainline philosophical circles toward panexperientialism (which should lead to rethinking sensationism, which might in turn open the way to considering religious experience).

69. Sterling Lamprecht, "Naturalism and Religion," in Yervant H. Krikorian, ed., *Naturalism and the Human Spirit* (Morningside Heights: Columbia University Press, 1944), 17-39, at 20.

70. John Herman Randall, Jr., "Epilogue: The Nature of Naturalism," in Krikorian, ed., *Naturalism and the Human Spirit*, 354-82, at 367.

71. James Bissett Pratt, *Naturalism* (New Haven: Yale University Press, 1939), 42.

72. William Drees, *Religion, Science and Naturalism* (Cambridge: Cambridge University Press, 1996), 14.

73. John B. Cobb, Jr., *Transforming Christianity and the World: A Way beyond Absolutism and Relativism*, ed. Paul F. Knitter (Maryknoll: Orbis, 1999).

74. Cobb, *Beyond Dialogue: Toward a Mutual Transformation of Christianity and Buddhism* (Philadelphia: Fortress, 1982).

75. David Tracy, "Kenosis, Sunyata, and Trinity," in John B. Cobb,

Jr., and Christopher Ives, eds., *The Emptying God: A Buddhist-Jewish-Christian Conversation* (Maryknoll, N.Y.: Orbis, 1990), 135-54, at 139; *Plurality and Ambiguity: Hermeneutics, Religion, Hope* [University of Chicago Press, 1987], 85.

76. *Plurality and Ambiguity,* 85.

77. Tracy, *Dialogue with the Other: The Inter-Religious Dialogue* (Louvain: Peeters Press, 1990), 90.

78. Quoted in R. Hooykaas, *Natural Law and Divine Miracle: A Historical-Critical Study of the Principle of Uniformity in Geology, Biology, and Theology* (Leiden: E. J. Brill, 1959), 114.

79. Francis Darwin, ed., *The Life and Letters of Charles Darwin,* 2 vols. (New York: D. Appleton, 1896), II: 6-7.

80. Richard Dawkins, *The Blind Watchmaker: Why the Evidence of Evolution Reveals a Universe without Design* (New York and London: Norton, 1987), 43.

81. Unless the different meanings of "naturalism" are clarified, says Lubarsky (in this volume), "those who are drawn to religious pluralism because of the implications of modern science will find themselves . . . doubting the whole enterprise of religion."

82. Whitehead, *Process and Reality,* 156

83. Whitehead, *Symbolism: Its Meaning and Effect* (1927; New York: Capricorn, 1959), 8.

84. C.I. Lewis, *Mind and the World Order* (New York: Charles Scribner's Sons, 1929), 38-39.

85. Ibid., 159.

86. Ibid., 157.

87. Ibid., 190. Whitehead's treatment of the "subjectivist principle" is arguably the most confusing part of his philosophy, which it took me many years to figure out. See "The Mystery of the Subjectivist Principle" (which I wrote with Olav Bryant

Smith), *Process Studies* 32:1 (Spring-Summer 2003): 3-36; re-printed in slightly revised form as the appendix to *Whitehead's Radically Different Postmodern Philosophy.*

88. Wayne Proudfoot, *Religious Experience* (Berkeley: University of California Press, 1985), 3.

89. *Reenchantment without Supernaturalism,* 340.

90. Whitehead, *Process and Reality,* 172, 180.

91. *Reenchantment without Supernaturalism,* 76.

92. Whitehead, *Process and Reality,* 162, 173.

93. Whitehead, *Symbolism,* 8.

94. Proudfoot, *Religious Experience,* 161.

95. Ibid., 219. In *Reenchantment without Supernaturalism,* I char-acterized Proudfoot's view thus: "Rather than religion's being a product, at least partly, of religious experience, so-called reli-gious *experience* is entirely a product of religious *beliefs*—which are themselves to be explained in nonreligious terms" (69). Frankenberry called this "a doubtful interpretation of Proud-foot's constructivism." These quoted passages, I believe, show the accuracy of my interpretation.

96. Ibid., 322.

97. Rorty, *Contingency, Irony, and Solidarity,* 5.

98. Paul Horwich, *Truth* (Oxford: Basil Blackwell, 1990), 1-2.

99. Donald Davidson, "The Structure and Content of Truth," *Journal of Philosophy* 87/6 (June 1990): 279-328, at 302. Fran-kenberry, commenting on this passage (note 17), suggested that I wrongly took it to show "Davidson's change of heart about rejecting correspondence theories." But no, I said only that he rejected the view that all correspondence theories could be rejected on the assumption of the truth of any of the epistemic theories. This rejection does, however, bear on the possibility of rejecting truth as correspondence, because

epistemic theories have always provided the main alternative. Moreover, what Davidson said to be the "correct objection to correspondence theories" is very weak—namely, that "such theories fail to provide entities to which truth vehicles [such as statements] can be said to correspond." However, Whitehead does provide such entities, namely, propositions (in the sense of non-physical entities that he calls "impure possibilities"). It is possible that he rules out this possibility on nominalistic grounds, as did Hilary Putnam, who wrote: "It is statements (not abstract entities called 'propositions') that are true or false" (Hilary Putnam, *Words and Life,* ed. James Conant [Cambridge: Harvard University Press, 1994], 302). This view, incidentally, led Putnam into self-contradiction, as shown by this statement: "While it is true that the stars would still have existed even if language users had not evolved, it is not the case that sentences would have existed. There would have still been a world, but there would not have been any *truths"* (ibid., 368).

100. Donald Davidson, "Truth Rehabilitated," in Davidson, *Truth, Language and History* (Oxford: Oxford University Press, 2005), 3.

101. Horwich, *Truth,* 1-2.

102. James Conant's introduction to Hilary Putnam, *Words and Life,* ed. Conant (Cambridge: Harvard University Press, 1994), xxvi.

103. Griffin, *Religion without Supernaturalism,* 321.

104. I have quoted this statement from memory.

105. Whitehead, *Science and the Modern World* (1925; New York: Free Press, 1967), 43.

106. "Parapsychology and Philosophy: A Whiteheadian Postmodern Perspective," *Journal of the American Society for Psychical Research* 87/3 (July 1993), 217-88 <http://www.anthonyflood.com/griffinparapsychology.htm>. My essay constituted the entire issue.

107. "Parapsychology and Philosophy," 272-75. With regard

to laboratory results, I quoted experimental parapsychologist Robert Morris' statement that "alternative, on-line interpretations do exist for all studies that offer evidence for retroactive influence."

108. "If ostensible psi events are authenticated, the modern worldview . . . would need to be modified to allow causal influence at a distance to and from minds" (ibid., 230).

109. Jule Eisenbud, *Parapsychology and the Unconscious* (Berkeley: North Atlantic Books, 1983), 46.

110. David Ray Griffin, "Ethics and the Fabric of the Universe," in Haruo Murata, ed., *Whitehead and Ethics in the Contemporary World: For Sustainability and the Common Good* (The Japan Society for Process Studies, 2010), 7-17.

111. Michael Walzer, *Thick and Thin: Moral Argument at Home and Abroad* (Notre Dame: University of Notre Dame Press, 1994), x, 11.

112. Griffin, "Ethics and the Fabric" (my paraphrase).

113. See John Mackie, *Ethics: Inventing Right and Wrong* (New York: Penguin, 1977), 24, and Bernard Williams, "Ethics and the Fabric of the World," in *Morality and Objectivity: A Tribute to J.L. Mackie,* ed. Ted Honderich (London: Routledge & Kegan Paul, 1985), 203-14, at 205. For similar positions, see Richard Rorty, *Contingency, Irony, and Solidarity* (Cambridge University Press, 1989), 20; Jürgen Habermas, *Justification and Application: Remarks on Discourse Ethics,* trans. Ciaran Cronin (Cambridge: Polity, 1993), 26, 29; John Rawls, *Political Liberalism,* with a new introduction and the "Reply to Habermas" (New York: Columbia University Press, 1996), 97.

114. Whitehead, *Adventures of Ideas,* 13.

115. Tu Weiming, "Epilogue: Human rights as a Confucian Moral Discourse," in William Theodore de Bary and Tu Weiming, eds., *Confucianism and Human Rights* (New York: Columbia University Press, 1998), 297-307, at 297, 302.

116. Gernot Köhler, *Global Apartheid* (World Order Models Project Working Paper Number 7) (New York: Institute for World Order, 1978); reprinted in Richard Falk, Samuel S. Kim, and Saul M Mendlovitz, eds., *Toward a Just World Order* (Westview Press, 1982), 315-25.

117. Titus Alexander, *Unraveling Global Apartheid: An Overview of World Politics* (Cambridge: Polity 1996).

118. Richard Falk, *On Humane Governance: Toward a New Global Politics* (University Park: Pennsylvania State University Press, 1995), 49-55.

119. Alan Cranston, *The Killing of the Peace: The Dramatic Chronicle of How the Will of the People Was Thwarted After One World War* (New York: Viking, 1945). The quote from Sharp is on page 51.

120. Robert C. Hilderbrand, *Dumbarton Oaks: The Origins of the United Nations and the Search for Postwar Security* (Chapel Hill: University of North Carolina Press, 1990), 51.

121. Ibid., x, 3.

122. Ibid., 3.

123. Whitehead, *Adventures of Ideas,* 5.

124. Ibid., 27.

125. Elizabeth Kolbert, *Field Notes from a Catastrophe* (Bloomsbury, 2006: 189); Lonnie Thompson, "Climate Change: The Evidence and Our Options," *Behavior Analyst* 33/2 [Fall 2010). Two more examples: The 20 previous winners of the Blue Planet Prize said: "In the face of an absolutely unprecedented emergency, society has no choice but to take dramatic action to avert a collapse of civilization (The Blue Planet Laureates, "Environment and Development Challenges: The Imperative to Act," February 20, 2012); Pulitzer Prize-winning journalist Ross Gelbspan: "[The Global Warming] problem is real. It threatens the survival of our civilization" ("U.S. Press Coverage of the Climate Crisis: A Damning Betrayal of Public Trust," The Heat Is Online (http://www.heatisonline.org/), May 5, 2010.

126. Falk, "Anarchism without 'Anarchism': Searching for Progressive Politics in the Early 21st Century" <http://mil.sagepub.com/content/39/2/381.full.pdf>.

127. Although Falk made this statement in an exposition of my views, he called it an "empirically grounded historical interpretation."

128. "The idea that America was attacked by foreign terrorists on 9/11 has been used," I argued, "to distract attention from the problem of global warming, which is the really serious threat to human civilization" (Griffin, "The Truly Distracting 9/11 Conspiracy Theory: A Reply to Alexander Cockburn," *Le Monde Diplomatique Norway,* English version, March 2007 <http://www.lmd.no/index.php?article=1408#fotnoter>; also at 9/11 Truth Europe <http://www.911truth.eu/index.php?id=0,8,0,0,1,0>).

129. 9/11 Consensus (http://www.consensus911.org/).

130. David Ray Griffin, *Christian Faith and the Truth behind 9/11: A Call to Reflection and Action* (Louisville: Westminster John Knox, 2006).

131. Ibid., 121.

132. "Smoke, Mirrors & Hot Air: How ExxonMobil Uses Big Tobacco's Tactics to Manufacture Uncertainty on Climate Science," Union of Concerned Scientists, January 2007; Naomi Oreskes and Erik M. Conway, *Merchants of Doubt: How a Handful of Scientists Obscured the Truth on Issues from Tobacco Smoke to Global Warming* (New York: Bloomsbury Press, 2010).

133. William F. Pepper, *An Act of State: The Execution of Martin Luther King* (New York: Verso, 2003; updated edition 2008).

134. Peter Phillips, et al., "Parameters of Power in the Global Dominance Group: 9/11 & Election Irregularities in Context," David Ray Griffin and Peter Dale Scott, eds., *9/11 and American Empire: Intellectuals Speak Out* (Northampton: Olive Branch Press [Interlink Books]), 2006). For a more recent example, see Kevin Ryan, "Another Nineteen: Investigating Legitimate 9/11 Suspects," Dig Within, August 11, 2012 <http://digwithin.net/>.

## CHAPTER 16. DAVID RAY GRIFFIN: MY INTELLECTUAL JOURNEY

1. Alfred North Whitehead, *Process and Reality,* corrected edition, ed. David Ray Griffin and Donald W. Sherburne (New York: Free Press, 1978 [orig. 1929]), xiii.

2. Wolfhart Pannenberg, *Jesus—God and Man* (London: SCM Press, 2010), 69 (originally published by Westminster Press, 1968).

3. David Griffin, "Schubert Ogden's Christology and the Possibilities of Process Philosophy," *The Christian Scholar* 50 (Fall, 1967), 290-303. Reprinted in *Process Philosophy and Christian Thought,* ed. Delwin Brown, Ralph E. James, Jr., and Gene Reeves (Indianapolis: Bobbs-Merrill, 1971), 347-61.

4. David Ray Griffin and Gene Reeves, "Bibliography of Secondary Literature on A.N. Whitehead," *Process Studies* 1/4 (Winter, 1971) (constitutes entire issue).

5. John B. Cobb, Jr., and Nicholas Gier, eds., *The Theology of Altizer: Critique and Response* (Philadelphia: Westminster Press, 1971).

6. David Ray Griffin and Thomas J.J. Altizer, eds., *John Cobb's Theology in Process* (Philadelphia: Westminster, 1977).

7. David Ray Griffin, "Introduction: Post-Modern Theology for a New Christian Existence," in Griffin and Altizer, eds., *John Cobb's Theology in Process,* 5-24.

8. John B. Cobb, Jr., and David Ray Griffin, eds., *Mind in Nature: Essays on the Interface of Science and Philosophy* (Washington, D.C.: University Press of America, 1977).

9. Griffin, *God, Power, and Evil: A Process Theodicy* (Philadelphia: Westminster, 1976). To my surprise, this book was taken seriously by fellow philosophers and theologians—so seriously, in fact, that I felt called upon to write a follow-up book, *Evil Revisited: Responses and Reconsiderations* (Albany: State University of New York Press, 1991), in which I responded to the various critiques that *God, Power, and Evil* had received.

10. See note 1, above.

11. John Hick, *The Myth of God Incarnate* (Philadelphia: Westminster Press, 1977).

12. Griffin, *Unsnarling the World-Knot: Consciousness, Freedom, and the Mind-Body Problem* (Berkeley: University of California Press, 1998).

13. John Beloff, *The Existence of Mind* (New York: Citadel Press, 1964).

14. See Chap. 5, "Religion and the Rise of the Modern Scientific Worldview," Griffin, *Religion and Scientific Naturalism: Overcoming the Conflicts* (Albany: State University of New York Press, 2000).

15. Whitehead, *Process and Reality,* 308.

16. Although given in 1981, this lecture was not published until a decade later: David Ray Griffin, "Parapsychology and the Need for a Postmodern Philosophy," *Exceptional Human Experience* 10/2 (December 1992), 155-62.

17. Ilya Prigogine and Isabelle Stengers, *Order Out of Chaos* (Boulder, Colorado: Shambhala, 1984).

18. "The real actual things that endure are all societies," Whitehead, *Adventures of Ideas* (1933; New York: Free Press, 1967), 204.

19. Andrew Bard Schmookler, *The Parable of the Tribes: The Problem of Power in Social Evolution* (Berkeley: University of California Press, 1984); William McNeill, *The Pursuit of Power: Technology, Armed Force, and Society since A.D. 1000* (Chicago: University of Chicago Press, 1984).

20. David Ray Griffin, ed., *Deep Religious Pluralism* (Louisville: Westminster/John Knox, 2005).

21. David Ray Griffin, *Parapsychology, Philosophy, and Spirituality: A Postmodern Exploration* (Albany: State University of New York Press, 1997).

22. Griffin, *Religion and Scientific Naturalism: Overcoming the Conflicts* (Albany: State University of New York Press, 2000).

23. *Reenchantment without Supernaturalism,* Ch. 6.

24. Griffin, *The Mysterious Collapse of World Trade Center 7: Why the Final Official Report about 9/11 Is Unscientific and False* (Northampton: Olive Branch [Interlink Books], 2009).

25. *Postscript:* After the conference, Ann and I spent a few weeks in China, where I gave several lectures on the ecological crisis on behalf of the Center's China Project, which has had an ongoing set of conferences and initiatives in both China and the USA on creating an "ecological civilization." In preparing for these lectures, I became even more aware than before of the urgency of dealing with global warming and the resulting climate disruption—the fact that it threatens, if we continue with "business as usual," with the destruction of civilization. Most immediately, therefore, I am working on a book on this issue, the tentative title for which is *Unprecedented.*

# Bibliography of David Ray Griffin

## BOOKS AUTHORED

1. *A Process Christology.* Philadelphia: Westminster, 1973. Reprinted with new preface, Lanham, Md.: University Press of America, 1990.

2. *God, Power, and Evil: A Process Theodicy.* Philadelphia: Westminster, 1976. Reprinted with a new preface, Lanham, Md.: University Press of America (Lanham, Md.), 1991; reprinted with a newer preface, Westminster John Knox (Louisville, Ky.), 2004.

3. *Process Theology: An Introductory Exposition* (with John B. Cobb, Jr.). Philadelphia: Westminster, and Belfast: Christian Journals, 1976. Also published in German (1979, trans. Marianne Muehlenberg), Japanese (1976, trans. Tokiyuki Nobuhara), Italian (Editrice Queriniana, 1978, trans. Giuseppe Grampa), and Chinese (Beijing: Central Compilation & Translation Press, 1999, trans. Yuehou Qu).

4. *How are God and Evolution Related?* (with Joseph A. Deegan). Claremont: Process and Faith Booklet, 1987.

5. *How Are God and Evil Related?* (with Joseph A. Deegan & Daniel E. H. Bryant). Claremont: Process and Faith Booklet, 1988, rev. 2001, 2088.

6. *God and Religion in the Postmodern World.* Albany: State University of New York Press, 1989. Also published in Korean (Seoul: ChoMyung Press, 1995; trans. SungDo Kang), Persian (Tehran: 2002; trans. and edited by Hamidreza Ayatollahy), and Chinese (Beijing: Central Compilation & Translation Press, 2003; trans. Mutian Sun).

7. *Varieties of Postmodern Theology* (with William A. Beardslee and Joe Holland). Albany: State University of New York Press, 1989.

8. *Primordial Truth and Postmodern Theology* (with Huston Smith). Albany: State University of New York Press, 1989. Also published in Turkish as "Ezeli Hakikat ve Post-Modern Hahiyat" in *Unutulan Hakikat* [Forgotten Truth], by Huston Smith/ David Rey [sic] Griffin, transl. Latif Boyaci (Istanbul: Insan Yayinlari, 1998).

9. *Evil Revisited: Responses and Reconsiderations.* Albany: State University of New York Press, 1991. 10. *Founders of Constructive Postmodern Philosophy: Peirce, James, Bergson, Whitehead, and Hartshorne* (with John B. Cobb, Jr., Marcus P. Ford, Pete A. Y. Gunter, and Peter Ochs). Albany: State University of New York Press, 1993. Also published in Chinese (Beijing: Central Compilation & Translation Press, 2001; trans. Yuehou Qu). French translation of my introduction ("Whitehead et la philosophie constructiviste postmoderne") published in Isabelle Stengers, ed., *L'Effet Whitehead* (Paris: Libraire Philosophique J. Vrin, 1994), 163-96.

11. *Parapsychology, Philosophy, and Spirituality: A Postmodern Exploration.* Albany: State University of New York Press, 1997. Also published in Turkish as *Parapsikoloji ve Felsefe: Postmodern bir perspektif,* trans. Yasemin Tokatli (Istanbul: Ruh ve Madde, 1998).

12. *Unsnarling the World-Knot: Consciousness, Freedom, and the Mind-Body Problem.* Berkeley & Los Angeles: University of California Press, 1998; Eugene: Wipf and Stock, 2008 (reprint).

13. *Religion and Scientific Naturalism: Overcoming the Conflicts.* Albany: State University of New York Press, 2000.

14. *Reenchantment without Supernaturalism: A Process Philosophy of Religion.* Ithaca, N.Y.: Cornell University Press, 2001. Also published in Korean, trans. by Wang Shik Jang, 2005.

15. *The New Pearl Harbor: Disturbing Questions about the Bush Administration and 9/11.* Northampton, Mass.: Olive Branch Press (Interlink Books), March, 2004; Updated Edition with a New Afterword, August, 2004. Translations (of Updated Version): Italian trans. by Giuseppina Oneto, *11 Settembre: Cosa C'è di Vero Nelle "Teorie del Complotto"* (Rome: Fazi Editore, 2004); Chinese trans. by Yan Ai, Daqiang Li, and Binyu Li, 2005; Danish trans. by Frank Sœholm Grevil, *Det Nye Pearl Harbor: Foruroligende spœrgsmål om Bush-administrationen og 11.September* (Randers: Progressive Publishing, 2005); Czech

trans., *Novy Pearl Harbor: 11. září a vláda George Bushe* (Prague: Volvox Globator, 2006); French trans. by Pierre-Henri Bunel, *Le Nouveau Pearl Harbor: 11 Septembre: Questions Gênantes à L'Administration Bush* (Paris: Éditions Demi-Lune, 2006); Dutch trans. by Jesse Goossens, *11 September: Een onderzoek naar de feiten* (Rotterdam: Lemniscaat, 2006); Japanese trans. by Yumi Kikuchi and Kiyoshi Toda, 2006; Arabic translation by Arab Scientific Publishers (Lebanon).

16. *Two Great Truths: A New Synthesis of Scientific Naturalism and Christian Faith.* Louisville: Westminster John Knox Press, 2004.

17. *The 9/11 Commission Report: Omissions and Distortions.* Northampton, Mass.: Olive Branch Press (Interlink Books), 2005. French trans. by Pierre-Henri Bunel, Geneviève Beduneau, and Evelyne Dablin, *Omissions et manipulations de la commission d'enquête sur le 11 Septembre* (Paris: Éditions Demi-Lune, 2006); Arabic translation by Arab Scientific Publishers (in Lebanon).

18. *The American Empire and the Commonwealth of God: A Political, Economic, Religious Statement,* co-authored with John B. Cobb Jr., Richard Falk, and Catherine Keller. Louisville: Westminster John Knox Press, 2006.

19. *Christian Faith and the Truth behind 9/11: A Call to Reflection and Action.* Louisville: Westminster John Knox, 2006.

20. *Evolution without Tears: A Third Way beyond Neo-Darwinism and Intelligent Design.* Claremont: Process and Faith Booklet, 2006.

21. *Whitehead's Radically Different Postmodern Philosophy: An Argument for Its Contemporary Relevance.* Albany: SUNY Press, 2007.

22. *Debunking 9/11 Debunking: An Answer to Popular Mechanics and Other Defenders of the Official Conspiracy Theory.* Northampton: Olive Branch (Interlink Books), 2007. Revised and Updated Edition, August 2007. (Bronze Medal, Independent Publishers Book Awards 2008.) French trans., *11 Septembre: La faillite des medias: Une conspiration du silence.* Paris: Éditions Demi-Lune, 2007.

23. *9/11 Contradictions: An Open Letter to Congress and the Press.* Northampton: Olive Branch (Interlink Books), 2008. Swedish transl., *Motsägelser om 11 september* (2008).

24. *The New Pearl Harbor Revisited: 9/11, the Cover-Up, and the Exposé.* Northampton: Olive Branch (Interlink Books), 2008.

(Publishers Weekly's "Pick of the Week," November 24, 2008.) French translation, *Un Autre Regard sur le 11-Septembre*, trans. by Aurélien Pouponneau, Arno Mansouri, and Thierry Lhomme. Éditions Demi-Lune, 2011.

25. *Osama bin Laden: Dead or Alive?* Northampton: Olive Branch (Interlink Books), 2009.

26. *The Mysterious Collapse of World Trade Center 7: Why the Final Official Report about 9/11 Is Unscientific and False.* Northampton: Olive Branch (Interlink Books), 2009.

27. *Cognitive Infiltration: An Obama Appointee's Plan to Undermine the 9/11 Conspiracy Theory.* Northampton: Olive Branch (Interlink Books), September 2010.

28. *9/11 Ten Years Later: When State Crimes Against Democracy Succeed.* Northampton, Olive Branch (Interlink Books), 2011.

BOOKS EDITED

1. *Mind in Nature: Essays on the Interface of Science and Philosophy* (with John B. Cobb, Jr.). Washington, D.C.: University Press of America, 1977.

2. *John Cobb's Theology in Process* (with Thomas J. J. Altizer). Philadelphia: Westminster, 1977.

3. *Process and Reality: An Essay in Cosmology,* by Alfred North Whitehead. Corrected Edition (with Donald W. Sherburne). New York: Free Press, 1978.

4. *Physics and the Ultimate Significance of Time: Bohm, Prigogine, and Process Philosophy.* Albany: State University of New York, 1986.

5. *The Reenchantment of Science: Postmodern Proposals.* Albany: State University of New York, 1988. Also published in Chinese (Beijing: Central Compilation and Translation Press, 1995; trans. Jifang Ma).

6. *Spirituality and Society: Postmodern Visions.* Albany: State University of New York Press, 1988. Also published in Chinese (Beijing: Central Compilation and Translation Press, 1998; trans. Chengbing Wang), and in Indonesian as *Visi-Visi Postmodern Spiritualitas & Masyarakat* (Yogyakarta: Penerbit Kanisius, 2005; trans. A. Gunawan Admiranto).

7. *Archetypal Process: Self and Divine in Whitehead, Jung, and Hillman.* Evanston: Northwestern University Press, 1989.

8. *Sacred Interconnections: Postmodern Spirituality, Political Economy, and Art.* Albany: State University of New York Press, 1990.

9. *Theology and the University: Essays in Honor of John B. Cobb, Jr.* (with Joseph C. Hough, Jr.). Albany: State University of New York Press, 1991.

10. *Postmodern Politics for a Planet in Crisis: Policy, Process and Presidential Vision* (with Richard A. Falk). Albany: State University of New York Press, 1993.

11. *Jewish Theology and Process Thought* (with Sandra B. Lubarsky). Albany: State University of New York Press, 1996.

12. *Deep Religious Pluralism.* Louisville: Westminster/John Knox, 2005.

13. *9/11 and American Empire: Intellectuals Speak Out* (with Peter Dale Scott). Northampton: Olive Branch Press (Interlink Books), 2006

## ARTICLES AND CHAPTERS

1. Translation of Wolfhart Pannenberg, "Appearance as the Arrival of the Future," *Journal of the American Academy of Religion* 35/2 (July, 1967), 107-18. Reprinted in Wolfhart Pannenberg, *Theology and the Kingdom of God* (Philadelphia: Westminster Press, 1969), 127-43.

2. "Schubert Ogden's Christology and the Possibilities of Process Philosophy," *Christian Scholar* 50 (Fall, 1967), 290-303. Reprinted in Delwin Brown, Ralph E. James, Jr., and Gene Reeves, ed., *Process Philosophy and Christian Thought* (Indianapolis: Bobbs-Merrill, 1971), 347-61.

3. "The Process Theology of Norman Pittenger: A Review Article," *Process Studies* 1/2 (Summer, 1971), 136-49.

4. "Is Revelation Coherent?" *Theology Today* 28 (October, 1971), 278-94.

5. "The Possibility of Subjective Immortality in Whitehead's Philosophy," *University of Dayton Review* 8 (Winter, 1971), 43-56. Reprinted in *Modern Schoolman* LIII/I (November, 1975), 39-57.

6. "Bibliography of Secondary Literature on A. N. Whitehead" (with Gene Reeves), *Process Studies* 1/4 (Winter, 1971) (constitutes entire issue).

7. "The Essential Elements of a Contemporary Christology," *Encounter* (Indianapolis) 33 (Spring, 1972), 170-84.

8. "Philosophical Theology and the Pastoral Ministry," *Encounter* (Indianapolis) 33 (Summer, 1972), 230-44.

9. "Whitehead's Contributions to a Theology of Nature," *Bucknell Review* 20 (Winter, 1972), 3-24.

10. "Hartshorne's Differences From Whitehead," in Lewis Ford, ed., *Two Process Philosophers* (American Academy of Religion, 1973), 35-57.

11. "Whitehead and Niebuhr on God, Man, and the World," *Journal of Religion* 52 (April, 1973), 149-75.

12. "Gordon Kaufman's Theology: Some Questions," *Journal of the American Academy of Religion* 41/4 (December, 1973), 554-72.

13. "Divine Causality, Evil and Philosophical Theology: A Critique of James Ross," *International Journal of Philosophy of Religion* 4/3 (1973), 168-86. A slightly revised version constitutes chapter 14 ("James Ross: All the World's A Stage") of David Ray Griffin, *God, Power, and Evil* (Philadelphia: Westminster, 1976).

14. "A New Vision of Nature," Donald Scherer, ed., *Proceedings for Earth Ethics Today* (Bowling Green State University, 1973). Reprinted in *Encounter* (Indianapolis) 35 (Spring, 1974), 95-107.

15. "Human Liberation and Reverence for Nature," Anticipation (Church and Society, World Council of Churches) 16 (March, 1974), 25-30.

16. "Faith, Reason, and Christology: A Response to Father Meilach," The Cord 24 (1974), 258-67.

17. "Buddhist Thought and Whitehead's Philosophy," *International Philosophical Quarterly* XIV/3 (September, 1974), 261-84. Reprinted in *Twentieth Century Literary Criticism,* Vol. 97 (GRI/ International Thomson Publishing, 2000).

18. "A Process Theology of Creation," *Mid-Stream* (Indianapolis: Council on Christian Unity) XIII/1-2 (Fall-Winter, 1973-74), 48-70.

19. "Holy Spirit, Compassion, and Reverence for Being," in Bernard M. Lee, S. M., and Harry James Cargas, eds., *Religious Experience and Process Theology: The Pastoral Concerns of a Major Modern Movement* (Paulist, 1975), 107-20.

20. "Christ in Evolutionary Context: A Review Article" (Eugene TeSelle's *Christ in Context*), *Encounter* (Indianapolis) 37/1 (Winter, 1976), 91-101.

21. "Relativism, Divine Causation, and Biblical Theology," *Encounter* (Indianapolis) 36/4 (Autumn, 1975), 342-60. Reprinted in Owen C. Thomas, ed., *God's Activity in the World: The Contemporary Problem* (AAR Studies in Religion No. 31, Scholars Press, 1983), 117-36.

22. "Response to George W. Coats and Bernard M. Loomer," *Encounter* (Indianapolis) 36/4 (Autumn, 1975), 376-78.

23. "Whitehead's Philosophy and Some General Notions of Physics and Biology" (122-34) and "Some Whiteheadian Comments on the Discussion" (97-100), in John B. Cobb, Jr., and David Ray Griffin, eds., *Mind in Nature: Essays on the Interface of Science and Philosophy* (University Press of America, 1977).

24. "Introduction: Post-Modern Theology for a New Christian Existence," in David Ray Griffin and Thomas J. J. Altizer, eds., *John Cobb's Theology in Process* (Westminster, 1977), 5-24.

25. "The Subjectivist Principle and Its Reformed and Unreformed Versions," *Process Studies* 7/1 (1977), 27-36.

26. "John B. Cobb, Jr." in Piersandro Vanzan and Hans Jurgen Schultz, eds. *Lessico dei teologi del secolo* XX (Brescia, Italy: Editrice Queriniana, 1978), 727-34 (in Italian).

27. "Values, Evil, and Liberation Theology," *Encounter* (Indianapolis) 40/1 (Winter, 1979), 1-15. Reprinted in John B. Cobb, Jr., and W. Widick Schroeder, eds., *Process Philosophy and Social Thought* (Chicago: Center for the Scientific Study of Religion 1981), 183-96. Also published as "Dios, el mal, los valores y la teologia de la liberacion," in Jorge V. Pixley and Jean-Pierr Bastian, eds., *Praxis Christiana y produccion teologica* (Salamanca, Spain: Ediciones Sigueme, 1978), 101-17.

28. "North Atlantic and Latin American Liberation Theologians," *Encounter* (Indianapolis) 40/1 (Winter, 1979), 17-30. Reprinted in John B. Cobb, Jr., and W. Widick Schroeder, eds., *Process Philosophy and Social Thought* (Chicago: Center for the Scientific Study of Religion, 1981), 197-209.

29. "Ordination for Homosexuals? Yes," *Encounter* (Indianapolis) 40/3 (Summer, 1979), 265-72.

30. "The Holy, Necessary Goodness, and Morality," *Journal of Religious Ethics* 8/2 (Fall, 1980), 330-49 (http://anthonyflood. com/griffinholygoodnessmorality.htm).

31. "Creation out of Chaos and the Problem of Evil," in Stephen T. Davis, ed., *Encountering Evil: Live Options in Theodicy* (John Knox, 1981), 101-17 (http://www.anthonyflood.com/griffinconsciousness.htm). Partially reprinted in Stephen H. Phillips, *Philosophy of Religion: A Global Approach* (Harcourt Brace, 1996), 251-56.

32. Critiques of John Roth (26-29), John Hick (53-55), Stephen T. Davis (87-89), and Frederick Sontag (152-54), in Stephen T. Davis, *Encountering Evil: Live Options in Theodicy* (John Knox, 1981).

33. Response to Critiques from John Roth, John Hick, Stephen Davis, and Frederick Sontag, in Stephen T. Davis, *Encountering Evil: Live Options in Theodicy* (John Knox, 1981), 128-36 (http://www.anthonyflood.com/griffincv.htm).

34. "Whitehead, God, and the Untroubled Mind: A Review Article" (Lawrence Wilmot's *Whitehead and God*), *Encounter* (Indianapolis) 42/2 (Spring, 1981), 169-88.

35. "Actuality, Possibility, and Theodicy: A Response to Nelson Pike," *Process Studies* 12/3 (Fall, 1982), 168-79.

36. Contributions to S. M. Lamb, J. B. Cobb, Jr., D. R. Griffin, J. O. Regan, and A. Basu, *Whitehead and Lamb: A New Network of Connection* (Claremont Graduate School, Spring, 1982), 16-18, 21-24, 31, 39-41, 43-47.

37. "Power Divine and Demonic: A Review Article" (Arthur McGill's *Suffering*), *Encounter* (Indianapolis) 45/1 (Winter, 1984), 67-75.

38. "The Rationality of Belief in God: A Response to Hans Küng," *Faith and Philosophy* 1/1 (January, 1984), 16-26 (http://www. anthonyflood.com/griffinreviewskueng.htm).

39. "Mind in Nature: Nobel Conference XVII" (a review article), *Zygon* 19/1 (March, 1984), 106-10.

40. "Edward Farley's *Ecclesial Reflection: An Anatomy of Theological Method*" (a review article), *Religious Studies Review* 10/3 (July, 1984), 244-47.

41. "John B. Cobb, Jr.," in Dean G. Peerman and Martin E. Marty, eds., *A Handbook of Christian Theologians* (Abingdon Press,

1984), 691-709. Reprinted, in slightly altered and enlarged form, as "John B. Cobb, Jr.: A Theological Biography," in David Ray Griffin and Joseph C. Hough, Jr., eds., *Theology and the University: Essays in Honor of John B. Cobb, Jr.* (Albany: State University of New York Press, 1991), 225-42.

42. "Bohm and Whitehead on Wholeness, Freedom, Causality, and Time," *Zygon* 20/2 (June, 1985), 165-191. Reprinted in slightly revised form in David Ray Griffin, eds., *Physics and the Ultimate Significance of Time*, ed. (Albany: State University of New York Press, 1986), 127-53 (http://www.anthonyflood. com/griffinbohm.htm).

43. "Introduction: Time and the Fallacy of Misplaced Concreteness," in David Ray Griffin, ed., *Physics and the Ultimate Significance of Time* (Albany: State University of New York Press, 1986), 1-48 (http://www.anthonyflood.com/griffin-timemisplacedconcreteness.htm).

44. "Creativity in Post-Modern Religion, in Michael Mitias, ed., *Creativity in Art, Religion and Culture* (Amsterdam: Editions Rodopi B.V., 1985), 64-85. Reprinted in revised form as "Creativity and Postmodern Religion" in David Ray Griffin, *God and Religion in the Postmodern World* (Albany: State University of New York Press, 1988), 29-49; partially (37-49) reprinted in Charles Jencks, ed., *The Post-Modern Reader* (London: Academy Editions; New York: St. Martin's Press, 1992), 373-82.

45. "Faith and Spiritual Discipline: A Comparison of Augustinian and Process Theologies," *Faith and Philosophy* 3/1 (January, 1986), 54-67. Reprinted in revised form as "Spiritual Discipline in the Medieval, Modern, and Postmodern Worlds," in David Ray Griffin, *God and Religion in the Postmodern World* (Albany: State University of New York Press, 1988).

46. "Whitehead and Mind-Body Interaction: A Response to Steven Rosen," *Journal of Religion and Psychical Research* 9/1 (January, 1986), 4-10.

47. "Robert S. Brumbaugh's *Unreality and Time*" (a review article), *Process Studies* 15/1 (Spring, 1986), 53-58.

48. "Lewis Ford's *The Emergence of Whitehead's Metaphysics, 1925-1929*" (a review article), *Process Studies* 15/3 (Fall, 1986), 194-207.

49. "What Process Theology Has to Offer: A Perspective," *Parish and Process* 2/1 (April 1987), 3-8.

50. "Creation *Ex Nihilo,* the Divine *Modus Operandi,* and the *Imitatio Dei,"* in George Nordgulen and George W. Shields, ed., *Faith and Creativity: Essays in Honor of Eugene Peters* (St. Louis: CPB Press, 1988), 95-123.

51. "Of Minds and Molecules: Medicine in a Psychosomatic Universe," Marcus P. Ford, ed., *A Process Theory of Medicine: Interdisciplinary Essays* (Edwin Mellen, 1988), 115-55. Reprinted in slightly revised form as "Of Minds and Molecules: Postmodern Medicine in a Psychosomatic Universe" in David Ray Griffin, ed., *The Reenchantment of Science: Postmodern Proposals* (Albany: State University of New York Press, 1988), 141-63. Excerpt published in *Noetic Sciences Review* 9 (Winter, 1989), 17-18.

52. "On Ian Barbour's *Issues in Science and Religion:* A Review Essay," *Zygon* 23/1 (March, 1988), 57-81.

53. "Introduction to SUNY Series in Constructive Postmodern Thought." Contained in each volume of the series, beginning with *The Reenchantment of Science* (1988). A revised version appears in each volume from 2000 on, beginning with Jerry Gill's *The Tacit Mode.*

54. "Introduction: The Reenchantment of Science," in David Ray Griffin, ed., *The Reenchantment of Science: Postmodern Proposals* (Albany: State University of New York Press, 1988), 1-46. Partially (pp. 13-30, 38-45) reprinted in Charles Jencks, ed., *The Post-Modern Reader* (London: Academy Editions; New York: St. Martin's Press, 1992), 354-72. Partially reprinted in Lawrence E. Cahoone, ed., *From Modernism to Postmodernism: An Anthology* (Blackwell, 1996), 665-86.

55. "Introduction: Postmodern Spirituality and Society," David Ray Griffin, ed., *Spirituality and Society: Postmodern Visions* (Albany: State University of New York Press, 1988), 1-31. Slightly revised version reprinted in *Dialogue and Humanism* 2 (1991). Chinese translation (by Wenyu Xie) of this reprinted version published in *Foreign Social Sciences* (Beijing) 11 (1992).

56. "Peace and the Postmodern Paradigm," in David Ray Griffin, ed., *Spirituality and Society: Postmodern Visions* (Albany: State University of New York Press, 1989), 143-54.

57. "Introduction: Varieties of Postmodern Theology," in David Ray Griffin, William A. Beardslee, and Joe Holland, *Varieties*

*of Postmodern Theology* (Albany: State University of New York Press, 1989), 1-8.

58. "Postmodern Theology as Liberation Theology: A Response to Harvey Cox," in David Ray Griffin, William A. Beardslee, and Joe Holland, *Varieties of Postmodern Theology* (Albany: State University of New York Press, 1989), 81-94.

59. "Liberation Theology and Postmodern Theology: A Response to Cornel West," in David Ray Griffin, William A. Beardslee, and Joe Holland, *Varieties of Postmodern Theology* (Albany: State University of New York Press, 1989), 129-49.

60. "Postmodern Theology and A/theology: A Response to Mark C. Taylor," in David Ray Griffin, William A. Beardslee, and Joe Holland, *Varieties of Postmodern Theology* (Albany: State University of New York Press, 1989), 29-62.

61. "Charles Hartshorne's Postmodern Philosophy," in Robert Kane and Stephen Phillips, ed., *Hartshorne, Process Philosophy and Theology* (Albany: State University of New York Press, 1989), 1-33. Reprinted in David Ray Griffin et al., *Founders of Constructive Postmodern Philosophy* (Albany: State University of New York Press, 1993), 197-231.

62. "Introduction: Archetypal Psychology and Process Theology: Complementary Postmodern Movements," in David Ray Griffin, ed., *Archetypal Process* (Evanston: Northwestern University Press, 1989), 1-76.

63. "A Metaphysical Psychology to Un-Locke Our Ailing World," in David Ray Griffin, ed., *Archetypal Process* (Evanston: Northwestern University Press, 1989), 239-49.

64. "Life After Death in the Modern and Post-Modern Worlds," in Arthur S. Berger and Henry O. Thompson, ed., *Religion and Parapsychology* (Barrytown, N.Y.: Unification Theological Seminary, 1989), 39-60.

65. "Toward a Postmodern Science," *IS Journal* 7/8 (1989), 76-83.

66. "Reply: Must God be Unlimited? Naturalistic vs. Supernaturalistic Theism," in Linda J. Tessier, eds., *Concepts of the Ultimate* (London: Macmillan, 1989), 23-31.

67. "Redefining the Divine: An Interview with David Ray Griffin," *In Context* 24 (Late Winter 1990), 20-25.

68. "Life After Death, Parapsychology, and Post-Modern Animism," in Stephen T. Davis, ed., *Death and Afterlife* (London: Macmillan Press, 1990), 88-109.

69. "The Restless Universe: A Postmodern Vision," in Keith J. Carlson, ed., *The Restless Earth: Nobel Conference XXIV* (San Francisco: Harper & Row, 1990), 59-111.

70. "Response from David Ray Griffin," in Keith J. Carlson, ed., *The Restless Earth: Nobel Conference XXIV* (San Francisco: Harper & Row, 1990), 198-201.

71. "Introduction: Sacred Interconnections," in David Ray Griffin, ed., *Sacred Interconnections: Postmodern Spirituality, Political Economy, and Art* (Albany: State University of New York Press, 1990), 1-14.

72. "Process Theology as Empirical, Rational, and Speculative: Some Reflections on Method," *Process Studies* 19/2 (Summer, 1990), 116-35 (http://www.anthonyflood.com/griffinprocesstheologymethod.htm).

73. "Professing Theology in the State University," in David Ray Griffin and Joseph C. Hough, Jr., eds., *Theology and the University: Essays in Honor of John B. Cobb, Jr.* (Albany: State University of New York Press, 1991), 3-34.

74. "How are God and Evolution Related?" (with Joseph A. Deegan), in David P. Polk, ed., *What's a Christian To Do?* (St. Louis: Chalice Press, 1991), 23-45.

75. "How Are God and Evil Related?" (with Joseph A. Deegan & Daniel E. H. Bryant), in David P. Polk, ed., *What's a Christian To Do?* (St. Louis: Chalice Press, 1991), 47-68.

76. "Steiner's Anthroposophy and Whitehead's Philosophy," *Revision* 14/1 (Summer 1991), 1-22.

77. "Postmodern Theology as First-World Liberation Theology," in *Religion and the Postmodern Vision: Paine Lectures 1991* (Columbia: University of Missouri-Columbia, 1992), 1-22.

78. "Griffin Response to Peters" (to Ted Peters' review of David Ray Griffin, ed., *The Reenchantment of Science and Spirituality and Society*), *Zygon* 27/3 (September 1992), 343-44.

79. "Green Spirituality: A Postmodern Convergence of Science and Religion," *Journal of Theology* (Dayton, Ohio: United Theological Seminary), 1992), 5-20.

80. "Process Theology," in Donald W. Musser and Joseph L. Price, eds., *A New Handbook of Christian Theology* (Nashville: Abingdon Press, 1992), 383-88.

81. "Hartshorne, God, and Relativity Physics," *Process Studies* 21/2 (Summer, 1992), 85-112.

82. "Augustine on God and Evil" (reprint of Chap. 6 of God, Power, and Evil), in Michael L. Peterson, ed., *The Problem of Evil: Selected Readings* (University of Notre Dame Press, 1992).

83. "Parapsychology and the Need for a Postmodern Philosophy," *Exceptional Human Experience* 10/2 (December 1992), 155-62.

84. "Introduction: Constructive Postmodern Philosophy," in David Ray Griffin et al., *Founders of Constructive Postmodern Philosophy* (1993), 1-42. Also published (in slightly abridged form) as "Whitehead et la philosophie constructiviste post-moderne," trans. Isabelle Stengers, in L'Effet Whitehead, ed. Isabelle Stengers (Paris: Libraire Philosophique J. Vrin, 1994), 163-96.

85. "The 'Vision Thing,' the Presidency, and the Ecological Crisis, or the Greenhouse Effect and the 'White House Effect,'" in David Ray Griffin and Richard A. Falk, eds., *Postmodern Politics for a Planet in Crisis* (Albany: State University of New York Press, 1993), 67-101.

86. "What is Consciousness and Why is it so Problematic?" in K. Ramakrishna Rao, ed., *Cultivating Consciousness: Enhancing Human Potential, Wellness, and Healing* (Westport, Conn.: Praeger, 1993), 51-70.

87. "Parapsychology and Philosophy: A Whiteheadian Postmodern Perspective," *Journal of the American Society for Psychical Research* 87/3 (July 1993), 217-88 (http://www.anthony-flood.com/griffinparapsychology.htm).

88. "Whitehead's Deeply Ecological Worldview," in Mary Evelyn Tucker and John Grim, eds., *Worldviews and Ecology: Bucknell Review* 37/2 (Lewisburg, Penn.: Bucknell University Press, 1993), 190-206. Volume reprinted as *Worldviews and Ecology: Religion, Philosophy, and the Environment* (Maryknoll: Orbis Books, 1994).

89. "Postmodern Theology for the Church" (three-part lecture series containing "Liberal But Not Modern: Overcoming the Liberal-Conservative Antithesis" [201-22], "Why Demonic Power Exists: Understanding the Church's Enemy" [223-

40], and "Overcoming the Demonic: The Church's Mission" [241-60]), *Lexington Theological Quarterly* 28/3 (Fall 1993), 201-60 <http://www.anthonyflood.com/griffinpostmod-theol00.htm>.

90. "Parapsychology and Post-Modern Process Theology," Part I: *Creative Transformation* 3/1 (Autumn 1993), 1, 8, 10-11; Part II: *Creative Transformation* 3/2 (Winter, 1994), 1, 3-4.

91. "Dualism, Materialism, Idealism, and Psi: A Reply to John Palmer," *Journal of the American Society for Psychical Research* 88/1 (January 1994), 23-39.

92. "Parapsychology, Psychokinesis, Survival, and Whitehead: A Reply to Frederick Ferré," *Journal of the American Society for Psychical Research* 88/3 (July 1994), 255-74.

93. "The Mind-Body Relation as Key to the Science-Religion Relation," *Proceedings of the Institute for Liberal Studies: Science, Technology, & Religious Ideas,* Vol. 5 (Frankfort: Kentucky State University (Fall, 1994): 1-15.

94. "Foreword" for Jerry D. Korsmeyer, *God-Creature-Revelation: A Neoclassical Framework for Fundamental Theology* (Lanham, Md.: University Press of America, 1995), ix-xii.

95. "Introduction to the Chinese Version of *The Reenchantment of Science*" (in Chinese, trans. Wenyu Xie), in David Ray Griffin, ed., *The Reenchantment of Science* (in Chinese), trans. Jifang Ma (Beijing: Central Compilation and Translation Press, 1995).

96. "Process Theodicy, Christology, and the *Imitatio Dei,*" in Sandra Lubarsky and David Ray Griffin, eds., *Jewish Theology and Process Thought* (Albany: State University of New York Press, 1996), 95-125 <http://www.anthonyflood.com/griffintheodicychristology00.htm>.

97. "Modern and Postmodern Liberal Theology: A Response to Alvin Reines," in Sandra Lubarsky and David Ray Griffin, eds., *Jewish Theology and Process Thought* (Albany: State University of New York Press, 1996), 289-308.

98. "Why Critical Reflection on the Paranormal is So Important—and So Difficult," in Michael Stoeber and Hugo Meynell, eds., *Critical Reflections on the Paranormal* (Albany: State University of New York Press, 1996), 87-117.

99. "Charles Hartshorne," in Donald W. Musser and Joseph L. Price, eds., *Handbook of Christian Theologians* (Nashville: Abingdon Press, 1996).

100. "Postmodern Science," in Susan E. Mehrtens, ed., *Revisionary Science: Essays Toward a New Knowledge Base for Our Culture* (Waterbury, Vermont: The Potlatch Group, 1996), 54-112.

101. "God is Creative-Responsive Love" (a portion of chapter 3 of *Process Theology: An Introductory Exposition,* co-authored with John B. Cobb, Jr.), in Michael Peterson, William Hasker, Bruce Reichenbach, and David Basinger, eds., *Philosophy of Religion: Selected Readings* (Oxford: Oxford University Press, 1996), 134-41.

102. "A Naturalistic Trinity," Joseph A. Bracken and Marjorie Hewitt Suchocki, eds., *Trinity in Process: A Relational Theology of God* (New York: Continuum, 1997), 23-40.

103. "Nicolas Nissiotis and Process Theology" (with John B. Cobb, Jr.),in Marina N. Nissiotis and Mihail P. Grigoris, eds., *Nikos A. Nissiotis: Religion, Philosophy and Sport in Dialogue* (Athens: Athnai, 1994 [actually 1997]), 356-61.

104. "Divine Goodness and Demonic Evil," in William Cenkner, ed., *Evil and the Response of World Religion* (St. Paul: Paragon House, 1997), 223-40.

105. "Panexperientialist Physicalism and the Mind-Body Problem," *Journal of Consciousness Studies* 4/3 (1997), 248-68 (http://www.anthonyflood.com/griffinpanexperiential-ism00.htm).

106. "Process Theology," in Philip L. Quinn and Charles Taliaferro, eds., *A Companion to Philosophy of Religion* (Cambridge, Mass., and Oxford: Blackwell, 1997), 136-42.

107. "A Richer or a Poorer Naturalism? A Critique of Willem Drees's *Religion, Science and Naturalism," Zygon* 32/4 (December 1997): 593-614.

108. "Science, Religion, and Metaphysics: A Response to Haught," *Center for Theology and the Natural Sciences Bulletin* 18/1 (Winter 1998): 13-15.

109. "Being Bold: Anticipating a Whiteheadian Century," *Journal of Whitehead Studies* (Seoul: The Whitehead Society of Korea) 1 (1998): 15-34. Also in *Process Studies in China* 1 (2004): 226-44, and in *Process Studies* 31/2 (2002).

110. "Christian Faith and Scientific Naturalism: An Appreciative Critique of Phillip Johnson's Proposal," *Christian Scholar's Review* 28/2 (Winter 1998): 308-28.

111. "Process Philosophy," in Edward Craig, ed., *Routledge Encyclopedia of Philosophy* (London: Routledge, 1998), Vol. 7: 711-16 (http://www.anthonyflood.com/griffinprocessphilosophy.htm).

112. "Global Government: Objections Considered," in Errol E. Harris and James A. Yunker, eds., *Toward Genuine Global Governance: Critical Reactions to "Our Global Neighborhood"* (Westport, Conn.: Praeger, 1999), 69-92.

113. "Materialist and Panexperientialist Physicalism: A Critique of Jaegwon Kim's *Supervenience and Mind*," *Process Studies* 28/1-2 (Spring-Summer 1999): 4-27.

114. "Reply to Jaegwon Kim," *Process Studies* 28/1-2 (Spring-Summer 1999): 35-36.

115. "Religious Experience, Naturalism, and the Social Scientific Study of Religion," *Journal of the American Academy of Religion* 68/1 (March 2000): 99-125.

116. "Rejoinder to Preus and Segal," *Journal of the American Academy of Religion* 68/1 (March 2000): 143-49 (http://www.anthonyflood.com/griffinrejoinderpreussegal.htm).

117. "Process Philosophy and Theology," in Gary Ferngren, ed., *The History of Science and Religion in the Western Tradition: An Encyclopedia* (New York: Garland, 2000), 214-19.

118. "A Conversation with Ervin Laszlo," *Process Perspectives* 23/2 (Fall 2000): 5-6.

119. "Process Theology and the Christian Good News: A Response to Classical Free Will Theism," in John B. Cobb, Jr., and Clark H. Pinnock, eds., *Searching for an Adequate God: A Dialogue between Process and Free Will Theists* (Grand Rapids: Eerdmans, 2000), 1-38.

120. "In Response to William Hasker," in John B. Cobb, Jr., and Clark H. Pinnock, eds., *Searching for an Adequate God: A Dialogue between Process and Free Will Theists* (Grand Rapids: Eerdmans, 2000), 246-62.

121. "Traditional Free Will Theodicy and Process Theodicy: Hasker's Claim for Parity," *Process Studies* 29/2 (Fall-Winter 2000), 209-26.

122. "On Hasker's Attempt to Defend His Parity Claim," *Process Studies* 29/2 (Fall-Winter 2000), 233-36.

123. "Science and Religion: A Postmodern Perspective," in William Desmond, John Steffen, and Koen Decoster, eds., *Beyond Conflict and Reduction: Between Philosophy, Science and Religion* (Leuven: Leuven University Press, 2001), 45-65.

124. "Creation out of Nothing, Creation Out of Chaos, and the Problem of Evil," in Stephen T. Davis, ed., *Encountering Evil: Live Options in Theodicy*, 2nd edition (Louisville: Westminster John Knox, 2001), 108-25.

125. Critiques of John Roth (25-28), John Hick (52-56), Stephen Davis (93-97), and D. Z. Phillips (164-67), in Stephen T. Davis, ed., *Encountering Evil: Live Options in Theodicy*, 2nd edition (Louisville: Westminster John Knox, 2001).

126. Rejoinder to Critiques (from John Roth, John Hick, Stephen Davis, and D. Z. Phillips), in Stephen T. Davis, ed., *Encountering Evil: Live Options in Theodicy*, 2nd edition (Philadelphia: Westminster/John Knox, 2001), 137-44.

127. "Divine Activity and Scientific Naturalism," in John S. Park and Gayle D. Beebe, eds., *Religion and Its Relevance in Post-Modernism: Essays in Honor of Jack C. Verheyden* (Lewiston, N.Y.: Edwin Mellen Press, 2001), 33-51.

128. "Process Philosophy of Religion," *International Journal for the Philosophy of Religion* (50th anniversary issue, ed. Eugene T. Long) 50 (2001): 131-51 (http://www.anthonyflood.com/griffinprocessphilrel.htm).

129. "Time in Process Philosophy," *KronoScope: Journal for the Study of Time* 1/1-2 (2001): 75-99.

130. "Is the Universe Designed? Yes and No." *Cosmic Questions*, Annals of the New York Academy of Sciences, Vol. 950, ed. James B. Miller (New York: New York Academy of Sciences, 2001), 191-205 (http://www.anthonyflood.com/griffindesign.htm).

131. "White Crows Abounding: Evidence for the Paranormal" (in Chinese). Translation (by Yingqian Lu, Liang Zhao, and Shan Song) of portions of Ch. 2 of *Parapsychology, Philosophy, and Spirituality. In Chinese and International Philosophy of Medicine* 2001 (special issue on "Qigong and the Human Body: Philosophical Explorations"), 61-98.

132. "Scientific Naturalism, the Mind-Body Relation, and Religious Experience," *Zygon: Journal of Religion and Science* 37/2 (June 2002): 361-80.

133. "Foreword" to Persian translation of *God and Religion in the Postmodern World*, trans. by Hamidreza Ayatollahy (2002).

134. "Being Bold: Anticipating a Whiteheadian Century," *Process Studies* 31/2 (Fall-Winter 2002): 3-15.

135. "Of Meontic Freedom and Panexperientialism: An Interview with David Ray Griffin," Metanexus Views, June 13, 2002 <http://www.metanexus.net/metanexus_online/show_article.asp?6602>.

136. "Whitehead, China, Postmodern Politics, and Global Democracy in the New Millennium" (in Chinese), *Culture Communication*, June, 2002. Also published in *Seeking Truth*, No.5, 2002, and in *China Process Studies*, No.1, 2003.

137. "The Postmodern Turn and the Hope of Our Planet" (interview conducted by Xiaohua Wang), *Social Sciences Abroad*, No. 3, 2003: 82-86; also published in *Chinese Self-Study Guide* No. 3, 2003: 17-20, and in *Century China*, Jan. 25, 2003: 1-7 (all in Chinese). Also published as "The Postmodern Turn and Democratic Global Government," *Culture Communication*, February 2003; also published in *China Weekly* No. 68 (2003): 1-3 (Part I), and No. 69 (2003): 16-19 (Part II) (all in Chinese).

138. "The Mystery of the Subjectivist Principle" (with Olav Bryant Smith), *Process Studies* 32:1 (Spring-Summer 2003): 3-36.

139. "Reconstructive Theology," *The Cambridge Companion to Postmodern Theology*, ed. Kevin J. Vanhoozer (Cambridge: Cambridge University Press, 2003), 92-108 (http://www.anthonyflood.com/griffinreconstructivetheology.htm).

140. "The Moral Need for Global Democracy," *Belonging Together: Faith and Politics in a Relational World*, ed. Douglas Sturm (Claremont: P&F Press, 2003), 119-39.

141. "A Process Alternative to Pax Americana" (with John B. Cobb, Jr.), Center for Process Studies website <www.ctr-4process.org>, 2003.

142. "Truth as Correspondence, Knowledge as Dialogical: On Affirming Pluralism without Relativism," *Truth: Interdisciplinary Dialogues in a Pluralist Age*, ed. Christine Helmer and Kristin De Troyer with Katie Goetz (Leuven: Peeters, 2003), 233-50.

143. "Panentheism: A Postmodern Revelation," *In Whom We Live and Move and Have Our Being: Reflections on Panentheism*

*for a Scientific Age,* ed. Philip Clayton and Arthur Peacocke (Grand Rapids: Eerdmans, 2004), 36-47.

144. "Scientific Naturalism: A Great Truth that Got Distorted," *Theology and Science,* 2/1 (April 2004), 9-30.

145. "Morality and Scientific Naturalism: Overcoming the Conflicts," in *Philosophy of Religion in the New Century: Essays in Honor of Eugene Thomas Long,* ed. Jeremiah Hackett and Jerald Wallulis (Kluwer Publications, 2004), 81-104.

146. "Feeling and Morality in Whitehead's System," *Schleiermacher and Whitehead: Open Systems in Dialogue,* ed. Christine Helmer, with Marjorie Suchocki, John Quiring, and Katie Goetz (Berlin and New York: Walter de Gruyter, 2004), 265-94.

147. "Response to Chip Berlet's Review of *The New Pearl Harbor,*" PublicEye.org, May 1, 2004 <http://www.publiceye.org/conspire/Post911/dubious_claims.html>.

148. "A Philosophy Professor Leads the Charge: G&G Talks with David Ray Griffin," Garlic and Grass, June 26, 2004 <http://www.garlicandgrass.org/issue6/PerfectCircle_Griffin.cfm>.

149. "Comments on the Responses by Van Till and Shults," *Theology and Science* 2/2 (November 2004), 181-85.

150. "Resurrection and Empire: A Sermon," *Creative Transformation* 13/4 (Fall 2004), 12-13, 16-17. Reprinted as Ch. 9 of *The American Empire and the Commonwealth of God: A Political, Economic, Religious Statement,* co-authored with John B. Cobb Jr., Richard Falk, and Catherine Keller. Louisville: Westminster John Knox Press, 2006.

151. "Foreword" to Olav Bryant Smith, *Myths of the Self: Narrative Identity and Postmodern Metaphysics* (Lanham, Md.: Lexington Books, 2004), ix-xi.

152. "Preface to the Westminster John Knox Edition" of *God, Power, and Evil: A Process Theodicy* (Louisville: Westminster John Knox, 2004), 1-10.

153. "Panentheism's Significance in the Science-and-Religion Discussion," *Science & Theology News,* May 2005 (35, 41), written as Guest Editor of this issue's "Science & Religion Guide to Panentheism," 34-41 <http://www.anthonyflood.com/griffinpanentheism.htm>.

154. "9/11 and the American Empire: How Should Religious People Respond?" Originally broadcast by BookTV on C-Span

2, April 30, 2005; text published at Garlic & Grass, Jan. 23, 2006 <http://www.garlicandgrass.org/issue9/David_Ray_Griffin. cfm>. A DVD is available at KenJenkins@aol.com.

155. "The 9/11 Commission Report: A 571-Page Lie," *Global Outlook,* April 2006: 100-106; originally posted at 911Truth. org, May 22, 2005 <http://www.911truth.org/article. php?story=20050523112738404>.

156. "What If Everything You Know about 9/11 Is Wrong?" Interview with Bruce David and Carolyn Sinclair, *Hustler Magazine,* August, 2005: 32-35, 108 (available at <http:// www.911truth.org/article.php?story=20050604140153943> [text only] and <http://911truth.org/docs/drgHfull.pdf> (with graphics).

157. "Truth and Politics of 9/11: Omissions and Distortions of *The 9/11 Commission Report,*" *Global Outlook* (www.GlobalOutlook. ca), Issue 10, ed. Ian Woods (Spring-Summer 2005), 45-56. Reprinted in *9/11: solving the Greatest Crime of All Time: The Best of Global Outlook,* Vol. 1, ed. Ian Woods (307-18).

158. "9/11: A Christian Theologian's Response: Deceptions of Empire and the Anti-Imperial Gospel of Jesus," *Zion's Herald,* July/August 2005: 5-6, 39-40 (http://www.anthonyflood. com/griffin911xntheologiansresponse.htm) (http://www. venusproject.com/ethics_in_action/David_Ray_Griffin. html).

159. "9/11 and the Mainstream Press: Address given at the National Press Club, July 22, 2005," 9/11 Visibility Project, July 29, 2005 (http://www.septembereleventh.org/newsar-chive/2005-07-29-pressclub.php).

160. "Getting Agnostic about 9/11" (an interview conducted by Mark Ehrman), *LA Times Magazine,* August 28, 2005 (http://www.latimes.com/features/printedition/magazine/ la-tm-crgriffin35aug28,1,3835884.story?coll=la-head-lines-magazine) (http://www.anthonyflood.com/griffin-gettingagnosticabout911.htm).

161. "Whitehead, China, Postmodern Politics, and Global Democracy." *Whitehead and China: Relevance and Relationship,* ed. Wenyu Xie, Zhihe Wang, and George E. Derfer (Frankfurt/ New Brunswick: Ontos Verlag, 2005), 25-28.

162. "Response to Ian Markham" (to Markham's review of *The New Pearl Harbor), Conversations in Religion and Theology,* 3/2

(November, 2005): 220-236. Both essays reprinted, with an introduction, in "Two Theologians Debate 9/11: David Ray Griffin an Ian Markham (http://www.scholarsfor911truth. org/ArticleTwoSpeak02May2006.html) (http://www.anthonyflood.com/griffintimemisplacedconcreteness.htm).

163. "Theism and the Crisis in Moral Theory: Rethinking Modern Autonomy." *Nature, Truth, and Value: Exploring the Thought of Frederick Ferré,* ed. George Allan and Merle Allshouse (Lanham, Md: Lexington Books, 2005), 199-220.

164. "Flights of Fancy: The 9/11 Commission's Incredible Tales about Flights 11, 175, 77, and 93," *Global Outlook,* April 2006; also chapter 4 of Griffin, *Christian Faith and the Truth behind 9/11;* previously posted as "Flights 11, 175, 77, and 93: The 9/11 Commission's Incredible Tales," 911Truth. org, December 5, 2005 (http://www.911truth.org/article. php?story=20051205150219651).

165. "The Destruction of the World Trade Center: Why the Official Account Cannot Be True," *The Hidden History of 9-11-2001,* ed. Paul Zarembka (Amsterdam: Elsevier, 2006), 79-122; also published (in slightly different form) at 911Review.com (http://911review.com/articles/griffin/nyc1.html) and as chapter 3 of Griffin, *Christian Faith and the Truth behind 9/11.*

166. "Explosive Testimony: Revelations about the Twin Towers in the 9/11 Oral Histories," 911Truth.org, January 18, 2006 (http://www.911truth.org/article. php?story=20060118104223192); reprinted as Chap. 2 of Griffin, *Christian Faith and the Truth behind 9/11.*

167. "Moral Values and Global Democracy," *Creative Transformation,* 15/1 (Winter 2006), 25-35 (http://www.processandfaith.org/publications/CT/Volume%2015/15.1/moral%20values%20issue.pdf).

168. "9/11: The Myth and the Reality," 911Truth. org, April 5, 2006 (http://www.911truth.org/article. php?story=20060405112622982) (http://www.anthonyflood.com/griffin911mythandreality.htm); slightly revised version in James H. Fetzer, ed., *The 9/11 Conspiracy: Experts and Scholars Speak Up for Truth* (Peru, Ill.: Open Court, 2007), 13-42.

169. "America's Non-Accidental, Non-Benign Empire," in Griffin et al., *The American Empire and the Commonwealth of God,* 3-22.

170. "Global Empire or Global Democracy: The Present Choice," in Griffin et al., *The American Empire and the Commonwealth of God,* 103-19.

171. "9/11, American Empire, and Christian Faith," 911Truth. org, April 28, 2006 (http://www.911truth.org/article. php?story=20060501003040487).

172. "Religious Pluralism," *Handbook of Process Theology,* ed. Jay McDaniel an Donna Bowman (St. Louis: Chalice Press, 2006), 49-58.

173. "9/11, the American Empire, and Common Moral Norms." In David Ray Griffin and Peter Dale Scott, eds., *9/11 and American Empire: Intellectuals Speak Out* (Northampton: Olive Branch, 2006).

174. "David Griffin Replies to NY Times 'Conspiracy Theories 101,'" Muslim-Jewish-Christian Alliance for 9/11 Truth, July, 2006 (http://www.mujca.com/griffinandfish.htm).

175. "9/11 Live or Fabricated: Do the NORAD Tapes Verify *The 9/11 Commission Report?"* 911Truth.org, September 4, 2006 (http:// www.911truth.org/article.php?story=2006091418303369).

176. "9/11 Under Attack: David Ray Griffin: Why the Official Story Just Doesn't Make Sense." Interview by Abigail Lewis. *Whole Life Times,* September 2006: 53-54.

177. "Rokende Pistolen Gezocht: De Echte Daders Achter 9/11" (Interview), *Penthouse* (Dutch), December, 2006: 088-091.

178. "Interpreting Science from the Standpoint of Whiteheadian Process Philosophy," in Philip Clayton, ed., *The Oxford Handbook of Religion and Science* (Oxford and New York: Oxford University Press, 2006), 453-71.

179. "Evolution without Tears: A Third Way beyond Neo-Darwinism and Intelligent Design," Claremont: Process and Faith (booklet), 2006.

180. "False-Flag Operations, 9/11, and the New Rome: A Christian Perspective," in Kevin Barrett, John B. Cobb Jr., and Sandra Lubarsky, eds., *9/11 and American Empire: Christians, Jews, and Muslims Speak Out* (Northampton: Olive Branch, 2007).

181. "The Truly Distracting 9/11 Conspiracy Theory: A Reply to Alexander Cockburn," *Le Monde Diplomatique Norway,*

English version, March 2007 (http://www.lmd.no/index. php?article=1408#fotnoter).

182. "The David Ray Griffin Interview: DRG Answers Your Questions," RINF Forum, February 5, 2007 (http://www. rinf.com/forum/911-truth-forums/the-david-ray-griffin-interview-drg-answers-your-questions-t431.0.html).

183. "Did George W. Bush Engineer the 9/11 Terrorist Attacks? An Interview with David Ray Griffin" [conducted by John B. Whitehead] (http://www.rutherford.org/Oldspeak/Articles/ Interviews/oldspeak-Griffin.html).

184. "Neocon Imperialism, 9/11, and the Attacks on Afghanistan and Iraq," Information Clearing House, February 27, 2007 (http://www.informationclearinghouse.info/article17194. htm).

185. "The American Empire and 9/11," *Tikkun,* March-April 2007) (http://www.tikkun.org/magazine/tik0703/frontpage/ empire911; this online version is longer than the magazine version and has notes); reprinted in *Journal of 9/11 Studies,* Vol. 11, May 2007 (http://www.journalof911studies.com/ volume/200704/DavidRayGriffin911Empire.pdf).

186. "Morons and Magic: A Reply to George Monbiot," Information Clearing House, March 7, 2007 (http://www.infor-mationclearinghouse.info/article17256.htm).

187. "Barbara Olson's Alleged Call from AA 77: A Correction About Onboard Phones," Information Clearing House, May 7, 2007 (http://www.informationclearinghouse.info/ article17659.htm).

188. "Could Barbara Olson Have Made Those Calls? An Analysis of New Evidence about Onboard Phones," co-authored with Rob Balsamo, Pilots for 9/11 Truth, June 26, 2007 (http:// www.911blogger.com/node/9627).

189. *"Il Rapporto della Commissione sull'11 Settembre: Il* capolavoro di omissione e mistificazione de Philip Zelikow" *("The 9/11 Commission Report*: Philip Zelikow's Masterpiece of Omission & Distortion"), Giulietto Chiesa, ed., *Zero: Perché la versione ufficiale sull'11/9 è un Falso* (Casale Monferrato, Italy: Piemme, 2007), 29-52.

190. "New Evidence that the Official Story about 9/11 is Indefensible," *The Canadian,* October 9, 2007 (http://www.911truth. org/article.php?story=20071009102819394).

191. "Was Deena Burnett Really Not Duped? A Reply to Andrew Kornkven's Suggestion about Alleged Cell Phone Calls," 911Blogger, October 10, 2007 (http://911blogger.com/node/11930).

192. "Process Theology: What It Is and Is Not," *Mormonism in Dialogue with Contemporary Christian Theologies,* ed. David L. Paulsen and Donald W. Musser (Macon, Ga.: Mercer University Press, 2007), 161-87.

193. "Neo-Darwinism and Its Religious Implications," in John B. Cobb, Jr., ed., *Back to Darwin: A Richer Account of Evolution* (Grand Rapids: Eerdmans, 2007), 268-87.

194. "Whitehead's Naturalism and a Non-Darwinian View of Evolution," in John B. Cobb, Jr., ed., *Back to Darwin: A Richer Account of Evolution* (Grand Rapids: Eerdmans, 2007), 264-90.

195. "Consciousness as a Subjective Form: Whitehead's Nonreductionistic Naturalism," in *Subjectivity, Process, and Rationality,* ed. Michel Weber and Pierfrancesco Basile (Ontos Verlag, 2007) (http://www.anthonyflood.com/griffinconsciousness.htm).

196. "Process Eschatology," *The Oxford Handbook of Eschatology,* ed. Jerry L. Walls (Oxford: Oxford University Press, 2007), 295-310.

197. "9/11 Contradictions: Bush in the Classroom," *The Canadian,* January 12, 2008 (http://www.agoracosmopolitan.com/home/Frontpage/2008/01/07/02080.html).

198. "9/11 Contradictions: When Did Cheney Enter the Underground Bunker," *The Canadian,* January 23, 2008 (http://www.911blogger.com/node/13506#new).

199. "Foreword" to Bob Aldridge, *America in Peril* (Pasadena: Hope Publishing House, 2008). Published separately at 911Blogger (http://911blogger.com/node/14223).

200. "9/11 Contradictions: Mohamed Atta's Mitsubishi and His Luggage," Global Research, May 9, 2008 (http://www.globalresearch.ca/index.php?context=va&aid=8937).

201. "Half Great, Half Terrible," Review of Philip Shenon, *The Commission: The Uncensored History of the 9/11 Investigation,* Amazon.com, March 19, 2008 (http://www.amazon.com/review/product/0446580759/ref=cm_cr_dp_hist_3?%5Fencoding=UTF8&showViewpoints=0&filterBy=addThreeStar).

202. "Ted Olson's Report of Phone Calls from Barbara Olson on 9/11: Three Official Denials," Global Research, April 1, 2008 (http://www.globalresearch.ca/index.php?context=va&aid=8514).

203. "Saving Civilization: Straussian and Whiteheadian Political Philosophy," in Michel Weber and Will Desmond, eds., *Handbook of Whiteheadian Process Thought* (Frankfurt: Ontos Verlag, 2008), 521-32.

204. "Tim Russert, Dick Cheney, and 9/11," Information Clearing House, June 17, 2008 (http://www.informationclearinghouse.info/article20108.htm).

205. "The Destruction of the World Trade Center: Why the Official Account Cannot Be True," in Paul Zarembka, ed., *The Hidden History of 9-11*, 2nd Edition (New York: Seven Stories, 2008), 75-117.

206. "Update: "The Destruction of the World Trade Center: Why the Official Account Cannot Be True," *The Hidden History of 9-11*, 2nd Edition (New York: Seven Stories, 2008), 315-26.

207. Foreword to Charles E. Lewis, "What I Heard LAX Security Officials Say During the 9/11 Attacks," 911truth.org, September 7, 2008 (http://911truth.org/article.php?story=2008071025531345).

208. "Reported Cell Phone Calls from the 9/11 Planes: Further Reflections Evoked by a Critique," Global Research, September 7, 2008 (http://www.globalresearch.ca/index.php?context=va&aid=10103).

209. "Was America Attacked by Muslims on 9/11?" OpEdNews, September 9, 2008 Global Research, September 10, 2008 (http://www.globalresearch.ca/index.php?context=va&aid=10142).

210. "What Really Happened on September 11? An Interview with David Ray Griffin," by Sam Vaknin, The Conservative Voice, September 8, 2008 (http://www.theconservativevoice.com/article/34340.html#).

211. "21 Reasons to Question the Official Story about 9/11," Global Research, September 11, 2008 (http://www.globalresearch.ca/index.php?context=va&aid=10145). In Italian as "21 Ragioni per contestare la versione ufficiale dell' 11 settembre" (http://www.megachip.info/modules.php?name=Sections&op=viewarticle&artid=9115).

212. "Did American Flight 77 Strike the Pentagon? The Debris Deficit," *The Canadian,* September 13, 2008 (http://www.agoracosmopolitan.com/home/Frontpage/2008/09/15/02611. html).

213. "The 9/11 Interview with Michael Hess: Evidence that NIST Lied about When He and Barry Jennings Were Rescued," WantToKnow.Info, Updated August 2009 (http://www.wanttoknow.info/008/hessjenningswtc7explosiontvbroadcast).

214. "Bush Doctrine Enters American Vocabulary," *San Francisco Chronicle,* September 25, 2008 (http://www.sfgate.com/cgi-bin/article.cgi?f=/c/a/2008/09/25/EDGR135ERL.DTL).

215. "The Bush Doctrine & *The 9/11 Commission Report:* Both Authored by Philip Zelikow," Information Clearing House, October 4, 2008 (http://www.informationclearinghouse. info/article20947.htm).

216. "The Ultimate 9/11 'Truth' Showdown: David Ray Griffin vs. Matt Taibbi," AlterNet, October 6, 2008 (http://www.alternet. org/rights/100688/the_ultimate_9_11_'truth'_showdown:_david_ray_griffin_vs._matt_taibbi/?page=entire).

217. "The Lies of the Mighty," Foreword to Mark H. Gaffney, *The 9/11 Mystery Plane and the Vanishing of America* (Walterville, OR: Trine Day, 2008), ix-xi.

218. "9/11: Time for a Second Look," Voltaire.net.org, April 18, 2009 (http://www.voltairenet.org/article159749.html).

219. "Panexperientialism: How It Overcomes the Problems of Dualism and Materialism," *Pschoscience,* June 2009 (http://www.psychoscience.net/panexperientialism.htm).

220. "Inside Job: Everything You Weren't Allowed to Ask about 9/11: An Interview with David Ray Griffin," by Joan d'Arc, *Paranoia: The Conspiracy and Paranormal Reader,* Issue 50 (Spring 2009), 52-59.

221. "9/11 Let's Get Empirical," *Prescription for a World in Crisis: Global Outlook,* Issue 13, ed. Ian Woods (Annual 2009), 87-102.

222. "9/11 and America's Blind Nationalist Faith," *Prescription for a World in Crisis: Global Outlook, Issue* 13, ed. Ian Woods (Annual 2009), 159-70. Also available as "9/11 and Nationalist Faith: How Faith Can Be Illuminating or Blinding" at Religious Leaders for 9/11 Truth.

223. "The Mysterious Collapse of WTC 7: Why NIST's Final 9/11 Report is Unscientific and False," Global Research, September 14, 2009 (http://www.globalresearch.ca/index. php?context=va&aid=15201).

224. "Osama Bin Laden: Dead or Alive?" Global Research, October 9, 2009 (http://www.globalresearch.ca/index.php?-context=va&aid=15601); revised version, Veterans Today, October 22, 2009 (http://www.veteranstoday.com/modules. php?name=News&file=article&sid=9079).

225. "Osama bin Laden as Responsible for the 9/11 Attacks: Is This Belief Based on Evidence?" Veterans Today, October 30, 2009 (http://www.veteranstoday.com/modules. php?name=News&file=article&sid=9194#at).

226. "Consciousness as Subjective Form: Whitehead's Nonreductionistic Naturalism," in Michel Weber and Anderson Weekes, eds., *Process Approaches to Consciousness in Psychology, Neuroscience, and Philosophy of Mind* (Albany: SUNY Press, 2009), 175-200.

227. "A Deeply Flawed Book," review of John Farmer, *The Ground Truth: The Untold Story of America Under Attack on 9/11*, Amazon. com, November 27, 2009.

228. "Phone Calls from the 9/11 Airliners: Response to Questions Evoked by My Fifth Estate Interview," Global Research, January 12, 2010 (http://www.globalresearch.ca/index. php?context=va&aid=16924).

229. "The IRD's Attack on my 'Silly' 9/11 Theories," 911Truth.org, April 21, 2010 (http://911truth.org/article. php?story=20100421004106172).

230. "Did Osama bin Laden Confess to the 9/11 Attacks, and Did He Die, in 2001?" Global Research, April 30, 2010 (http://www. globalresearch.ca/index.php?context=va&aid=18923).

231. "Ethics and the Fabric of the Universe," *Whitehead and Ethics in the Contemporary World: For Sustainability and the Common Good*, ed. Haruo Murata (The Japan Society for Process Studies, 2010), 7-17.

232. "Building What? How SCADs Can Be Hidden in Plain Sight," 911Truth.org, May 27, 2010 (http://911truth.org/article. php?story=20100527162010811); reprinted as "Building What? How State Crimes Against Democracy (SCADs) Can Be Hidden in Plain Sight," *Censored 2011: The Top 25 Censored*

*Stories,* ed. Mickey Huff and Peter Phillips with Project Censored (New York: Seven Stories, 2010).

233. "William A. ('Bill') Christison (1928-2010)," 911Truth. org, June 20, 2010 (http://911truth.org/article. php?story=20100620115516747).

234. "Did 9/11 Justify the War in Afghanistan? Using the McChrystal Moment to Raise a Forbidden Question," Global Research, June 24, 2010 (http://www.globalresearch.ca/ index.php?context=va&aid=19891).

236. "Obama Says 'Justice Has Been Done': Bin Laden Scholar Says No," PR Newswire, May 6, 2011 (http://www.prnewswire.com/news-releases/obama-says-justice-has-been-done-bin-laden-scholar-says-no-121381654.html).

237. "A Response to Paul Zarembka about Phone Calls from the 9/11 Planes," ITHP, October 25, 2011. Also at 911Truth.org (http:// www.911truth.org/article.php?story=20111025080659853).

238. "Is a Global Ethic Possible?" in Luis Cabrera, ed., *Global Governance, Global Government: Institutional Visions for an Evolving World System* (Albany: State University of New York Press, 2011), 101-26.

239. "Whitehead's Moral Philosophy" (in Chinese), in Liqun Ding and Xiaojuan Li, eds., *World and China: Selected Writings on Frontier Issues in World Philosophy* (Harbin, China: Heilongjiang University Press, 2011), 30-43.

240. "Whitehead, China and Global Democracy in the New Millennium" (in Chinese), in Liqun Ding and Xiaojuan Li, eds., *World and China: Selected Writings on Frontier Issues in World Philosophy* (Harbin, China: Heilongjiang University Press, 2011), 147-58.

241. "Lynn Margulis: 1938-2011," 911Truth.org, November 23, 2011 (http://911truth.org/article.php?story=20111123153456439).

242. "Lynn Margulis: Scientist, Scholar, and Friend," *Process Perspectives: News Magazine of the Center for Process Studies* 34/1 (Winter 2012), 9.

243. "Lynn Margulis and on Spirituality and Process Philosophy" (with John B. Cobb, Jr.), in Dorion Sagan, *Lynn Margulis: The Life and Legacy of a Scientific Rebel* (White Ricer Junction, VT: Chelsea Green, 2012).

244. "Process Thought and Natural Theology," in Russell Manning, ed., *Oxford Handbook of Natural Theology* (Oxford: Oxford University Press, 2013).

245. "Deep Religious Pluralism," in Kevin Schilbrack, ed., *The Wiley-Blackwell Companion to Religious Diversity* (London: Wiley-Blackwell, 2013).

## BOOK REVIEWS

1. Kenneth Cauthen, *Christian Biopolitics: A Credo and Strategy for the Future,* in *Encounter* (Indianapolis) 33/2 (Spring, 1972), 210-11.

2. Anders Nygren, *Meaning and Method: Prolegomena to a Scientific Philosophy of Religion and a Scientific Theology,* in *The Review of Books and Religion* 2/6 (Mid-March 1973), 12.

3. Alan Richardson, *The Political Christ,* in *Religious Education* LXIX/6 (November-December 1974), 753-54.

4. W. Sibley Towner, *How God Deals with Evil,* in *Religious Education* LXXIII (January-February 1978), 98-100.

5. Lawrence F. Wilmot, *Whitehead and God: Prolegomena to Theological Reconstruction,* in *Transactions of the Charles S. Pierce Society* 16/1 (Winter, 1980), 86-88.

6. Bonnell Spencer, *God Who Dares to Be Man: Theology for Prayer and Suffering,* in *Process Studies* 13/3 (Fall, 1983), 237-40.

7. "Rupert Sheldrake's *A New Science of Life"* (a review article), *Process Studies* 12/1 (Spring, 1982), 38-40.

8. Nicholas Rescher, *The Riddle of Existence: An Essay in Idealistic Metaphysics,* in *Canadian Philosophical Reviews,* December, 1986, 531-32.

9. Marjorie Suchocki, *The End of Evil: Process Eschatology in Historical Context,* in *Process Studies* 18/1 (Spring 1989), 57-62.

10. Frederic B. Burnham, ed., *Postmodern Theology: Christian Faith in a Pluralist World,* in *Theology Today* 47/2 (July, 1990), 220, 222.

11. Kai Nielsen, *God, Scepticism, and Modernity,* in *Journal of the American Academy of Religion* 59/1 (Spring, 1991), 189-90.

12. Joanna Macy, *Mutual Causality in Buddhism and General Systems Theory,* in *Process Studies* 20/4 (Winter 1991), 244-48.

13. Stephen T. Franklin, *Speaking from the Depths: Alfred North Whitehead's Hermeneutical Metaphysics of Propositions, Experi-*

*ence, Symbolism, Language, and Religion,* in *Journal of Religion* 72/1 (1992), 124.

14. Milic Capek, *The New Aspects of Time: Its Continuity and Novelties,* and A. D. Papanicolaou and Pete A. Y. Gunter, ed., *Bergson and Modern Thought,* in *Journal of the History of the Behavioral Sciences* 28 (October 1992), 382-86.

15. Hans Schwarz, *Evil: A Historical and Theological Perspective,* in *Interpretation* 51/3 (July 1997), 326-28.

16. Milic Capek, *The New Aspects of Time: Its Continuity and Novelties: Selected Papers in the Philosophy of Science,* ed. Robert S. Cohen, in *Process Studies* 27/3-4 (1998): 345-48.

17. Lewis Ford, *Transforming Process Theism,* in *Journal of Religion* 81/4 (October 2001), 668-70 (http://www.anthonyflood. com/griffinreviewsford.htm).

18. "A National Disgrace Riddled with Omissions and Distortions," review of *The 9/11 Commission Report: Final Report of the National Commission on Terrorist Attacks upon the United States,* Amazon.com, November 25, 2004.

19. "Abundant and Compelling Evidence," review of Four Arrows and James H. Fetzer, *American Assassination: The Strange Death of Senator Paul Wellstone,* Amazon.com, Dec. 5, 2004.

20. "A Deeply Flawed Book," review of John Farmer, *The Ground Truth: The Untold Story of America Under Attack on 9/11,* Amazon. com, November 27, 2009.

# Contributors

JOHN BUCHANAN, PhD, Independent Scholar

PHILIP CLAYTON, Dean, Claremont School of Theology; Provost, Claremont Lincoln University; Professor of Theology at Claremont School of Theology, Claremont Lincoln University, and Claremont Graduate University

JOHN B. COBB, JR., Avery Professor of Theology Emeritus, Claremont School of Theology and Claremont Graduate University; Founding Director, Center for Process Studies

DANIEL DOMBROWSKI, Professor of Religion, Seattle University; editor, *Journal of Process Studies*

GARY DORRIEN, Reinhold Niebuhr Professor of Social Ethics, Union Theological Seminary; Professor of Religion, Columbia University

RICHARD FALK, Albert G. Milbank Professor of International Law Emeritus, Princeton University; Research Professor, Global Studies, University of California, Santa Barbara

TOD FLETCHER, former Instructor of Geography at the University of California (Berkeley) and San Francisco State University, and former Adjunct Professor of Geography at Laney College

MARCUS FORD, Professor of Humanities Emeritus, Northern Arizona University

NANCY FRANKENBERRY, John Phillips Sousa Professor of Religion, Dartmouth College

DAVID RAY GRIFFIN, Professor of Philosophy of Religion and Theology Emeritus, Claremont School of Theology and Claremont Graduate University; an original director of the Center for Process Studies

BETH JOHNSON, Minister of Palomar Unitarian Universalist Fellowship in Vista, California. She received the Doctor of Ministry Degree at Claremont School of Theology, where David Griffin was her mentor

CATHERINE KELLER, Professor of Theology, Drew University's Theological and Graduate School

SANDRA LUBARSKY, Professor of Sustainable Development and Director of Sustainable Development Program, Appalachian State University

GENE REEVES, Distinguished Professor, Renmin University (China); International Advisor, Rissho Kosei-kai (Japan)

PETER DALE SCOTT, Professor Emeritus, Department of English, University of California, Berkeley

ZHIHE WANG, Executive Director of the Institute for Postmodern Development of China; former associate professor at the Chinese Academy of Social Sciences; and vice-editor-in-chief of Social Sciences Abroad

23508219R00251

Made in the USA
Charleston, SC
25 October 2013